COMMUNICATION

Patterns and Incidents

COMMUNICATION
Patterns and Incidents

By WILLIAM V. HANEY, Ph.D.

Associate Professor of Business Administration
School of Business
Northwestern University

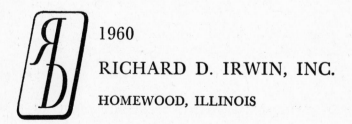

1960

RICHARD D. IRWIN, INC.

HOMEWOOD, ILLINOIS

First Printing, June, 1960
Second Printing, December, 1961
Third Printing, January, 1963
Fourth Printing, November, 1963
Fifth Printing, July, 1964
Sixth Printing, September, 1965
Seventh Printing, December, 1965

Library of Congress Catalogue Card No. 60–11751

PRINTED IN THE UNITED STATES OF AMERICA

Every writer is a product of his experiences. In the case of this book so much is due to the author's contact with one outstanding personality that special mention must be made of it. The author is deeply grateful for eight years of study and friendship with the late

PROFESSOR IRVING J. LEE

of Northwestern University. Those who have been stimulated by his writings and inspired by his person will recognize the influence of Dr. Lee on virtually every page. It is to the continuation of his teachings and values that this book is respectfully dedicated.

PREFACE

ACCORDING to its title this book is about communication. The title will appear appropriate or inappropriate, I suppose, to the extent that the reader's visualization of "communication" coincides with the author's. Perhaps it would be helpful to indicate what this book is *not* about. It does not, for example, deal with much of the subject matter usually developed in texts of public, conversational, conference, and business and professional speaking. It does not serve the purposes of texts of composition or of business writing, reports, and letters. Nor is it a book on reading or listening. These vital aspects, phases, and media of communication are treated skillfully and thoroughly in many fine works. Some of them are listed in the bibliography at the end of this book.

The book *is* concerned with equally vital phases of communication which have not been treated so comprehensively and are, perhaps, not so well understood and appreciated. It focuses on what it is that happens *inside* a communicator *before* and *as* he talks, writes, etc., and *as* and *after* he listens, reads, etc. Some might call these processes "thinking" and dissociate them from the communication experience. Others, including this writer, have felt no need to make such a distinction and, indeed, question the wisdom of drawing an arbitrary line between "thinking" and "communicating." It seems to this writer that perceiving, evaluating, visualizing, and interpreting are as involved in the communication process as are phonation, articulation, spelling, grammar, etc.

Rationale

The book's rationale is that communication is a serial process involving the phases of encoding, sending, medium, receiving, and decoding. Each step, like a link in a chain, is crucial. Because they are by far the least understood, this book focuses on the encoding and decoding phases.

Each chapter deals with one or more "patterns of miscommunication" which arise in the encoding and/or decoding phases. The miscommunications stem largely from various fallacious assumptions unconsciously held by the communicators—be they speakers or writers, listeners or readers. The usual chapter format includes a definition of the miscommunication pattern, the range and types of its consequences, some of its probable causes, and finally, the suggestion of techniques for correcting the miscommunication and for preventing its recurrence.

If the book's purpose were only to provide the reader with a body of information and theory about communication it would seem sufficient to restrict it to the textual material. The fond hope, however, is that readers will be able to use the book to move beyond the level of acquaintance with content to the improvement of their own communication processes. And this is where the function of the "incidents" begins.

The Incidents

The late communication authority, Irving J. Lee, used to say that the road to becoming a competent practitioner of communication (and of the avoidance and correction of miscommunication) was marked by five milestones. First, one acquaints himself with the subject matter—the studies, the theories, the methods, and the experiments. In other words he acquires the current knowledge of the field. Second, he learns to recognize proficiencies, shortcomings, and defects in the communication of others. Third, and somewhat more difficult, he comes to perceive and understand them in his own behavior. Fourth, he develops skills in prescribing for improved communication on his own part. Fifth, and by far the most formidable accomplishment, he learns to prescribe for the communicative problems of others.[1]

The text of this book, at most, can only contribute to the reader's realization of Step One. The incidents[2] which follow each of the succeeding chapters, however, give him the opportunity to practice at the level of Step Two.[3]

Most of the incidents are simply reports of actual happenings in which communications somehow went awry. They are presented be-

---

[1] Lee listed these "steps" in their order of difficulty rather than suggesting they be strictly adhered to chronologically. He never insisted, for example, that Step One had to be mastered before practicing Step Two, etc. Nor did he discourage one's developing skills on two or more levels simultaneously.

[2] I have used the term *incidents* to distinguish them from *cases*, a term usually associated in collegiate business education with comparatively long, detailed accounts replete with factual and, often, statistical data. While virtually all of the *incidents* contained in this book are factual, they are relatively short and limited in background information.

[3] Explorations into Steps Three and Four may be within grasp for some at this point. It is recommended, however, that Step Five, the Messianic enthusiasm of a few undergraduates notwithstanding, be approached with considerable caution and constraint.

cause there is often a decided gap between one's *acquaintance* with a subject matter and his *application* of it. The incidents afford the opportunity to move beyond a superficial understanding of the patterns of miscommunication to a deeper, more enduring appreciation of them.

It is suggested that the reader will benefit from the incidents to the extent that he "bores into them." He should not be content with an appraisal of the obvious. To the incidents he should bring questions rather than preconceived answers: What is going on in the incident? What has happened? Why did it occur? What were the underlying assumptions of the communicators involved? What could have been done to prevent it or at least to diminish its consequences? What could be done now?

The incidents were allocated to the chapters because they appeared to this writer and to most of his students (virtually all of the incidents have been "class tested") to exemplify in some manner or other the content of the chapter to which they are appended. This is not to suggest that other patterns of miscommunication (either within or outside this book) cannot or should not be perceived in the incidents. On the contrary, the reader is encouraged to probe, to examine, to analyze, and to dissect as far as his insights and skills will permit.

In sum, the purpose of this book is not unlike that of medical training. While there is no pretense of turning out "Doctors of Communication," there is the earnest hope that the reader, after acquiring some background from a given chapter, will proceed to "practice" on the appended incidents. In them he will find the opportunity to develop a heightened sensitivity to the communicative processes of others and, perhaps, to his own. And it is genuinely hoped that he will begin to acquire awarenesses and techniques for avoiding and coping with these patterns of miscommunication in "real life."

ACKNOWLEDGMENTS

My deepest appreciation goes to M. Kendig, Director of the Institute of General Semantics, Lakeville, Connecticut, for her critical discussion of the draft of most of the chapters, and to Robert R. Hume, Assistant Director, Public Information and Publications, International Association of Chiefs of Police, Washington, D.C., for his invaluable editorial assistance with the final manuscript.

Serving as unofficial editors (because of the state of the material when it reached them) were Joyce Larsen, Carter Crowen, and Verna Kummer who generously and expertly typed the manuscript.

I want to thank, too, the students of Northwestern and DePaul Universities and the administrators and professionals of numerous business, professional, government, and industrial organizations who permitted me to share theories and techniques with them.

Not the least of my gratitude goes to my wife Arlene who somehow managed to shield me from our three wonderful but very active sons.

Finally, and it should go without saying, any errors and shortcomings in this book are uniquely my own and undoubtedly result from good advice unheeded.

WILLIAM V. HANEY

NORTHWESTERN UNIVERSITY
March, 1960

TABLE OF CONTENTS

CHAPTER   PAGE

  I. INTRODUCTION 1

 II. MISEVALUATION AND MISCOMMUNICATION 5

III. THE INFERENCE-OBSERVATION CONFUSION 12

   INCIDENTS

     56 Minutes before Pearl Harbor 25
     The Case of the Ledgers 29
     General Patton and the Sicilian Slapping Incidents 32
     False Armistice 37
     The Man and the Desk 40

 IV. BY-PASSING 41

   INCIDENTS

     Was There a Noise? 63
     The Product-Information Program 63
     Ammons v. Wilson & Co. (A), (B) 65
     Construction of a Sailplane 67
     Jack McGuire 70
     Room 406 71
     The Sturdy Corporate Homesteader 72

  V. ALLNESS 75

   INCIDENTS

     The Kiss and the Slap 85
     Big Business—Pro and Con 85
     Aldermanic Election 91
     Interview with Miss Winkler 93
     Intelligence Is for Commanders 97
     The Hayden Company 98

 VI. DIFFERENTIATION FAILURES I (INDISCRIMINATION) . . 100

   INCIDENTS

     The Dixon Company 112
     Full Circle 113
     What's Wrong with the Men? 114

CHAPTER   PAGE

Wright Cleaners and Dyers, Ltd. 115
The Wayland Company 117
On a Bus 119
The New Neighbor 120

VII.   DIFFERENTIATION FAILURES II (POLARIZATION) . . . 122

Incidents

Deadly Force 134
Evans and Borne 135
The Student Answers 136
Mayhall House 136
The Case of the Storage Shelves 139
Two Factions 140

VIII. DIFFERENTIATION FAILURES III (THE FROZEN
       EVALUATION) 143

Incidents

Ordeal in London 156
Money Troubles 157
The "Good Old Days" 158
The Knight Manufacturing Company 159
Spring Wooing 160

IX.   INTENSIONAL ORIENTATION I (A GENERAL STATEMENT) 162

Incidents

The "Water-American" 170
"Get Off Route 25, Young Man" 170
Report from Rainbow Land 173
The Trials of Galileo 174
The Hall-Barwell Letters (A), (B), (C) 176
Negro-White Differences 180
Profits—The Importance of How Much 181
Making Glamor Sell Glamor 182
The Star Spangled Banner 183

X.   INTENSIONAL ORIENTATION II ("POINTING" AND
       "ASSOCIATING") 185

Incidents

Galvanized Sheets 199
Case of the Growing Boy 200
Seek to Change Name of Cicero 200
Sticks and Stones 201
The Manatee 202
The Four Goals of Labor 202

CHAPTER   PAGE

    Name It a Name 203
    Prestige Foods 203
    Flight from Scorn 206
    McCall College 207

  XI.   INTENSIONAL ORIENTATION III (BLINDERING) 209

    INCIDENTS

    The Rawley Company 221
    The Name of the Situation as Affecting Behavior 223
    Arno Annello, Machinist 226
    You Get What You Want 229
    The Roberts Machine Company 233
    Flies, Typhoid, and Publicity 236

  XII.   TRIGGER TO DISPUTE 239

    INCIDENTS

    Is This Man Mad? 253
    The Cocktail Party 254
    The Accident 255
    "They Don't Do It Our Way" 257
    On a Certain Blindness in Human Beings 260
    Speech Experts Vary in Rating MacArthur 262

  XIII.   UNDELAYED REACTIONS 264

    INCIDENTS

    The Logan Company 273
    The Mid-Western Telephone Company 275
    Air Judge's Charge of Abuse by Police 277
    Your Eyes Can Deceive You 279
    Torment in a Neighborhood 281
    Dyer Public Relations, Inc. (C) 284

  XIV   OVERVIEW 289

A BIBLIOGRAPHY ON COMMUNICATION AND RELATED AREAS 295

INDEX 315

INDEX TO INCIDENTS 319

Chapter I

INTRODUCTION

IT IS AXIOMATIC that clear and effective communication is essential in business—and in government, hospitals, schools, homes—anywhere people deal with one another. It is difficult, in fact, to imagine even the simplest, most elementary interpersonal activity which does not depend upon communication in one form or another.

The concern for communication in business, in particular, has grown enormously. Among the scores, if not hundreds, of factors responsible for this burgeoning interest must surely be the insights being developed by management. Today's administrator is aware that the efficiency of a group depends to a great extent on how well the efforts of its individual members can be co-ordinated. But he also appreciates that co-ordination does not just "happen." He realizes, for example, that satisfactory communication is necessary if he and his employees are to achieve understanding and co-operation; if he is to cope with the problems which come with geographical decentralization and departmental specialization; if he is to present a desirable image of his organization to its various publics, etc. In dealing with these and many other concerns the modern administrator has become, characteristically, a *communicator*. Studies indicate that aside from communicating—speaking, writing, listening, reading, and thinking (*intra*personal communication)—top administrators do virtually nothing! Even middle- and lower-management personnel devote the great bulk of their working hours to the processes and problems of communication.[1]

With all this increased interest, one might expect improvements in the communicative process. And, indeed, there has been fantastic advancement—in some areas. With the aid of modern electronic equipment it is possible to send, receive, and store prodigious amounts of information with incredible speed—and reach unlimited numbers of people in the process.

---

[1] Milton M. Mandell and Pauline Duckworth, "The Supervisor's Job: A Survey," *Personnel,* Vol. XXXI (1955), pp. 456–62.

Quantity, speed, and coverage, however, are not the only require-ments of communication. It is also imperative that we communicate *clearly* and *precisely*. But, in contrast to the technological improve-ments, progress toward greater *understandability* has come much more slowly. It is still entirely possible for persons to fail to understand one another, even though they speak the "same" language; for firms to snarl orders and lose customer confidence; for nations to break off diplomatic relations and even declare wars because of distortions in communication. As veteran Federal Mediator Douglas Brown put it: "At least 99 per cent of the union-company difficulties I deal with either start with or are complicated by poor or inadequate or omitted communication."

PATTERNS OF MISCOMMUNICATION

What happens when men talk together, write to and for one an-other? Why are they sometimes unsuccessful in exchanging their thoughts clearly, understandably, and effectively? When Green speaks, why does White fail to "get" him, even though White tries to under-stand? How is it possible for an executive, earnestly wanting to com-municate with his employees, to make costly errors in terms of money and morale? How is it that a military commander can issue orders which can be misinterpreted so as to lead to incalculable disasters? This is the nature of the problems which concern us in this book. But let us delineate the book's scope more specifically. We can begin by examining the communicative process.

Imagine a very ordinary and simple communication situation. Mr. A feels warm and asks Mr. B to open a window, which he does. Con-sider, now, the steps involved in this communication. First of all, A had something to communicate—a desire to have B open a window. His next step was to *encode* this desire into a set of symbols (words, in this case) which he felt B would understand. He then proceeded to express or *send* (orally, in this instance) the message to B. The message then took the form of vibrations in the air (we will call this phase the *medium*). B *received* these vibrations with his auditory equipment which forwarded them in the form of electrochemical impulses, which B experienced as sounds, to his brain. B then *decoded* these sounds into words and then to a visualization of what A was asking him to do. Finally, B *responded* to his decoding by performing an action which led A to believe the communication had been successful.

The communication process is extraordinarily subject to the maxim that a chain is only as strong as its weakest link. In other words, for the process to have been impaired, distorted, or even prevented, only one phase, or link, need have been affected. The communication could have been vitiated in the *sending* stage if A had failed, for example, to articulate the sounds loudly, slowly, or distinctly enough; or in the *medium* stage if the vocal vibrations had been obstructed by, say, a double or triple pane of glass such as separates a TV studio from its control room or overwhelmed by competing vibrations, as in a noisy factory; or in the *receiving* stage if B suffered from a hearing loss.

Each of these phases is crucial because, to repeat, an interference or breakdown in *any* of them could effectively damage or prohibit the over-all process. But there are two other phases which are equally critical and much less understood—*encoding* and *decoding*. It is with these steps of the process that this book is primarily concerned. But we need to delimit the book's focus still further.

Encoding and decoding are subject to a great many difficulties. The sender may be unable to encode an adequate message because, for example, he is afflicted with aphasia or he has grammatical or logical difficulty in formulating his thoughts, or he is hampered by a limited vocabulary, or (and this is of special concern in this book) his communication is conditioned by certain fallacious and unconsciously held assumptions.[2]

In summary, then, the *patterns of miscommunication* to which this book addresses itself are *those which arise in the encoding and decoding phases of the process and which emanate in large part from certain faulty and often unconsciously held premises on the part of the communicator—be he sender and/or receiver.* Let us return to Mr. A and Mr. B to illustrate.

Suppose in transmitting his desire about opening the window, A chose to say: "Let's get a breath of fresh air in here!" By this he intends to convey simply that he feels warm and that he would like B to open the window. Now note some of the assumptions which may be underlying A's remark and of which he may be quite unaware. He could be assuming that because he is warm, B also feels warm and will welcome the idea of opening a window. He could be assuming that because B is closer to the window, he is the "logical" one to open it and that B will

---

2 The *receiver* may also be affected by aphasic, grammatical, logical, or vocabulary problems in decoding words. Furthermore, he is equally liable to the insidious influence of erroneous assumptions of which he may be unaware.

understand and agree with this. He could be assuming that because he means something by his words, B will understand them as A intends them.

Actually, none of these assumptions is *necessarily* warranted. B may be quite comfortable or even chilly with the window closed and thus be offended by A's apparent selfishness. Furthermore, he may fail to see A's logic about B's proximity to the window and instead resent A's "pushing him around." B may even fail to interpret A's words as they were intended. He may, conceivably, hear A's remark as an indictment against B's failure to open the window previously. It is even possible that B may feel that A is not interested in opening a window at all but is sarcastically alluding to B's habits of personal hygiene! B as the receiver, of course, is just as prone to contribute to a miscommunication, influenced as he is by his own unconscious false assumptions.

What are some of these insidious assumptions? Where do they spring from? How do they affect our communications? What are their consequences? How can we recognize and cope with them? These are key questions, and in the next chapter we shall begin to explore them.

Chapter II

MISEVALUATION AND
MISCOMMUNICATION

IT IS USEFUL to think of man's communication as a form of his behavior—a most essential and complex form, to be sure. Therefore,
the following postulates about human behavior in general are intended
to apply as well to communication in particular.

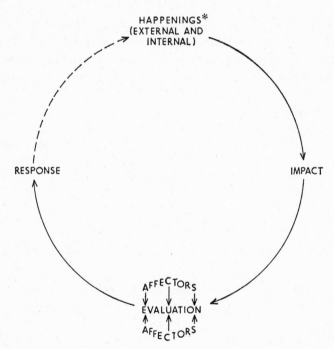

* This simplified diagram does not apply to simpler behaviors such as reflexes which do not involve
an evaluation phase.

First of all, behavior is caused. That is, man always acts in response
to some stimulation. These *happenings* may occur *outside* the person,
as, for example, the scene of a boy digging for worms, the roar of a
plane overhead, or the aroma of frying bacon. Or they may occur
within the individual as, say, a feeling of nausea or euphoria, a mem-

ory, the "flash" of an insight, etc. These external and internal stimuli make an *impact* on the individual's nervous system as visual, auditory, olfactory, tactile, gustatory, organic, etc., sensations. He is continuously *evaluating*[1] ("sizing up," assessing, interpreting) the impacts of these happenings, although he may often be quite unaware that he is doing so. Largely on the basis of his evaluation of the impact of the happenings, the individual *responds* by talking, smiling, blushing, walking, fighting, or perhaps by not overtly acting at all. These responses may now serve, in turn, as new happenings. These happenings may make an impact, may be evaluated, etc. The entire sequence (happenings-impact-evaluation-response) goes on incessantly and may occur, of course, in a fraction of the time it has taken to describe it here.

THE ROLE OF AFFECTORS

But there is more to the story. First, it needs to be underscored that one's responses in many situations are immediately preceded by and, to a great extent, determined by his *evaluations*.

Before the war it was customary to allow civilians aboard Navy ships during visiting hours on Sunday. The Saratoga, which was anchored in the San Pedro–Long Beach area, attracted a lot of these visitors, and usually they found its decks as steady as their own front porches. Occasionally, however, a freak wind would raise swells behind the breakwater, and if these swells hit the Saratoga broadside, she would roll most heartily. When this happened, the visitors were loaded into running boats and taken quickly ashore.

One stout matron was so resentful at having her visit cut short in this way that the officer of the deck had to have her escorted to the accommodation ladder in order to get her off on the last visitors' boat. This ladder is simply a set of open steps leading down the side of the ship from the deck to a small platform near the water, from which the visitors step into the shoregoing boats. The O.D. carefully cautioned the lady to stay off this platform until he gave the word, but she was too angry to pay attention. Head high, she stepped briskly down to the platform and waited for the boat.

Meanwhile the Saratoga had completed its swing in one direction and was rolling back. The platform started down, hit the water; the O.D. shouted another warning, but by this time the chill harbor water was well above the woman's ankles.

Gasping with surprise and indignation, she glared up at the helpless O.D. "You young whippersnapper!" she roared. "You did that on purpose!"[2]

---

[1] In the communicative process *evaluation* occurs in the encoding and decoding phases.

[2] *Saturday Evening Post*, May 1, 1948. Reprinted by permission of the author, Captain Marcus A. Peel, U.S.N.

The lady with the wet feet responded in precise accord with her evident *evaluation* of the situation!

Another important aspect of the behavioral process is that one's *evaluations* are by no means determined solely by the nature of the *happenings* or stimuli which make an *impact* on his nervous system. Evaluations of pain make good illustrations of this fact.

Dr. Henry K. Beecher, during World War II, was able to make comparative studies of soldiers and male civilians undergoing pain from similar operations. He found that only 32 per cent of the soldiers (all of whom had been wounded in combat) said "Yes" when asked if the pain was severe enough to require something for relief. On the other hand, 83 per cent of the civilians recovering from noncombat operations (despite the fact that the surgical trauma is less than in combat operations) asked for a hypodermic injection for relief.[3]

It seems quite evident that stimuli alone do not account for differences in response. The *meaning* that the pain has for the patient is a very considerable factor in determining the extent of his suffering. Unbolstered by the assurance of security if disabled and by the glory of having served his country and by the sense of relief at having escaped a far greater calamity, the civilian patient apparently *evaluates* his pain as markedly more severe than his uniformed counterpart.

One's evaluations, then, which usually have such a direct bearing on one's responses, are themselves subject to influencing factors. To appreciate the role of these *affectors*, as we shall call them, read these phrases.

Almost everyone reads these as "Snake in the grass." "Busy as a beaver," and "Paris in the spring." But look again—it is "Snake in the *the* grass," etc. Silly? Perhaps, but why do we read them incorrectly? One possible answer relates to our past experience with these very familiar phrases. Let someone say "snake in the _____" and "grass" will immediately occur to most of us. Another reasonable explanation is our habit of reading clusters of words rather than word-by-word, and thus we are more prone to skip over individual words—especially those we usually consider inconsequential, such as the short articles "a" and "the." Chances are that we would have caught the trick if "important" words such as "snake," "grass," "beaver," etc., had been repeated. Again, the separation of the repeated words, which is seemingly legitimatized by the triangles, could have thrown us off. The same words stretched out on a straight line don't fool as many people. We could have been misled, too, by our predisposition to gloss over apparent "typographical errors."

Any or all of these factors or others could have *affected* our *evaluation* of the situation, which then led us to respond inappropriately. This, then, is what is meant by *affectors*—one's habits, prejudices, experiences, abilities, physiological-emotional state, likes and dislikes, education, hereditary factors, attitudes, etc. These and many other factors may influence our evaluations and thus, indirectly but importantly, our responses.

There is a category of affectors which merits special attention. These are the assumptions that we develop partially, at least, from our language system. Some of these assumptions about ourselves, other people, situations—about everything, actually—are really quite dangerous and for three reasons: (1) Many of them are downright false. The succeeding chapters will deal with some of the more important of these fallacious assumptions. (2) They are often unknown to the person who holds them. He has acquired them, for the most part, as a child and has taken them so for granted that he is rarely aware of them and virtually never questions them. The consequence, then, is that his evaluations are frequently tainted by these insidious erroneous notions. (3) Finally, their influence is effective, i.e., they significantly affect the way we think and feel and act. Let me illustrate. One of these fallacies is that words are, rather than merely arbitrary tags for things, somehow inextricably linked with what they represent.[4] This is sheer nonsense, of course, but we do not always behave as if it were. In fact, our reaction to the "thing" is sometimes distinctly colored by its label.

An incident occurred several years ago while the late Professor Irving J. Lee was giving his exceedingly popular course, "Language and Thought," at Northwestern University. Dr. Lee had several graduate assistants who were occasionally given the opportunity to lecture before a class of two to three hundred undergraduates. On one such occasion an assistant set out

---

[4] This fallacy will be developed more fully in Chapter 10, "Pointing" and "Associating."

to "dramatize" the tendency to react to labels rather than to what the labels represent.

He distributed bits of food which resembled dried biscuit and assured the class that the food was sanitary and nutritious and added that most of them had probably never eaten this type of food before. Each student was to taste the food and decide how much he liked or disliked it. Most students found it relatively tasteless and reported an indifferent reaction. A few said they liked it slightly and even fewer expressed a mild dislike. *Not one* said he liked or disliked it extremely.

The assistant tabulated the results on the blackboard and suggested that perhaps the food would be more tasty with cream and sugar. He added that it was quite inexpensive and readily available. At this point he reached behind his desk and held up a large, distinctly labeled box and said "Just go to your grocer's and ask for _____ Dog Biscuits!"

The reaction was precisely what he had hoped for—a great deal of groaning, shrieking, laughing, feigned nausea (and some not so feigned). Whereupon he triumphantly cried out: "Now, just what are you reacting to—those innocuous bits of food—or to the words on this box!"[5]

THE MAP-TERRITORY ANALOGY

For focusing attention on the insidious role that language plays in influencing human behavior we are primarily indebted to the late Alfred Korzybski.[6] Korzybski contended that the relation of our as-

---

5 Elated by his success, the assistant repeated his "dramatization" in the next term. But soon the word spread and students came to expect such things from the course "where they served dog biscuits." Undiscouraged, he changed his tactic. He baked some "special" cookies, passed them out to the class, and tabulated the results. The cookies were sweet and the reactions were unanimously favorable.

"Glad you liked them. I'll give you the recipe," he volunteered, "so you can bake some at home if you wish."

The recipe: So much flour, sugar, shortening . . . and two cups of carefully cleaned grasshoppers!

He admitted later that, even had he been able to restore order, he would not have dared to ask: "Now, what are you reacting to . . . ?"

6 Korzybski's *Science and Sanity: An Introduction to Non-Aristotelian Systems and General Semantics* (Lancaster, Pa.: Science Press Printing Co., 1933; in the 4th edition [1958] it is distributed by the Institute of General Semantics, Lakeville, Conn.) is considered the inaugural of the discipline of general semantics. Voluminous, difficult reading for many, but profound, the book's theses have been "translated" and applied by such able writers as J. Samuel Bois, *Explorations in Awareness* (New York: Harper & Bros., 1957); S. I. Hawakawa, *Language in Thought and Action* (New York: Harcourt, Brace & Co., 1949); Wendell Johnson, *People in Quandaries* (New York: Harper & Bros., 1946) and *Your Most Enchanted Listener* (New York: Harper & Bros., 1956), and Irving J. Lee, *Language Habits in Human Affairs* (New York: Harper & Bros., 1941), and *How to Talk with People* (New York: Harper & Bros., 1952). Two journals (*ETC.: A Review of General Semantics*, edited by S. I. Hayakawa, and the *General Semantics Bulletin*, edited by M. Kendig) publish theoretical and experimental studies concerning or relating to the discipline. Two organizations, the Institute of General Semantics (Lakeville, Conn.), with summer and winter seminar-workshops and numerous other training activities, and the International Society for General Semantics (400 W. North Ave., Chicago, Ill.), with chapters throughout the world, use Korzybski's formulations as their focal point.

sumptions, unconscious or otherwise, to the phenomena with which they were concerned (people, things, theories, processes, relationships, etc.) is analogous to the relationship of maps to the territories they are used to represent. Geographical maps are "pictures," or abstractions, of their territories. Our assumptive maps, similarly, are "pictures" of the "territories" they are used to represent. Man relies on both kinds of maps as guides in his dealings with their respective territories.

But there is an essential difference between our geographical and our assumptive maps. Cartography has advanced to the point that most geographical maps can be followed with great confidence. On the other hand, our assumptive maps are often inadequate and distorted representations of their territories. And we are misled by them because we rely upon them so unquestioningly.

There is another important difference between the two types of maps. Distortions in a geographical map can usually be checked against the territory itself. Suppose you get hold of a faulty road map. As you travel, you discover that the roads, bridges, and railroads are not where the map indicated they should be. Your first inclination might be to suspect the map and search for a "good" one. While it is not necessarily more difficult to check our assumptive maps against their territories, we seldom *do* question them. The fact of the matter is that we usually take them as much for granted as we do the air we breathe.

And so Korzybski perceived that we go through life driving on "roads" and crossing "bridges" which exist only on our assumptive maps, but not in the "territories" they represent—i.e., people, objects, processes, relationships, happenings, etc., as they actually exist and occur. Rarely suspecting these treacherous maps, we are led to treat and react to their territories in immature, foolish, and dangerous ways.

SUMMARY

In these first two chapters we have attempted to delineate the scope of the book and to set out a rationale for its succeeding chapters. In short, as we have indicated, the book focuses upon the encoding and decoding phases of human communication. More specifically, we are concerned with the evaluations (and misevaluations) of the communicator (sender and receiver), which sometimes lead to miscommunications and thus to stupid, immature, dangerous, unsane behavior.

The thesis is that a study of the communicator's evaluations as they are influenced by affectors, such as the fallacious and unconsciously held assumptions that he develops partially through his language system,[7] offers promise for preventing or ameliorating miscommunications and the tension, anguish, friction, misery, and danger which so frequently follow them.

---

[7] *General Information Bulletin,* No. 6, of the International Society for General Semantics asserts the influence of language succinctly and lucidly:

"Nor do we realize how grammar warps our 'thinking.' When we make sentences, we force symbols (words) into certain set relationships. Yet the things which these symbols represent often have quite different relationships. This happens because our grammar preserves many ancient wrong guesses about the world we live in; such as: similar things may be treated as identical; the 'essences' of things never change; parts may be considered without relation to the whole; qualities are properties of 'things'; an event has 'a cause.' Such notions once fit man's knowledge of the world. But our century has seen the birth of the relativity theory and atomic fission. Today, primitive language habits serve only to widen the frightening chasm between our lagging civilization and our leaping technology."

Chapter III

THE INFERENCE-OBSERVATION CONFUSION

Suppose we get into the first of our patterns of miscommunication by inviting you to test yourself.

Instructions

Read the following little story. Assume that all the information presented in it is definitely accurate and true. Read it carefully because it has ambiguous parts designed to lead you astray. No need to memorize it though. You can refer back to it whenever you wish.

Next read the statements about the story and check each to indicate whether you consider it true, false or "?". "T" means that the statement is *definitely true* on the basis of the information presented in the story. "F" means that it is *definitely false*. "?" means that it may be either true or false and that you cannot be certain which on the basis of the information presented in the story. If any part of a statement is doubtful make it "?". *Answer each statement in turn, and do not go back to change any answer later and don't re-read any statements after you have answered them. This will distort your score.*

To start with, here is a sample story with correct answers:

Sample Story

You arrive home late one evening and see that the lights are on in your living room. There is only one car parked in front of your house, and the words "Harold R. Jones, M.D." are spelled in small gold letters across one of the car's doors.

Statements about Sample Story

1. The car parked in front of your house has lettering on one of its doors.   (T) F ?

   (This is a "definitely true" statement because it is directly corroborated by the story.)

2. Someone in your family is sick.   T F (?)

   (This could be true and then again it might not be. Perhaps Dr. Jones is paying a social call at your home or perhaps he has gone to the house next door or across the street.)

3. No car is parked in front of your house. T (F) ?

(A "definitely false" statement because the story directly contradicts it.)

4. The car parked in front of your house belongs to a man named Johnson. T F (?)

(May seem very likely false, but can you be sure? Perhaps the car has just been sold.)

So much for the sample. It should warn you of some of the kinds of traps to look for. Now begin the actual test. Remember mark each statement *in order*—don't skip around or change answers later.

THE STORY[1]

A business man had just turned off the lights in the store when a man appeared and demanded money. The owner opened a cash register. The contents of the cash register were scooped up, and the man sped away. A member of the police force was notified promptly.

STATEMENTS ABOUT THE STORY

1. A man appeared after the owner had turned off his store lights. T F ?

2. The robber was a *man*. T F ?

3. The man did not demand money. T F ?

4. The man who opened the cash register was the owner. T F ?

5. The store-owner scooped up the contents of the cash register and ran away. T F ?

6. Someone opened a cash register. T F ?

7. After the man who demanded the money scooped up the contents of the cash register, he ran away. T F ?

8. While the cash register contained money, the story does *not* state *how much*. T F ?

9. The robber demanded money of the owner. T F ?

10. The story concerns a series of events in which only three persons are referred to: the owner of the store, a man who demanded money, and a member of the police force. T F ?

11. The following events were included in the story: someone demanded money, a cash register was opened, its contents were scooped up, and a man dashed out of the store. T F ?

If you will permit me to withhold the answers for a few pages I

---

[1] The story and statements are a portion of the "Uncritical Inference Test," copyrighted, 1955, by William V. Haney.

would like to describe a classic study[2] to you. It was conducted over forty years ago and has been repeated in many forms since but always, to the best of my knowledge, the results of the Otto experiment have been corroborated.

The scene is a University of Wisconsin classroom. A carefully planned incident is about to occur. Of the seventy-five students present, only four, A, B, C, and D (and the instructor), are "in" on the stunt. At a given signal the following events occur: (1) While the instructor is collecting papers from students in the front row, A suddenly hits B with his fist, and B retaliates by striking A with a book, and the two fall to quarreling very loudly; (2) at the same time C throws two silver dollars into the air, permits them to fall to the floor, and scrambles after them as they roll away from him, and picks them up; (3) the instructor now orders A, B, and C from the room; (4) as he does so, D simply gets up and walks from the room at a normal gait; (5) as A, B, and C are preparing to leave, the instructor walks to the

2 M. C. Otto, "Testimony and Human Nature," *Journal of Criminal Law and Criminology,* Vol. IX (1918), pp. 98–104.

blackboard at the front of the room, glances at his watch, writes "9:45" on the blackboard, erases it, and writes it again; (6) A, B, and C leave the room, and the instructor turns to the class and says, in effect: "You have all seen what has happened, and you know that you may very well be called upon to give testimony.[3] Let us now take time to write out reports of what we have observed." And with the instructor's assistance the class composes a series of questions to give order to their reports. The following are some of those questions and some of the answers to which these eye witnesses were willing to testify.

Q: Where was the instructor when the disturbance began?

Twenty-two of the students reported that he was near the front of the room; twenty that he was about in the middle; and twenty-one that he was in the rear. A number of students scattered all over the room said they would have testified under oath that the instructor was at his (the student's) desk collecting his paper!

Q: Where was the instructor and what was he doing when the boys left the room?

Only five of the seventy-five reported the "9:45" business with any accuracy. The attention of the others was obviously fixed elsewhere. However, only six said they did not know. The others gave very definite testimony. Three said the instructor was holding the door open for the students to pass through. One said he was standing in the middle of the room muttering, "I'll break this up, or know the reason why." Three remembered him sitting dejectedly at his desk with his face buried in his hands. The consensus of the remaining students was that he was sitting at his desk nervously toying with, variously, the papers he had collected, class cards, his watch chain, a piece of chalk, etc. He appeared "as if not knowing what to do," and "his face wore an expression of embarrassment and uneasiness."

Q: What did C do?

You will recall that C had thrown two silver dollars into the air. They fell to the floor, and he hurried to pick them up. Some students reported that either A or B, in their fighting, had dropped some money; that these coins had rolled to the front of the room; and C had scrambled to pick them up. Other students said an adjustable desk arm from one of the classroom seats had been broken off (and A, incidentally, had tried to poke B with it) during the fighting; the little ratchet-ball inside had fallen out and had rolled to the front. It was this ball that C had rushed to pick up. The stu-

---

[3] At this time the university was on a student self-governing basis. This meant that any student disciplinary case, as this incident was to all appearances, would be submitted to a student court and testimony would be taken. In other words, it is most likely that the students saw the situation as quite real and one for which they might very well be asked to appear in court to give testimony.

dent sitting next to C, ironically enough, insisted he had seen a little steel ball come rolling out between C's feet and that C grabbed it and put it in his pocket.

Q: How did A, B, and C look as they left the room?

The reports corresponded directly with the observer's attitude toward the instructor's action. If the student felt the instructor had been fair and justified in sending the boys from the room, then they tended to look "embarrassed" and "ashamed." If, however, the student thought the instructor too severe, the boys looked "angry," "injured," and "abused." C's neighbor, referred to previously as perceiving C do nothing more heinous than pocket a steel ball, reported that C had looked "very angry," while A and B appeared "sheepish."

Q: What did D do?

This question was quite accidental. While the class was deciding the questions to be answered for their reports, one student asked: "Are we to include the fact that D rushed from the room at the beginning of the disturbance?" The instructor replied noncommittally: "Please report what you saw as completely as you can, but report no more."

It seems highly likely that, with a vociferous struggle being waged in an opposite section of the room, only a few at most would even have noticed D's casual departure. Yet the suggestion of the student's question plus the obvious fact that D was now absent was apparently enough to convince over 85 per cent of the students that they *had* seen D leave, and most of them were quite confident about the specific manner in which he left—saying, variously, that he had "rushed," "hurried," "bolted," or "made a wild dash from the room."

Mr. Otto, who was concerned with the bearing of this sort of behavior on the taking of legal testimony, seems amply justified in his alarm:

The importance of these facts is obvious. If it is impossible for a witness to reproduce an occurrence as it took place in his presence, even when asked to do so directly after the occurrence; if it is his very nature to demand consistency in such items as he does get, to the point of rejecting some and creating others; if such a thing as sending three men from a room at the same time may act as a suggestion around which is built up what the witness believes himself to have observed concerning them; what are the chances of arriving at the truth under conditions[4] which often obtain where testimony is taken?[5]

It may seem incredible that people could be capable of observing,

---

[4] Referring to such factors as the time lapse between the observation and the giving of testimony (involving sometimes hours, days, weeks, or even years), the "third-degree" tactics of examining authorities, the leading and suggestive questions of cross-examining attorneys, etc.

[5] Otto, *op. cit.,* p. 104.

remembering, and reporting an incident so distortedly—that they could fail so utterly to distinguish between what they had observed and what they only guessed.

OBSERVATIONAL AND INFERENTIAL STATEMENTS

One vital facet of this phenomenon is the form of language we use when we report. Practically speaking, there are two kinds of declarative statements I can make about what I observe (see, hear, smell, taste, etc.). Assuming that my vision and the illumination are "normal," I can look at a man wearing a red tie and say: "That man is wearing a red tie." This is called a *statement of observation* because it corresponds directly to what I have observed. On the other hand, I can look at the same man and say just as confidently: "That man bought that tie." Unless I actually observed him purchasing the tie, this statement is for me a *statement of inference*. I *inferred* he bought the tie because (1) he's wearing it; (2) he looks honest; (3) he appears to be the kind of person who would select his own ties; etc. I may be right—but I may be wrong. Perhaps someone gave him the tie—or loaned it to him. Perhaps he found it. He may even be the type that prefers to shop after the stores have closed! The point is that, since I did not *observe* him buying the tie, the statement for me is necessarily an inferential one.

Observational and inferential statements are often extremely difficult to distinguish. Certainly the structure of their language offers no indication of their differences. There may be no grammatical, syntactical, orthographical, or pronunciational distinctions between them whatsoever. Moreover, the tones or inflections in which they are uttered may sound equally "certain." Recall the plight of the stout matron on the "Saratoga" (Chap. II). What could sound more assured—what could have more of the ring of authority in it than her bellow: "You young whippersnapper! You did that on purpose!" And yet that statement is necessarily an inference—she couldn't possibly have *observed* the O.D.'s "purpose."

In other words, there is nothing in the structure of our language that makes it inescapable that we discriminate between inferential and observational statements. It seems reasonable to assume, then, that our failure to distinguish on these verbal levels may contribute appreciably to the difficulty we have on pre-verbal levels, namely, our propensity to confuse *inference* and *observation*. In short, we find it enticingly easy to make inferences and to utter inferential statements

with the false assurance that we are dealing with "facts"—and the consequences of acting upon inferences *as if* they were observations are
often less than pleasant.

"Mother, I wish I didn't look so flat-chested," said my 15-year-old daughter as she stood before the mirror in her first formal dress.
I remedied the matter by inserting puffs of cotton in strategic places.
Then I hung around Mary's neck a string of seed pearls—just as my grandmother had done for my mother and my mother for me.
At midnight her escort brought her home. The moment the door closed
behind him Mary burst into tears.
"I'm never going out with him again," she sobbed. "Mother, do you
know what he said to me? He leaned across the table and said, 'Gee, you
look sharp tonight, Mary. Are those real?' "
"I hope you told him they were," I said indignantly. "They've been in
the family for three generations!"
My daughter stopped sobbing. "Oh, the pearls. Good heavens, I'd forgotten all about them."[6]

—Mrs. J.L.H. *(Alabama)*

Lest the reader feel that the inference-observation confusion pertains
only to stout matrons, teen-age girls, and University of Wisconsin students of 1918, let us bring the matter somewhat closer to home. Here
are the answers to the test I trust you took at the beginning of the
chapter.

1. ? Do you *know* that the "business man" and the "owner" are one
   and the same?
2. ? Was there *necessarily* a robbery involved here? Perhaps the man
   was the rent-collector—or the owner's son—they sometimes demand money.
3. F An easy one to keep up morale.
4. ? Was the owner a *man?*
5. ? May seem unlikely but the story does not definitely preclude it.
6. T
7. ? Of course, we don't know who scooped up the contents of the
   cash register or that the man necessarily *ran* away.
8. ? The dependent clause is doubtful—the cash register may or
   may not have contained money.
9. ? Again, a robber?
10. ? Only three persons if you count the businessman and the owner
    as one—but can you?
11. ? "Dashed?" Could he not have "sped away" on roller skates or in
    a car? And do we know that he actually left the store?

6 From "Life in These United States," *Reader's Digest,* September, 1951. Reprinted by
permission.

THE UNCALCULATED RISK

We need to dig deeper into this formulation we call the inference-observation confusion.

"Taking a calculated risk" is a familiar phrase we ordinarily use to describe a situation in which a person has decided to take an action which *may* have undesirable consequences—embarrassment, loss of money, injury, etc. But we imply that he is *aware* of these potential effects and, furthermore, has assessed the likelihood that they will occur. Generally speaking, when one takes a *calculated* risk, he is apt to be in a better position to avoid the hazards or at least to adjust to them, should they occur.

The inference-observation confusion, on the other hand, frequently involves the taking of what we might call "uncalculated risks." An actual traffic accident case[7] will serve as a departure point.

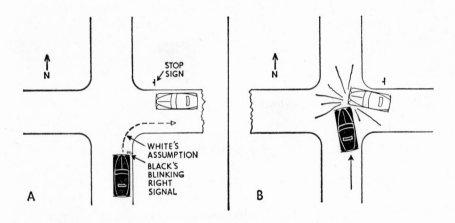

Diagram A shows Driver White halted at a stop sign. Driver Black is approaching the intersection from the south. His right directional signal is blinking. White *assumes* Black is going to turn right at the intersection and, acting on this inference *as if* it were fact, starts to cross the intersection. Black does *not* turn but continues northward and is unable to avoid a costly collision with White (Diagram *B*). The directional signal? Black had intended to turn right into a driveway —fifty yards *beyond* the intersection. Which was liable for the per-

---

7 See William V. Haney, "Are Accident-Prone Drivers Unconscious-Inference-Prone?" *General Semantics Bulletin*, Nos. 20 and 21 (1957). Reprinted in *Traffic Digest and Review*, Vol. V (March, 1957).

sonal injuries and property damage?—White for failing to yield the right of way.

Let us go back and examine White's behavior more closely. We shall presume that he saw Black approaching and that he noted the blinking directional signal. At about this time he must have made his key assumption that Black was going to turn right at the intersection. Somehow in the process, however, this inference became merged with his observations. Perhaps he forgot that he had, in fact, guessed—or perhaps he was never fully aware that he was in the realm of inference. At any rate, his crucial error occurred at the moment he treated the inference *as if* it were not.

It was at this point that he took his *uncalculated risk*. White, in entering the intersection with Black approaching, was taking a very definite risk. But, since he apparently failed to perceive his inference *as an inference*—i.e., as a situation involving a degree of uncertainty—he did not realize the risk he was taking and thus was hardly prompted to calculate its probability.[8]

In sum, the inference-observation confusion apparently occurs as follows: (1) Someone makes an inference, (2) fails to recognize or remember that he has done so, (3) thus does not calculate the risk involved, (4) proceeds to act upon his assumption *as if* it were "certain," and (5) ends by taking an unrecognized and uncalculated risk which may sometimes prove costly, dangerous, or even fatal.

CORRECTIVES

The basic procedure for avoiding the inference-observation confusion is twofold: (1) we must be aware when we are inferring, as distinguished from observing, and (2) we must calculate the degree of probability that our inferences are correct.

I venture an estimate that the bulk of our difficulty with guesses, predictions, assumptions, hunches, conjectures—inferences, generally—is not so much that we perform inadequately at 2 but rather

---

[8] Thomas Fansler, of the National Safety Council, described the phenomenon in this manner: "In checking over case histories of traffic accidents, an observer cannot help being impressed with the number of times the idea of suddenness or unexpectedness occurs. After the accident, the driver will report, 'Suddenly the man ran in front of my car,' or 'I expected the other fellow to stop but instead . . .' The inference that may be drawn from this is that there was an *expected* pattern of circumstances in the minds of the drivers and that the change from the *expected* pattern to a 'sudden' or 'unexpected' pattern was partly responsible for the accident." From "The Dynamics of a Traffic Accident," by Thomas Fansler in a Research Memorandum of the National Safety Council (reprinted in the *Traffic Review*, Vol. III, No. 3 [Summer, 1949]).

that we fail at 1 and thus never reach 2. For example, if I am unaware that "the man bought the tie" is an inference on my part, I am hardly likely to be prompted to assess the probability of my inference, since I don't perceive it as an inference in the first place. That is, I will never consider asking myself, "How *likely* is such and such?" if "such and such" has been my observation—*or* an inference I unconsciously consider as my observation.

It was suggested earlier that an important contributor to the confusion of inference for observation was the difficulty that we have in discriminating *statements* of inference from *statements* of observation. Studies[9] indicate that one *can learn* to make this distinction habitually and thus markedly increase his "inference-awareness."

How, then, does one go about it? The first step is to learn the characteristics of statements of observation and statements of inference.

Statements of Observation	*Statements of Inference*
1. Can be made only *after* observation.	1. Can be made at any time.
2. Must stay with what one has observed—must not go beyond. (I observed the man *wearing* the tie —his *buying* it, if he did so, was beyond my observation.)	2. Can go beyond observation— well beyond. We can infer to the limits of our imaginations.
3. Can be made only by the observer. (The observational statements of another are still my inferences, assuming that I have not observed what he has.)	3. Can be made by anyone.

These three requisites of observational statements are vital. You simply do not have a statement of observation if each of these criteria is not satisfied. A fourth pair of chacteristics provides a helpful, but not an essential, contrast:

4. Statements of observation approach "certainty."	4. Statements of inference involve only degrees of probability.

Anyone who has experienced the fantastic Ames perception demonstrations[10] now housed at Princeton University will certainly realize

9 William V. Haney, "Measurement of the Ability to Discriminate between Inferential and Descriptive Statements," unpublished Ph.D. dissertation, Northwestern University, 1953. A précis of the above appeared in *General Semantics Bulletin,* Nos. 16 and 17 (1955). See also my article, "Police Experience and Uncritical Inference Behavior," *General Semantics Bulletin,* Nos. 22 and 23 (1958).

10 See William H. Ittelson, *The Ames Demonstrations in Perception* (Princeton, N.J.: Princeton University Press, 1952).

the necessity for the term "approaches." We can never get quite "all the way" to certainty. Our senses are restricted and imperfect, and our perceptions are subject to suggestion and distortion. But in the practical day-to-day world in which most of us live and work, our observations (and our observational statements) come as close to "certainty" as we frail, fallible human beings can get.

As for inferential statements, think of a continuum with an infinite number of gradations. Label one end "the extremely probable," and the other "the extremely improbable." We are constantly going through the process of "pegging our inferences" (provided that we recognize them as such and try to assess their probability) somewhere on this scale. For instance, the inference that the earth will continue to turn on its axis tomorrow seems so *extremely probable* that we feel quite secure in literally "betting our lives" on it. Or we will stake our lives on the *improbability* of the inference that the sun will be destroyed within the week. To return to my inference about the man with the red tie—that he bought it—I might peg this guess at the 50-50 mark. I might be willing to wager a quarter that he bought the tie, but probably not a dollar and certainly not five. But suppose in answer to my question the man says in all apparent sincerity: "Yes, I bought the tie." This still does not make it an observation for *me,* of course, but his remark may have the practical effect of causing me to change the point on the probability scale. If I know and trust the man, I may now be willing to risk a hundred dollars or even a thousand on the inference. This, then, is the vital process of probability assessment, but, remember, we must be *aware* of when we are dealing with inferences before we can even enter this phase.

I have a short check list I carry around in my head to use when I think it is important to distinguish inference and observation. Perhaps you will find it useful, too:

1. Did I *personally* observe what I am talking or writing about?
2. Do my observational statements stay with, and not go beyond, my observations?
3. When I deal with important inferences, do I assess their probabilities?
4. When I communicate with others, do I label my inferences as such and get them to label theirs?

Not long ago I was discussing this check list with a group of industrial engineers. Afterward one of the men came up and said: "Say, am I glad you made that fourth point. That's the core of my problem. I have a man who is constantly giving me his inferences *as if* they were his observations. Maybe he's afraid to tell me they are only guesses, but, in any event, I go upstairs and report them as observations to my superior—and sometimes they're wrong and I'm in hot water. I think I know now how to deal with this fellow. I'll tell him: 'Look, management doesn't expect us to *know* everything, but they do expect us to know the *difference* between what we know and what we're only guessing at.' "

POSTSCRIPT

I sometimes feel that in urging the distinction between inference and observation I may appear to be implying: "Don't make inferences. Stay away from them. They are dangerous. They only get you into trouble." Nothing could be further from my purpose. In the first place we could not avoid inferences if we tried. We assume incessantly. You and I are assuming that the chairs we are seated on (I am assuming you are sitting on one) will not collapse beneath us. We are assuming that the next breath we take will not be noxious and kill us. When we eat our respective dinners tonight, we will be making a host of inferences about the source and preparation of the food. Whenever we use the Postal Service we make inferences about the speed and safety of our mail. Whenever we take advice from a doctor, attorney, or cleric and whenever we read a newspaper, magazine, or book (this one included), we make inferences about the credibility of their statements. One might be able to reduce the number of his inferences if he resigned from life and lived in bed as a vegetable. But, even so, he would have to make inferences about those who attended him.

In short, we live in a world of risk; some risks we can avoid, many we cannot. In fact, the refusal to take some risks may be quite absurd. The story is told of one of our former statesmen—a man reputed for his extreme caution and precision. He and a friend were traveling through the flatlands of the Midwest when the friend, who had been viewing the scenery, said: "Isn't that a fine flock of sheared sheep over there?" The statesman looked and remarked: "Well, they are sheared on this side, at least."

This chapter is not designed to advocate inaction and indecision. The capacity to infer, after all, is essential in the arts and in the sciences. Analysis, problem solving, planning—all involve inference. Think of any creation—a skyscraper, a portrait, an electronic computer, or a picnic; without inferences, none would have been possible.

The point is this: Since we must make inferences anyway, is it not better (1) to be aware that we are making them so that (2) we will be prompted to calculate the risk involved? The story of the dining-car waiter makes the point:

It seems a prosperous-looking man walked into the train's diner, sat down, and ordered a meal. When he finished, he was presented with a check for $2.45. He fished three one-dollar bills out of his wallet and handed them to the waiter. Shortly afterward the waiter returned with his change on a plate—a half dollar and a nickel. The man gave a grunt of annoyance and pocketed the half-dollar and looked up expecting to see a resentful waiter. Instead the waiter grinned widely: "That's all right, Boss —just gambled and lost!"

Aside from miscalculating his "risk," the waiter showed considerable maturity. There is a world of difference between professional and novice "inferencers." The novice goes out to the race track, say, and bets his life's savings on what he is completely convinced is a "dead-sure thing." The "pro" may bet the same amount (which he can just as ill afford to lose), but he knows the odds against him. Both may lose their money, but the novice is likely to lose a great deal more than money.

Let me add an important adjunct here. Much of our risk-taking is not of the simple, one-chance, win-or-lose, horse-racing variety. A good deal of it occurs in a process—a flow of events—which can be modified or to which our behavior can be modified in mid-stream, so to speak. Take the automobile collision of White and Black, for instance. If sometime during the process, beginning with White's noting of Black and ending with the crash, White had become aware that he was taking a bad risk, there were numerous actions he could have taken to avoid, or at least diminish, the consequences. He might, for example, have speeded up to get through the intersection before Black reached it; sounded his horn or arm-signaled to alert Black of the danger; braked his car sooner; veered off to his right; etc. In other words, even a poor decision is not necessarily an injurious one if one keeps himself alerted to the effect of changing circumstances upon his inferences and risk calculations.

*   *   *   *

"We are never deceived; we deceive ourselves."

-GOETHE

INCIDENTS

56 MINUTES BEFORE PEARL HARBOR[11]

By Hugh Russell Fraser

My task was to investigate the 56 minutes of warning we had of the Jap air attack on Pearl Harbor, Dec. 7, 1941. What I learned amazed me. I reported every detail to the Assistant Chief Signal Officer—specifically, Maj. Gen. James A. Code.

Now, nearly seventeen years later, I can tell that story. The facts, incredible as they are, became a part of my history of the U.S. Signal Corps in World War II. To most Americans who know merely that we had some radar warning of the sneak Jap attack on the "Day of Infamy," the history of those 56 minutes will come as a shock.

Radar could, and did, detect the approach of the Jap air fleet. But not, of course, as it should have been detected, and not as it would have been detected if authorized radar equipment had been installed. Actually, the island of Oahu was to have been ringed with permanent radar-warning installations. It was not. As early as November of the year before, the Corps of Engineers was directed to install six permanent radar-warning sets to be operating around the clock beginning July 1, 1941.

These sets were not installed by July 1. They were not installed by December, nor by December 7. Four mobile radar warning units, mounted in trucks were provided in their place. Regarded generally by the men assigned to them as toys to experiment with, they were in operation only from 4 A.M. to 7 A.M. Why were these hours chosen? Probably it was because those were the three hours out of the 24 when the enemy—any enemy—was most likely to attack. If this was the theory, then it came very close to being 100% right!

The Opana mobile radar set, manned by Privates Joseph Lockard and George Elliott, was the one that detected the approach of the Jap air armada. Singularly enough, it was supposed to be shut down promptly at seven o'clock on the morning of December 7, but, by one of those fortunate accidents of history, the truck coming at that time to take the two men back to base camp and to breakfast was late. So Lockard and Elliott decided to leave the set on until it arrived.

---

11 *American Mercury*, August, 1957, pp. 80–85. Reprinted by permission.

Thus, after 7 A.M., the Opana unit was the only radar unit on the island operating. The other mobile sets, also mounted in trucks, had shut down promptly. One was located at Punaluu on Kahana Bay, 20 miles to the southeast; another on the extreme west side of the island near Makua, and the fourth near Waipahu on the southwest coast, 11 miles west of Pearl Harbor itself.

The Opana unit, which made history, was located about 22 miles due north of Pearl Harbor and about 28 miles northwest of the city of Honolulu. In other words, it was north of the mountains on the island of Oahu, which itself is about 43 miles long and 30 miles wide.

As the seconds after seven o'clock ticked off, Lockard—who kept his eye idly on the machine, noted nothing unusual until, suddenly, at 7:02 A.M., there appeared what he later described as "huge blip of light—bigger than anything I had ever seen before on the set—moving slowly from the extreme left side of the scope to the right. It was, you might call it, a pillar of light. It startled me, for the flight of one plane is represented by a mere dot, several planes a collection of white dots, but here was something different. The whole left side of the scope suddenly took on light!

"My natural reaction," he continued, "was to infer the radar unit was out of order. So I asked the mechanic, Elliott, to check it. He did so in a couple of minutes and reported it was working all right. By then it was 7:04 A.M. Something unusual, I knew, was before my eyes. Elliott thought so, too, although neither of us could imagine what it might be.

"Quickly we plotted it. The calculations were easily made, and it appeared to be definitely a large flight of planes approaching from due North, three points East and about 137 miles away.

"We looked at each other, and Elliott was the first to reach for the phone. At first he couldn't get anybody at the Army Information Center at Fort Shafter. The line was dead. Then he tried another line. It was open, and soon Private Joseph McDonald at the switchboard answered. Tersely, Elliott told him what we were seeing on the scope. McDonald's answer was: 'Well, what do you expect me to do about it? There's nobody around here but me.' Elliott told him to find somebody and then hung up.

"What happened, I learned later, was that there was an officer reading a book in the next room. McDonald had supposed he had gone. He was Lt. Kermit Tyler.[12] McDonald told him what Elliott had re-

12 [The following paragraph was contained in a report of the Army Pearl Harbor Board which was published in the *Army and Navy Journal,* September 15, 1945: "The

ported. Lieutenant Tyler looked up from his book, thought awhile as if to take it all in, then said: 'It's all right, never mind.'

"Joe McDonald then called back and I answered the phone. He told me what Tyler had said. I thereupon insisted on talking to the officer myself. I was a little excited and puzzled and didn't want to let the matter end with McDonald. Joe then asked the lieutenant if he would be good enough to talk to me. The officer then came on the phone and said, 'What is it?'

"I made my reply as brief as possible. 'The scope,'' I said, 'indicates a large flight of planes approaching Oahu from due North, three points East, about 137 miles away at the last reckoning.'

"There was a pause for a few seconds, then Tyler said, 'That is probably our B-17s coming in from San Francisco.' I knew there was such a flight coming in, but I knew also those planes would hardly be approaching us from due North.

"At once I made this point clear, and he replied, 'Well, there is nothing to worry about. That is all.' The last words he said with some emphasis and I judged he didn't want to hear anything further about it, so I said: 'All right, sir,' and hung up.

"Meanwhile, somewhat startled by the whole business, although not alarmed, as now the matter was out of my hands, I continued to watch the set. The pillar of light, or 'blip,' as I call it, continued to move steadily from left to right and the truck still had not arrived. At 7:25 A.M. we made a quick computation and the flight of planes, whatever it consisted of was 62 miles out. At 7:39 A.M., just as we heard the truck arriving outside, I made my last computation and the flight was 22 miles away!

"It was at 7:39 A.M. that we closed down the radar unit and climbed into the truck for a long ride back to base. I was still turning over in my mind what we had seen on the scope as the truck bounced over the badly rutted road. I said nothing to the driver about it, nor did Elliott —not because we were alarmed but because I knew that what didn't make sense to us would hardly make sense to him.

"After we had been driving about twenty minutes, the driver called our attention to a heavy black pall of smoke that lay on the Pearl

Navy was supposed to have detailed officers in the Information Center to be trained as liaison officers, but had not yet gotten around to it. In the Information Center that morning was a Lieutenant Kermit A. Tyler, a pursuit officer of the Air Corps, whose tour of duty thereat was until 8 o'clock. It was Tyler's second tour of duty at the Center and he was there for training and observation, but there were no others on duty after 7 o'clock except the enlisted telephone operator. He was the sole officer there between 7 and 8 o'clock that morning, the rest of the personnel that had made the Center operative from 4:00 to 7:00 had departed." (Reprinted by permission.)]

Harbor horizon to the South. 'Looks like oil smoke,' he commented. Soon we were hearing what sounded like explosions and even anti-air-craft fire. It was all very puzzling and somebody suggested it was a practice raid on Pearl Harbor.

"However, on we went over the rugged road. Actually, it was only twenty miles back to base camp, but because of the road it took al-most forty minutes. As we hove into view of the camp and the truck slowed down, we saw a lot of soldiers running towards us, shouting questions the words of which I couldn't quite at first make out. Finally, it was plain they were asking, 'What happened?' 'Did you report it?' and the like. I never saw a camp so collectively excited.

"As we started to get out of the truck, a major came elbowing his way through the group of men surrounding us and said, sharply, to us: 'Shut up! Don't say a word! I'll talk to you.'

"With that he took us off to his office and questioned us for fifteen minutes. It was not until then I realized the Japs were at that very moment attacking Pearl Harbor, and that what we had seen on the screen was the Jap air fleet approaching.

"Now, as I look back, the position of the flight, the vast number of planes, made sense. I learned later the enemy aircraft carriers had sailed far to the North so that when the planes took the air they would be coming in from an unexpected direction."

Lockard at one point told me that except for the brief questioning by the major on the island of Oahu on the morning of December 7, 1941, I was the first to interrogate him in detail as to those 56 minutes —namely from 7:04 A.M. when Elliott reported the set was not out of order, to the time the first bomb fell on Pearl Harbor.

The tracing of the history of these 56 minutes, however, led me into a further investigation of why the permanent radar sets had not been installed on the island of Oahu by July 1. Here I ran into a curious and amazing story which I tried in vain to have the Congressional In-vestigating Committee explore.

My investigation disclosed that the colonel in the Corps of Engi-neers, who was charged with the duty of having these permanent radar sets installed and operated around the clock by July 1, 1941, had spent most of his time in the summer of 1941 drinking. His entire record demonstrates incredible negligence of duty. Not only did he fall down on his job but the toll in lives and ships that we had to pay for his fail-ure was heartbreaking.

I tried to bring my evidence before the committee. To that end I prepared a long memorandum, setting forth the facts as I saw them.

I requested that this colonel be summoned and be cross-examined under oath.

To my surprise, the Democratic members of the committee, whom I knew personally and regarded highly, handled my request—made in my capacity as a citizen—as if it was a "hot potato." They not only refused to act on it in any way, or request that he be summoned, but they told me in essence "to forget it"!

Amazed that members of my own party would take this view, I turned to the Republicans. I knew only one personally. He was Representative "Bud" Gearhart of California. Mr. Gearhart read my memorandum carefully and promised to do his best to get the colonel summoned. Later he reported back he had failed, but he had tried his best.

"Why won't they go into this question of radar units?" I asked. "Surely, you know their importance!"

"Yes," he said, "of course. My opinion is that somebody failed and failed terribly, but I ran up against a stone wall. The chairman flatly refused me, and when I asked one of my Democratic friends what was the real reason for what I thought, and still think, was an obvious run-around, he said, 'Look, Bud, you can do what you please and maybe you can get somewhere, but don't forget I'm a Democrat and a loyal one, and I take my orders from my Commander-in-Chief, and my Commander-in-Chief happens to be President of the United States!' "

THE CASE OF THE LEDGERS[13]

By W. C. Lohse

Alfred Gregory, bank examiner, and his two assistants were making a routine examination of a country bank. The procedure in such bank examinations is to see that all of the various bank ledgers are proved by adding machine to see that they reflect the same figures as shown on the bank's statement for that particular day. In examination circles it is customary to refer to the Loan Ledger as a Liability Ledger; Checking Accounts as Commercial Ledgers; and the General Books, in which all entries ultimately arrive and from which the daily state-

---

13 All names have been disguised. Reprinted by permission.

ment is made, are called the General Ledger. One of the two assistant examiners had been on the examination force for only a period of two or three months, and as a novice, it became his lot to do the majority of the machine work.

Mr. Gregory and his two assistants, Bill, the recruit, and Mac, the experienced assistant, entered the bank promptly at 7:30 A.M. as Leonard Brace, the Cashier and Vice-President, was opening the bank for business. The examiners' credentials were shown to Brace and the examination proceeded as scheduled. At this point it might be pointed out that no banker is ever aware of when an examination might take place.

GREGORY: "Bill, as soon as you have counted the cash, run the Liability Ledger and then report to Mac."

BILL: "Okay!" With that Bill was elated because he had been put on his own for the first time.

Bill succeeded in counting the cash and balancing it in a fairly short time, and proceeded to hunt up the Liability Ledger. This bank was considerably different from those Bill had been in before. Here, they kept all the ledgers in one place and they were not labeled. Bill picked up a ledger and proceeded to run it on an adding machine.

Gregory and Mac were working in the Directors' Room, whose open door faced the open door of Brace's office. Bill entered the Directors' Room and went over to Mac with the total he had on his adding machine tape.

BILL: "Here you are, Mac. I ran the Liability Ledger and this is the total that should be on the statement."

MAC (looking at the statement): "Boy, you sure goofed. This isn't even close. Run it over again."

BILL: "Okay!"

GREGORY: "Say, Mac, you better have him stick with it; good experience."

Bill returned to his work, tabulated the ledger again, reported to Mac, and was again dismissed as having the wrong total. This procedure was repeated several times more before the morning was over. From where he sat in his office, Brace could see the repeated trips Bill made between Mac and the ledger. At noon, Mr. Gregory explained to Brace that the examiners would have to leave for lunch and since Bill had been unable to strike a balance with the Liability Ledger, the ledger would have to be sealed until they could check it out after lunch.

After lunch the examiners came back to the bank and Bill was sent to Mr. Brace's office to pick up the Liability Ledger that Brace had sealed up. Bill returned to the Directors' Room apparently distressed.

GREGORY: "What's the matter, boy?"

BILL: "Boy, I've really messed this up."

GREGORY: "What do you mean?"

BILL: "I have been running the wrong ledger all morning. I was running the Commercial Ledger—no wonder I couldn't balance."

GREGORY: "That's all right, son, no harm done. Here take this Liability Ledger back and run it now."

Bill was passing Mr. Brace's door with the ledger, when Brace called to him to wait a minute.

BRACE: "Wait a minute. I'd like to talk to Mr. Gregory and you fellows."

Bill and Brace walked back to the Directors' room.

BRACE *(perspiring heavily):* "Well, I guess the jig's up, Mr. Gregory."

GREGORY *(thinking Brace was joking, as most bankers do with examiners, answers):* "Yep."

BRACE *(continues):* "I didn't think that some young fellow would catch me. If I had to be caught I hoped it would be an old timer like yourself."

GREGORY *(now that it is clear that Mr. Brace is serious):* "Well, now that we know of this situation, would you please aid us in ascertaining how far it has gone?"

Mr. Brace readily agreed and proceeded to show the examiners where, over the past eight years, he had embezzled $28,000 and the methods used to perpetrate the defalcation. Gregory asked what had given him the idea that the examiners had discovered the defalcation. Mr. Brace said that when he had seen Bill repeatedly going to the Ledger, he figured something was wrong because in all the years that he had been under various examinations, it had never taken an examiner more than an hour to run and balance his ledger.

Brace was subsequently tried and convicted. Despite his family's reimbursement of the major portion of the embezzlement he was fined $25,000 and sentenced to ten years.

Gregory admitted privately that it was quite unlikely that the defalcation would have been detected by the routine examination.

GENERAL PATTON AND THE SICILIAN
SLAPPING INCIDENTS[14]

By Henry J. Taylor

Headquarters Seventh Army
A.P.O. #758, U.S. Army
29th August, 1943

MY DEAR GENERAL EISENHOWER:

Replying to your letter of August 17, 1943, I want to commence by thanking you for this additional illustration of your fairness and generous consideration in making the communication personal.

I am at a loss to find words with which to express my chagrin and grief at having given you, a man to whom I owe everything and for whom I would gladly lay down my life, cause for displeasure with me.

I assure you that I had no intention of being either harsh or cruel in my treatment of the two soldiers in question. My sole purpose was to try and restore in them a just appreciation of their obligation as men and soldiers.

In World War I, I had a dear friend and former schoolmate who lost his nerve in an exactly analogous manner, and who, after years of mental anguish, committed suicide.

Both my friend and the medical men with whom I discussed his case assured me that had he been roundly checked at the time of his first misbehavior, he would have been restored to a normal state.

Naturally, this memory actuated me when I inaptly tried to apply the remedies suggested. After each incident I stated to officers with me that I felt I had probably saved an immortal soul....

Very respectfully,
(*Signed*) G. S. PATTON, JR.
Lieut. General, U.S. Army

General D. D. Eisenhower
Headquarters AFHQ
APO #512—U.S. Army

---

[14] From the book *Deadline Delayed* by Members of the Overseas Press Club. Copyright, 1947, by E. P. Dutton and Co., Inc., New. Reprinted by permission

When General Patton gave me a copy of this letter he lay back on the bed in his field-trailer and said, "What does that sound like to you?"

"It sounds to me like only half of the story," I said.

So, first, let's see what actually happened.

Private Charles H. Kuhl (in civilian life a carpet layer from South Bend, Indiana), ASN 35536908, L Company, 26th Infantry, 1st Division, was admitted to the 3rd Battalion, 26th Infantry aid station in Sicily on August 2, 1943, at 2:10 p.m.

He had been in the Army eight months and with the 1st Division about thirty days.

A diagnosis of "Exhaustion" was made at the station by Lieutenant H. L. Sanger, Medical Corps, and Kuhl was evacuated to C Company, 1st Medical Battalion, well to the rear of the fighting.

There a note was made on his medical tag stating that he had been admitted to this place three times during the Sicilian campaign.

He was evacuated to the clearing company by Captain J. D. Broom, M.C., put in "quarters" and given sodium amytal, one capsule night and morning, on the prescription of Captain N. S. Nedell, M.C.

On August 3rd the following remark appears on Kuhl's Emergency Medical Tag: "Psychoneuroses anxiety state—moderately severe. Soldier has been twice before in hospital within ten days. He can't take it at front evidently. He is repeatedly returned." (signed) Capt. T. P. Covington, Medical Corps.

By this route and in this way Private Kuhl arrived in the receiving tent of the 15th Evacuation Hospital, where the blow was struck that was heard round the world.

"I came into the tent," explains General Patton, "with the commanding officer of the outfit and other medical officers.

"I spoke to the various patients, especially commending the wounded men. I just get sick inside myself when I see a fellow torn apart, and some of the wounded were in terrible ghastly shape. Then I came to this man and asked him what was the matter."

The soldier replied, "I guess I can't take it."

"Looking at the others in the tent, so many of them badly beaten up, I simply flew off the handle."

Patton squared off in front of the soldier.

He called the man every kind of a loathsome coward and then slapped him across the face with his gloves.

The soldier fell back. Patton grabbed him by the scruff of the neck and kicked him out of the tent.

Kuhl was immediately picked up by corpsmen and taken to a ward.[15]

Returning to his headquarters Patton issued the following memorandum to Corps, Division and Separate Brigade Commanders two
days later:

> Headquarters Seventh Army
> APO #758 U.S. Army
> 5 August, 1943

It has come to my attention that a very small number of soldiers are
going to the hospital on the pretext that they are nervously incapable
of combat.

Such men are cowards, and bring discredit on the Army and dis-
grace to their comrades whom they heartlessly leave to endure the
danger of a battle while they themselves use the hospital as a means
of escaping.

You will take measures to see that such cases are not sent to the
hospital, but are dealt with in their units.

Those who are not willing to fight will be tried by Court-Martial for
cowardice in the face of the enemy.

> (*Signed*) G. S. PATTON, JR.
> *Lieut. General, U.S. Army*
> *Commanding*

Five days later General Patton, not a medical man, again took
matters into his own hands.

He slapped another soldier.

Private Paul G. Bennett, ASN 70000001, C Battery, Field Artillery,
was admitted to the 93rd Evacuation Hospital on August 10th at
2:20 P.M.

Bennett, still only twenty-one, had served four years in the Regular
Army. He had an excellent record. His unit had been attached to the
II Corps since March and he had never had any difficulties until four
days earlier when his best friend in the outfit, fighting near by, was
wounded in action.

Bennett could not sleep that night and felt nervous. The shells
going over "bothered" him. "I keep thinking they're going to land
right on me," he said. The next day he became increasingly nervous
about the firing and about his buddy's recovery.

A battery aid man sent him to the rear echelon, where a medical

---

15 There Kuhl was found to have a temperature of 102.2° F., gave a history of chronic
diarrhea for the past month, and was shown by a blood test to have malaria.

officer gave him some medicine which made him sleep. But he was still nervous, badly disturbed.

On August 10th the medical officer ordered him to the 93rd Evacuation Hospital, although Bennett begged not to be evacuated because he did not want to leave his unit.

General Patton arrived at the hospital that day.

Bennett was sitting in the receiving tent, huddled up and shivering.

Patton spoke to all the injured men. He was solicitous, kind and inspiring. But when he and Major Charles B. Etter, the receiving officer in charge, reached Bennett and Patton asked the soldier what his trouble was, the soldier replied, "It's my nerves," and began to sob.

Patton turned on him like a tiger, screaming at him:

"What did you say?"

"It's my nerves," sobbed Bennett. "I can't take the shelling anymore."

In this moment Patton lost control of himself completely. Without any investigation of the man's case whatever, he rushed close to Bennett and shouted: "Your nerves, hell. You are just a . . . coward, you yellow b____."

Then he slapped the soldier hard across the face.

"Shut up that . . . crying," he yelled. "I won't have these brave men here who have been shot seeing a yellow b____ sitting here crying."

Patton struck at the man again. He knocked his helmet liner off his head into the next tent. Then he turned to Major Etter and yelled, "Don't admit this yellow b____, there's nothing the matter with him. I won't have the hospitals cluttered up with these SOB's who haven't got the guts to fight."

Patton himself began to sob. He wheeled around to Colonel Donald E. Currier, the 93rd's commanding Medical Officer. "I can't help it," he said. "It makes me break down to see brave boys and to think of a yellow b____ being babied."

But this was not all. In his blind fury, Patton turned on Bennett again. The soldier now was managing to sit at attention, although shaking all over.

"You're going back to the front lines," Patton shouted. "You may get shot and killed, but you're going to fight. If you don't, I'll stand you up against a wall and have a firing squad kill you on purpose.

"In fact," he said, reaching for his revolver, "I ought to shoot you myself, you _____ whimpering coward."

As he left the tent Patton was still yelling back at the receiving officer to "send that yellow SOB back to the front line."

Nurses and patients, attracted by the shouting and cursing, came from the adjoining tent and witnessed this disturbance.

Patton made no initial report of these affairs to his superior, General Eisenhower, who was then in his Headquarters at Tunis on the North African mainland.

"I felt ashamed of myself," General Patton told me, "and I hoped the whole thing would die out."

But an official report by Lieut. Colonel Perrin H. Long, Medical Corps consulting physician, was already on the way to Allied Headquarters through Medical Corps channels.

"The deleterious effects of such incidents upon the well-being of patients, upon the professional morale of hospital staffs and upon the relationship of patient to physician are incalculable," reported Lieut. Colonel Long. "It is imperative that immediate steps be taken to prevent a recurrence of such incidents."

General Eisenhower received this report on August 17th. His communication to General Patton was sent off that night.

In his message, which Patton showed me, the Commanding General told Patton of the allegations, told him that he could not describe in official language his revulsion, informed Patton that he must make, on his own initiative, proper amends to the soldiers involved and take steps to make amends before his whole army.

"This all happened practically on the eve of a new attack in which I had been written in for a large part of the plans, already issued," Patton explained, "and General Eisenhower stated therefore that he would temporarily reserve decision regarding my relief of command until he could determine the effect of my own corrective measures.

"Then Eisenhower did four things: He sent Maj. General John Porter Lucas to Sicily to make an investigation of the charges, sent the Theatre's Inspector General to investigate command relationships in my entire army, sent another general officer to interview the two soldiers and made a trip to Sicily himself to determine how much resentment against me existed in the army.

"Eisenhower's problem was whether what I had done was sufficiently damaging to compel my relief on the eve of attack, thus losing what he described as my unquestioned military value, or whether less drastic measures would be appropriate.

"I went to see both Kuhl and Bennett," Patton continued, "explained my motives and apologized for my actions.

"In each case I stated that I should like to shake hands with them; that I was sincerely sorry. In each case they accepted my offer.

"I called together all the doctors, nurses and enlisted men who were present when the slappings occurred. I apologized and expressed my humiliation over my impulsive actions.

"Finally, I addressed all divisions of the 7th Army in a series of assemblies, the last of which was an address before the 3rd Division on August 30th.

"I praised them as soldiers, expressed regret for any occasions when I harshly treated individuals and offered my apologies as their Commanding General for doing anything unfair or un-American.

"Beyond that, except to leave the Army and get out of the war, I do not know what I could have done."

FALSE ARMISTICE[16]

The papa of all the blunders that have been made in the entire history of American journalism is the false armistice report of World War I. On November 7, 1918 (four days before the actual end of the war), a cable was sent over the wires of the United Press Association by its president, Roy Howard. Worded in concentrated cablese, it read: "Paris urgent armistice allies Germany signed eleven smorning hostilities ceased two safternoon sedan taken smorning by Americans."

Believing it had the scoop of the century, UP in New York immediately sent the welcome news out on its wires. Newspapers subscribing to the service rushed extras to the streets, proclaiming the glad tidings in giant headlines. The public began the wildest celebration in the nation's history. Offices and schools were empty in no time. Embacing each other in the streets, people crowded together, paraded, got drunk.

Other news services could get no confirmation. Even the wires of the UP provided no follow-ups. Some papers put out later editions saying the report was false. In a few instances, newsboys selling these papers were mobbed by angry celebrants who didn't want to believe the bad news, and the festivities continued unabated through the night.

It was not until late the next morning that the appalled UP received and released a second dispatch from Howard stating that the news was now said to be unconfirmed.

---

16 From Betsy Simon's "It's a Beaut!" *Cosmopolitan Magazine*, March, 1951. Reprinted by permission.

Although the UP has since been completely exonerated, they had a hard time trying to track down the source of the false report. The most commonly accepted explanation is that a German secret agent, believing that the American people were as ready to quit as the Germans, had made the original telephone call to American General Headquarters in Paris. A Naval attaché there had relayed the information to Vice Admiral Henry B. Wilson, commander of United States Naval forces in France. Admiral Wilson, in Brest at the time, had no reason to doubt the authenticity of the news, and he gave it to Howard. Two hours after Howard had cabled the report, Admiral Wilson informed him that the news was unconfirmed. Howard immediately sent a second cable, killing the story, but by this time the transatlantic cables were jammed, and the message was delayed twenty-four hours.

On April 28, 1945, twenty-six and a half years later, the Associated Press fell victim to the same kind of armistice error. Nine days before V-E Day, the AP sent a bulletin from San Francisco; "Germany has surrendered to the allied governments unconditionally and announcement is expected momentarily, it was stated by a high American official today."

The announcement touched off a small facsimile of the 1918 excitement. Radio news announcers picked up the report, and the news was spread across the nation. On the front pages of dozens of newspapers (undaunted by AP's qualifying "announcement is expected momentarily") bold headlines screamed: "Nazis Quit" . . . "Germany Surrenders" . . . "Germany Gives Up" . . . "Surrender!" Even a London paper declared exultantly: "All Over, This Is V-Day."

But an hour and a half after the first news bulletin, President Truman announced that the rumor had "no foundation."

The AP, divulging its source, stated that the original announcement had come from Senator Tom Connally, who was attending the San Francisco conference. Senator Connally has never divulged *his* source.

The red-faced, eat-crow quota has also risen perceptibly over the following faux pas: the Hughes-Wilson election in 1916, when newspapers glibly announced the election of Mr. Hughes only to find, the following morning, that Mr. Wilson was president; the Truman-Dewey election, when magazines, commentators (Drew Pearson: "Dewey is sure to be elected. . . ."), pollsters, and newspapers (*Chicago Tribune* headline: "Dewey Defeats Truman") all tried to second-guess the electorate; the Landon-Roosevelt election, which caused the abrupt demise of the *Literary Digest*, which had made a specialty of accurate straw-vote predictions (it had guessed right in the 1920, '24, '28, and '32 elections).

American papers are not alone in being vulnerable to error. The European press has also contributed more than a fair share of boners for the book. One of the most flagrant, and at the same time one of the saddest examples of this, was the way the French press handled the Nungesser-Coli attempt to fly the Atlantic Ocean in 1927. Twenty-five thousand dollars had been offered to the first pilots to make a non-stop Paris–New York flight, and when the French team of Nungesser and Coli took off from Le Bourget on the morning of May 8, 1927, French hopes went with them.

Early in the afternoon of May ninth, rumors began to circulate throughout Paris that the two men had landed at New York to wild acclaim. One of the leading Paris afternoon papers printed an eyewitness account of the landing. A short time later, the rest of the afternoon papers published similar stories. Many of these accounts told dramatically how the plane had circled the Statue of Liberty three times before finally alighting on American waters.

Paris went wild. Newspapers were sold out on every street corner, and people laughed and wept for sheer joy. Champagne flowed in the streets; never had France been so proud. But at midnight no official confirmation had been received. The crowds began to sober up and become angry, and they directed their anger at the newspapers.

The following morning the papers carried the bitter truth—the flyers had not arrived. In true French journalistic tradition, the blame for the false report was placed on the Ministries of Commerce, War, and Interior. Of all the Paris papers, *Le Temps* had been the only one to withstand the temptation to print the unconfirmed reports.

Tracing the origin of the rumors was difficult. New York news services had sent nothing but denials, so, Q.E.D., the reports must have originated in Paris. One explanation had it that Myron T. Herrick, the popular American ambassador, had innocently repeated a rumor that the plane had been sighted over Newfoundland. Although he had stated it was a rumor, Paris was so full of wishful thinking that the rumor was quickly turned into fact. Actually, the French plane, with fuel for only forty hours, was last sighted off the Irish coast, and the fate of the two flyers has never been determined.

To their everlasting credit, however, the French, on May twenty-first, just twelve days later, greeted the arrival of Charles A. Lindbergh as enthusiastically as they would have received their own Messrs. Coli and Nungesser.

THE MAN AND THE DESK[17]

By F. J. Roethlisberger and William J. Dickson

The personnel of one of the departments interviewed was moved from one building to another. In the new location, because of lack of space, it was found necessary to seat four people across the aisle from the remainder of the group. It happened that there were three women in the department who were to be transferred to other work. These women were given desks across the aisle so that their going would not necessitate a rearrangement of desks. The fourth person, a man, was given a desk there simply because there was no other place for him to sit. In choosing the fourth person, the supervisor was undoubtedly influenced by the fact that he was older than the rest of the group and was well acquainted with the three women. But, beyond that, nothing was implied by the fact that he was chosen. Now see how this employee interpreted the change in his seating position. He felt that his supervisor evaluated him in the same way in which he evaluated the women. The women were being transferred to other types of work; consequently, he felt that he too would be transferred before long. Two of the women were being returned to jobs in the shop. He felt that he himself might be transferred to the shop; and there was nothing he dreaded more. Having dwelt on speculations like these for a while, the employee recalled with alarm that his name had been omitted from the current issue of the house telephone directory. This omission had been accidental. The house telephone directory, however, constituted a sort of social register. Names of shop people below the rank of assistant foreman were not printed unless they were employed in some special capacity requiring contacts with other organizations. With the exception of typists and certain clerical groups, the names of all office people were listed. The fact that his name had been omitted from the directory now took on new significance for the employee. It tended to reinforce his growing conviction that he was about to be transferred to a shop position. He became so preoccupied over what might happen to him that for a time he could scarcely work.

---

[17] *Management and the Worker* (Cambridge: Harvard University Press, 1939), pp. 544–45. Reprinted by permission.

Chapter IV

BY-PASSING

DEFINITION

Belden, West and Bartell[1] is a medium-sized brokerage firm with approximately 95 employees. The accounting department has 17 employees, of whom three are middle-aged women who operate the bookkeeping machines. With the average volume of business, all three were normally finished with their posting about one hour before the usual quitting time.

On February 21st one of the bookkeepers, Elizabeth Morley, phoned in to say she was ill and would be unable to report for duty. The other two pitched in and completed about 75 per cent of the absent woman's posting before the normal quitting time. The supervisor then approached one of the bookkeepers, Jane Dover, and said: "Elizabeth just called and said she'll be absent again tomorrow, so the balance of her work (25 per cent of her normal work load) will have to be completed the first thing in the morning."

Miss Dover, a very conscientious and somewhat unassertive woman, said nothing. The following morning the supervisor found that Miss Dover had worked until 8:30 P.M. the previous evening to complete Miss Morley's posting. The supervisor had intended that she and the other bookkeeper continue with the remainder of Miss Morley's work in the morning before starting on their own posting.

* * * *

A foreman told a machine operator he was passing: "Better clean up around here." It was ten minutes later when the foreman's assistant phoned: "Say, boss, isn't that bearing Sipert is working on due up in engineering pronto?"

"You bet your sweet life it is. Why?"

"He says you told him to drop it and sweep the place up. I thought I'd better make sure."

"Listen," the foreman flared into the phone, "get him right back on that job. It's got to be ready in twenty minutes."

... What (the foreman) had in mind was for Sipert to gather up the oily waste, which was a fire and accident hazard. This would not have taken more than a couple of minutes, and there would have been plenty of time to finish the bearing.[2]

* * * *

---

1 All names have been disguised.

2 Quoted from *The Foreman's Letter*, February 8, 1950, published by the NFI, a Division of VISION Incorporated, with permission of the editor.

A motorist was driving on the Merritt Parkway outside New York City when his engine stalled. He quickly determined that his battery was dead and managed to stop another driver, a woman. She consented to push his car to get it started.

"My car has an automatic transmission," he explained to her, "so you'll have to get up to 30 to 35 miles per hour to get me started."

The woman smiled sweetly and walked back to her car. The motorist climbed into his own car and waited for her to line up her car behind his. He waited—and waited. Finally, he turned around to see what was wrong.

There was the woman—coming at his car at 30 to 35 mph!

The damage to his car amounted to $300!

*   *   *   *

In each of the preceding instances there was talking and there was listening. There were people "sending" words and other people "receiving" them. But somehow the communication went awry. The speaker didn't "get through"—the listener didn't "get him." The listener presumably heard the same words that the speaker said, but the communicators seem to have "missed" one another.

This communication phenomenon is called *by-passing*, and it can be expressed with a diagram. Here is a sketch of part of the communication between Sipert and his foreman:

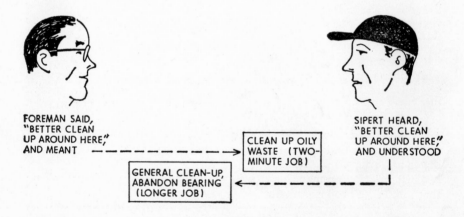

FOREMAN SAID, "BETTER CLEAN UP AROUND HERE," AND MEANT

SIPERT HEARD, "BETTER CLEAN UP AROUND HERE," AND UNDERSTOOD

CLEAN UP OILY WASTE (TWO-MINUTE JOB)

GENERAL CLEAN-UP, ABANDON BEARING (LONGER JOB)

It is evident that the foreman had one meaning for "better clean up around here" and Sipert had another. Their meanings *by-passed* one another without meeting. *By-passing*, then, is the name for the miscommunication pattern which occurs when the *sender* (speaker, writer, etc.) and the *receiver* (listener, reader, etc.) *miss each other with their meanings*.

Same Words—Different Things

Before going on, it should be noted that the three *by-passing* illustrations took the form of some persons "sending" and others "receiving" the *same words* but attributing *different meanings* to them. Miss Dover, for example, heard the *same words* her supervisor had said but interpreted them quite differently from what he had intended. This is a very common type of *by-passing,* but it has an equally prevalent counterpart.

Different Words—Same Things

By-passing may occur just as readily when people are using *different words* to represent the *same thing.* I recently witnessed with thinly disguised amusement a heated and fruitless argument between my twelve-year-old nephew and a Massachusetts soda fountain clerk, only a year or two older. Jimmy, born and reared in Illinois, was visiting the East Coast for the first time.

The conversation went something like this:

JIMMY: Do you have pop?

CLERK: What?

JIMMY: Pop.

CLERK: I don't know what you're talking about.

JIMMY (*scornfully*): You never heard of pop?

CLERK: No, and neither did you!

JIMMY: Listen, it's that stuff that comes in a bottle—you shake it up and it fizzes out!

CLERK: Oh! You mean a soda!

JIMMY: No! I don't want a soda! (A "soda" where Jimmy lives is made with ice cream, flavoring, and soda water.)

CLERK: Well, then, what *do* you want?

JIMMY: Never mind! You wouldn't have it anyway!

At this point I partially reconciled the two antagonists by suggesting that they were both talking about the same thing. Jimmy, incidentally, finally got his "pop," "soda," "tonic," "minerals," or whatever you care to call it.

Both types of *by-passing* (same words—different things and different words—same things) have a common basis, of course. Both involve people missing one another's meanings, and their consequences are equally worthy of consideration.

SOME CONSEQUENCES

By-passing may occur under such a variety of circumstances that it may be helpful to suggest something of the range of its consequences.

The Range of Consequences

By-passing is certainly one of the most prevalent and potentially costly and dangerous patterns of miscommunication in business or virtually anywhere else, for that matter. But *by-passing* isn't always serious, hazardous, or even important. Much of the time its effects are trivial and quite inconsequential. And at other times its results may be amusing or even hilarious. In fact, much of our humor is based on *by-passing*. Permit me to make the point with a personal story. It happened on my first day of college teaching a number of years ago. Mustering as much dignity as possible for a neophyte, I walked into the classroom and announced that I was going to seat the class alphabetically. I explained that I had difficulty in associating names with faces, and in seating them thus "I would get to know them by their seats." You may be quite sure the class *by-passed* me!

But I was not to have the only red face that day, for twenty minutes later a young, innocent Freshman miss rose to describe her initial campus impressions. She said she was particularly fond of the serenades— when the fraternity boys would come as a group to sing beneath the girls' dormitory windows. "We girls love it so," she emphasized, "we wish the boys could stay all night!"

Unfortunately, not all *by-passings* end so delightfully (at least from the audience's point of view). *By-passings* occurring every day in industry, in government, and in homes, result in enormous wastes of time, money, effort, and tempers. History is full of examples of *by-passing* which have lead to catastrophes. There is even disturbing evidence to suggest that a *by-passing* on a word in the Japanese response to the World War II Potsdam ultimatum may have led to the dropping of the atomic bombs on Japan and Russia's declaration of war on Japan—events which have had irrevocable effect upon world affairs.[3]

---

[3] William J. Coughlin, "Was It the Deadliest Error of Our Time?" *Harper's Magazine,* March, 1953, pp. 31–40.

Immediate Consequences

Before we leave this cursory review of *by-passing* we should note that the *immediate* effects of this breakdown in communication generally fall into one or the other of two broad classifications.

Apparent Agreement. Most of the *by-passing* illustrations we have been considering have had *apparent agreement* as their immediate consequence. That is, the initial result of the *by-passing* was such that those involved felt they were in harmony with one another. Sipert and his foreman, Miss Dover and her supervisor, the stalled motorist and the woman driver, etc., believed that they had had an adequate understanding. The *by-passing*, however, concealed an *actual disagreement* (i.e., the people involved differed on meanings).

It is acting on the false assurance of agreement which so frequently leads us into trouble.

Jeannie, 9, called to her mother upstairs: "Mom, may I fix the Easter eggs?" "Yes, dear," mother called back, "just put three dozen eggs into the kettle and be sure to cook them for at least fifteen minutes."

Jeannie placed the eggs in the largest kettle she could find and filled it with cold water. Then she set the kettle on the stove and turned on the gas.

After fifteen minutes of eager clock-watching, Jeannie removed the eggs from the water (which had not yet begun to boil) and set them on the table.

While she was preparing the Easter egg dyes, her brother Tom, 14, walked into the kitchen and picked up an egg. "Are you sure you cooked these long enough?" he asked. "Sure. Exactly fifteen minutes, just like Mom said." "Well, okay—say, want to see what a hard head I have?" And with that Tom cracked a very un-cooked egg on his head!

Apparent Disagreement. But *by-passing* which conceals *actual agreement* by manifesting *apparent disagreement* can also be disconcerting.

Major Gregory Klimov, for two years an official of the Soviet Military Administration in Occupied Berlin and who later fled to the West, recounts the first meeting of the Allied Control Commission, Economic Directorate. After routine matters had been settled, the head of the American delegation proposed that the first item on the agenda should be: "The working out of basic policy for the economic demilitarization of Germany."

The interpreters now translated the chairman's phrase into Russian as: "Working out the policy of economic demobilization." Another of those borderline cases in linguistics! The English formula had used the word "policy." The interpreters translated this literally into the Russian word "politik," although the English word had a much wider meaning, and the Russian phrase for "guiding principles" would have been a more satisfactory translation.

At the word "politik" General Shabalin sprang up as though stung. "What 'politik'? All the political questions were settled at the Potsdam Conference!"

The American chairman, General Draper, agreed: "Quite correct, they were. Our task is simply to translate the decision into action, and so we have to lay down the guiding policy . . ."

The interpreters, both American and English, again translated with one accord: ". . . 'politik.' "

General Shabalin stuck to his guns: "There must be nothing about politics. That's all settled. Please don't try to exert pressure on me."

"But it's got nothing to do with politics," the interpreters tried to reassure him. "The word is 'policy.' "

"I see no difference," the general objected. "I have no intention of revising the Potsdam Conference. We're here to work, not to hold meetings."[4]

And this futile battle over the awkward word *policy* was the beginning of the first of many long and similar arguments around the conference table.

Whether the immediate consequence of *by-passing* is an *apparent agreement* or an *apparent disagreement*, the subsequent effect *can* be unpleasant, unproductive, and even fatal. Let us now look into some of the contributing factors of this often troublesome pattern of miscommunication.

TWO FALLACIES

If we are to cope with harmful *by-passing*, we must explore some of its underlying assumptions. Let us return to the Sipert-foreman incident for further analysis. We have already ascertained that Sipert and his foreman *by-passed* one another. That is, they missed one another with their meanings. The critical question now is *why*? We can presume that neither intended to *by-pass*. Certainly, the foreman did not use "big," foreign, or unfamiliar words. Why, then, did the communication go askew?

Suppose we had the opportunity to ask Sipert and the foreman what they thought went wrong in their communication. Judging from in-

---

4 Gregory Klimov, *The Terror Machine: The Inside Story of the Soviet Administration in Germany* (New York: Frederick A. Praeger, Inc., 1953), pp. 146–47. Reprinted by permission.

numerable explanations by others involved in similar communication breakdowns, their responses would follow this pattern:

SIPERT: I was sure I knew what the boss meant. I never thought he was talking about cleaning up the waste.

FOREMAN: I was certain Sipert would understand what I was driving at. It never occurred to me that he would put a different interpretation on my remark.

"I was sure . . . I never thought . . ."; "I was certain . . . It never occurred to me. . . ." These men are revealing the colossal assumption which underlay their behavior—the assumption that *"words mean the same to the other fellow as they do to me."* Most of us unconsciously act on this assumption, a great deal of the time—and usually, fortunately, the assumption happens to be correct. That is, more often than not, people *do* understand our words as we intend them—but *sometimes* they *misunderstand,* and we have already suggested the scope of the consequences.

The assumption is supported by two pernicious fallacies. One is that *words have meanings.* The other is that words are used in only one way ("the way I am using them")—that *words have mono-usage.* I shall attack each of these fallacies, for they lie at the foundation of *by-passing.*

The Fallacy That Words Have Meanings

The prevailing delusion that words have meanings possibly stems from what Irving J. Lee called the "container myth":

If you think of words as vessels, then you are likely to talk about "the meaning of a word" as if the meaning were *in* the word. Assuming this, it is easy to endow words with characteristics. Just as you may say that one vessel is costlier or more symmetrical than another, you may say that one word is intrinsically more suitable for one purpose than another, or that, in and of itself, a word will have this or that meaning rather than any other. When one takes this view, he seems to say that meaning is to a word as contents are to a container.[5]

He suggested that when one acts upon his unconscious assumption that words *contain* meanings, he is insidiously led to assume that when he talks (or writes) he is handing his listener (or reader) so many *con-*

---

5 Irving J. Lee, "On a Mechanism of Misunderstanding," *Promoting Growth toward Maturity in Interpreting What Is Read,* ed. Gray, Supplementary Educational Monographs, No. 74 (Chicago: University of Chicago Press, 1951), pp. 86–90. Copyright 1951 by the University of Chicago.

tainers of meanings. If this is the case, the recipient is "bound to get the correct meanings."

Words, of course, do not "contain" or "have" meanings. Apart from people using them, words are merely marks on paper, vibrations in the air, raised dots on a Braille card, etc. Words really do not *mean* at all— only the *users* of words can mean something, with the words they use. This is a sensible enough statement to accept—*intellectually*. Unfortunately, our *behavior* with words very frequently does not abide by it.

The Fallacy That Words Have Mono-Usage

The second of the fallacies underlying *by-passing* is the assumption of mono-usage. The notion that words are used for one and only one meaning is so patently ridiculous that it hardly seems worthwhile to refute it. Yet so much of our communication seems based on this misconception that I must comment on it.

To begin, let me ask a question: How many words are used in only *one* way? Excepting certain technological terms, virtually *all* of our common words (so far as I have ever been able to determine) are used in more than one way. That is, the words we usually use in our day-to-day communications almost invariably have multi-usage. In fact, the 500 most commonly used words in our language have an aggregate of over 14,000 dictionary definitions! Take the word *fast*, for instance:

> A person is *fast* when he can run rapidly.
> But he is also *fast* when he is tied down and cannot run at all.
> And colors are *fast* when they do not run.
> One is *fast* when he moves in suspect company.
> But this is not quite the same thing as playing *fast* and loose.
> A racetrack is *fast* when it is in good running condition.
> A friend is *fast* when he is loyal.
> A watch is *fast* when it is ahead of time.
> To be *fast* asleep is to be deep in sleep.
> To be *fast* by is to be near.
> To *fast* is to refrain from eating.
> A *fast* may be a period of non-eating—or a ship's mooring line.
> Photographic film is *fast* when it is *sensitive* (to light).
> But bacteria are *fast* when they are *insensitive* (to antiseptics).

And note the versatility of *call* in this gripping narrative:

> Jim *called* on Joe to *call* him out for *calling* him up at midnight and

calling him down, but their wives *called* in friends who got the fight *called* off.[6]

If one recognizes the phenomenon of *multi-usage* in our language, he will anticipate that words are quite likely to be understood differently by different people. *Parade Magazine* made this point quite graphically some years ago when it conducted an interesting demonstration. Each of three artists was given a copy of a paragraph from the *Encyclopaedia Britannica*. The paragraph described (words only, no pictures) an animal which none of the artists had ever seen:

> The body is stout, with arched back; the limbs are short and stout, armed with strong, blunt claws; the ears long; and the tail thick at the base and tapering gradually. The elongated head is set on a short, thick neck, and at the extremity of the snout is a disc in which the nostrils open. The mouth is small and tubular, furnished with a long extensile tongue. A large individual measured 6 ft. 8 in. In colour it is pale sandy or yellow, the hair being scanty and allowing the skin to show.[7]

From this purely *verbal* description the artists were asked to draw what they conjured up from the words. The results are shown on the next page.

The animal (No. *4*), is an aardvark, or anteater. As bizarre and as diverse as these drawings appear, note one extremely significant point: Each is *a legitimate interpretation* of the paragraph. Note that while a detail may be interpreted *differently*, it is, nevertheless, consistent with *a* common usage of the term. Who can deny, for example, that in each instance the back is "arched," that the ears are "long," or that the tail is "thick at the base and tapering gradually"?

The Phenomenon of Multi-Usage. If we consider the causes of multiple usage, a very widespread phenomenon in our language, we may be alerted to some of the potential areas of *by-passing*. Among these causes are (*a*) etymological shifts, (*b*) regionalisms, and (*c*) technical/common usage.

a) Etymological Shifts. A great many of our older words have undergone etymological shifts. That is, they have acquired new usages as they have been passed down through time. Some of the usages drop out after a time, but many remain, and the result is often a formidable accumulation of definitions, all of which are operating presently. The

---

6 The sentence hardly suggests the multi-usages of *call*. Webster's Unabridged lists 40 different definitions for the word. Other kaleidoscopic words: *turn* (54 definitions), *fall* (50), *touch* (46).

7 From "Aardvark," *Encyclopaedia Britannica* (1957) p. 4. Reprinted by permission.

No. 2

No. 4

No. 1

No. 3

word *mess* is a good example. A Latin term, it originally stood for *something sent*. This usage is still reflected in words such as *message* and *messenger*. Later *mess* came to represent food *sent* from the kitchen to the dining table; then a quantity of soft food (*mess* of porridge); then a sufficient quantity of a certain kind of food for a dish or meal (*mess* of peas). Still later, *mess* referred to the people sitting about the dining table (soldiers were at *mess*). Finally, *mess* came to denote the various dinnerware, glasses, and dishes with the unfinished food still clinging to them which were piled together in a heap after dinner, and thus represents any general disorganization (what a *mess!*).[8]

We have a great knack for using old words in new ways. "Beat" (generation), "Bikini," "nervous," and "square" are among the hundreds of words which have acquired new usages during the last few years. Incidentally, I have found that whether one approves of them or not, it is generally wise to keep abreast of these new usages. Recently, my office was chilly, and I walked into my secretary's office to ask: "Are you cool in here?" "Crazy, man!" she responded gleefully.

The rapidity of the etymological shifts is one reason why learning English is so difficult for foreigners. While they may have mastered the grammar and conventional usages (which remain relatively constant), they may have trouble keeping up with the ever-changing idiom. Not long ago a student from India enrolled at Northwestern University. On his first day at the university, an American student generously escorted him about the campus, helpfully pointing out the buildings in which the new student would be having classes, the cafeterias, library, etc. Finally, they returned to the Indian's dormitory room. When the American had seen that the newcomer was comfortably situated, he left with a cheery, "See you later!" The Indian stayed up until 3 o'clock in the morning, for he did not want to be so impolite as to retire when his new friend had obviously promised to return!

A Thailander enrolled at another midwestern university. He eagerly waited for an opportunity to meet the president, a renowned scholar. Finally, he was granted an appointment and, with the utmost of humility and solemnity, walked into the president's office. He bowed deeply to the president and said: "I am most honored to meet with you, sir. I know that you are a very wise guy."

b) Regional Variations. Word usages vary, not only from time to

---

8 Adapted from "Meanings of 'Mess,'" by Dwight Everett Hawkins, *Word Study* (published by G. & C. Merriam Co., Springfield, Mass.), October, 1956.

time but from geographical region to region. Jimmy in his quest for "pop" learned this the hard way. What is a "sweet roll" in some areas is a "bun" in others and a "danish" in still others. "Evening" in the southern states is the period from noon through twilight. In the rest of the country, however, it generally refers to the period from sunset or the evening meal to ordinary bedtime.

And no one will be able to convince the American motorist that the English speak "English."

This summer my wife and I rented a little Morris Minor Saloon and traveled about 3500 miles in England, Wales and Scotland. Previously I had read the highway regulations, but we were most of the summer learning the British way of addressing the automobile driver and tourist. If we saw a sign ROAD UP, we came to learn that it meant "Road Taken Up" or "Road Repairs Ahead." Near Chepstow we were asked to detour (the British call it DIVERSION) because, said the man who directed us, there had been a BUMP down the road. We could see two cars locked together in a collision.

It is a little shocking to see a sign BENDS FOR ONE-HALF MILE, meaning curves, or DOUBLE BEND, for S-curve. CONCEALED TURNING means "Blind Corner" in England. Nearing London, you may find a warning DUAL CARRIAGEWAY, meaning "Divided Highway," and at the other end TERMINATION DUAL CARRIAGEWAY, meaning, of course, the end of the divided highway. Instead of "No Passing" the sign reads NO OVERTAKING. When the danger zone is passed, you come to END OF PROHIBITION! You are told not to "Stop" but HALT at highway intersections. If you try to park in a no-parking area, you find a sign NO WAITING.

In town you can get a HACKNEY CARRIAGE just as quickly as you can get a taxi over here. If you want to travel with a trailer, you go down and rent or buy a CARAVAN. You should carry a TORCH with you in your car always, since you might have trouble at night and need a flashlight. If the day is hot, you can stop and get some MINERALS, i.e., cold drinks (though we seldom found them really cold). Sometime during your tour you will need to visit the GENTLEMAN'S HAIRDRESSER (barbershop). As we toured, we POPPED IN at one small hotel after another, either to eat or spend the night, and we learned that the next morning the maid always TURNED THE ROOM OUT to prepare for the next guest.[9]

c) Technical/Common Usage. Specialists (and almost everyone is a specialist to some degree) tend to develop their own "private language." Salesmen speak of "closure" (the completion of a sale); plumbers of "wiping a joint" (applying molten lead with a pad to join pipes); publishers of "fillers" (short items to fill out columns); television di-

---

9 Clyde S. Kilby, "Signs in Great Britain," *Word Study*, December, 1955. Copyright 1955 by G. & C. Merriam Co., publishers of the Merriam-Webster Dictionaries. Reprinted by permission.

rectors of "stretching" (slowing up to consume time); and laundry men of "mangling the wash" (smoothing it by roller pressure). Ordinarily, these specialists use these terms to good effect when communicating with their fellow specialists. Many of these words and phrases, however, are *also* used by the general public, but in quite different ways. Let the technician forget that the outsider is not accustomed to these words in his specialized sense, and the results are likely to be confusing at best.

I learned something of the intricacies of plain English at an early stage in my career. A woman of thirty-five came in one day to tell me that she wanted a baby but that she had been told that she had a certain type of heart-disease which might not interfere with a normal life but would be dangerous if she ever had a baby. From her description I thought at once of mitral stenosis. This condition is characterized by a rather distinctive rumbling murmur near the apex of the heart, and especially by a peculiar vibration felt by the examining finger on the patient's chest. The vibration is known as the "thrill" of mitral stenosis.

When this woman had been undressed and was lying on my table in her white kimono, my stethoscope quickly found the heart-sounds I had expected. Dictating to my nurse, I described them carefully. I put my stethoscope aside and felt intently for the typical vibration which may be found in a small but variable area of the left chest.

I closed my eyes for better concentration, and felt long and carefully for the tremor. I did not find it and with my hand still on the woman's bare breast, lifting it upward and out of the way, I finally turned to the nurse and said: "No thrill."

The patient's black eyes snapped open, and with venom in her voice she said: "Well, isn't that just too bad? Perhaps it's just as well you don't get one. That isn't what I came for."

My nurse almost choked, and my explanation still seems a nightmare of futile words.[10]

Miscommunication is also possible, of course, from specialty to specialty. The dentist's "closure" (the extent to which the upper and lower teeth fit together when the jaw is closed) differs from that of the salesman. And the parliamentarian's "closure" (a method for ending debate and securing an immediate vote on a measure) differs from both. Consider the machinist who ordered a tree. "What caliper size do you want?" inquired the nursery man. "About six or seven inches," said the machinist, whose calipers measure *diameters*. The tree man brought a sapling only two inches across, for his calipers measure *circumferences*.

---

[10] Frederic Loomis, M.D., *Consultation Room* (New York: Alfred A. Knopf, 1939), p. 47.

The Humpty-Dumpty Attitude (Egocentrism). Despite the fact that the overwhelming majority of our words have multi-usage, people still communicate, as exemplified so many times in this chapter, as if *their* words had mono-usage. One extremely important reason for this inconsistency is evident in this passage from Lewis Carroll's *Through the Looking Glass:*

Humpty-Dumpty said: "There's glory for you." "I don't know what you mean by 'glory,'" Alice said. Humpty-Dumpty smiled contemptuously. "Of course you don't till I tell you. I meant, 'There's a nice knock-down argument for you.'" "But 'glory' doesn't mean a 'nice knock-down argument,'" Alice objected. "When I use a word," Humpty-Dumpty said in a rather scornful tone, "it means just what I choose it to mean, neither more nor less."

Few of us are as frank as Humpty, although we are frequently as arrogant. We would not call it "arrogance" (unless we were talking about the other fellow) because we are largely *unaware* of the prevailing egocentrism which so frequently accompanies our use of words. If a person were to resolve to watch scrupulously his own language use during a twenty-four-hour period, he would almost certainly catch himself talking or listening (writing or reading) dozens of times with the Humpty-Dumpty attitude. He would find himself assuming, "I *knew* what the other person understood or meant simply because that was the way *I* used or would have used the words."

THE MOTIVES OF BY-PASSERS

Up to this point we have been presuming that the communicators, regardless of their degree of success or failure, *intended* to understand one another. Of course, this is not always a warranted assumption. The speaker (or writer) may very purposely *desire* to be *by-passed.* Or the listener (or reader) may just as earnestly contrive to miss meanings. The motives of the communicators, therefore, must be considered in any analysis of the factors of a *by-passing.*

The story is told of the Congressman, running for re-election, who was speaking before a group of his constituents. At the conclusion of his prepared talk, a question came from the floor:

"Congressman, you didn't say anything about Social Security. Just how do you feel about Social Security?"

Realizing that his audience was evenly and irreconcilably divided on the issue, he responded with a wink and a knowing smile:

"Don't worry about that subject, young man—I'm *all right* on that one!"

And everyone applauded!

And a certain used-car dealer used purposeful *by-passing* to his advantage with this advertisement: "Money cheerfully refunded in 24 hours if not satisfied." Some wishful-thinking buyers were convinced that they were being offered an unlimited guarantee on their purchase and that it would require only a day for the dealer to refund their money. Weeks later, when some of the secondhand autos began to break down, expectant owners approached the dealer, who retorted: "The advertisement? Oh, that meant I was giving you a one-day guarantee!"

For truly "professional" *by-passing* observe it at the level of international affairs:

Belatedly from the Brussels Fair comes a story of the Russians' genius at the game of semantics—the skillful use of words to conceal facts or pervert meaning.

In the Russian exhibit was their small car, the Ziss. In the U.S. display was an American small car. Somebody got the idea of having a neutral automotive engineer compare the two, point by point, and decide which was the better.

After conscientious checking, the engineer gave his opinion: The American car was the better. The official Russian news agency boastfully reported the matter to the homefolks, thus:

"In comparative tests of Russian and foreign automobiles, the Russian Ziss placed second, while the American car was next to last."[11]

Purposeful *by-passing* can be used constructively as well. Take the case of a certain labor-management conciliator. The union contract had only a week to run. The union had adamantly refused to discuss terms with management and was preparing to strike. When the conciliator asked union officials why they had refused to bargain, he was told: "Why, we want a *substantial* increase [they told him confidentially that this meant 15 to 20 cents per hour], and we're dead sure management won't go along with us, so why waste time?" Nothing the conciliator could say would persuade them to meet with management. Finally, he turned to the company, where he was told in confidence that it was willing to give 5 or 6 cents. "Would you say this would be a 'substantial increase,'" he asked. "It certainly would be," he was assured. He then returned to the union officials and reported that the

11 "Russian Genius" (Editorial), *Chicago Daily News,* April 7, 1959, p. 16. Reprinted by permission.

company was willing to talk in terms of a "substantial increase." With that, he was able to coax the union's representatives to meet with the company's. With his guidance, the two parties were able to reach a compromise in time to avert a strike that neither side wanted.

Parade Magazine. Reprinted by permission.

"Reverend Benson says for you to call later. He just got into the bathtub."

Of course, the *receiver* of communication may *by-pass* intentionally just as readily as the *sender*. Our legal system takes this into account by insisting that a law must be obeyed not only in accord with its *letter* (words) but with its *spirit* (intent). The law recognizes that the *letter* of even the most cautiously written statute may be subject to willful misinterpretation.

But whether the *by-passing* be purposeful or not, the pattern of the miscommunication is essentially the same, and the methods of avoidance are applicable in either case.

CORRECTIVES

There is no panacea for curing harmful *by-passing*, but these time-tested techniques can decrease or prevent a great deal of it:

1. Be person-minded, not word-minded.
2. Query and paraphrase.
3. Be sensitive to contexts.

Make these techniques *habitual*. Make them your conditioned response to a communication situation. Consider them as the finely tempered muscles of the athlete. Even after these habits have been established, they must be practiced and strengthened daily.

Be Person-Minded—Not Word-Minded

The communicator who habitually looks for meanings in the *people* using words, rather than in the *words* themselves, is much less prone to *by-pass* or to be *by-passed*. He realizes that the important question in communication is not what the *words* mean, but what the *user* means by them. When an alert communicator talks or writes, he is aware that his listeners or readers may *not* necessarily interpret his words as he means them. When he listens or reads, he is aware that the speaker or writer may be intending words other than as he is interpreting them at the moment.

To keep person-minded in his communications he frequently asks himself:

This is what it means to *me*, but what does it, or will it, mean to *him*?
What would I mean if I were in his position?
Does my interpretation of his words coincide with his viewpoint (as I see it)?

• Query and Paraphrase

Query the Speaker or Writer.   Some of the best parental advice a child ever receives somehow becomes lost as he grows older. Almost everyone has been told: "If you don't understand the teacher, ask her what she means." But as time goes on, something happens to us. We evidently become too inhibited or proud or embarrassed to ask another person what he means.

A common complaint among my colleagues in college teaching is that students do not ask enough questions in the classroom—the very place where questions should abound![12] It is almost as if we believed that asking a question of a speaker or writer (assuming that circumstances permit) would lead him to doubt our intelligence! Nothing could be farther from the truth. Professors and executives alike indicate that they respect a thoughtful question. To them it indicates interest and a sense of responsibility rather than stupidity.

To be sure, some managers (and teachers) resent questions from

---

12 Business executives express much the same concern. "What do you have to do to get people to ask questions," a vice-president of a manufacturing firm asks. "If people would only make *sure* they got it straight, we'd save a hundred thousand dollars a year."

subordinates. They may feel so insecure or so poorly versed in their fields that they interpret a question as a threat that they must ward off. Such an executive is an extremely poor communication risk, and his firm is the worse for it. So, ask questions when:

1. You don't understand or can't make sense out of what you have heard or read.
2. You think there may be a legitimate interpretation other than the one which first occurred to you.
3. You sense something out of alignment—something which doesn't quite mesh with the rest of your knowledge of a situation.

Paraphrase the Speaker or Writer. Putting a speaker's or writer's communication into your own words and asking him if he will accept your paraphrasing is one of the oldest, simplest, most useful, and most neglected techniques in communication.

I recently observed a fascinating series of business meetings in which the technique of paraphrasing was put to a special use. The meetings were the regular executive conferences of a certain firm, but a new touch had been added. An outsider was engaged to serve as moderator. The requirements were that he be reasonably intelligent, that he have a good memory for spoken communication, and that he develop the knack of paraphrasing the statement of another *without* embellishments, judgments, deletions, or additions of his own.

This is how it worked. The agenda having been set up previously, the meeting began with the moderator in charge. "Gentlemen," he would say, "the meeting is convened. Who would like to begin?" Some of the men raised their hands, and the moderator recognized, say, Executive A, who then made a statement. Then, *before* anyone else was permitted to speak, the moderator *paraphrased* A's remark. A would now either accept the moderator's rephrasing as accurate (in which case the next person would be permitted to speak) or correct it. In the latter case the moderator would then paraphrase A's correction, which A would either accept or correct, etc., until A accepted the moderator's paraphrasing *without qualification*.

After A and the moderator agreed on A's communication, any other member was permitted to query or paraphrase what had been said if he were still in doubt about A's meaning.

The procedure sounds laborious, and, indeed, it was for the first few meetings. But after a brief period of practice this group of executives was holding conferences (which had been somewhat notorious for their miscommunications) with startling equanimity and progress.

This writer has never experienced group discussions with so few instances of *by-passing*; moreover, many *potential by-passings* were revealed by the moderator's rewordings. An additional benefit, according to the men involved, was that with the moderator's paraphrasings the speaker was assured that at least one other person in the room understood fully what he was trying to say—a very satisfying and previously infrequent experience!

The meetings, it is true, were somewhat longer[13] than usual, but who can estimate the amounts of time and the money, effort, and nervous tension saved thus by the prevention of miscommunications?

The Responsibilities of the "Sender."   So far we have been discussing the techniques of querying and paraphrasing from the "receiver's" point of view; that is, how the listener or reader should use them. But communication is a two-way street, with responsibilities at both ends. The "sender" (speaker, writer) should do his utmost to make querying and paraphrasing possible. He should not only permit it or make himself approachable—he should *encourage* it, *invite* it—even, on some occasions, *insist* on it.

Be Sensitive to Contexts

Dictionaries define *context* as (*a*) "the part of a discourse in which a word or passage occurs and which helps to explain the meaning of the word or passage" (verbal context), and (*b*) "the whole situation, background, or environment relevant to some happening or personality" (situational context). We shall want to use both of these definitions.

Verbal Context.   The words or remarks which surround a word or phrase in question often, but not infallibly, help to determine the intended meaning of that word or phrase. If you and I are discussing track and field events and I comment, "I understand your sister is quite fast," you may thank me for the compliment. But if we have been speaking of ladies of doubtful character, and I should make the same remark, you might feel fully justified in punching me in the nose. If so, you would have interpreted my statement largely in terms of the *verbal context* in which it occurred.

Lifting words or even sentences, paragraphs, or chapters, out of context is a well-known trick of propagandists and others who seek to distort communication. A pointed example was the circular that

---

13 Frequently, of course, B's reaction to A's statement was delayed by the moderator's interposition. For the special value of such delays read p. 272.

Clarke[14] described as having been used by Republicans in the campaign of 1928:

They quoted an article from the presumably unbiased *Encyclopaedia Britannica* (11th ed., Vol. XXVI, p. 392), to show the corruption of Tammany Hall, and the danger of putting a member of the Tammany Society in the presidential chair. They quite failed, however, to quote the very relevant final sentence of the *Britannica* article, namely: "The power of the organization in the state and in the nation is due to its frequent combination with the Republican organization, which controls the state almost as completely as Tammany does the city" [*Nation*, Vol. CXXVII, pp. 438–39].

Some advertisers use similar tactics to their advantage:

The case of the paper filter. Early this year, the *Reader's Digest* furnished grist for another cigaret advertiser's mill. A January *Digest* article—titled "How Harmful Are Cigarets" was a thoughtful and detailed piece, an objective and factual examination of the effects of smoking. It cited medical and other expert testimony and quoted findings of clinical research and other scientifically developed statistics. The impression it left was that smoking would do no one's health any good, but would not do any serious harm if not carried to excess. The author's own conclusion: "Smoking is a very pleasant, very foolish habit. Most people can indulge in it with no apparent danger. Eight cigarets a day, apparently, harm no normal person." That was the only reference in the entire article to the advisability of smoking only eight cigarets a day. Elsewhere, the article discussed the value of filters. It said using another cigaret as a filter removes 70 per cent of the nicotine and using a silicagel cartridge removes 60 per cent. It nowhere said anything about the efficacy of paper filters. Further, the nicotine factor was only one of over a half-dozen discussed in the article, and the article seriously questioned the over-all advantage of using filters of any kind ". . . with a filter one is likely to smoke a cigaret until it is shorter than if a filter had not been used—usually 20 per cent shorter—and that extra length is the nicotine-filled butt."

Brown and Williamson used this article as a basis for a campaign on its Viceroy filter-tip cigarets. The headline said: "Read January *Reader's Digest* to Find Out Why Filtered Cigaret Smoke Is Better for Your Health." A short bloc of copy said: ". . . if you smoke over eight cigarets a day—you will want to switch . . . to the cigaret which filters your smoke."

The discrepancies are obvious. The *Digest* article did not say that filtered smoking is better for one's health. What it did say about filters had nothing to do with the paper type of filter that Viceroy uses. The reference to smoking eight cigarets a day had nothing to do with anything the article said about using filters.[15]

---

14 Edwin Leavitt Clarke, *The Art of Straight Thinking: A Primer of Scientific Method for Social Inquiry* (New York: D. Appleton–Century Co., 1929), p. 348. Reprinted by permission of Appleton-Century-Crofts, Inc.

15 "Advertising Abuses and the Digest," *Tide,* December 15, 1950, pp. 13–14. Reprinted by permission.

As prevalent as intentional miscommunications of this sort are, those which are inadvertent are more common. Classified advertisers, for example, in an effort to minimize costs, frequently reduce the contexts of their ads to a point where it is difficult *not* to *by-pass:*

FOR SALE—Large Great Dane, pedigree, will eat anything. Especially fond of children.

ROOMS FOR RENT—For a successful affair, it's the _____ Hotel.

FOR RENT—Lovely furnished room for young lady with southern exposure.

HELP WANTED—Man to drive dynamite truck. Must be prepared to travel unexpectedly.

An answer to the problem of insufficient verbal contexts is, of course, for the sender to provide and/or the receiver to obtain enough related information to determine the intent of the excerpt.[16]

In conclusion, be sensitive to verbal contexts, the surrounding words and sentences which may help to determine the meaning of any word, phrase, or passage. Ask yourself: Is this word, phrase, etc., taken out of its verbal context? Might I interpret it differently if I knew what went before or after it? Am I giving my receiver sufficient (but not too much) information for him to understand my communication?

Situational Context.   What lies beyond the context of words and phrases? How does this communication fit into the larger framework of people and happenings? Make a habit of orienting yourself toward the total context of a situation.

---

16 It is possible, of course, to err in the other extreme. Discretion must be exercised especially by the sender, who must avoid unnecessarily long and repetitious communications, for they can be as confusing as if they were intended to deceive. In short, it *is* possible to overcommunicate.

Dr. George Russell Harrison, dean of the Massachusetts Institute of Technology, recalled this incident:

"A plumber of foreign extraction wrote the National Bureau of Standards and said he found that hydrochloric acid quickly opened plugged drainage pipes and inquired if that was a good thing to use. A scientist at the bureau replied that 'the efficacy of hydrochloric acid is indisputable, but the corrosive residue is incompatible with metallic permanence.'

"The plumber wrote back thanking the bureau for telling him that hydrochloric acid was all right. The scientist was disturbed about the misunderstanding and showed the correspondence to his boss—another scientist—who wrote the plumber: 'We cannot assume responsibility for the production of toxic and noxious residue with hydrochloric acid and suggest you use an alternative procedure.'

"The plumber wrote back that he agreed with the Bureau—the hydrochloric acid works fine. Greatly disturbed, the scientists took their problem to the top boss. He broke with scientific jargon and wrote the plumber: 'Don't use hydrochloric acid. It eats hell out of pipes." From "Inside Washington" by the Chicago Sun Washington Bureau, *Chicago Sun,* February 17, 1947, p. 10.

Suppose we re-enact the Sipert-foreman case, with one change—Sipert now has a sensitivity about the "bigger picture":

FOREMAN: Better clean up around here.

SIPERT: Okay. (Then moments later after the foreman has left)—Wait a minute! The Boss has me working on this bearing. It's supposed to be a rush-order job. Now he tells me to drop it and clean up my work area. Something is wrong somewhere—I'd better check.

And, of course, if he *had* "checked," the delay and embarrassment could have been so easily avoided.

SUMMARY

By-passing occurs when communicators miss one another's meanings. It may take place when they use the same words to mean different things or when they use different words to mean the same thing. The effects of *by-passing* may range from the trivial and humorous to the serious and even catastrophic. In general, the immediate consequence of a *by-passing* may be either an apparent agreement on meanings when actually a disagreement exists, or an apparent disagreement when an actual agreement is the case.

Basically a person by-passes because of the assumption, often unconscious, that words mean the same to the other person as they do to him. Underlying this assumption are two insidious fallacies. The first fallacy, that words have meanings, probably owes a considerable share of its influence to the pervasive "container myth." The second fallacy, that words have mono-usage, thrives despite the manifest multi-usage nature of our language. A prime contributor to the fallacy of mono-usage is the egocentric attitude, expressed so candidly by Humpty-Dumpty: "When I use a word it means just what I choose it to mean." Our egocentrism in the use of words, of course, is so habitual that we are scarcely aware of the invalid premise which underlies so much of our communication, namely: "He can understand my words only one way—the way *I* mean them." (In considering the causes of *by-passing* we must also recognize that people often *by-pass* by design.)

Three common-sense but uncommonly used techniques are effective in curbing *by-passing*. (1) Be person-minded—not word-minded. (2) Query and paraphrase. (3) Be sensitive to contexts.

To be truly effective, these techniques must become deeply imbedded habits which, in a sense, are on the alert even when we are not.

INCIDENTS

WAS THERE A NOISE?[17]

In Sweet Esther, Wisconsin, Bert Johnson and Fred Carr were haled into court on a disorderly conduct charge. They had been picked up fighting in a drugstore. When the judge asked them for their story Johnson replied:

"Well, your honor, we're neighbors and Carr, here, told me he was going down to the drugstore—did I want anything. I said I'd go along with him.

"Well sir, on the way down Carr says: 'I got a puzzle I bet a buck you can't figure out—suppose lightning strikes a tree in the middle of the forest and the tree falls down. Now, there ain't no animals or birds or people anywhere near the tree. Was there a noise when it fell?'

"Well, quick as a wink I says: 'Sure there's a noise—it don't matter if people ain't there.' Then Carr gets on one of them superior grins and says: 'I guess you ain't as bright as you think you are—there ain't no noise if nobody can hear it.' "

The two men glared at each other and Johnson continued: "Well, you know how it is your honor—I'm saying there's a noise and Carr saying there ain't and we start talking louder and louder—one thing leads to another—I give Carr a little shove—then he takes a cut at me —and so on and so on—only by this time we're in the drugstore and I guess we messed the place up a bit."

THE PRODUCT-INFORMATION PROGRAM[18]

The Meridian Corporation is one of the nation's leading manufacturers of television and radio receivers as well as other electronic instruments. It had been the policy of the firm to hold an annual national conference to which its two hundred district distributors were

---

17 All names have been disguised.
18 All names have been disguised.

invited at company expense. One of the most important events of the convention was the Product-Information Program. This program consisted of a speech coupled with whatever visual aids (motion pictures, sound-slide films, etc.) were appropriate. The purpose of the program was to introduce the new models and to explain their features.

The policy was to provide each distributor with a duplicate set of materials (script, films, recordings, etc.) so that he could stage a similar Product-Information Program for the salesmen in his own district.

To accomplish this, the materials were reproduced two hundred times and shipped to the distributors' respective home addresses while they were still in conference. Thus, on returning home they would be able to commence their own Product-Information Program meetings immediately. Beginning the meetings immediately was essential if the salesmen were to be able to capitalize upon the national advertising campaign conducted by the firm simultaneously with the conclusion of the convention.

Daniel Steger, merchandising manager of Meridian, was usually in charge of preparing and presenting the Product-Information Program at the national convention. He would write the script and ordinarily engaged the Raymond Co., a visual aids firm, to prepare his other materials. On this occasion he needed a rather lengthy sound-slide film. A month before the convention, Ted Robbins, a technician from Raymond, and Steger went over the plans for the film in great detail. Robbins submitted sketches for each frame which Steger approved.

Two weeks later Steger phoned Robbins.

S: Say, Robbins, is it too late to add another frame to our film?

R: No, I don't think so—what do you have in mind?

S: Well, this comes after the 16th frame, so we'll call it frame number 17. I would like a picture of a stationary core with three or four small dots circling around it—do you get what I mean?

R: Sure, I got you—any other changes?

S: No, that'll just about do it.

R: Okay, fine, we'll add 17 and you'll have the finished product the day before the convention.

S: Can't make it any sooner?

R: 'Fraid not—we're swamped already.

S: Okay then—make that change and I'll see you in two weeks.

The sound-slide film was delivered on schedule on the day before the convention. Steger previewed it and when frame number 17 appeared, he stared in amazement. This is what he saw:

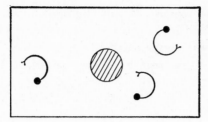

This is what he had in mind when he phoned Robbins two weeks previously:

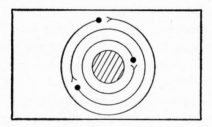

Steger jumped to the phone and demanded that the frame be changed. The Raymond Company assigned a double crew which worked the rest of the day, all of the night and half of the next morning to deliver a copy of the revised film to a badly shaken Steger, barely in time for him to make his appearance before the Convention. The total cost of replacing the two hundred sound-slide films was $1,250.

AMMONS v. WILSON & CO.[19]

Supreme Court of Mississippi   176 Miss. 645, 170 So. 227
1936

(A)

... Appellant was engaged in the wholesale grocery business at Beulah in Bolivar County. Appellee was engaged in the business of meat packing, part of which was the manufacture and sale of shortening. Appellant made the following case by his evidence: Appellee had one Tweedy as its travelling salesman in the territory including Bolivar County. On or about the 9th, 10th or 11th of August, 1934, Tweedy "booked" him for 60,000 pounds of shortening at 7½ cents per pound tierce basis. The booking meant nothing more than that appellee was willing to receive orders from appellant for shortening up to that amount at 7½ cents per pound tierce basis, such orders subject to acceptance by appellee, and that by the booking appellant was not bound to order all or any part of the 60,000 pounds, nor was appellee bound to accept orders for all or any part thereof. In other words, the evidence showed that the booking neither constituted a contract nor an absolute offer to contract—it was merely tentative. On the 23rd and 24th of August appellant, through appellee's travelling salesman, Tweedy, ordered for prompt shipment 942 cases of shortening, aggregating 43,916 pounds. These orders were sent in by Tweedy. Appellant heard nothing from them until the 4th of September following, when he was advised by appellee, in response to his inquiry as to when the shipment would be made, that the orders had been declined. At that time the price of shortening was 9 cents instead of 7½ cents a pound. In other words, appellee waited 12 days from the time the orders were given before declining to accept them. Tweedy had represented appellee in that territory for 6 or 8 months, and during that time he had taken several orders from appellant for certain of appellee's products, which orders in every case had been accepted and shipped not later than one week from the time they were given.

The orders here involved, as well as prior ones, were in writing and contained this provision: "This order taken subject to acceptance by seller's authorized agent at point of shipment." Under this stipulation the orders constituted mere offers to purchase on appellant's part and were not binding on appellee until received and accepted. It is also true, as contended by appellee, that its travelling salesman, Tweedy, was without authority to make a binding contract for it. The extent of his authority was to solicit and transmit orders to his principal for approval.

The question in the case is whether or not, under the law, appellee should be charged with an implied acceptance of the orders by its silence.

[How would you rule—for or against the appellant? Why?]

(B)

... As above stated, all of appellant's previous orders had been accepted and the goods shipped not later than a week from the giving of such orders, while appellee was silent for 12 days after the giving of the orders here involved, and then refused to accept them in response to appellant's request for shipment. We think the sound governing principles are laid down in Restatement, Contracts, subsection 1 (c) of section 72, the applicable part of which is as follows:

"(1) Where an offeree fails to reply to an offer, his silence operates as an acceptance in the following cases and in no others: * * *

"(c) Where because of previous dealings or otherwise, the offeree has given the offeror reason to understand that the silence or inaction is intended by the offeree as a manifestation of assent, and the offeror does so understand."

We are not aware of any decisions of our court in conflict with these principles; certainly those relied on by appellee are not.

We are of the opinion that it was a question for the jury whether or not appellee's delay of 12 days before rejecting the orders, in view of the past history of such transactions between the parties, including the booking, constituted an implied acceptance. The evidence was rather uncertain as to the damages suffered by appellant on account of the alleged breach of the contract. If there was a breach, appellant was entitled to at least nominal damages. If there were actual damages, it devolves on appellant to trace them directly to the breach of the contract and make them definite enough to comply with the governing rules of law. Reversed and remanded [in favor of appellant].

CONSTRUCTION OF A SAILPLANE[20]

By Dr. W. B. Klemperer

It happened, as I recall, in 1924 in Germany. An existing sailplane design was to be enlarged and equipped with a 7 horsepower two-cylinder motorcycle engine driving a propeller through a special reduction gear. There was nothing symmetrical about the motor; hence the front bulkhead of the fuselage to which the engine was to be bolted

---

[20] Reprinted by permission of Dr. Klemperer, Staff Advisor to Chief Engineer, Missiles and Space Systems, Douglas Aircraft Company, Inc.

was a somewhat complicated asymmetrical structure built up of several tiers of plywood separated by wooden webs. The design was made by a small crew in Friedrichshafen; the engine was already located in Fulda where the plane was to be assembled. The fuselage, however, was being built by the Aachener Segelflugzeugbau-Gesellschaft in Aachen which was still under Belgian occupation, over five years after the end of World War I, a condition which rendered postal communications with this station somewhat cumbersome and made it necessary to minimize the shipping back and forth of bulky drawings.

In an attempt to make sure that the bulkheads would be manufactured correctly, each component drawing was marked "port" and "starboard" on the appropriate side. Furthermore all bulkhead components were shown in the conventional aspect as seen in the direction of flight and this was confirmed by the remark printed on every pertinent drawing "von hinten gesehen" (as seen from the rear). Inexplicably when fuselage and engine were finally confronted with each other, they did not fit; the whole nose of the fuselage was built in mirror image. Faces were red and when questioned how they could possibly have misread all the information, the shop crew explained, "We are landlubbers and did not know what 'port' and 'starboard' stood for; we did not bother to look up these nautical terms because it said very plainly, 'as seen from the rear.' So we held the vellums up to a bright light and read through them from the back. This was rather awkward, so we had all vellums printed in reverse, although we had to make an extra right-side print in order to read the legends and dimensions." There was nothing else to do but to cut the whole nose of the fuselage off, splice four new fuselage spar ends and build a new motor bulkhead. This caused a delay of two weeks.

Another comedy of errors occurred in the course of the construction of the same aircraft, although not at the same shop. To save weight we had designed a special wheel rim to be made out of strong aluminum alloy (Duralumin) instead of the conventional steel tire wheel rims. There was some concern about whether it was possible to make these shapes by spinning out of a large flat sheet because of the self-hardening properties of the material under cold working, and it was realized that it might be necessary to re-anneal between several spinning operation steps. I enclose a somewhat simplified replica[21] of the sketch which I furnished the workman who promised to do his best without wasting too many blanks of the then rather precious material.

---

21 The drawing appears on p. 69.

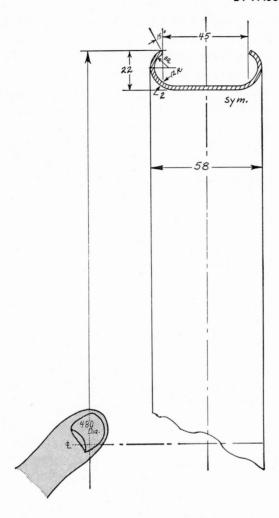

When he finally got around to do the job, he phoned me that he was having trouble because he had to make a wooden form which he had to destroy every time he wanted to take the job off for annealing. When he told me that he had already made four unsuccessful tries, I had a horrible vision of tremendous waste of material and labor cost and rushed over to the shop, where I expected to find four unfinished, unsuitable wheels which were supposed to be about 20″ in diameter. But when I got there, I saw nothing of the sort but four little ashtrays about 2″ in diameter with incurled lips, not quite as far closed as would have corresponded to the profile of the rim. Obviously he had spun the work around the *vertical* axis instead of around the *horizontal* axis. Relieved, I drew his attention to the absence of horizontal rear contour lines at the upper lip level which would have had to be shown on the drawing if this had been a body of revolution around the vertical axis. To this he replied, "Oh yes, I know, but those lines are the ones that engineers usually forget to draw." Then I called his attention to the notation "480 Dia." (of course, all dimensions were given in millimeters) and pointed out that it should have been obvious that this was a body of revolution about the horizontal center-line, even though only half of the object was shown. His alibi was, "Oh, that's where I always hold the thumb of my left hand, when I hold a number one size drawing at my best seeing-distance." There was no trouble remaking the rims after that experience.

JACK McGUIRE[22]

The company I work for is engaged in selling metals to industrial accounts. These metals are steel, aluminum, brass, copper, stainless steel, nickel, monel and nickel alloys for foundry work, as well as for fasteners (machine screws, washers, nuts, etc.), pipe fittings, rivets, and other items, such as nails, studs, etc.

The policy of the company in regard to sales personnel is to hire a man and train him in the plant for about a month to familiarize him with the products sold. The next step is to have him come in the office where he learns office procedure, basic facts about metals, pricing setup, company policy in regard to returned goods and other matters. An important step in this process is listening to a veteran salesman handle customers on the phone, as well as observing how customers who come into the office are handled.

Jack McGuire, a personable young sales trainee, had recently gone through this procedure and was now handling customers by phone. Jack had joined the company immediately after his graduation from high school where he had been an outstanding athlete.

In preface, it should be noted that during an average week a salesman receives about one or two calls wherein the customer has contacted the wrong company or the customer has a misconception about the products handled by the company.

One day McGuire received a call from the purchasing agent of one of our large industrial accounts.

---

22 All names have been disguised. Printed by permission of the author, whose name has been withheld by request.

BUYER *(without announcing his company's name):* "Do you have any track spikes in stock?"

McGUIRE *(with a little chuckle):* "No, I am afraid you called the wrong place. You will have to try a sporting goods house like Dooner's.

BUYER *(angrily):* "Thank you for the information," and he banged down the receiver.

One week later, our regular salesman, Frank Clifford, called on the account and was confronted by the buyer in an angry manner, "What are you hiring now, wise guys? I called up for track spikes to be used in our scrap metal yard and your salesman told me to go to Dooner's.

Clifford explained that the man was new and that it probably was an honest error. Later, Clifford explained to McGuire that what the buyer had wanted were railroad track spikes which are used like steel nails where heavy timber is involved.

ROOM 406[23]

It was 4:56 P.M. on Tuesday, January 3, 1959, on the surgical floor of John Randolph Memorial Hospital. Nurse Rhoda Fleming, an efficient woman with fifteen years' service in the hospital was in charge of the floor that afternoon. She was making her final check of the rooms prior to the arrival of her relief, who came on at 5:00 P.M. In Room 406 she found that Mr. Henry Youstra, who had undergone surgery the week before, and who had not responded after surgery, had finally died. She pulled the sheet over the face of the body and made a mental note to tell her relief to empty the room for a new patient, for bed space was a tremendous problem at the hospital. After finishing her check she returned to the floor desk which was located near the elevators. The night nurse, Ann Simmons, starting her third day at the hospital, had already arrived and was waiting at the desk.

"Anything new, Rho?" she asked.

"406 just died, so that room's all set to go again. I hate to see them go that way, but we can certainly use the space."

"That's for sure. How about 411, did you give her her shot yet?"

"No, and you'd better do that right away. Old Doc Anders might be up, and he'd have a conniption if she hadn't had it yet."

"Does the office know that 406 is ready?"

---

23 All names are disguised. Printed by permission of the author whose name has been withheld by request.

"No, you can call them after you get things cleaned up."

Nurse Fleming then left, and Nurse Simmons gave 411 her shot and went about her other routine duties. At about 6:30 P.M. Nurse Simmons called the office and told them that room 406 was ready for occupancy, though she had not checked that room herself. She was told that a Mr. Leopold would be down from emergency surgery later on and would be given that bed. She then went on about her duties.

Visitors' hours began at 7:00 P.M. at Randolph Hospital, and as was her custom Mrs. Henry Youstra left home at 6:00 P.M. so as to arrive just at 7:00. Over the weeks of visiting her husband, she had acquired the habit of asking for her visitor's card by the room number, as the cards were issued by room number. The girl at the front desk gave her the card prepared for visitors of Mr. Leopold, and she took the elevator to the fourth floor. Nurse Simmons was at the fourth floor desk when Mrs. Youstra arrived there. Nurse Simmons recognized Mrs. Youstra as a nightly visitor and smiled professionally at her, not recalling which patient she visited, nor looking at the name on the card. Nurse Simmons placed the card in the desk file and Mrs. Youstra went down the hall.

At 8:00 P.M. the end of visiting hours, Nurse Simmons checked each room to see that all visitors had left. In Room 406 she found Mrs. Youstra dead on the floor beside the bed containing her husband's body.

THE STURDY CORPORATE HOMESTEADER[24]

In a happier time, so a U.S. Chamber of Commerce speaker tells us, the government used the public domain to "give every man a chance to earn land for himself through his own skill and hard work." This is the sturdy homemaker sob with which the air will presently resound when this gentleman's associates get to work on Congress. He may have been thinking of the California redwood forest. It was so attractive a part of the public domain that in this generation we have had to raise millions of dollars from rich men and school children to buy back a few acres of it here and there for the public.

Under a measure called the Timber and Stone Act, a homemaker who had his first citizenship papers could buy 160 acres of redwood

24 From Bernard DeVoto's "The Easy Chair," *Harper's Magazine*, May, 1953, pp. 57–58. Reprinted by permission.

forest from the government for $2.50 an acre, less than a panel for your living-room costs. Agents of a lumber company would go to a sailors' boarding house on the San Francisco waterfront. They would press a gang of homemakers and lead them to a courthouse to take out first papers. Then they went to a land office and each filed claim to 160 acres of redwood: a quarter-section whose number the lumber company had supplied. At a lawyer's office they transferred to the lumber company the homesteads they had earned by skill and hard work, received $50 for services rendered, and could go back to the boarding house. "Fifty dollars was the usual fee," a historian says, "although the amount soon fell to $10 or $5 and eventually to the price of a glass of beer."

Under this Act four million acres of publicly owned timber passed into corporate ownership at a small fraction of its value, and 95 per cent of it by fraud. Under other Acts supposed to "give every man a chance to earn land for himself," enormously greater acreages came to the same end with the sturdy homemaker's help.

The laws stipulated that the homemaker must be in good faith. Erecting a "habitable dwelling" on his claim would prove that he was. Or if it was irrigable land, he had to "bring water" to it, for a homemaker would need water. Under a couple of dozen aliases apiece, employees of land companies or cattle companies would file claim to as many quarter-sections or half-sections of the public domain and after six months would "commute" them, get title to them at $1.25 per acre.

The sworn testimony of witnesses would prove that they had brought water to the claim; there was no reason for the witnesses to add they had brought it in a can. Or the witnesses swore that they had "seen water" on the homestead and so they had, having helped to throw it there cupful by cupful. Or to erect a "twelve by fourteen" cabin on a claim would prove good faith. Homemaker and witnesses neglected to mention that this "habitable dwelling" was twelve by fourteen inches, not feet. Alternatively, a "shingled residence" established that the homemaker intended to live on his claim; or could be created by fastening a couple of shingles to each side of a tent below the ridgepole. Sometimes a scrupulous corporation would build a genuine log cabin twelve by fourteen feet, mount it on wagon wheels, and have the boys drive it from claim to claim, getting the homemaker a lot of public domain in a few hours. In a celebrated instance in Utah the efficiency of this device was increased by always pushing the truck over the corner where four quarter-sections met.

In six months the homemakers, who meanwhile had been punching cows or clerking in town commuted their two dozen parcels of the public domain. They transferred them to their employers and moved on to earn two dozen more quarter-sections apiece by their skill and hard work. Many millions of acres of publicly owned farmland and grazing land thus passed economically into the possession of corporate homemakers. If the corporation was a land company it might get half a million acres convenient to a railroad right-of-way or within a proposed irrigation district. Or a cattle company could thus acquire a hundred thousand acres that monopolized the water supply for miles and so graze a million acres of the public domain entirely free of charge.

Lumber companies could operate even more cheaply. Their employees need not pay $1.25 per acre or wait to commute their claims. They could pay a location fee, say $16 per 320 acres and the company could forwith clear-cut the timber and let the claims lapse. At twenty cents an acre virgin stands of white or ponderosa pine, Douglas fir, or Norway or Colorado spruce were almost as good as some of the damsites which, our propagandist hopes, will presently be offered to the power companies.

These are typical, routine, second-magnitude land frauds in the history of the public domain out West—to describe the bigger ones would require too much space. Enough that in the golden age of landgrabs, the total area of the public domain proved up and lived on by actual homesteaders amounted to only a trivial fraction of the area fraudulently acquired by land companies, cattle companies, and lumber companies. Among the compelling reasons why the present public-land reserves had to be set aside was the headlong monopolization of the public domain that was threatenting the West with peonage. Those reserves were also made to halt the waste of natural resources which the United States has dissipated more prodigally than any other nation. They had to be made so that a useful part of our national wealth could be preserved, developed, wisely managed, and intelligently used in future times. They had to be made so that the watersheds which control the destiny of the West could be safeguarded. But no one should forget for a moment that they were, besides, necessary to prevent Eastern and foreign corporations from taking over the whole West by fraud, bribery, and engineered bankruptcy.

Chapter **V**

ALLNESS

HAVE you noticed the tone of finality and completeness in the talking of some people? When they speak, it is almost as if they were declaring: "What I am saying is all there is to say about the subject—there is nothing more." It is hardly a rare characteristic. Stop in at your barber shop or beauty salon, as the case may be, and listen to the ease and dispatch with which the intricate problems of national and international affairs are neatly and conclusively solved. Listen to the talking of quarrelers, and you will find a similar note of arrogance, of unseemly assurance and know-it-allness (we shall call it "allness" for short).

Underlying much of this dogmatic, unqualified, categorical, closed-minded thinking and communication are two assumptions—both are fallacious and both are usually held unconsciously by the communicator.

TWO FALSE ASSUMPTIONS

(1) *It is possible to know and say everything about something.* (2) *What I am saying (or writing or thinking) includes all that is important about the subject.* These assumptions are so patently ridiculous that it seems pointless to refute them. And yet a very considerable proportion of communication is apparently based upon them. Perhaps, as Bois[1] has said, we need to crack through the hard shell of the obvious.

We can go about it this way. Pick up a simple object, say a piece of schoolroom chalk. Examine it; study it. What could you say about it? You might mention that it is white, small, light weight, cylindrical, nonedible, inexpensive, a writing instrument, tasteless, hard, smooth, about four inches long, about a third of an inch in diameter, a piece of matter, and related to our national economy. You might add that it is a mineral, capable of squeaking on a blackboard, brittle, a manufactured product, a schoolroom necessity, calcium carbonate, used in

---

[1] J. Samuel Bois, *Explorations in Awareness* (New York: Harper & Bros., 1957).

children's games, a domestic product, powdery when crumbled, likely to soil dark clothing, usually shipped in sawdust or in a protective box, breakable when dropped on hard surfaces, inorganic, etc., etc., etc.

While you might be quite willing to stop talking about the subject, you would not contend that you had said *everything* about it. But just how long would it take to say *everything* about it? A half hour? An hour? Two hours?[2] A day? When we consider the origin of the material, its countless evolutions, and its dynamic atomic structure, it is evident that to say or know *all* about even the simplest object is impossible. This charming story about Agassiz, the great naturalist, is pertinent:

A scientist, he thought, was a man who sees things which other people miss. . . . One of his students has left an account of how he trained them:
"I had assigned to me a small pine table with a rusty tin pan upon it. . . . When I sat me down before my tin pan, Agassiz brought me a small fish, placing it before me with the rather stern requirement that I should study it, but should on no account talk to anyone concerning it, nor read anything relating to fishes, until I had his permission so to do. To my inquiry 'What shall I do?' he said in effect: 'Find out what you can without damaging the specimen; when I think that you have done the work I will question you.' In the course of an hour I thought I had compassed the fish; it was rather an unsavory object, giving forth the stench of old alcohol. . . . Many of the scales were loosened so that they fell off. It appeared to me to be a case of a summary report, which I was anxious to make and get on to the next stage of the business. But Agassiz, though always within call, concerned himself no further with me that day, nor the next, nor for a week.
"At first, this neglect was distressing; but I saw that it was a game, for he was . . . covertly watching me. So I set my wits to work upon the thing, and in the course of a hundred hours or so thought I had done much—a hundred times as much as seemed possible at the start. I got interested in finding out how the scales went in their series, their shape, the form and placement of the teeth, etc. Finally, I felt full of the subject and probably expressed it in my bearing; as for words about it then, there were none from my master except his cheery 'Good morning.' At length, on the seventh day, came the question 'Well?' and my disgorge of learning to him as he sat on the edge of my table puffing his cigar. At the end of the hour's telling he swung off and away, saying 'That is not right.'
"It was clear that he was playing a game with me to find if I were capable of doing hard, continuous work without the support of a teacher, and this stimulated me to labor. I went at the task anew, discarded my first notes, and in another week of ten hours a day labor I had results which astonished myself and satisfied him."

2 One of my colleagues, conducting a training course in communication for executives, kept his group going for three hours listing the details of a piece of chalk!

After this arduous assignment was over, Agassiz did not praise his pupil. At least, he did not emit words of admiration. Instead, he gave him a gallon tank full of bones and told him to see what he could do with them. The young man examined them, and found (from the jaws) that they came from a number of fish of different species. So he started to fit them together so as to reconstruct the skeletons. After two months or more, he succeeded. Once more Agassiz did not praise him, but gave him a more difficult task of observation and comparison. This was all the praise the pupil could expect, for it meant: "You are becoming a more competent scientist."[3]

Having established (to your satisfaction, I trust) that we can never know or say *all* about anything, we still have not discussed how these fallacious assumptions arise nor what can be done to cope with them.

THE PROCESS OF ABSTRACTING

The structure of our language contributes to the problem of *all-ness*. Just what do we do when we use language—when we talk, write, listen, read, think, etc.? We abstract. Let me demonstrate this by first of all listing a few details about a certain person I know. Among many, many other things he is:

a male	red-headed
over 21	a salesman
a husband	a father
a veteran	a human being
a citizen	a car owner
a tax exemption	a taxpayer
a golfer	a bridge player
a Scout leader	a possessor of Civil Rights
a moderate drinker	an avid detective-story reader
a properly registered voter	a teller of droll jokes
a churchgoer	a "lover" of music, rose growing and
a baseball fan	swimming
a Rotary member	a student of current political
a "hater" of soap operas, women	campaign issues
drivers, and tardy people	a newspaper reader
a consumer	a son

ETCETERA (for I could never list *all* about him).

Now, what happens when I *say* something about this person? Suppose I say: "He is a good voter." What I am doing, in effect, is calling your attention and mine to *some* details about this person; perhaps to such details as "over 21," "a citizen," "a properly registered voter," "a student of political campaign issues and candidates," etc. But, at the same

3 From Gilbert Highet, *The Art of Teaching* (New York: Alfred A. Knopf, 1950), pp. 242–43. Reprinted by permission.

time, I am *neglecting* and inducing you to neglect that he is "red-headed," "a husband," "a father," "a veteran," "a car owner," "a golfer," "a churchgoer," and literally thousands of other details that our attentions might have been called to.

This characteristic of language use—this process of focusing-on-some-details-while-neglecting-the-rest—is called *abstracting*. When we talk, write, listen, read, etc., we are *necessarily* abstracting. However, this is often difficult to remember. And when we are unaware that we are attending to some details about a situation, a person, etc., while simultaneously overlooking a host of others, it becomes extremely easy to assume that what we know or what we say is *all* that we really need to know or say. John G. Saxe has depicted the obfuscating property of abstracting on a physical rather than a verbal level in his charming verse about the six blind professors and the elephant.

> It was six men of Indostan
>   To learning much inclined,
> Who went to see the elephant
>   Though all of them were blind
> That each by observation
>   Might satisfy his mind.
>
> The first approached the elephant
>   And, happening to fall
> Against the broad and sturdy side,
>   At once began to bawl:
> "Why, bless me! But the elephant
>   Is very much like a wall!"
>
> The second, feeling of the tusk,
>   Cried: "Ho! what have we here
> So very round and smooth and sharp?
>   To me, tis very clear,
> This wonder of an elephant
>   Is very like a spear!"
>
> The third approached the animal,
>   And, happening to take
> The squirming trunk within his hands
>   Thus boldly up he spake:
> "I see," quoth he, "The elephant
>   Is very like a snake!"
>
> The fourth reached out his eager hand
>   And felt about the knee:
> "What most this wondrous beast is like
>   Is very plain," quoth he:
> "Tis clear enough the elephant
>   Is very like a tree!"

> The fifth who chanced to touch the ear
>   Said: "E'en the blindest man
> Can tell what this resembles most—
>   Deny the fact who can:
> This marvel of an elephant
>   Is very like a fan!"
>
> The sixth no sooner had begun
>   About the beast to grope
> Than, seizing on the swinging tail
>   That fell within his scope,
> "I see," quoth he, "the elephant
>   Is very like a rope!"
>
> And so these men of Indostan
>   Disputed loud and long,
> Each in his own opinion
>   Exceeding stiff and strong;
> Though each was partly in the right,
>   And all were in the wrong.[4]

Of course, this kind of difficulty is not uncommon even among those of us with 20/20 vision!

PROBLEMS OF ALLNESS REACTIONS

More specifically, what sorts of problems does *allness* contribute to? (The following are intended only to suggest some of the various manifestations of the *allness* attitude rather than to serve as rigid and mutually exclusive categories.)

Judging the Whole by Its Part

Sidney Harris develops this aspect of *allness* most eloquently:

Some weeks ago, I presided as toastmaster at a large luncheon sponsored by the National Conference of Christians and Jews. A few hours later, I flew to New York to visit some friends living in Greenwich Village.

As I taxied into New York from the airport, the relationship between these two events suddenly struck me. To the average mind the phrase "Greenwich Village" conjures up a definite set of images, most of them bad, and most of them false.

To the reader of sensational journals or to the casual tourist, Greenwich Village is a weird neighborhood in lower Manhattan, composed largely of ranting poets, crazy artists, ridiculous perverts and "Bohemians" of the lowest order of depravity.

---

4 By John G. Saxe and printed in Lowrey and Johnson, *Interpretative Reading* (New York: D. Appleton–Century, Inc., 1942), pp. 44–45.

Actually, this is only a part of the truth and not the large part. Anyone who has stayed in the Village for more than a few weeks learns that the painters, the poets and the perverts are only the most obvious tenants of the neighborhood.

The great bulk of the population in the Village is made up of substantial citizens living in well-kept homes, with well-tended children, dogs, and back gardens. The houses along 10th St. are charming and almost austerely Early American. Washington Square is bursting with roller skates, softballs and all the springtime signs of bourgeois maternity.

Now, what the ignorant majority thinks of "Greenwich Village" is exactly what it thinks of other races and creeds. It is always the obvious undesirables that, in the public mind, characterize a group or a neighborhood. It is the deplorable habit of human nature to identify any object with its worst attribute.

If a man drinks, we describe him as a "drinker," never adding that he is kind, humorous, brave and truthful. The part we dislike becomes the whole—until we get to know the whole. And, until "brotherhood" among people becomes a reality, we will be as unfair toward other races and creeds as we are in our partial judgment of Greenwich Village.[5]

Intolerance of Other Viewpoints

We all know how difficult it is to concede points of view which differ from our own. One afflicted with *allness* cannot abide such differences, for in his warped logic his viewpoint is the *only right* one and thus others may appear to him as stupidities, hindrances, or even as threats. Davis has an interesting diagram[6] of how a production expert's perception of a problem tends to differ from that of a sales expert.

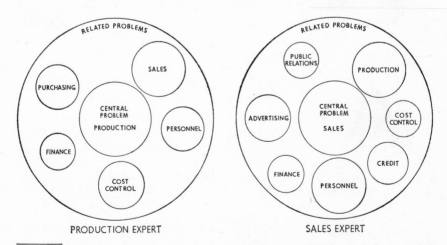

PRODUCTION EXPERT   SALES EXPERT

---

[5] Sidney J. Harris, "The Village Is Sadly Misjudged," from his column "Strictly Personal," *Chicago Daily News,* April 14, 1954. Reprinted by permission.

[6] By permission from *Human Relations in Business,* by Keith Davis. Copyright, 1957. McGraw-Hill Book Company, Inc.

Each sees his own bailiwick as the central problem area and places differing emphases on the related problems.

The "All Wall"

"I can't get through to him." "He simply won't listen to reason." "His mind is made up; he doesn't want to be confused by facts." Familiar expressions? They are generally directed at the person with extreme *allness* who appears to have drawn up an insular wall around himself.

The person within his "all wall" finds it well nigh impossible to learn. He has so thoroughly shielded himself from anything new or different that he warrants the reprimand of Epictetus: "It is impossible for anyone to begin to learn what he thinks he already knows." The old Stoic, I suspect, would be especially concerned with the student (to use a term loosely) who "knows" what his teacher is about to try to teach him. Aside from the disruptive effect that such a person can have on his classmates, he is wasting his time, his instructor's effort, and his father's money.

(Lest these remarks be construed as pertaining only to college students, let us recognize that we are students all of our lives—or should be. An academic *commencement*, after all, is intended to designate a *beginning*, not an *ending*.)

The relationship between the height of one's "all wall" (the degree of his *allness*) and his ability to learn might be expressed in this manner:

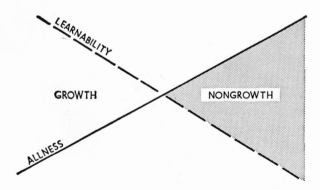

As one's *allness* increases, his *learnability* decreases and vice versa. Growth and development tend to cease as his *allness* exceeds his *learnability*. The diagram, however, does not take time into account. It is evident that one's *allness-learnability* ratio fluctuates from time to time and from subject to subject. Let us chart in an oversimplified way a certain day in the life of a not too typical (we trust) undergraduate:

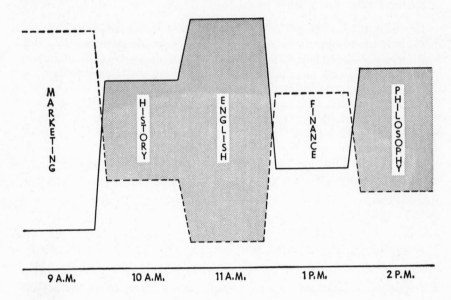

| 9 A.M. | 10 A.M. | 11 A.M. | 1 P.M. | 2 P.M. |

If this student were to express his fluctuating attitude through the day it might sound something like this:

"Marketing—Now there's a field for you! I'm really fascinated by the ways they find out what the public wants to buy. I'm going to be able to *use* this course.

"History—Frankly, this bores me. What good is it to know what happened so long ago? Times have changed. Life is different now, so why dig up the dead?

"English—I positively can't stand this! I've had this stuff drilled into me for twelve years. When will they let up? When I go into business, I'll have a secretary writing my letters.

"Finance—This is all right, but it's plenty stiff. Some of it is practical, but a lot of it I'll never use.

"Philosophy—Boy, is this stuff up in the clouds! I just hope I can bluff through the exams."

A college student with this much shaded area isn't getting his money's worth out of his education. An employee with this much shaded area isn't giving his employer his money's worth.

It would seem that frequently the less we know about something, the more certain we are that we know it *all*. Prejudice, as it was once defined, is often a matter of "being down on something you're not up on."

Stuart Chase asserted the point thus:

Chester Bowles in *Ambassador's Report* observes that after three months in India it would have been easy to write the book, for he learned all the pat answers by that time. After eighteen months it was much harder, for by then he knew that most of the pat answers were wrong. The longer he stayed, the more complicated India became. Messrs. Cohn and Schine, Lieutenants of Senator McCarthy, were bothered by no such problem when they breezed through Europe in a few days, uncovering Communist conspiracies or evidence of "disloyalty" in various cities.[7]

Was it not Bertrand Russell who said: "One's certainty varies *inversely* with one's knowledge"?[8]

CORRECTIVES

For reducing *allness*, perhaps the following check list will be helpful:

1. Develop a sincere humility—a deep conviction that you can never know or say everything about anything. Disraeli said: "To be conscious that you are ignorant is a great step toward knowledge." Lawrence A. Appley, President of the American Management Association, holds a similar view with reference to management training:

   "He believes that before the executive can communicate effectively or, in fact, handle any of the other tasks of management, he must first know that he doesn't know. When a man develops the humility to admit that perhaps he doesn't know all the answers after all, then he is ready to begin to learn. It's at this point that management training becomes a wise investment."[9]

2. Be wary of building an "all wall." Watch for the moments when you feel too assured, too certain. To close yourself off from continued learning and development is fatal (at least between your ears). Dwight D. Eisenhower asserted that one of the key problems of the military commander (it is equally pertinent for the civilian administrator) is "to keep his mind open, to avoid confusing necessary firmness with stubborn preconception or unreasoning prejudice."[10]

---

7 Stuart Chase, *Guides to Straight Thinking* (New York: Harper & Bros., 1956), pp. 43–44. Reprinted by permission.

8 *Ibid.*, p. 25.

9 "Is Management Training Worth It?" *Nation's Business*, November, 1957, p. 115. Reprinted by permission.

10 Dwight D. Eisenhower, *Crusade in Europe* (New York: Doubleday & Co., Inc., 1948), p. 256.

3. Remember, that whatever you know or say it is never all there is to know or say. The Crouse-Hinds Company in Syracuse, for example, makes a practice of consulting its employees before making any installation or building changes. A plan for rearranging and installing foundry equipment was shown to the foundry employees. The result was a "goldmine of ideas that never would have occurred to anyone but the workers closest to the job."[11]

4. Recall as you communicate that you are inevitably abstracting (attending to some details while neglecting a multitude of others).

   a) Recognize the possibility that the part with which you are acquainted may not be representative of the whole. It is difficult to resist judging a man by his clothes or the car he drives, a firm by the brashness of one of its salesmen, a university by a handful of its graduates; but generalizations on such meager samples are apt to be quite misleading.

   b) Anticipate the chance that your "communicatee" may not be abstracting as you are. Consider this poignant example of a communicator's failure to empathize with another's abstractions—to gain his point of view.

   > "Tell me," said the blind man, "what is white like?"
   > "It is like newly fallen snow," replied his sighted friend.
   > "Lightweight and damp?"
   > "No, it is more like paper."
   > "It rustles, then?"
   > "No, no—it is like an albino rabbit."
   > "I understand—soft and furry."

5. When you use language, add an *etcetera* to remind yourself and others that there is always more:

   > "The important thing about etcetera is that we should think it even when we don't say it. When we make a statement and think of the 'and so forth' at the end of it, we show we realize that we have not said all that is possible to say about the subject, that we have uttered an approximation, a fragment, a partiality. The use of etcetera is an exhibition of the consciousness of ignorance, a humility, a sincere modesty."[12]

---

11 See *Personnel Policies and Practices Report,* August 6, 1957. Copyrighted 1957 by Prentice-Hall, Inc.

12 Leo Lerner, "And So On and So Forth" from "The First Column," *Lerner Newspapers,* September 27, 1955, p. 1.

INCIDENTS

THE KISS AND THE SLAP[13]

In a railroad compartment, an American grandmother with her young and attractive granddaughter, a Romanian officer, and a Nazi officer were the only occupants. The train was passing through a dark tunnel, and all that was heard was a loud kiss and a vigorous slap. After the train emerged from the tunnel, nobody spoke, but the grandmother was saying to herself, "What a fine girl I have raised. She will take care of herself. I am proud of her." The granddaughter was saying to herself, "Well, grandmother is old enough not to mind a little kiss. Besides, the fellows are nice, I am surprised what a hard wallop grandmother has." The Nazi officer was meditating, "How clever those Romanians are! They steal a kiss and have the other fellow slapped." The Romanian officer was chuckling to himself, "How smart I am! I kissed my own hand and slapped the Nazi."

BIG BUSINESS—PRO AND CON

"Big Business Is Dangerous"[14] by Emmanuel Celler, Chairman of the Judiciary Committee of the House of Representatives.

Under our ancient common law your neighbor must not point a gun at you, even though he has never shot anyone. Similarly, our antitrust laws were intended to protect businessmen not only from violence but from fear of violence. They are not working perfectly.

As a Congressman I have to listen to all sorts of stories. One story that came to me told of sudden terror in the refrigerator industry. The independents were telephoning each other the bad news that General Electric was on the warpath. The Tecumseh Company, which supplies some independents with compressors, was to be killed off and

---

13 Alfred Korzybski, "The Role of Language in the Perceptual Processes," *Perception: An Approach to Personality,* edited by Robert R. Blake and Glenn V. Ramsey. Copyright 1951 The Ronald Press Co. Reprinted by permission.

14 *Reader's Digest,* June, 1950. Reprinted by permission of the author and the *Reader's Digest.*

they would be left at the mercy of GE. Just to make sure, a phone call was put through to Mr. Herrick, president of Tecumseh. He said he had talked with Charles Wilson, president of GE, and there was nothing to the story.

A week later, in Washington, Mr. Wilson told us what had happened. Yes, one of his salesmen had gone to one of Tecumseh's customers and offered to sell compressors "at any price regardless of cost." Mr. Herrick had called up Mr. Wilson in great distress and wanted to know if GE had decided to put him out of business. "I told him it was the bunk and that the salesman had been talked to." So all was well. But was it?

I don't like to see men first terrorized and then relieved to find that Charles Wilson is feeling kindly and won't let his men shoot. What may his successor decide to do? GE has been guilty several times of antitrust violations, but the law had not succeeded in making Mr. Herrick or the refrigerator men feel protected. GE's next conviction might be for slaughtering them, a poor comfort to the dead.

No one suggests that this country can do without big companies to handle certain kinds of work. You can't build automobiles or develop the mercury boiler on a shoestring. But our evidence seems to show that many articles are as well-made by small companies as by big ones. Big companies often invade fields where bigness is not necessary for efficiency. Our witnesses tell us that the big fellows at times use their power to cut off supplies from the smaller independents, or to prevent retailers from carrying their goods, so that the consumer does not have a fair chance to discover and choose the best products. "Independents" are often allowed to live if they do not act independently, but the public does not get the benefit of their active competition. And how independent is a man whose livelihood depends on acting as supplier or agent-dealer for a single big company?

The law is supposed to prevent abuses of power in business. But the abuses are so easy to get away with that if we try to stop them by policing alone the job might well take more police than would be safe for a free country. *I believe it is more practical to outlaw any concentration of power that cannot be shown to be so useful as to justify the cost of policing it against abuse.*

I agree with the dissenting opinion of Justices Douglas, Black, Murphy and Rutledge in the recent case in which U.S. Steel was allowed to buy the Consolidated Steel plant on the West Coast. The justices pointed out that U.S. Steel was frankly buying this fabricating plant "to insure itself of a market for its own rolled steel in case demand should fall off." In other words, it wanted to shut out the smaller companies that had been competing for this business and, as the justices say, "competition is never more irrevocably eliminated than by buying the customer."

"Size in steel," they say, "is the measure of the power of a handful of men over our economy. That power can be benign or it can be dangerous. The philosophy of the Sherman Act is that it should not exist.

"Industrial power should be scattered into many hands so that the fortunes of the people will not be dependent on the whim or caprice, the political prejudices, the emotional stability of a few self-appointed men."

A free country cannot afford to let anyone have great power unless he is checked by an automatic force like free competition or by some democratic legal control to make him serve the public. Since no checks work perfectly, I do not believe power is justified merely by showing that the man who has it is not abusing it right now. Power, I think, is justified only when there is no other practical instrument for serving the public interest.

If we have big private powers in business, every now and then we run into a national crisis where the people demand that the Government step in. In Europe, where the people have carelessly accepted bigness as a good thing in itself, they have come out with some form of socialism. I believe socialism comes from not being careful about bigness.

Big business, run by men like the du Ponts who care about production, has often given us good service to set off against its abuses of power. But big concerns have often been put together by financial operators, not to serve the public but to give the insiders power to take the profits away from small stockholders. Some people still remember Samuel Insull and the collapse of his utility empire. We have had experience in breaking up finance-controlled big business under the Public Utility Holding Company Act of 1935. The big utility holding companies have now been pretty well split up, and the results look good. When Commonwealth & Southern started to take the treatment in 1938, the total market value of its securities was 125 million dollars. By 1949 investors had received, in the breakup, cash and securities worth 415 million dollars. At the same time, consumers are getting electricity at lower rates. If that is ruining an industry, we might ask if there are any more that need the same kind of ruin.

I believe the most efficient system for the United States has to include both big and small companies in the places where they do the most good. But I also believe that the best results come from having as much freedom as possible. This means not only freedom from socialistic management of business by bureaucrats. It means also freedom from control by outside financial interests or big competitors, suppliers or customers.

It may be that abuse of power can largely be prevented by requiring more publicity about the affairs of big concerns. Good lighting cuts down the need for policemen. When the public knows more about what goes on, I hope that small businessmen who are threatened by big ones may feel as safe in standing up to protest as our citizens do when they feel injured by big government.

"Big Business Is Essential to Our Economy"[15] by Crawford H. Greenewalt, President of E. I. du Pont de Nemours & Co.

All of us in America want an expanding economy—more goods, higher living standards, a more abundant life for all of our people. We can reach that end only through a strong industry—cooperative and harmonious in all its parts—fruitful in peace, decisive in war. Yet Mr. Celler wants to chip away at the foundation of our industrial strength, to weaken the companies which through their competitive success have become large, to remove the incentive to greater progress by saying "so far and no farther."

Mr. Celler's argument runs something like this: Large companies have a power that *might* be used against the public interest. There are laws to prevent that abuse but enforcement is too difficult. So, regardless of the company's contribution to the economy, no matter how well it discharges its responsibilities, we'll call it guilty whether it has done anything bad or not, and let it prove itself innocent if it can.

This is an idea new to citizens of a free country—that power to do something is the same as doing it, and that you are guilty until proved innocent. And the remedy is as novel as it is dangerous: that the way to control such power is to eliminate it. Mr. Celler wants to eliminate

---

15 *Reader's Digest,* June, 1950. Reprinted by permission of the author and the *Reader's Digest.*

the handful of businesses which can be called "big" on the remarkable theory that law enforcement with respect to them might "take more police than would be safe for a free country."

If the large companies really had this "economic power" that Mr. Celler thinks they have, wouldn't there be fewer small businesses as time went on? Actually there are more—many more per thousand of population today than there were 20 years ago.

If they really had that power, don't you think the big ones would have a steadily increasing percentage of the nation's business? Actually the 25 largest manufacturing corporations have about the same percentage of the nation's business today that they had 20 years ago.

And how about the power to perpetuate one's self in business—the "once big, always big" theory? You have only to look at the list of the 25 largest manufacturing companies over the last 50 years to see how the competitive process has laid many away and brought others forward to take their place.

If we look at fact rather than fancy, aren't we forced to conclude that the "economic power" of big business resides largely in Mr. Celler's imagination?

The fact is that corporations are not soulless entities. They are just people who have teamed up to do a big job. And just as people on the average are decent and law-abiding, so are corporate people, sharing not only Charles E. Wilson's kindly feeling but also his desire to observe the law.

To say that corporations never err would be like saying that people never make mistakes. Business will have its occasional Samuel Insulls just as Congress has its Andrew J. Mays. Neither provides a basis for eliminating either business or the Congress. Both are examples of human frailty, and we have laws to take care of them in all spheres of activity. In business the antitrust laws provide ground rules that are adequate to serve the public interest, and let us never say with Mr. Celler that it is impracticable to enforce them.

Can anyone seriously doubt that big business is essential to our American economy? Radios, automobiles, refrigerators and the thousand and one articles we demand for our comfort require mass production for cheapness and universal availability. Mass production needs large pools of capital, of technical skills, of resources of many types. Mass production is nothing more than a team of stockholders and employes doing a large job. That has been the secret of American industrial success—willingness to work together.

The idea that big and small businesses are in conflict just doesn't hold water. In our industrial economy they need each other. There is scarcely a product made by a large business that doesn't create opportunities for thousands of small businesses in the long road that reaches eventually to the consumer. Let me give you one example.

My company manufactures nylon, a textile fiber of unusual properties and, fortunately for us, of unusual popularity. This fall a dress manufacturer will offer a line of nylon dresses for which the customer will be asked to pay $49.95. For the nylon that goes into one of those dresses the du Pont Company gets $1.92. The difference between that and the retail price represents the contribution added by many smaller businesses—the company that makes the yarn, the company that weaves it into cloth, the company that dyes it and finishes it, the dress manufacturer, and finally the retail store. And the consumer gets the lion's share of the benefit, since these dresses can be washed, hung out to dry and worn without pressing a few hours later.

Many more examples could be cited to point up the mutual opportunities brought about by large and small businesses working together. Du Pont could never have put nylon over without the assistance of small business. Small business could never have made the investment necessary to produce nylon.

Business growth comes about only through success in pleasing the customer. We have no way to influence him in the exercise of his judgment except to offer a better product or the same product at a lower price. Business success is simply a measure of the votes of thousands of satisfied customers. If they like the product and the price, the business will grow. If not it will fail. It is as simple as that. And when government arbitrarily limits growth it is not only penalizing success but is also penalizing the customer by thwarting the free exercise of his judgment.

We in business are much like Mr. Celler. He pleads for the votes of his constituents—we plead for the votes of our customers. And let me assure you that dissatisfied customers can sink even a big company as quickly, surely and devastatingly as dissatisfied voters can sink a public servant.

Mr. Celler would hardly try to prevent political voters from registering. It is just as contrary to our democratic structure to prevent economic voters from registering.

[What do you make of the differing abstractions of these two writers?]

ALDERMANIC ELECTION[16]

Allenshire, population 50,000, a suburb of a large city in New England, is largely Republican and predominantly Protestant. Many of its citizens are well-to-do executives and professional people. The per capita income of the suburb is well above the national average.

In a recent aldermanic election these two leaflets were distributed respectively by supporters of the two candidates for Alderman of the 3rd Ward:

ALLENSHIRE YOUNG REPUBLICAN CLUB

COMPARE YOUR ALDERMANIC CANDIDATES

Then—VOTE for Alderman Martin J. Stewart—April 7

Alderman Martin J. Stewart	*Ronald Green*
Residence	
212 Grey. Home owner. Allenshire resident 24 years.	609 Wilson. Home owner. Allenshire resident 8 years.
Family Status	
Married. 2 children, 4 grandchildren.	Married. 2 children.
Occupation	
Business man. President, National Office Supplies Co.	Lawyer. Partner, law firm of Green, Weisman and Epstein. Former OPA lawyer.
Political Activities	
Assistant Secretary, Allenshire Republican Club.	Vice President, Allenshire Democratic Club. Active in last November's campaign for Levine, Democratic nominee for Sheriff.
Local Government Experience	
Alderman the past two years. 12 years on Park District Board without salary. Now President.	None
Civic Activities	
Deacon, First Methodist Church. Charter member, Northwest Allenshire Community Club. Air Raid Warden during the war. Civilian Defense Chairman for Allenshire during the war.	Member, Temple Beth Israel. "Active participant in community and charitable activities."

---

[16] All names have been disguised.

Endorsements

Allenshire Young Republican Club.
Allenshire Women's Republican Club.
3rd Ward Young Republican Club.
3rd Ward Women's Republican Club.
Service as Alderman rated very highly in poll of fellow alderman and City Department Heads.
3rd Ward Residents for Stewart.

Allenshire Democratic Club.
3rd Ward Independent Citizens for Green.
Committee of 100 Nonpartisan 3rd Ward Neighbors.

Vote April 7   6 AM–5 PM

VOTE FOR ALDERMAN MARTIN J. STEWART

3rd Ward Young Republican Club

Biographical Sketch
of
RONALD GREEN

Candidate for
ALDERMAN — 3RD WARD

Allenshire   Election: April 7

Born: (Nearby city), 1914.

Married: One son, 7 years old; one daughter, 6 months old.

Residence: 609 Wilson Avenue, Allenshire (own home). Allenshire resident 8 years.

Education: (Local university), 1936, School of Law, 1938 (Scholarship student—top man in class).

Community and charitable activities:
   Participated in community activities such as factory zoning problem in south end of ward, Northwest Allenshire transportation problem, and represented community (without fee) in litigation concerning the Jackson School corner—gasoline station zoning problem. Member of several Allenshire civic, social and religious organizations; lecturer on municipal, governmental and legal problems; member, participant and attorney for charitable organizations.

Experienced Educator:
   Member of faculty (local university School of Law) since 1947. Presently serving as member of that faculty.

Governmental Experience:
   Formerly Assistant Regional Attorney, U.S. Government Emergency War Agencies (4 New England states).

Professional Experience:
   Practicing attorney since 1938. Admitted to practice before state and Federal Courts, U.S. Court of Appeals, and U.S. Supreme Court.

Professional Associations:
   Member, Allenshire Bar Association; State Bar Association; Federal Bar Association; (list of national and local honorary legal fraternities).

INTERVIEW WITH MISS WINKLER[17]
By Schuyler Dean Hoslett

This conversation takes place in the office of Mr. Zurch, Director of Personnel for an organization employing about 3,500 persons. Miss Winkler has been reported by her supervisors as doing unsatisfactory work; they ask that she be transferred on the basis of a list of charges outlined in a memorandum. Mr. Zurch has sent for Miss Winkler, who enters his office while he is talking to an assistant about another matter. Also present in the office at the time of the interview, but presumably not able to hear the conversation and doing other work, were Mr. Zurch's secretary, his assistant, and the recorder of the interview. Inasmuch as Miss Winkler spoke in a low tone, all of her comments were not audible to the recorder, especially as she became more emotional and finally tearful but the conversation was substantially as follows:

W: Did you send for me, Mr. Zurch?

Z: Yes, I did; I'll be with you in just a minute. (Mr. Zurch continues to talk to his assistant for seven minutes. During this time there is considerable confusion in the office, with the telephone ringing often, and with Mr. Zurch becoming more and more concerned over some matter about which he talks loudly, interspersing his rather definite comments with considerable swearing. This, it may be noted, is his usual manner under stress. Mr. Zurch continues:) Now, look, Miss Winkler (takes several minutes to look over her file and to talk to his assistant about another matter), you remember we talked together in March and at that time B Division was not satisfied, and since you have been with Mr. Newton, and he was not altogether satisfied.

W: He didn't tell me anything like that. (Speaks in a low, courteous voice.) He told me after I left that he wanted me back. . . .

Z: Now you have been in C Division and there is a report on your work there. Now Miss Winkler, we take each employee and try to fit

---

17 Reprinted from "Listening to the Troubled or Dissatisfied Employee," *Personnel*, July, 1945, pp. 54–56, by permission of the American Management Association.

her in where she can do the best job. We realize that people sometimes can't get along because of the supervisor, or fellow employees, and we try to make adjustments. (This comment is given in Mr. Zurch's usual direct and rather belligerent manner.) Now you have been in a number of positions. How many have you occupied?

W: (After thinking a moment) Four or five.

Z: Do you agree with the comments made in this report? (Quotes from report before him on the desk.) "Shows little interest in work and says she doesn't care for filing."

W: (Miss Winkler's voice is growing husky now and her response is almost inaudible, but she explains that she doesn't like filing, and that she wasn't hired to do that kind of work. She was to be a stenographer.)

Z: We don't have the work always to everyone's satisfaction.

W: But I wasn't told that was what the job would be.

Z: But we can't give everyone a job he wants . . . (Interview has turned into something of an argument at this point; Mr. Zurch presents next charge.) "Deliberately slows down on the job."

W: No, I do not. (Miss Winkler seems quite incensed at this charge.)

Z: "Uses business hours to write letters."

W: I did that once.

Z: "Doesn't keep up to date with her work."

W: They put in a new system up there and the supervisor asked me to help with it and I said I would. But I couldn't keep up to date on my own work and do that too. The supervisor asked me to do this at the same time that I had more than enough work of my own to do. (Though deeply disturbed at these charges, Miss Winkler's responses are direct; by this time, however, she is on the verge of tears.)

Z: "Leaves fifteen minutes before 12 and returns twenty to twenty-five minutes late."

W: If I went before 12, I returned earlier.

Z: "Uses rest-room facilities on 2nd floor instead of 3rd as required by the rules."

W: They were dirty on the 3rd floor.

Z: We can't be in those rooms every minute of the day. When I went in there (apparently at an earlier complaint) it wasn't dirty—only a few papers thrown around. It wasn't like any bathroom at home, but it wasn't dirty.

W: I have seen it at times when you couldn't use it.

Z: Why didn't you report it?

W: I did—But that's a petty thing (i.e., the complaint.)

Z: Yes, but it means five to ten minutes more away from your desk. Listen, Miss Winkler, I think the supervisor doesn't have an axe to grind; maybe all of these things aren't true, but a certain amount is.

W: I did the work I was told to do, but some had to be left over. They expected me to get the mail out, and certain work had to be left.

Z: That's right, but there are those times when you were away from your work. (Mr. Zurch explains the limitations on the number of persons the organization may hire; that each girl must do her work, or the organization will get behind.)

W: I still think the charges aren't fair.

Z: Well, tell me, are there any differences between you and Jones (her immediate supervisor)?

W: I'd rather not say.

Z: Don't you get along?

W: Oh, sometimes.

Z: Please tell me the story. . . . (When apparent there will be no response) Did you go over this with Miss Counce (the counselor)?

W: (Miss Winkler replies that she did, but by this time she is crying softly, and the exact words were not heard.)

Z: We have a reputation of being fair. We try to analyze every factor in a report of this kind. . . . You have been here two years, long enough to know the whole story. . . . Do you think you aren't in the right job?

W: I want to leave the job.

Z: (In a milder tone) Now that's not the right attitude. We won't get anywhere that way. Has Mr. Achen (a higher supervisor) ever talked to you?

W: Not once.

Z: Has the Principal Clerk of the department talked to you about it?

W: Yes, once. (Two sentences not heard.)

Z: Do you think your work too heavy?

W: I can keep it cleaned up at times, but not all the time. There are days when with dictation, etc., I can't.

Z: Well, why don't we have the job analyzed on a week's basis and see if there is too much for one person.

W: A week wouldn't be right; once I was behind for three weeks.

Z: Honestly, haven't you taken extra time off?

W: No, absolutely not. I've noticed other girls going out when they weren't supposed to, though.

Z: Are you getting along with other employees?

W: Yes.

Z: Well, I'll tell you, you go back upstairs after you get set (i.e., after she has made repairs on her face because of the crying). Do you have any other comment to make?

W: I feel he (supervisor) has been very unfair about my slowing down on my work.

Z: All right, O.K., now you stay down until, let's see, it's 3:30 now, until 3:45. I'll call them to expect you at 3:45.

Mr. Zurch's comment after the interview: "This girl comes from a good family and environment and apparently feels that she has a better head than the other workers. Our problem is to get her adjusted. I disagree with this report that she purposely slowed down on the job. The fact that she didn't like filing is nothing against her; we have that trouble all the time. But there is no question that she takes time off. I think 50–60 per cent of the charges are correct and the rest is put on for a good story. We'll find that the supervisor hasn't talked to her correctly. She would be a better employee under a girl who could handle her or a smart-looking man. You noted that she was especially indignant at charges of slowing down, but not so indignant on spending extra time out."

Mr. Zurch calls the immediate supervisor and the next higher supervisor into his office to discuss the situation.

Z: What is it all about, this Winkler case?

Mr. Achen: Her attitude is wrong. She wants to be a stenographer and she was hired as a clerk-typist and there isn't a 100 per cent steno job up there. We give her some dictation, but can't give her full time. She doesn't want to do filing.

Jones: She gets behind. (Telephone call interrupts.)

Mr. Achen: She said to someone, "I'll let this filing pile up and just see what happens." I think for the good of the department she should be transferred. (Another telephone call interrupts.)

Z: But we can't transfer her all the time.

Mr. Achen: We spoke to her about the restrooms, but she disregards the rules. We have given her a fair chance.

Z: O.K., thanks a lot. (Apparently the decision is to transfer Miss Winkler to another department. Mr. Zurch goes off to a meeting.)

INTELLIGENCE IS FOR COMMANDERS[18]

"The consideration overshadowing all others in the minds of the Hawaiian commanders was the belief and conviction that Pearl Harbor would not be attacked. . . . It explains the reason for no effective steps being taken to meet the Japanese raiders on the morning of December 7th." (From the Report of the Joint Committee on the Investigation of the Pearl Harbor Attack, Congress of the United States.) With these words the congressional committee handed down its judgment. Their verdict is plain—an intelligence deficiency resulted in a command failure.

History is replete with examples of those ominous twins: intelligence failure and military disaster. There is the story of the field marshal who stood on a hill north of Rossomme surveying the battlefield through his telescope. The enemy appeared to be withdrawing. All that was needed to complete the marshal's victory was a final blow by the splendid French cavalry drawn up in the valley below. The ground was heavy from recent rains, but no obstacle to a mounted charge could be seen. Turning to Lacoste, a timid but hostile native tied to a hussar's saddle, the commander asked in substance: "Is the way between here and the village over there (Mont St. Jean) clear for my cavalry?" The native nodded, "Yes." The marshal hurriedly dispatched a messenger to Paris announcing a victory. Without further consideration he ordered the cavalry to carry the plateau of Mont St. Jean. Over the first ridge swept twenty-six French squadrons—forty-five hundred men mounted on huge horses. They crossed the last valley at a gallop. Up the slope they rode and over the crest—when suddenly the leading horses reared in sudden terror. Before them yawned an awful chasm—the sunken road of Ohain—fifteen feet down its precipitous banks to the bottom. It was too late! Rank after rank was hurled into the trench by its own impetus and by the pressure of the ranks behind. Local tradition says that two thousand horses and fifteen hundred men were buried in the road of Ohain. The field marshal was Bonaparte. The battle—Waterloo. For Napoleon, served by inaccurate intelligence of the terrain, it was the beginning of defeat. St. Helena was only a step away.

---

18 From the Introduction, *Intelligence Is for Commanders*, by Lt. Col. Robert R. Glass and Lt. Col. Phillip B. Davidson (Harrisburg, Pa.: Military Service Publishing Co., 1948). Reprinted by permission.

There are examples from our own Civil War. On the morning of 2 May 1863, the Blue general realized that the enemy was capable of enveloping his right, and warned the commander of the XI Corps located on that flank. The line of march taken by the enemy *might* have meant either an envelopment of the Blue right or a retreat on the town of Gordonsville. Apparently, in view of the disparity in numbers and the wide dispersion of the enemy forces which would result from an envelopment, a retreat to Gordonsville was more logical from the Blue standpoint. And yet throughout the afternoon evidence kept piling up that the enemy was marching against the flank of the XI Corps. Numerous officers came in from the picket and reported to the division or corps commander that the Greys were moving around that flank. The mildest reaction on the part of these commanders was to laugh at it. In one case Corps headquarters even rebuked an officer who was reporting the observation of his own eyes, and warned him not to bring on a panic. In another instance an officer was called a coward and was ordered back to his regiment. And thus, "Fighting Joe" Hooker, refusing to believe that the enemy would attack his flank, suddenly found the Confederates rolling up his right. His campaign suffered a serious but avoidable loss. Within a month the Army of the Potomac had a new commander.

THE HAYDEN COMPANY[19]

The Hayden Company, headquartered in Dayton, Ohio, has numerous divisions in unrelated industries throughout the United States. These divisions for the most part are autonomous in their operations.

Guy Horton is attached to the Personnel Department in the headquarters office of the Hayden Company. He reports to the personnel director. He serves in an advisory capacity and gives assistance in problems of office and laboratory personnel to the office managers in the various divisions of the firm.

These divisions do not have personnel officers as such, and all recruiting, selecting and training is carried on through their respective office managers.

An acute problem had arisen in the Memphis division. Because of separations and expanded operations several additional research men

---

19 All names are disguised.

would be needed within five to six weeks. The research these men would do would be in the field of farm chemistry and the application of farm products to industry.

Mr. Horton's search to find manpower to fill this need took him to several midwestern universities where he was permitted to look through alumni records and also to talk to graduating seniors who qualified. One of the schools he visited was the Rogers Institute of Technology, an institution with a high scholastic rating.

Mr. Horton sent the following report to his superior, relating his experiences at Rogers.

"I visited R.I.T. yesterday morning and was permitted to interview several seniors and also to look at alumni records for candidates for the Memphis Laboratory. The students I talked to gave me a very unfavorable impression, their dress and speech could have been much better. After speaking to a number of them I did not think it worth while to interview others. My next step was to seek out the alumni records, and believe me I did not get a great deal of cooperation on this. Some clerk showed me an enormous card file and without further word he left. I leafed through this card file for a while but gave it up as a waste of time. I judge this school as being no more than a trade school and it would be a waste of time to visit it in the future."

Chapter VI

DIFFERENTIATION FAILURES I
(INDISCRIMINATION)

THE following accounts may seem quite diverse but they are alike in at least one important respect.

* * * *

For a camera bug's 50th birthday, a White Plains woman decided to present him with 50 flash bulbs. She knows little about cameras, but she purchased a box camera with a flash attachment for herself at the same time she bought the bulbs. And before wrapping each bulb in gold paper she carefully tested it in the attachment. She was delighted that every bulb "worked," and happily sent them off to her friend—who still hasn't had the heart to tell her the facts of life about cameras.[1]

* * * *

Grand Falls, N.B., Jan. 9 (AP)—The foamy white waste products of a starch factory looked like snow to Frederick Boucher, 7, so he jumped into an eight foot ditch filled with it. Two classmates on their way home from school with Frederick called for help but by the time rescuers arrived the boy was dead.[2]

* * * *

The young Negro doctor, fresh from Nashville's Meharry Medical College, learned what he was up against as soon as he started to practice in Sanford, in the heart of Florida's orange-grove country. His first emergency was the case of a woman suffering from what he decided was a ruptured ectopic (outside the womb) pregnancy. When he arrived with the ambulance at the hospital, the head nurse, a white woman, demanded scornfully: "Who told you that you could make a diagnosis?"

Dr. George Henry Starke had to turn his patient over to the white doctor on duty; no Negro was allowed to practice in the biracial hospital. The white doctor let him sit in on the operation, which saved the woman's life, and confirmed Starke's diagnosis. When it was over, the head nurse

---

[1] From "Our Town," *Reporter Dispatch* (White Plains, N.Y.).

[2] *Chicago Sunday Tribune*, January 10, 1954, Part 2, p. 16. Reprinted by permission of the Associated Press.

snapped: "Well, you're the first Negro I ever saw that could make a diagnosis. . . ."[3]

$*$ $*$ $*$ $*$

In each case a person failed to discriminate—to separate like things from one another. Whether it was electric bulbs, piles of white material, or Negroes, someone overlooked important differences and saw only similarities. The head nurse, for example, seemed to have had difficulty in differentiating among Negroes. To her they evidently appeared as indistinguishable as the proverbial peas in a pod.

We shall use the term, *indiscrimination*, to represent the behavior which occurs when one fails to recognize variations, nuances, differences; when one is unable or unwilling to distinguish, to differentiate, to separate apparently like things from one another. *Indiscrimination* may be defined, then, as the *neglect of differences*, while *overemphasizing* similarities. It is one of three forms of differentiation failure that we shall examine in this book.

"HARDENING OF THE CATEGORIES"

One of the most troublesome consequences of *indiscrimination* is an evaluational "disease" we might appropriately label "hardening of the categories." Most of us have a penchant for categorizing—for classifying. Show someone something he has never seen before—an unusual butterfly, a peculiar tree leaf, a strange rodent—and one of his first questions is likely to be: "What *kind* is it?" We meet a new person and we are uneasy until we can pigeonhole him—What *is* he?—how is he classified? Is he a salesman, plumber, farmer, teacher, painter? Is he Protestant, Catholic, Jew, atheist? Democrat, Republican, Independent? Lower, middle, upper "class"?

Categorizing, per se, is not undesirable. Under some circumstances, as we shall discuss later, it is quite essential. But we are concerned here with categorization when the categories become hardened, unyielding, when they tend to deter further analysis and investigation when such would be desirable. Joe White,[4] for example, as an office manager for a meat packing firm, has developed a category for women workers over fifty years old. "They're insecure, inefficient, ineffectual, and temperamental," he will tell you. Thus, when Mary Grey, fifty-two, a widow, applied for a clerical position, Joe did not even bother

---

[3] "Negro in Florida," *Time*, January 19, 1952, p. 71. Reprinted by permission.
[4] The names are fictitious, but the incident actually occurred.

to interview her. He knew her "kind." Fortunately, another manager of the company *did* interview her and hired her on the spot. She has since proved to be a stable, energetic, intelligent worker who is likely to give many more years of service than most of the inexperienced eighteen-year-olds Joe is prone to hire.

Stereotypes

The word *stereotype* is a useful one for our purposes. Originally a printing term, it stood for a plate which printed the "same" picture, drawing, etc., over and over again. Thus a sociological or psychological stereotype is a fixed, conventional image or picture. One who stereotypes applies his image of the group to any individual he assigns to that group. He disregards, consciously or otherwise, any differences or distinctions the individual may have which set him apart from the stereotyped group.

Consider the prevailing stereotype of "poet" in America. Such adjectives as "thin," "effeminate," "meek," "sensitive," "delicate," and "eccentric" may come quickly to mind. The stereotype can exist only so long as the exceptions are suppressed. But the generalized image dissipates when one considers some of our contemporary poets—for example, warm, wiry Carl Sandburg; barrel-chested former backwoodsman, the late Lew Sarett; and Robert Frost:

> His Vermont neighbors take no special notice of the heavy-set man with the big head of unkempt white hair. Occasionally they meet him on a back-country road, trudging along with an oddly catlike grace, wearing an old blue denim jacket and blue sneakers. They recognize the heavy, big-knuckled hand shaped to ax-helve scythe. Vermonters find nothing outlandish or alarming about Robert Frost.
>
> Neither do U.S. readers, to most of whom the word "poet" still carries a faint suggestion of pale hands, purple passions and flowing ties.[5]

Of course, stereotypes can be expedient devices at times. Many television, pulp, and movie writers cherish them because they serve as short cuts to characterizations. Merely depict a lean, lanky, sad-faced Negro shuffling through a scene, and you have tapped a familiar mold. His personality and behavior are completely predictable because his writers generally permit no deviations from the established pattern.

The story is told of Metropolitan Opera Company prima donna, Dorothy Kirsten, who was making her debut in motion pictures. Having always worn her hair down, Miss Kirsten was surprised when the

---

5 "Pawky Poet," *Time*, October 9, 1950, p. 76. Reprinted by permission.

studio requested her to change to an upswept coiffure. Reason: "They wanted me to look like a prima donna!" And Hollywood actor John Wayne was given his first opportunity when Director Raoul Walsh decided he measured up to the requirements: "To be a cowboy star, you gotta be six feet three or over; you gotta have no hips and a face that looks right under a sombrero."

And so stereotypes can save time and effort. They obviate any additional analysis or investigation. There is no need to look for *differences*—a stereotype precludes them. Stereotyping permits us to set up neat, well-ordered, and oversimplified categories into which we can slip our evaluations of people, situations, or happenings.

The Battle of the Categories

Few of us go very far in life without having to fight the "battle of the categories." Try to change your line of work, to transfer from one subject major to another in college, to compete for a dramatic role in the school play when you have been classified as an "athlete" or a "campus politician," and you invariably find people resisting your attempt to "break through their categories."

A few months ago a very capable actor committed suicide—why? Apparently out of despondency over being unable to find work. Film executives evidently felt that the public would not accept George Reeves as anyone other than "Superman," a role he had played in television movies for years.

*   *   *   *

As one hardens his categories, as he habitually goes by stereotypes, he is progressively less able to "search out the differences." His characteristic response to a new person, situation, thing, or idea is to find the "proper category"; slip the object of his attention into the pigeonhole; then he need attend to it no longer. Some persons are terribly uneasy until they can "tack on a label." Is he a union man? A Jew? A Democrat? A Sigma Sigma? An ex-convict? They can relax when they find the "right" tag.

A key danger with *hardened categories* is that the categorizer is prone to evaluate with faulty analogies. Situation (or person) A is new, but seems similar to situation B. Anxious to do his pigeonholing, the categorizer sweeps A into B's category with the dangerous assumption that the way to behave in situation A is the way he behaved in B.

When his outfit was deactivated Sgt. Vincent Bonura[6] was reassigned to another camp. He reported to his new company commander, Captain Carl Barnes, and the men exchanged salutes.

"At ease, Sergeant, smoke if you like."

"Thank you, sir."

"Well, Sergeant, I want to get the best from every one of my men, so I'll want to check you on all your past experience so I can see best where I can use you. Let's see . . . Bonura. That's Italian, isn't it?"

"No sir, I'm Sicilian."

"Ooooh, a Sicilian. . . . Well, Sergeant, I've had Sicilians in my outfits before, and I want to get one thing straight. I don't like any trouble makers in my company."

"Sir, I'm not a trouble maker!"

"Don't interrupt me, Bonura!"

"Sorry, sir."

"In France in '45 I had this man. . . . Mazaaro . . . Marzano . . . something like that and from the time he came to me until I got rid of him he gave me nothing but trouble. Now I don't know why you got shipped out of your old outfit. . . ."

"Sir!"

"Sergeant! I don't know why you got shipped out but if you're the hot-headed type I'll make it plenty rough for you around here—and give you plenty of time for cooling off!"

LANGUAGE: A CONTRIBUTING FACTOR

Why do people behave in these irrational, rigid ways we call *indiscrimination*? By definition, it is because they neglect differences and overemphasize the similarities. Why, then, do they do so? Fear, greed, insecurity, and other destructive feelings and attitudes undoubtedly play important roles in contributing to indiscrimination. But one factor in particular is especially worthy of attention, not simply because it is important but because it offers a remedial approach to the problem. It constitutes a factor which *can* be altered and thus effect an important change in the outcome. I am speaking of language. We can demonstrate the point if you will study the box on the next page. Now, before you read any further, make a statement (write it down, speak it aloud, or simply "say" it to yourself) about what you see there.

If you responded without too much consideration, the chances are that your statement described how the figures were *alike*. Such phrases as "geometric figures," "straight-line drawings," "patterns," "forms," etc., are common responses. Our little game illustrates what linguistic specialists have recognized for years, that English-speaking persons

---

[6] The names have been disguised.

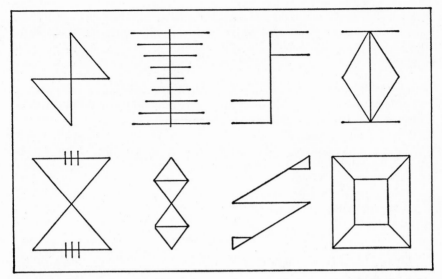

find it relatively easy to perceive and to speak in terms of similarities in "reality." We are often more prone to *generalize* than to *differentiate*.

Our propensity to see similarities may be explained partly by the abundance of mass nouns and verbs in our language.[7] We may use the word *wood*, for example, to stand for anything within a myriad of objects ranging from a sliver to a giant Sequoia. Consider the enormous variety of fabrics that *cloth* may be used to represent. Think for a moment of the almost infinite variations in form, size, shape, color, etc., that such words as *Negro, furniture, Catholic, student,* and *animal* may be used to represent.

Here is a curious and revealing comparison. In English we can use the word *snow* to refer to a snowflake, a snowball, a flurry, blizzard, avalanche, lightly or heavily falling snow, snow which is dry, wet, caked, loose, compact, shifting, still, etc. But the Eskimo, astonishingly, has *no one word* for all of these! To be sure, he has a large vocabulary of words for many *specific* forms of snow. But he has no *one general* word, such as our *snow*, for all of them.[8] This is fortunate, in a way, for the Eskimo. With his abundance of specific nouns and a dearth of general nouns, he is led to focus upon the *differences* in his environment. Take the case of snow, for example. The Eskimo has to

---

7 We have no monopoly on general words (or on the ability to generalize). Our language is outstanding in this respect when compared with certain other languages, particularly those of some of the more primitive cultures.

8 Lister Sinclair, "Word in Your Ear," *Ways of Mankind*, ed. Walter Goldschmidt (Boston: Beacon Press, 1954), p. 27.

be constantly on the alert for the *differences* in drift patterns, textures, crust strengths, etc. If he does not attend to them, he may not provide a full dinner table for his family—he may not even get home to them at all. And so his language which encourages him to perceive *differences,* may be a definite boon in this respect.

Our preponderance of mass verbs is another case in point. We have a large number of verbs which represent, to many foreigners at least, a perplexing variety of actions. *Get, make, do, carry,* and *use* are just a few of these. *Go* is a particularly interesting example. We use this word for going on foot and also for when we are transported as by a vehicle. But the German has no comparable verb. When he *goes* on foot, *gehen* is appropriate. But one does not *gehen* by vehicle. This requires an entirely different verb, *fahren.*

The language of the Navaho Indian goes much further along this line. When he travels by horse, the Navaho simply cannot express the general notion of "going by horseback." His language requires that he specify the speed of the animal whether it be, for example, at a walk, a trot, a gallop, etc. Moreover, his language insists upon another kind of dividing the generic process of "going." The Navaho must distinguish between starting to go, going along, arriving at, returning from a point, etc. "It is not, of course, that these distinctions *cannot* be made in English but that they *are not* made consistently.[9]

The general nature of the difference between Navaho thought and English thought—both as manifested in the language and also as forced by the very nature of the linguistic forms into such patterns—is that Navaho thought is prevailingly so much more specific, so much more concrete.[10] The nature of their language forces The People to notice and to report many other distinctions in physical events which the nature of the English language allows speakers to neglect in most cases, even though their senses are just as able as those of the Navaho to register the smaller details of what goes on in the external world.[11]

Conversely, it appears that the plethora of general verbs[12] (and

---

[9] Clyde Kluckhohn and Dorothea Leighton, *The Navaho* (Cambridge, Mass.: Harvard University Press, 1948), p. 201.

[10] *Ibid.,* p. 199.

[11] *Ibid.,* p. 201.

[12] English certainly has no dearth of specific verbs, especially with respect to those aspects of our culture on which we place a great deal of emphasis. Sports is an example in point. These synonyms for "defeat" were gleaned from just one week's scanning of newspaper sports pages:

bash	edge	nip	slaughter	stifle	triumph over
batter	mangle	scuttle	slip by	top	trounce
blast	massacre	shade	smash	trample	wallop
crush	maul	sink	smother	trim	whip
down	nick	skin	squeeze by	trip	white-wash

nouns) in our language both reflects and encourages our inclination to see relationships and similarities among phenomena.

The crux of this chapter is that the process of *noting similarities* generally involves the *neglecting of differences*. Recall your reaction to the drawings a few pages back. When one says or visualizes: "They are all geometrical designs, figures, drawings, etc.," he is calling his attention to the ways in which the units are *alike* and suppressing his cognition of their *differences*. He neglects, for the moment at least, that the second figure, top row, reminds him of a row of telephone poles reflected in water; that the fourth figure, bottom row, is the only rectangle, etc.

A language which prompts us to note similarities, then, may tend to discourage us from observing the differences. And the failure to see differences, as we have discussed, may lead to the destructive and dangerous patterns of *indiscrimination*. Let us now examine some of the possible preventives and remedies that we may use in coping with *indiscrimination*.

CORRECTIVES

A difficult aspect in the treatment of *hardened categories* is that the categorizer is usually *unaware* that his stereotypes are affecting his behavior. He becomes so oblivious of his overemphasis on similarities and neglect of differences that he takes the rigidly categorized world of his own making for granted.

Of course, we all carry our sets of categories around with us. You are a rare person if some sort of stereotyped image does not occur to you at the mention of at least some of these terms:

doctors	white-collar workers
Southerners	dam-yankees
divorcees	management
union officials	Jews
Negroes	artists
professor	teen-ager

But the mere occurrence of conventionalized images to someone does not necessarily make him a chronic stereotyper. One may be quite aware that his generalized image is just that, and often with little or no basis in fact. He says to himself, in effect: "Sure, you mention 'professor' and I think immediately of the pedantic, absent-minded fuddy-duddy, carrying a rolled up umbrella and wearing spats. But that's just the stereotype. Actually, very few of the professors I have known even approach this caricature."

The problem of *indiscrimination* arises when a person is *unaware of* or *unwilling to recognize* his stereotypes as such—when, in other words, his categories become hardened. Thus an approach to the dissolution of stereotypes—to the softening of categories—is to work toward the *awareness* of them. What can one do to alert himself to the influence of stereotypes upon his evaluations and communications?

Become Sensitive to Differences

Recall that this chapter holds that the overemphasis on similarities with the corresponding neglect of differences leads frequently to stereotyping. In fact, stereotypes cannot exist *without* the neglect of differences. The moment one begins to take differences into account, his stereotypes begin to disintegrate. As one makes a deeply ingrained habit of looking for differences, he approaches a self-awareness which makes possible mature, intelligently discriminating behavior in dealing with people, situations, happenings, relationships, etc. "The more we discriminate among," Irving J. Lee said, "the less we will discriminate against."

Accept the Premise of Uniqueness. Perhaps the first step toward developing a heightened awareness of differences is to disavow the erroneous notion of "identicalness." No two things have ever been found to be exactly similar in all respects—or even in one respect. Those two peas in the pod are actually quite dissimilar, even to the naked eye, if one observes closely. "Nature" apparently abhors identicalness. No two snow flakes, no two blades of grass, no two grains of sand—no two of anything—have ever been shown to be completely identical. An important technique of identification is based on the presumption that no two fingerprints are exactly the same. Consider that there are presently close to three billion persons on earth with approximately ten fingers each and add all the people who have gone before us and are yet to come—it is an astounding presumption. Yet it has never been disproved.

Nor has man contrived two of anything completely identical. A machinist friend tells me that possibly the most precise man-made objects are Johannson blocks. "Jo" blocks are used to check the accuracy of micrometers (extremely exact instruments in themselves). I have seen "Jo" blocks so precise that two of them placed together formed such a close union that a partial vacuum was created and a man found it impossible to pull them directly apart! He had to twist and slide them to separate them. Are "Jo" blocks identical, then? They are incredibly alike—machined within a tolerance of plus or minus two millionths of an inch! But note, these are *tolerances*—that is, even "Jo" block machinists must admit that they can only *approach* identicalness, never attain it.

Because no two of anything have been found to be *absolutely* the *same* we have a useful premise: *There is always uniqueness; never identicalness.* Thus, if you are deeply convinced that there are *always* differences, you may not be so prone to overlook them. You will be less likely to "disregard the individuality of nature, and substitute a generality which belongs to language."[13]

Index Your Evaluations. One simple device which has proved successful in developing the awareness of differences is the *INDEX*. Indexing is hardly a new process. The housewife indexes her recipes; the executive his correspondence; the librarian his papers and books. Each is *separating* items according to the essential differences among them. The habit of *indexing* people, things, situations, etc., is equally, if not more, useful. The salesman who habitually indexes will react to Purchasing Agent$_1$ as if he were different from Purchasing Agent$_2$—he is.

Make a habit of *indexing*. The next time you hear someone (or yourself) making statements such as these below, ask yourself *Which?*

"Union officials are corrupt!"	*Which* officials of *which* unions?
"Women shouldn't be allowed to drive automobiles!"	*Which* women drivers?—and might there be some men you would prohibit?
"Doctors are mercenary!"	*Which* doctors? Would you include your home-town physician? Those who contribute half their time to charity cases? Those who work in laboratories at a fraction of the income they could command?

Doctor$_1$ is different from Doctor$_2$, of course, and Doctor$_2$ is different from Doctor$_3$, etc. Use the little subscript as a mental exercise, as an habitual memory jogger to call your attention to the differences.

---

13 A. B. Johnson, *A Discourse on Language* (Utica, N.Y.: William Williams, 1832), p. 10.

As the next two chapters will describe two other types of *indexing,* we should *index* the *indexes.* To distinguish them, this chapter advocates the use of the *Which* Index.

THE VALUES OF SEEING SIMILARITIES

To digress for a moment, I trust I have not given the impression that one should focus on differences at the *expense* of similarities. The ability to see similarities is essential in generalizing, categorizing, organizing, classifying, arranging, cataloguing, etc. These activities, in turn, are indispensable in learning, analyzing, problem solving, innovating, decision making, etc. For example, a child learns about fractions when his teacher shows how the *parts* of a pie, when put together, make a *whole* pie. From this he can *generalize to* (i.e., see the similarities with) fractions of a plot of land or a container of milk. He eventually generalizes to the visualization of "fractions" as an abstract "idea."

Take another case. Suppose a certain businessman plans to build a motel and wants to find the optimum location for it. His basic approach is to analogize—that is, he will look for *similarities* with respect to location among successful existing motels. He may find that they are usually located on major highways within easy access of motorists driving through. Moreover, they tend to be situated on the outskirts of cities, far enough out to avoid high real estate taxes and competition from hotels and yet close enough to utilize the inexpensive urban power and water, etc. Thus he may be able to make a wiser decision because he has been able to abstract key similarities out of a myriad of differences among the motels.

Categorization, cataloguing, and classifying (all based on seeing the similarities) are imperative in modern business. Imagine the chaos in the offices of the comptroller, the purchasing agent, the production control manager, etc., if they were somehow prevented from classifying and organizing the multitudinous data and details with which they deal.

Scientific advance (or progress on any frontier) is intimately related to the perception of similarities. We learn about the unknown largely on the basis of the known. Someone must have been able to generalize from perhaps a rolling log to the notion of a wheel, from a boiling kettle to a steam engine, and from a flying kite, bird, etc., to the visualization of an airplane.

This chapter hardly proposes to minimize the value of seeing similarities. Our goal is to achieve better-*balanced* perceptions—to see the differences *as well as* the similarities. To accomplish this, most of us need training in looking for differences. Thanks to our formal education, language structure, etc., we are already fairly adept at noting the similarities.

SUMMARY

In life there are differences as well as similarities. Our language structure, however, which subtly influences our evaluating and communicating patterns, encourages us to overemphasize the similarities and to neglect the differences. The frequent result is that we often behave in terms of stereotypes (neglect of differences) and react to essentially *different* and *unique* people, situations, and things as if they were "identical" with our self-manufactured stereotypes. One can develop a greater sensitivity to differences by accepting the premise of uniqueness and by applying the *Which Index* in his evaluations of people, situations, etc. The deeply ingrained habit of asking "Which?" will diminish one's tendencies to overgeneralize that so frequently lead to stupid, unsafe, and unsane behavior.

Remember, there are differences which make a difference—take them into account.

INCIDENTS

THE DIXON COMPANY[14]

In 1958 the Dixon Company, a national restaurant chain, found itself short of the cash funds necessary to establish several new restaurants. Albert Bullock, president, instructed Walter Green, the company's sixty year old treasurer, to enter into negotiations with a local bank for a $600,000 loan. The bank indicated that the loan would be granted provided the company submit a satisfactory audit report by an independent public accounting firm.

Mr. Green requested the public accounting firm of Wilscher and Wunderlich to perform the audit. Edward Thorndike, a partner in W & W, assigned Tom Scott to supervise the audit. Scott, twenty-six, had been with W & W for seven years and had proven to be a highly capable Certified Public Accountant although inclined to be somewhat over-confident in his manner.

Within the first few days of the audit Scott uncovered several company accounting policies which were not in agreement with generally accepted accounting principles. After lengthy discussions with Mr. Green, Scott was able to have these exceptions corrected.

During the final week of the audit Scott took another apparent accounting principle variance to Green.

SCOTT: I've got another book adjustment for your approval, Mr. Green.

GREEN: All right, Tom, what is it?

SCOTT: As you know, accounting depreciation principles are based on the theory that certain assets purchased and used in the business produce income. If such an asset is usable over a period of more than one year its cost should be systematically and consistently prorated over its estimated useful life. Thus, each year's income is charged with a proportional part of the cost of the equipment used to produce such income. I've discovered that while you follow this principle in regard to most assets you do not consistently and systematically depreciate class 10 equipment (dishes, glassware, etc.). In 1955, '56, and '57, you charged off 5%, 8%, and 3%, respectively. If you had followed a correct policy the percentages would all be the same.

GREEN: *(Smiling)* Well, Tom, I've gone along with all your other

---

14 All names have been disguised.

adjustments but you're off base on this one. I guess you still have a little to learn about the restaurant business.

SCOTT: *(Suddenly flushing with anger)* Why any elementary accounting text book will tell you you can't vary your depreciation rate policy.

GREEN: You go out and find yourself a modern, up-to-date book on depreciation methods, young man. Then, you will realize you are wrong.

The conversation grew more heated and finally Scott walked angrily from Green's office, saying: "Well, I'm sorry if I can't make you understand this but I'm going to report this to my supervisor and I'm sure we'll have to note this exception in our report to the bank."

Scott phoned Thorndike and reported his disagreement with Green. Mr. Thorndike replied: "Tom, a dish does not *wear* out; its life ends suddenly with a crash. The normal depreciation principle often cannot be applied to a restaurant's class 10 equipment. Variable depreciation rates based on such factors as actual glassware inventory counts or current glassware purchases are acceptable. These factors give some indication of the rate of loss as the result of breakage."

When he had concluded the phone conversation with Scott, Thorndike made this notation in his assignment files: *"If we get the Dixon job next year we will have to find someone else to handle the field work. Scott seems to have clashed with the company's treasurer."*

FULL CIRCLE[15]

By Henry J. Taylor

I travel the whole world, and whenever I come home countless friends ask: "Why do Europeans dislike us Americans so much? Because of our aid? Because America is rich? Why?"

I think we should relax, and worry less about our alleged "failure to be loved." For I maintain that *Europeans do not dislike us any more than they dislike each other.* Prove it yourself:

Take a circular trip, country by country. Did you ever find a Scotsman who is on fire with friendliness for the English or the Irish, or vice versa? Cross the Channel. Most British have little more than contempt

---

15 Copyright 1956 by The Reader's Digest Assn. Reprinted with permission.

for the French, and—again—vice versa. The French do not like the Spaniards and, as for liking Italians, many Frenchmen get livid at mere mention of the name. The dislike of Italians, in turn, for Frenchmen, Yugoslavs, Albanians and Greeks is historic; and they have been fighting Austrians for hundreds of years. Austrians, in turn, detest the Czechs and Poles. The Poles detest the Austrians and Czechs.

Go north in the circle. The Norwegians do not like the Swedes. ("You stayed neutral in the war while we fought," say Norwegians. "You would have stayed neutral too if you had not been attacked," reply the outraged Swedes.) The Dutch will tell you there is no excuse for Belgium. ("Northern Belgium should be Dutch. Southern Belgium should be French. Why a Belgium?") The Belgians like neither the Dutch, Danes nor the French. And as for liking the Germans, from one end of Europe to the other people love the Germans like a bulldog loves a tramp.

I hope we Americans make more friends in Europe, but we are wrong in thinking of ourselves as the special target for European displeasure; wrong in our mystification, wrong in our hurt feelings and wrong in excessive and futile measures to make ourselves loved by spending money. The fact is, we can easily be too preoccupied with the attitudes toward us of peoples abroad.

WHAT'S WRONG WITH THE MEN?[16]

ROME—(AP)—What's wrong with men, as green-eyed Gianna Maria Canale, Italian film star sees it:

AMERICANS: "They have too many muscles, always thinking of sports and not enough about their women. Besides, they drink too much."

ITALIANS: "They are exactly the opposite of Americans. They think only of women, but not in a nice way. They have a one-track mind."

SOUTH AMERICANS: "They resemble Italians."

ENGLISHMEN: "Really too cold to be good."

GERMANS: "They would want to order me around as though they were the commanding officers."

FRENCH: "They lose themselves in too many compliments. Frenchmen talk too much. They're boring."

---

16 *Chicago Daily News*, February 12, 1955, p. 36. Courtesy of Associated Press.

While waiting for a paragon to come up over her horizon, Miss Canale intends to continue working on pictures and buying valuable paintings, rugs and antique furniture for her 14-room villa overlooking Rome.

WRIGHT CLEANERS AND DYERS, LTD.[17]

Wright Cleaners and Dyers operates a number of retail branches throughout a large metropolitan area. Many of the branches are located in blighted and economically depressed neighborhoods, but a few, such as the store established in Whitesdale six months ago, are in quite well-to-do communities.

Richard Clark, 35, a rising executive in an electronics firm, lives with his wife and two sons, three and two years old, in Whitesdale. On Monday Clark left for a short business trip and instructed his wife to take several of his shirts to Wright's. Mrs. Clark did so and was promised by Mrs. Jackson,[18] sole clerk at Wright's, that the shirts would be ready by Wednesday.

Clark arrived home late Wednesday night. The next morning he drove with his sons to Wright's. He walked into the store with his boys at 9:15 A.M.

CLARK: Are my shirts ready yet?

MRS. JACKSON: Do you have your ticket?

CLARK: Ticket? No, I didn't know you had to have one.

MRS. JACKSON: Oh, yes—I can't find your laundry without a ticket number.

CLARK: Well, okay—I guess my wife has it at home.

Clark loaded his boys into the car, drove to his home a mile away, picked up the ticket, and returned with his children to Wright's.

MRS. JACKSON: (After glancing at the ticket number) Oh, that's not in yet.

CLARK: But my wife said they were promised for yesterday.

MRS. JACKSON: Well, actually they may have come in this morning, but they would be in large boxes in the back and it would take an hour

---

[17] All names have been disguised.

[18] Mrs. Jackson, sixty-one, a widow, had been forced by the death of her husband to secure employment. She has been working for Wright's for 6 months—her first job since her marriage in her early twenties. Except for a brief indoctrination period, she has spent all of this time at the Whitesdale store.

to unpack them. You come back in an hour and I'm sure I'll have them ready for you.

CLARK: But that will make me late for an appointment. Why don't you let me help you go through the boxes. I really need those shirts, now.

MRS. JACKSON: I can't do that—no one is allowed back of the partition (rear of store).

At this, Mrs. Jackson walked behind the partition, leaving a somewhat exasperated Clark.

In an hour Clark returned.

MRS. JACKSON: Here they are (the shirts)—I got them out for you. I'm sorry about the delay.

CLARK: (Angered, but under control) If you're sorry, may I assume that you wouldn't like to have this sort of thing happen again?

MRS. JACKSON: Why yes, of course.

CLARK: Well, whose rule is it that no one is allowed to help you sort out the laundry in an emergency?

MRS. JACKSON: The supervisor's—that's a store rule.

CLARK: Then I would suggest that you advise your supervisor, since you are closer to the situation, that this store is in Whitesdale—not in some derelict type of neighborhood. I think you can assume that people are honest here.

MRS. JACKSON: Oh, it isn't a question of honesty—do you know I had a woman in here a couple of weeks ago who was going through the cleaning bags hanging on the racks—tearing them open—to find her cleaning.

CLARK: I don't see the similarity—I had the ticket number—nothing would have had to be torn into.

MRS. JACKSON: Well, no one is allowed behind the partition. That's a store rule.

CLARK: I know, and most of the time it's probably a good rule—but don't you suppose there are some occasions—some emergencies—when there might be an exception—an instance when a rule might be broken?

MRS. JACKSON: No, that's what rules are for (and walks behind the partition).

Much later in the day, Clark telephoned Wright's main office and spoke to Anthony Conti, supervisor of stores.

CLARK: Mr. Conti, I didn't feel like doing you people a favor this morning but I'm a little more mellow now, and I'd like to tell you about a practice which may lose you customers. (Clark recounts the incident with Mrs. Jackson)

CONTI: (Speaking in slightly broken English) Well, I'll tell you, Mr. Clark—I'll tell you why that happened. You see, we train our girls all alike because we may have to transfer them from one store to another, and so on. Now, we tell them *never* and under *no* conditions to let anyone go back of the partition. And there are two reasons why we tell them this. Now we find that nine times out of ten whenever we let a customer back there fooling around with the cleaning there's going to be confusion. And the second reason is the safety of the girls. You know what I mean—we can't let a man back there with the girls.

CLARK: I know what you mean, but I don't think Mrs. Jackson should have been concerned. She's seen me several times in the store. And I don't exactly dress or look like an escaped convict—besides I had my two little boys with me.

CONTI: Well, you have to have a rule, though—you never know and those things can happen.

CLARK: Yes, but the probability of their happening in Whitesdale is pretty remote, don't you think?

CONTI: Well, maybe—but rules are rules and we make the girls live up to them.

THE WAYLAND COMPANY[19]

The Wayland Company, a large ore producer with its headquarters offices in New York City, maintains numerous lead, zinc, and feldspar operations. One of its larger feldspar centers is located at Bixby, Utah. Early in the spring of 1958, Robert Harris, plant manager at Bixby flew to New York for an annual meeting with Cal Douglas, production manager of the feldspar operations, and Fred Squires, chief cost accountant for Wayland's. Douglas and Squires were located in the New York offices.

The purpose of the meeting was to establish the standard costs[20] of

---

19 All names have been disguised.

20 "A forecast or predetermination of what costs should be under projected conditions, serving as a basis of cost control, and as a measure of productive efficiency when ultimately compared with actual costs." From Eric L. Kohler's *A Dictionary for Accountants* (New York: Prentice-Hall, Inc., 1952).

the Bixby plant for the coming fiscal year. Predictions were to be made as to the extent of such expenses as supplies, repair material, repair labor, fuel, and direct and indirect labor. Direct labor[21] costs were by far the largest expenditure in the plant. Direct labor is generally considered a *variable cost*[22] in that it varies directly with the quantity of production. Past experience at Bixby had shown, for example, that the direct labor required for producing one ton of feldspar was approximately one-half man-hour; for producing two tons, one man-hour, etc. A measure of the efficiency of the operation could be determined by the extent to which the actual direct labor cost ran above or below this norm. It was the company policy, therefore, to hold the plant manager responsible for maintaining his variable costs, direct labor included, at the lowest feasible level. He was not held responsible, however, for fixed costs, which were beyond his control.

Cal Douglas called the meeting to order and the three men began to go over the standard costs. As the conference reached the topic of direct labor, Fred Squires remarked: "According to our figures the direct labor cost incurred at Bixby should be ninety cents per ton and it should be 100% variable cost."

DOUGLAS: I don't think you're taking into consideration the fact that our Bixby plant has recently been organized. A clause in our contract with the union states that five men have to be paid for five hours a day regardless of production. In other words, if Bixby had 100% downtime these particular men would have to be paid for five hours for every day of the downtime period, whether it is for one day or for six months! It's my thinking, therefore, that all costs incurred when the plant is not operating should be classified as fixed and not be charged to the plant manager.

HARRIS: Mr. Douglas is correct about our plant being organized and I've got to pay those five men no matter what the production situation is. If their time is classified as variable cost then I would be held responsible for an expenditure over which I have no control. And I certainly agree with Mr. Douglas when he says these should be fixed costs.

SQUIRES: Mr. Harris, you don't seem to realize that what you're asking us to do is contrary to all established cost accounting principles. If we classify any of your plant's direct labor as fixed costs we would

---

21 Direct labor is that directly related to the product.

22 The obverse of *variable cost*, in accounting terminology, is *fixed cost*, i.e., cost incurred independently of the quantity of production, e.g., rent, property tax, depreciation, insurance, etc.

incur some serious problems with respect to accounting terminology. Based on my twenty-five years as a cost accountant this idea would certainly be a radical innovation and in my opinion it just cannot be done.

Cal Douglas, sensing that the meeting had reached an impasse, suggested that they break for lunch. After lunch the conference reconvened and the controversy grew more heated. Finally, Cal Douglas commented: "Gentlemen, it's evident that we reached a stalemate here. Frankly, we haven't the time to work it out. I think I can see both points of view and I realize that we're asking Fred to act against some established accounting principles but frankly, I think we must make an exception in this case. We simply must adjust our cost accounting procedure to accommodate our labor problem."

Mr. Squires replied with repressed anger: "Do you realize what repercussions this would lead to? It would change accounting terminology and procedures we've been abiding by for years. Cost accounting, by its nature, has to be consistent from period to period. If we inaugurate this procedure we'll be harming the accuracy of our total plant costing."

ON A BUS[23]

By Ruth Lebow Cogan

I was doing industrial nursing at the time of this story and if you have ever done industrial work you know you start to work at 8:00 A.M. not five minutes after, and you finish at 4:30 P.M. not five minutes earlier.

On this particular evening I had to go to school after work so instead of going home my usual way I caught a Jackson Blvd. bus going east. It must have been about twenty minutes to five before I caught the bus since I had to walk a block to catch the bus and had to wait a few minutes before it arrived. The bus reached State St. about five o'clock and it was at this time that I transferred, or tried to, to a north bound bus.

I was carrying an arm load of books and no other packages when I boarded the bus. I handed the driver the transfer and started to move

---

23 Printed by permission of the author.

to the back of the bus when the driver called me back. He said, in what appeared to me to be a very accusing voice, that my transfer was an hour overdue, that it was stamped for four o'clock. I told him the other driver must have made a mistake since I had not finished work till four thirty. At this point he accused me of lying and said I was shopping for an hour and tried to get by with an old transfer. By this time he was shouting and all the people in the bus were intently watching and listening for the outcome. He asked for another fare and seeing there was no future in arguing with him, I opened my purse and found I had no change—only a ten dollar bill. I told the driver I only had a ten dollar bill and asked if he could change it. His face was getting redder and redder and he finally burst out with "I'll change it and give you all your change in silver." By this time I was furious and told him I did not care how he changed it as long as he gave me my change.

At this point he really lost control and blared out that he knew people like me—always trying to cheat the bus lines out of a fare and I didn't pull the wool over his eyes and that he could see through my act. He said he changed his mind, that he would not cash my ten dollars and that I would just have to get off the bus. Under fire of accusations I had no alternative but to get off since technically he was within his rights to refuse to change a ten dollar bill.

THE NEW NEIGHBOR[24]

Oak Park Ill., (pop. 63,175) is one of Chicago's bigger & better suburban bedroom towns, a community which proudly labels itself "the middle-class capital of the world." Its houses are mostly a solid, two and three-story type built 20 years ago, and its residents are likewise solid and respectable.

"Did you know a nigger is moving into the neighborhood?" an Oak Park druggist whispered to his customers several months ago. The newcomer to the neighborhood around Chicago and East Avenues was indeed a Negro. He was also one of the nation's ablest chemists. Percy Levon Julian, A.M., Ph.D. (Harvard and the University of Vienna), the only Negro in his class at DePauw University, where he was valedictorian (and a classmate of David Lilienthal), is

24 *Time*, December 4, 1950, pp. 18–19. Reprinted by permission.

the highly paid chief of soyabean research for Chicago's Glidden Co. In that job and earlier, Percy Julian, the grandson of an Alabama slave, had made world-famous chemical discoveries. They ranged from processes for the synthetic manufacture of important body-regulating hormones (e.g., testosterone, progesterone) to a foam fire extinguisher which saved many U.S. naval vessels in World War II. But in Oak Park, there were people who attached more importance to the color of a man's skin than to his achievements. The town's only two Negro families lived in the northern section. Julian paid $34,000 for an ornate 15-room house in Chicago Avenue neighborhood and began spending $8,000 more for landscaping and improvements, intending to move his wife and two children in by Christmas. When the news got out, the water commissioner refused to turn on the water until the Julians threatened to go to court. Anonymous telephone callers made threats.

One afternoon last week, after the landscapers and renovators had gone for the day, a dark sedan pulled up at the Julians' house. Two men got out, broke into the house and poured gasoline through all its rooms. They laid a clumsy fuse of surgical gauze to the outside and lit it; it went out. Then they tossed a flaming kerosene torch through a window and drove away. Before the gasoline was ignited, neighbors called firemen and the house was saved.

Percy Julian, a proud, energetic man of 51, stood his ground and served notice that his family would move into the house by New Year's Day. He hired (for $36 a day) a private, round-the-clock guard to patrol the property with bulldog and shotgun. "We've lived through these things all our lives," said Percy Julian. "As far as the hurt to the spirit goes, we've become accustomed to that."

Chapter VII

DIFFERENTIATION FAILURES II (POLARIZATION)

POLARIZATION may be considered as a special form of *indiscrimination*, but it is prevalent enough and potentially destructive enough to warrant a separate chapter.

DEFINITION

To define *polarization*, we must distinguish between two kinds of situations which apparently present two, and only two, alternatives. One of these is a genuine dichotomy; the other a false dichotomy.

Contradictories

At any given time and place you will either marry or you will not marry; you will either be arrested for speeding or you will not; you will either receive a pay raise or you will not; you will either make the varsity basketball team or you will not; etc. These are authentic dichotomies or *contradictories*. Note their characteristics: (1) *One* alternative *must* occur, but (2) both cannot.[1] Take this statement: "People are either over six feet tall, or they are not." Everyone, at any given time and place, must (1) be in one camp or the other for there is no middle ground, and (2) he cannot be in both camps.

Now, it is quite safe, sound, and sane to make "either-or" statements about *contradictories*. But there is another type of situation about which "either-or" statements and evaluations can be quite misleading and dangerous.

Contraries

Examine this statement: "People are either tall or short." It has the "either-or" form, but it does not involve contradictories, for there is middle ground—countless people who are *neither* "tall" *nor* "short."

---

[1] Aristotle expressed these requirements as two of his Laws of Thought: (1) Something must be either A or non-A, and (2) nothing can be both A and non-A at the same time and place.

And this is the key distinction between contradictories and contraries. Contradictories permit no middle ground, no other alternatives; contraries do. Moreover, the middle ground may consist of gradations, shadings, degrees—an unlimited number of them in many cases. The temperature of the air around us is a good example—it isn't simply a "hot" *or* "cold" affair. The temperature varies by smooth, continuous changes that we express conveniently in arbitrary steps called *degrees*. Actually, there are an infinite number of gradations between zero and one hundred degrees Fahrenheit.

Many of the important relationships and phenomena which concern us involve contraries. Health-illness, wealth-poverty, loyalty-disloyalty, sanity-insanity, beauty-ugliness; intelligence-stupidity, bravery-cowardice, competence-incompetence, etc., are not simple either-or matters. But people sometimes have an irrational way of dealing with these and other contraries. We call this behavior *polarization.*

Polarization

Polarization occurs when one treats *contraries as if* they were *contradictories;* when one deals with a situation involving gradations and middle ground in strict, either-or *contradictory* terms. I recall quite vividly the intense conflict in a certain midwestern village over the issue of fluorine in the town's drinking water. Impressive scientific evidence had been presented to the effect that fluorine in proper proportion to the water markedly reduced dental decay, especially in children. But nothing could persuade the majority of citizens that the fluorine would not be poisonous, and the health measure was voted down.

The fluorine issue involved contraries; it was a matter of gradations. But the majority of the people treated it *as if* they were dealing with contradictories. "Fluorine," the polarized, "is either poisonous or it's safe. We know it's poisonous, so we're not going to have anything to do with it!"

Fluorine is, of course, a deadly poison—*in sufficient quantities.* But medical and dental research had demonstrated that in minute amounts (as with other "poisons," such as chlorine and arsenic) it was highly beneficial. It was the failure of some people to see the *graded* uses and effects of fluorine that cost the town a valuable health aid.

CONSEQUENCES

Let us examine some of the manifestations and effects of *polarization.*

Deluding Ourselves

Not the least of the negative effects of polarization is that we may deceive ourselves. While the following example may seem extreme, it does illustrate the extent to which one can beguile himself with his own *polarizations:*

A man of forty consulted a physician by reason of extreme obsessive (either-or) disability; his history showed that he had never contrived to adapt himself to easy association with his fellow-men and women. So far as women were concerned he had a series of reflections which horrified him. In interview he revealed a classification of all women into contrasting classes—the thin and virtuous, the fat and vicious. He felt that he should marry, and the idea of marriage to any but a thin and virtuous woman was inconceivable. Nevertheless, he was attracted only by fat women, and his few would-be virtuous approaches to thin women had been signally unsuccessful. The alternatives he proposed to himself were fantastic and utterly without warrant in the world of fact. But the endless internal argument that exhausted him was conducted entirely in these terms. For many years his intimate thinking of this important relation had been of this general character.[2]

As bizarre as this unfortunate man's perceptions may have been, are they really much different from the *polarizations* so many of us practice? I knew an aggressive young man who vowed while in college that his annual income at the age of thirty would be $25,000. Today he is thirty-five—bitter and disillusioned, for he is making "only" $12,000. In his eyes he is a dismal failure.

For several years the comptroller of a big firm, looking forward to his own retirement, had been grooming a man we'll call Smith as his successor. Smith was aware of this plan and worked so successfully toward the goal that he was also being considered as a candidate to step eventually from the comptrollership to the presidency. Then one day he went completely to pieces.

The comptroller asked him sympathetically what was the matter.

"I've just found out," Smith said after some coaxing, "that I've got diabetes."

Examination by a specialist showed that he had only a mild case and that with insulin shots and reasonable care in his diet he would have no trouble. This enabled him to get back to work with much of his old efficiency, but he insisted that he be dropped from consideration as the comptroller's successor.

---

2 Elton Mayo, *Some Notes on the Psychology of Pierre Janet* (Cambridge, Mass.: Harvard University Press, 1948), p. 80.

"Up to now," he explained, "I've hardly been sick a day in my life. Now I'll never again be able to think of myself as healthy."

Smith destroyed his career because he saw health as an absolute. That is, he saw himself as formerly absolutely healthy and now absolutely unhealthy. He had completely obliterated from his mind the possibility of a middle ground.[3]

Deluding Others

Polarization may, of course, be used to mislead others. In their famous debates on slavery, Stephen A. Douglas attempted to use *polarization* to his advantage when he threw an apparent contradictory at Abraham Lincoln. Lincoln sidestepped the horns of the false dilemma neatly by exclaiming: ". . . I protest against the counterfeit logic which concludes that because I do not want a black woman for a slave, I must necessarily want her for a wife. I need not have her for either. I can just leave her alone."

Polarization is also a favored treatment for "getting out from under," as per Captain Queeg's stock reply to those who criticized his unreasonably harsh treatment of subordinates: "Well, what do you want me to do—give him a commendation?"[4]

And parents often use it on children for "their own good." A friend of ours thought she had mastered the technique when she would ask her four-year-old: "Which would you rather do first, Johnny, take your bath or brush your teeth?" Johnny, of course, didn't want to do either, but how can you say no to a question like that?

But Johnny learned to retaliate in kind. One day while shopping with his mother, he pulled her over to the toy department and demanded: "What are you going to buy me, Mom, a bicycle or an electric train?"

Among the most effective *polarizers* in modern history were Adolph Hitler and his Nazi henchmen. "Everyone in Germany," declared Hitler, "is a National Socialist—the few outside the party are either lunatics or idiots."[5] The thesis they so successfully inculcated was that an enemy of the National Socialist party was necessarily an enemy of Germany. "Even if you loved Germany greatly," wrote Hayakawa, "but still didn't agree with the National Socialists as to what was good for Germany, you were liquidated."[6]

---

3 Robert Froman, "How to Say What You Mean," *Nation's Business,* May, 1957. Reprinted by permission.

4 Herman Wouk, *The Caine Mutiny* (Garden City, N.Y.: Doubleday, 1951).

5 *New York Times,* April 5, 1938.

6 S. I. Hayakawa, *Language in Thought and Action* (New York: Harcourt, Brace & Co., 1949), p. 224.

The Pendulum Effect

One of the most destructive **consequences** of *polarization* is the "pendulum effect." This hypothetical argument will demonstrate the way it operates:

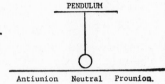

Antiunion   Neutral   Prounion.

Scene:	Two friends are drinking coffee at a restaurant counter. They have just begun to discuss the value of unions, a subject on which both are essentially neutral.

Tom:	Did you see the newspapers this morning? That Senate investigating committee is really digging up the dirt. I guess some of these unions are out for what they can get. (Mike perceives this as an "off-center" remark. He wants to move the pendulum back to <u>center</u> but to "counterbalance" he makes an equally "off-center" comment in the opposite direction.)

Mike:	Now, wait a minute. Sure, there are a few crooked unions--or at least a few crooked officials in them, but most of the unions have been a terrific boost for the workingman. (Tom sees this as a bit "extreme" and he must counterbalance it.)

Tom:	What do you mean, a boost for the workingman? Sure, the unions put more dough in his pockets, but what can he buy with it? Less than when he was getting half the money. And do you know why? Because the money comes from the companies and they get it right back from the workers as consumers with jacked-up prices. And who's scooping up the gravy while all this is going on? The unions!

Mike:	Says who! Don't forget the fat company executives who are raking in a half million or more a year--and with their stock options and delayed salaries and so on-- and don't forget about Uncle Sam's share, either!

Tom:	Listen you. . . !

By this time the alternating swings of the pendulum have reached an almost irreconcilable amplitude. The men are clearly at the futile "you are *all* wrong—I am *all* right" stage.

The "pendulum effect" is so pervasive that it is almost a "rhythm" of social affairs. Trace the pattern of an innovation, for example. The new formulation or method, the new science or art, the invention, etc., are typically introduced with enthusiasm and often with over-statement. If the claims are too exuberant, the public (lay or professional) is quite likely to resist. The more resistance, the more frantic become the efforts of the proponents and the pendulum swings in ever greater arcs.

Trouble over innovations is sometimes aggravated by the personality of the discoverer. Discoverers are often men with little experience or skill in human relations, and less trouble would have arisen had they been more diplomatic. The fact that Harvey (discoverer of the circulation of blood) succeeded eventually in having his discovery recognized, and that Semmelweis (discoverer of puerperal fever) failed, may be explained on this basis. Semmelweis showed no tact at all, but Harvey dedicated his book to King Charles, drawing the parallel between the King and realm, and the heart and body.[7]

Finally, as an example of the "pendulum effect" on a more prosaic level, I could not resist the following:

In Marlboro, Md., truck driver John Sanford, Jr., 33, was arrested for doing 50 mph in a 35-mph zone, was then charged with impeding traffic when he refused to drive more than 30 mph in a 50-mph zone on his way to the police station.[8]

CONTRIBUTING FACTORS

We have defined polarization as the confusion of *contraries* with *contradictories*. We shall now examine some of the reasons for this misevaluation.

Similar Grammatical Form

Contraries and contradictories are often stated in a similar grammatical form:

You either had coffee this morning or you didn't. (Contradictory.)
You are either a coffee fiend or a complete abstainer. (Contrary.)

That each is frequently expressed in the ". . . either . . . or" pattern probably accounts for some of the confusion between them.

Neglect of Middle Ground

A more complex and more important reason for *polarization* is the disregard or avoidance of the shadings and gradations between the

---

[7] W. I. B. Beveridge, *The Art of Scientific Investigation* (New York: W. W. Norton & Co., 1950), chap. 9.
[8] *Time*, May 16, 1955, p. 124. Reprinted by permission.

extremes. The tendency to neglect the middle ground may be attributed to a number of factors. Most of the important ones fall under the headings of *conditioning* and *expediency*.

Conditioning. All through life we are *conditioned* to *polarize*. It is altogether possible that our "training" in this respect begins even prenatally. Schilder has a theory about the role of simple motor activities in our conditioning:

> It is probable that the charm of thinking in polarities is due to the fact that simple motor attitudes can be expressed in this way. We turn to an object or we turn away from it, we may approach an object or run away from it. There are extensor reflexes and flexor reflexes; we master the motions of bending or stretching. We may swallow something or we may spit it out, but these are rather primitive actions and do not lead to a deeper appreciation of the outward world.[9]

Consider, too, our linguistic conditioning. Let me illustrate the point by inviting you to take a little test. First of all, give the opposites of the following words:

white — _____
good — _____
polite — _____
honest — _____
success — _____

It wasn't very difficult, was it? Opposites come very readily to mind. But now try the second part of the test: fill in the *gradational terms* between the extremes.

white	— ____ — ____ — gray — ____ — ____ — black
good	— ____ — ____ — ____ — ____ — ____ — bad
polite	— ____ — ____ — ____ — ____ — ____ — impolite
honest	— ____ — ____ — ____ — ____ — ____ — dishonest
success	— ____ — ____ — ____ — ____ — ____ — failure

You probably found this much more difficult. Actually, the cards were stacked against you. There are comparatively few "intermediate terms" in our language. Of course, we have the imprecise, quantifying adjectives and adverbs such as "slightly," "fairly," "medium," "average," "very," "extremely," etc., but using them requires extra thought and effort, and we frequently neglect them.

The paucity of middle terms tends to encourage *polarization*. If we cannot say a man is *entirely* honest, it is easiest to classify him at the opposite pole as "dishonest." We disregard the infinite gradations

---

9 Paul Schilder, *Goals and Desires of Man* (New York: Columbia University Press, 1942), p. 211. Reprinted by permission.

of "honesty" between the poles partially because we lack the quantifying substantive *words* to express them. Recently, a young high-school graduate hung himself because he had failed by a slim margin to be elected to the National Honor Society. It seemed to make little difference to him that he had been president of his class, that his parents had given him a new convertible as a graduation gift, that he had been awarded a college scholarship, and that he had been accepted by one of the foremost universities in the nation. In his state of depression it was impossible to conceive of anything short of "complete success" as other than "total failure."

There are *many* other factors in our environment which condition us to *polarize* with ease and alacrity. I shall touch upon just a few of them.

a) The "Two-Sided Question."   It seems as if someone is always attempting to temper a heated argument by admonishing: "Now remember, there are two sides to every question!" Our well-meaning friend may actually be more misleading than helpful, for few questions of any importance have only two sides—they are multisided. Are the problems of public school integration, atomic weapons control, or agricultural surplus simple pro and con affairs? Or, for that matter, can the problem of choosing a vocation or a mate, of raising children, or of earning a living be solved by a categorical "yes" or "no"?

And yet the "two-sided question" myth is a prevailing one. "Did you hear about the Smiths' breakup? It was all his fault." "No, she was to blame." Could not both of them have contributed to the strife, and could there not have been factors beyond the control of both—inability to have children, financial difficulties, in-law interference?

To be sure, there are legitimate two-sided questions—in law and in debate, for example. But the charges or resolutions are scrupulously phrased and defined in order to permit positions of "guilty" and "not guilty" (note the avoidance of the contraries "guilty" and "innocent"), "affirmative" and "negative."

b) Popular Songs.   One would not have to search long through the lyrics of popular songs to find exhortations to *polarize*—an influence, unfortunately, that most of us tend to underestimate. Note the utter disregard for gradations in such titles as "All or Nothing at All," "It Must Be Right; It Can't Be Wrong," etc.

c) Cheap Fiction.   Whether it occurs in the form of paper-back novels, pulp magazines, television, or the movies, cheap fiction is replete with *polarization*. The "beauty" is breath-taking, while the "beast" is grotesque; the rich are fabulously so, and the poor are penniless; the paragon of honesty invariably clashes with the despicably deceitful.

If there is anything adult about the current rash of "adult Westerns" on television it is probably the avoidance of depicting the "good guy" as insufferably all good and the "bad guy" as unfailingly bad.

Expediency. It is much easier to think of a person as either intelligent or stupid than to rate him more precisely along a continuum of mental ability. It might be considerably simpler for a teacher to "pass" or "fail" his students. But rating them along the range of A–B–C–D–F, percentages, etc., requires a good deal more consideration and judgment.

And, too, we are often pressured for decisions. We feel we haven't the time to investigate and analyze. And we are uncomfortable with the uncategorized, the unresolved—so "if it ain't this, it's gotta be that."

CORRECTIVES

To diminish *polarization,* habituate these techniques:

1. Detect the contrary.
2. Specify the degree—the HOW-MUCH INDEX.
3. Separate the double contraries.

Detect the Contrary

The first step in combating polarization is to detect the *contrary.* But how can one quickly, yet dependably, distinguish it from the *contradictory?* Aristotle's Laws of Thought are twenty-three centuries old, but, so far as they apply, they are still valid and practical. Use them to test an either-or situation.

An employer: "The biggest problem with secretaries is initiative. Some, when they see a job to be done, will always go right ahead and do it without having to be told. But the others—you literally have to lead them by the hand—especially if it involves anything outside of their regular routine."

Which is involved—*contraries* or *contradictories?* To qualify as a contradictory, the situation must measure up to both of Aristotle's requirements:[10] (1) Must a secretary either "always go right ahead and do it" or "be led by the hand"? Hardly, there is abundant middle ground. The situation fails on the first criterion of the contradictory and is, therefore, a contrary.

---

10 See n. 1, p. 122.

Specify the Degree—Apply the How-Much Index

Having determined that one is dealing with a contrary, the next step is to specify the degree between the extremes. In other words, it is no longer a question of *either-or* but of *how much*. To a great extent the method of applying the *How-Much Index* depends upon the nature of the contrary and the availability of terms to denote the degrees.

Use a Quantitative Index When Possible. Some objective contraries (e.g., tall-short, light-heavy, hot-cold, large-small, etc.) lend themselves to a quantifying index. *Time Magazine* writers, for example, often use the "telling detail" to specify. "The boy was tall (5 ft. 11 in.) for his age (13) . . ."; ". . . a small (annual gross: $300,000) management consulting firm . . ."; ". . . has the largest undergraduate enrollment (8,000) in the state."

Use Substantive Middle Terms When Available. Many contraries, of course, cannot be numerically quantified. One cannot describe a person as 89 per cent patriotic, $2\frac{1}{2}$ times more friendly than his neighbor, or $\frac{1}{4}$ ill. But some contraries do have a supply of substantive middle terms which may be helpful in specifying approximate degrees between the poles. The following adjectives, by no means as precise and as nonoverlapping as inches, pounds, or miles per hour, may suggest some of the gradations and nuances along the "beautiful-ugly" continuum:

attractive	gorgeous	piquant
becoming	gruesome	plain
coarse	handsome	pleasing
comely	hideous	presentable
cute	homely	pretty
drab	horrible	repulsive
exquisite	ill-favored	uncomely
fair	lovely	unprepossessing
frightful	nondescript	unseemly
ghastly	ordinary	unsightly
good-looking	passable	well-favored

Use Quantifying Terms. Certainly, words such as "very," "slightly," "moderately," "extremely," "generally," "seldom," "average," "fairly," "often," "medium," etc., do not approach the specificity of the numerical indexes, but they are obviously superior to the absence of quantification. Remove the quantifying terms, "most" and "generally," from the statement below, and note how much more harsh, unyielding, and "either-or-ish" it becomes:

Most American educators agree that the elective system in our colleges and high schools leads generally to an aimless nibbling at knowledge, or to excessive specialization.

Separate the Double Contraries

The *compound polarization* merits special consideration. Actually, it involves mistaking a double (or multiple) contrary for a contradictory. This bit of doggerel epitomizes a common *compound polarization:*

> Girls at college
>   Are of two strata:
> Those with dates
>   And those with data.[11]

The old "beautiful-but-dumb" cliché. The counterpart for males: "All brawn and no brain." Both notions are not only fallacious, but

---

[11] Richard Armour, *Reader's Digest*, January, 1952, p. 20. Reprinted by permission.

some evidence indicates that if there is a correlation between physical and intellectual superiorities it is a positive rather than a negative one.

But let us return to the double contrary—how can we deal with it? The first step is to cut it down to size—to separate the contraries and work on them individually. Suppose we take the "brawn-brain" fable. Expanded, it would appear: People are either brainy (and puny) or brawny (and stupid). It is immediately clear that there are two "continua" involved—intelligence and strength. We can now proceed to specify degrees on each of them with the *How-Much Index* as before. Graphically, our double value-determining might be expressed as shown on page 132.

Lest the foregoing treatment appear a bit frivolous, consider these *compound polarizations:*

There are two kinds of doctors: Those who are dedicated; those who are dollar-conscious.[12]

Is it not more likely that most doctors are some degree of both? And what do you make of the executive's evaluation in the incident below?

Eugene R. Long,[13] 51, a foreman at the Rugge Company was recently dismissed from the firm. Long had been with Rugge for 18 years. Wayne S. Finley, president, gave this reason for Long's dismissal: "He revealed his position as pro-Communist by his many outspoken attacks on Senator McCarthy and his wonderful work."

SUMMARY

Polarization tends to occur when contraries (situations involving graded variations, middle ground) are treated *as if* they were contradictories (strictly either-or affairs). We may be misled not only by our own *polarizations* but by the purposeful or unintentional polarizations of others. The factors contributing to *polarization* include the similar grammatical form of contradictories and contraries and, more importantly, our propensity to neglect the middle ground. Conditioning and expedience are among the influences accounting for the latter.

Polarization tends to be reduced when one develops habits, first, of distinguishing contraries from contradictories and, second, of specifying the degree (applying the How-Much Index). In the case of *compound polarizations* the initial step is to separate the contraries. Then the gradations can be specified on each continuum.

---

12 Attributed to a high-ranking officer of a national service and fraternal organization.
13 All names with the exception of Senator McCarthy's have been disguised.

INCIDENTS

DEADLY FORCE[14]

The use of deadly force in effecting the arrest of an alleged felon is a serious problem to the police officer and can place him in the position of judge and jury. He must at times decide the guilt or innocence of a person in a split second which ordinarily could take a court months of contemplation to decide.

* * * *

Ralph Rogers, an officer for less than a month, was patrolling his post on foot. Suddenly, he saw a man sprinting from a store with a woman chasing after him, screaming, "Stop that robber!" The man was running toward an idling automobile. Another man was at the wheel, evidently waiting for the runner. The officer realized that he could not possibly overtake the fleet runner and considered for a moment his terrible dilemma. He decided against shooting, and the man scrambled into the car which was already starting to move—a screech of tires and the car turned a corner and was out of sight.

The lady, breathless, ran up to the officer. She was furious. "Why didn't you stop him!" she snarled. "You could have shot him easily! He stole $700 from me!"

The officer's face grew crimson. "Look, lady," he choked, "what could I do? If I had shot and killed him I could have been tried for murder or manslaughter."

"But he robbed me of $700! Don't you have the right to shoot a robber?"

"Yes—but I didn't *know* he was a robber when I was chasing him. Maybe you don't know this but if he had stolen less than $15 that would be petty larceny and he would not be classified as a felon. That means that if I had killed the guy I could be tried for murder or manslaughter.

"So, do you see the position I'm in? If I shoot and possibly kill a man I am liable for a serious offense. If I let him get away I'm the goat. Don't worry, lady, you won't be the only one I get hell from. The

14 All names have been disguised. Printed by permission. The author's name has been withheld by request.

chief is going to have plenty to say and so are the newspapers! What a law we have when you're damned if you do—and damned if you don't!"

EVANS AND BORNE[15]

Evans and Borne is a partnership with branches in four cities, New York, Chicago, Boston and Los Angeles. Each branch is supervised by a vice-president. The firm is an investment banking firm which participates in securities underwritings and also acts as a dealer and agent in the sale or purchase of securities. The company has been rapidly increasing its value of business during the last five years and currently employs 400 persons.

Due to this expansion the Accounting Department has been responsible for an ever-increasing amount of record-keeping. (The Department also maintained an inter-office account which was necessary because each branch office kept its own accounting records.) Management decided that a consulting firm ought to look into the possibility of a basic change in procedure. Such a firm was engaged and, after a study of several weeks, submitted the following recommendation:

Evans and Borne has arrived at a point in its operations where a decision must be made as to whether to continue operations under the present system or to install an electronic accounting system. We recommend the latter.

The consulting firm was discharged and the president, James L. Borne called in his Executive Committee (the four vice-presidents) to discuss the recommendation. After about an hour's discussion of the pros and cons of the two alternatives, Mr. Borne, well known for his decisiveness, rose and spoke enthusiastically.

Judging from our talking here we are just about unanimously agreed that the electonic system is for us. I feel the same way. The growth of our business alone convinces me that a year from now we will have no choice. The size and complexity of our operation will force us into electronic accounting. And so I firmly feel that not only should we go into the new system but that we should do so immediately. As you know these new machines are a tremendous investment and I want them to start paying off just as soon as possible. So, what do you say? Shall we get into electronics as soon as possible?

---

15 All names are disguised. Reprinted by permission.

The system was installed within three months. It was quite evident within the first month that the company had gone in over its head. There had not been time to train personnel adequately and tempers flared continuously.

The turmoil in the Accounting Department was such that management was seriously considering discarding the system. But by this time the company had been irrevocably committed to it; there would be no turning back. It was almost a year before the department was restored to order.

THE STUDENT ANSWERS[16]

A newspaper reporter approached four college students with a question. . . . "Faced with tremendous increases in applicants, should colleges stiffen admission requirements or expand facilities?"

Their answers were as follows:

A GIRL: "As long as there is a demand for admission, colleges should expand facilities. Certainly the desire by so many to get a college education should not be fustrated because an institution does not have room to accommodate them."

A BOY: "Expand facilities, of course. Americans place a high value on education and we should not try to restrict opportunities of getting this education."

A BOY: "Everyone should have the opportunity to get a college education. If it means additional facilities, then they will have to be provided. The continuing needs of science and industry for skilled personnel obligate colleges and universities to expand if necessary to provide professional training."

A GIRL: "I don't think this a case of either. Expanding facilities to accommodate increased enrollments doesn't have to force a change of admission requirements. It would be of no value to let everyone go to colleges offering below standard instruction."

MAYHALL HOUSE[17]

Mayhall House is an independent men's dormitory on the campus of a large mid-western university. The grade-average of the dorm was

16 Taken from the *Chicago Sun-Times*, December 7, 1955, p. 65. Reprinted by permission.

17 All names are disguised. Printed by permission of the author, whose name has been withheld by request.

one of the lowest of any house on campus. This was mainly because almost all of our 65 residents were majoring in either Engineering or Commerce—generally acknowledged as the most difficult schools in the university. And, of course, we had our share of "goof-offs"—5 or 6 fellows who had ability but had never been able to apply themselves to their studies. We chalked them up as immature and hoped they would "see the light" before their academic probation ran out. But as long as they didn't disturb anyone we felt we could get along with them.

As a matter of fact, there was very little "disturbing" or "horsing around" in the house. I had visited a number of the other dorms and was rather surprised to see college men, or rather "boys," running up and down the halls yelling and chasing one another and playing silly pranks on one another. As I said, I had always considered our house remarkably calm and dignified—until this year. Now, you wouldn't know it. Everyone's calling it "Mayhem House."

The situation has become so out of hand that it's difficult to know how to describe it but I'll try to start at the beginning.

When we started school in September two important events (at least to me) occurred. I was elected President of Mayhall House and a new counselor moved in. His name was John Morrison, 23, a graduate student in theology. John seemed to be very pleasant but made it clear in his first meeting with the residents of the house that he had heard our grade average was low and hoped we could raise it. He gave quite a pep talk and said if we would all pull together we might put Mayhall near the top if not at the top of the list.

I agreed with this but I didn't see how there could be much improvement in view of the fact that most of us were in the toughest schools.

The first evidence that John meant what he said occurred when he established his "closed-door policy." The fellows had the custom of leaving the doors of their rooms open and of occasionally talking across the corridor to one another. If John happened to be passing by he would simply close the doors without saying a word. I suppose he thought the fellows would take the hint but they only got sore about the situation and started doing more "trans-corridor communication." It got to be quite a joke. John would start at one end of the corridor and close ten sets of doors as he walked to the other end. Two minutes after John was gone all the doors would be open and the talking would start in again—only louder and more of it. On one occasion, a student yelled, "Go to hell, John!" after John had closed his door. John opened the door again and put the student on formal warning.

Next was the radio episode. About the middle of November John posted a notice:

In order to provide proper study conditions no radios will be turned on after 7 P.M. Effective this date.

This seemed rather high-handed and unnecessary to me. Radios had never been a problem in the house before. A few students like to study with some soft music in the background. But if anyone objected they would turn them off.

The fellows seemed to accept this as a challenge. The same night the notice was posted about seven or eight men turned on their radios to get them warmed up but not loud enough for anyone to hear.

Then one radio blared up full blast for a second and then was snapped off. John came bolting down the corridor to find the radio. When he got near the room, another radio blared up for a moment at the opposite end of the hall. John wheeled and streaked back. At this moment two other radios opened up and John started twirling around in circles! It was the most ridiculous thing you ever saw and the fellows couldn't help bursting out laughing.

John was furious. "All right, *children!* If you can't take proper care of your *toys* someone will have to take care of them for you!"

He then started moving from one room to the next confiscating the radios. It took him about two hours but he picked up every radio in the house, put them into a storeroom, and locked the door. Maybe the seven or eight pranksters deserved this but he took *all* the radios—mine included!

Well, that was the sign for open warfare. What happened then was one continuous nightmare. The next night somebody brought some fire-crackers into the house and the mayhem started! Someone tied a fire-cracker to a burning cigarette and laid it in front of John's door. A few minutes later the cigarette burned down and ignited the fire-cracker. John threw open his door and not a soul was to be seen. He was fit to be tied. That was a night to be remembered! All night long, about every ten minutes a fire-cracker went off somewhere—outside the dorm, in the corridor, in somebody's room, or even outside John's door! John didn't even come out.

The next day it snowed and that night it was snowballs. I won't go into the gory details but the end result was the damage of various property including five broken windows!

This, of course, brought in the Dean of Men. I was only surprised that he hadn't come in before. I guess John never mentioned our situation to him. The rest is history. John has been transferred to another house and we are on social probation for the rest of the semester.

THE CASE OF THE STORAGE SHELVES[18]

A continual problem with most companies is that of records retention and storage. The problem arises out of increasing needs for storage space due to the growing amounts of paper work that must be retained.

For a number of years our firm had no systematized records retention program, but government requirements and business expansion necessitated an organized records system. The job was turned over to Mr. Rhodes, our office manager.

His first action was to appoint a Records Revision Committee. The committee consisted of four supervisors, including myself, with Mr. Rhodes as chairman. Mr. Rhodes assigned to each of us a number of research projects relating to the revision of records retention. Our procedure was to report to the others by memos whenever our research turned up anything significant.

One project, among others that Mr. Rhodes assigned to himself, was the choice of file containers for the records. After considerable study of the problem he sent out a memo to each of us.

To: Records Revision Committee   From: M. P. Rhodes
Subject: File Containers
From my research I would say there are two types of file containers which would suit our purpose.
    A. Transfer case with a top opening and cord to tie down the opening.
    B. Cardboard transfer case with a sliding drawer.
I personally prefer "A".
Check which of the two we think we ought to purchase.
    Type A_____
    Type B_____
Return your choice immediately as I want to get a purchase order out tomorrow.

Unfortunately, I was out of the office when the memo arrived and didn't receive it until 10 A.M. the next morning. The choices surprised me because I knew either of the file containers would require the pur-

---

18 All names are disguised. Permission to reprint given by the author, whose name has been withheld by request.

chase of some special and rather expensive shelves. I recalled another type of case, a metal reinforced cardboard transfer case, which lent itself to stacking on top of one another, thus eliminating shelving. I immediately phoned Mr. Rhodes, explaining my tardy receipt of his memo and offered my alternative suggestion.

MR RHODES: You're dead right and I suppose it's better to correct the matter now than after we've bought the containers—and the shelves. I know it's not your fault, but brother! how I wish you had told me this last night! The others had checked type "A". I suppose they figured that since I had done the research I knew what I was doing. So I went right ahead and sent out the purchase order. Now, I'll have to get Purchasing to back-track on it. I'll guarantee you—this won't make them happy!

TWO FACTIONS[19]

A problem of undeniable importance lies within the confines of the Police Department for which I work. I think that I can safely say that it has directly involved a large percentage of the members of this Department and, moreover, its effect has been felt by every citizen of our city.

The problem originated years ago, but instead of diminishing with time it has grown to be a complex and difficult situation. This problem is now evidenced by open dissension and strife within the ranks of those employed around me.

Approximately 10 years ago, the city's police administration tolerated gambling and the illegal sale of liquor (bootlegging) to a considerable extent. In all probability, this tolerance was the result of some political pressures plus the desires of a few corrupt people who were interested, not in better government, but in building large bank accounts.

This state of affairs continued unchallenged for several years until a group within the Department began to develop. About 25 or 30 officers, headed by 4 or 5 recognized leaders of no great rank, held a few informal meetings. They decided that all illicit forms of entertainment in the city would be closed. It was clear that some of the officers were motivated largely by public spiritedness while others joined the group because they had been excluded from the group receiving graft money and privileges.

---

[19] Printed by permission. The author's name has been withheld by request.

Thereupon, this group (with the exception of a few who agreed in theory but would not shoulder direct responsibility) began to act. In groups and simultaneously, they entered establishments, effected some arrests and closed the doors to further operation. These officers, for the most part, made these raids and arrests while on off-duty time.

Immediately, attempts were made to compromise the two factions, but they failed. The consequences were not long in coming. The leaders of the "Vigilante" group were fired upon the provisions that they had been acting without authority, due to the fact that they were not actually on duty, nor did they have their supervisor's consent to act.

Within the Police Department, the "Vigilantes" were met with both hatred and sympathy and a wide crack soon appeared within the organization.

Almost at once, the dismissed members began suit to regain their positions and after a year's legal debate, full re-instatement plus salary re-imbursement was ordered. All of the men resumed their positions with the Department.

Perhaps this solved their respective problems but it certainly was of no value with respect to the enmities created in the rank-and-file. In fact, the flames were fanned to the point where everyone was placed in an impossible situation—he must either associate with one group or another or be disliked by both.

These two factions, the "Vigilantes" and the "Anti-Vigilantes," have been at great odds since that date. Men refuse to speak to one another and open condemnations are the rule. Politics play a larger and larger part in the organizational structure of the Department. The Public Safety Commissioner (an elective position) if favorable to one faction will immediately, upon taking office, assign favored positions to his group and thus relegate the "out-group" members who had been holding these positions to more or less menial stations. It should be quite evident how this constant displacement of key personnel depreciates the value of our organization and also should show quite clearly that the breach in ranks grows deeper with each change.

Many new men have been added to our Department since the trouble originated, and a large percentage of them have been drawn into the struggle. I cite my own experience as an example: One of my best friends in the city happens to have been an active leader of the "Vigilante" group. Our friendship is based almost entirely on mutual interests outside our field of work, namely fishing and hunting, but because of my association with him, many say I am a sympathizer of the

Vigilante faction. I have lost several friends who say that because I enjoy this man's company, I am a believer in his theories and a backer of his principles.

Upon the completion of my probationary period, I was told that it would be impossible for me to be a "fence-sitter," in other words, that I would be forced to declare my sympathies for one group or another. I laughed then because I could not see why my choice of friends should be based on such damned foolishness. But I am no longer laughing for it has affected my working conditions and even threatens any future chance for advancement or promotion. This much has happened to me and, of a certainty, it is happening and has happened to many others.

Chapter VIII

DIFFERENTIATION FAILURES III (THE FROZEN EVALUATION)

This chapter deals with a third form of failure to differentiate. The previous two chapters were concerned with the necessity for indexing on a "horizontal" basis—that is, the need for differentiating among people, circumstances, attitudes, objects, etc., at *a given time*. The present chapter calls for a "vertical" sort of indexing, to take into account the way a person, a situation, a "thing," etc., *changes* with time.

THE CASE OF FRANK

I want to tell you about a personable man you would probably like and respect. Frank, to give him a name, began life with two strikes against him. To make a long sordid story short, an alcoholic, violent-tempered father, the frequent absence of a mother who was forced to work away from home, and the influence of a gang of young toughs which Frank joined at thirteen were sufficient to turn him into a brash, cynical, externally callous adolescent. After numerous scrapes he finally got into serious trouble in 1941. Caught stealing a car at eighteen, he was sentenced to two years in prison. Actually, the sentence was a fortunate development for Frank. Appalled by the grimness of prison life, his brashness quickly dissolved. Under the skillful guidance of the prison chaplain and a social therapist, Frank was beginning to gain insights about himself at the time of his release. With eleven months off for good behavior, Frank felt he had paid his debt to society —but there were those who did not agree. On his return home, his father cursed him and forbade him at first to enter the house, ironically, for bringing shame to the family's name. Some of the neighbors openly mocked him as he walked down the street; others pointedly ignored him. He tried to find work, but, even with an abundance of wartime jobs, no one would hire anyone with his record. Frank was understandably relieved when he was drafted a few months later.

He sank gratefully into anonymity, but even in the Army there were

143

incidents, as, for example, the time an officer's foot-locker had been burglarized. Frank, though innocent, was the first to be called in for questioning. But, on the whole, Frank's three years in the Army were helpful. It gave him time to think. He could now see how his environment had almost driven him into crime. He began to go to church, where he found solace and encouragement and resolved firmly to salvage the rest of his life.

When the war ended Frank received an honorable discharge and returned home. His father had died during the war. His brothers and sisters had all married, and three of them had moved away. A fourth lived in the family house with his wife and two children, and Frank's mother lived with them.

It was now over five years since Frank had stolen the car, but many had still not forgotten. There was no more open taunting, but many of the neighbors seemed cool and distant. Finding a job, too, was difficult. It became painfully clear that his record still followed him. Once he lied about his prison sentence and was hired—only to be fired under embarrassing circumstances a week later when he was found out. Police drove up to his home twice during his first month at home to take him into headquarters for questioning about auto thefts.

Finally, Frank moved to another section of the city, and life began to improve. A kindly man hired him as a mechanic's apprentice in his garage. Three years later with steady pay increases he married. Today, he is the likable manager of the garage, has a lovely wife and two lively youngsters. He still visits his mother from time to time, but he much prefers to have her come to his home. The old neighborhood hasn't forgotten the old Frank.

*   *   *   *

Frank has been the victim of a special form of failure to differentiate: the *frozen evaluation*. Some people made evaluations about the "Frank-of-1941." The "Frank-of-1960" is virtually another person, but the evaluations have remained unchanged—frozen.

Not all *frozen evaluations*, of course, are as poignant and enduring as those concerning Frank. I was recently the delighted[1] target of one. Hurrying for an appointment, I was fortunate enough to find the one remaining parking space in the area. The space was the one nearest to the corner. Thirty minutes later when I returned, the car in the space behind mine had left and a woman was trying energetically but

---

[1] "Delighted" only because I felt the incident would be an apt illustration for this chapter.

ineptly to park between my car and the one in the third space from the corner. As I unlocked my door, the woman leaned out and proceeded to unbraid me most indecorously for failing to park in the second space, thus depriving her of the corner space, a much easier space in which to park! In her frustration she had unconsciously frozen her evaluation of the parking situation. She had assumed, in other words, that the now vacant second space was also empty at the time I had parked!

The parking incident was an example of an evaluation made in the present and frozen to apply inappropriately to the past—a sort of "retroactive" frozen evaluation. The obverse—evaluations which are indiscriminately spread over the future without respect for change, as in the case about Frank—can also have undesirable consequences. Universities, hospitals, and other institutions which receive stipulated bequests and gifts are sometimes hamstrung by this kind of *frozen evaluation*. Several decades ago an eastern college was willed two hundred thousand dollars—a very considerable gift, especially in those days. The donor, an ardent railroader, decided that the industry would *always* flourish, as indeed it did at the time he wrote his will. Thus he stipulated that his gift was to be invested in ten particular railroad stocks in prescribed amounts. The investment was to remain undisturbed. Capital gains were to be reinvested in the stocks in which they occurred. Only the dividends were to be used by the college. A fool-proof plan, reasoned the benefactor: the college would have a continually increasing endowment with commensurate dividends. Unfortunately, his prediction was faulty. As the years passed, most of the railroads on the list met with difficult times, and a few failed. The college, unable to react to changing economic conditions, could only sit by helplessly and watch the investment shrink to a fraction of its original value.

When one unconsciously (or perhaps deliberately) spreads an evaluation over the future and/or over the past, then, *disregarding changes* in whatever he is judging (a person, group, situation, etc.), we say that he has frozen his evaluation. Some of our most destructive *frozen evaluations* are those we make about ourselves. Take this case of self-imposed torment, for example:

An attractive girl, aged 17, came to the attention of a certain clinic as a voluntary case. For several years her parents had been concerned over the abnormal shyness which she exhibited in the presence of young men or boys. In the presence of members of the opposite sex she would blush violently and lapse into a nervous silence after a few stammered remarks. Her behavior was arrogant when she was with girls of her own age, and at least confident in the presence of adult women.

The medical findings were negative. . . . The social investigation revealed nothing in the home environment at the moment which would seem to be responsible fo her mental condition. But social investigation did yield the significant fact that her shyness had developed quite suddenly three years before. The parents had no explanation to offer as to the possible cause of the condition.

The psychologist talked with the girl in a friendly and informal manner. In the course of the conversation it was observed that, while she discussed sports and school activities quite freely, she would invariably become emotional when the subject of boys was mentioned. . . .

Little by little the following story came out: Three years before at a children's party the girl had been playing with some boys. In some manner she caught her fingers in a door when it was slammed shut. This caused the child such extreme pain that she became ill and vomited. The incident was quickly forgotten by everybody but the little girl herself, to whom it remained a crushing misfortune. Although she tried not to think of it, the bitter memory was always there to be reinstated by the presence of boys![2]

THE ASSUMPTION OF NON-CHANGE

The frozen evaluation seems to occur most frequently when one somehow assumes *non-change*. Suppose John Brown, as a Freshman, failed one of my courses mainly through negligence and irresponsibility. And suppose someone comes to me four years later and asks my appraisal of Brown, whom I have neither seen nor heard of since. I can very confidently say, "Oh, Brown is a poor student," *if* I assume John has *not* changed. But how reliable is this assumption? I think you will agree that I might be doing Brown a great disservice with my obsolete evaluation.

This leads to a much broader question: How dependable is the general premise of *non-change*—the assumption which appears to underlie so many of our frozen evaluations? Actually, the notion that there is rest, pause, cessation, etc., is a pernicious, yet prevailing, fallacy.

On every stratum we can observe, or at least presume, process. Everywhere about us we can see evidences of incessant change—of aging, of wearing out, of growing, of eroding, of regenerating, of decaying, etc. Even the "solid" earth undergoes perpetual change. Aside from dramatic changes like earthquakes and volcanic eruptions and

---

2 From *Psychology and Life*, third edition by Floyd L. Ruch. Copyright, 1948 by Scott Foresman and Company, Chicago. Reprinted by permission.

the slower ravages (wind, rain, glacial movements, etc.), the surface of the earth is in continuous motion.

The land surfaces of the world are no more in a state of absolute quiet than its water surfaces. Minute waves called microseisms are continuously moving through the rocks over the entire surface of the earth as can be seen by examining a sensitive seismograph record obtained in any part of the world.[3]

And on submicroscopic levels, modern-day physicists postulate, there is never-ceasing change. This "inert" book you are reading is presumed to be composed of infinitesimal particles whirling about at the speed of light—the "mad dance of electrons," as Korzybski called it.

Changes in People

And people change—often imperceptibly, sometimes markedly. Infants become children, adolescents, young adults, middle-aged, and finally elderly people, experiencing gradual, sometimes abrupt, changes beyond enumeration. The periods in which people live change, too. Consider the attitude shifts of "the public." In 1922, for example, *Good Health* published an article which typified current public opinion about smoking:

Tobacco benumbs all the finer sensibilities. That's why men smoke. A man who loves his wife and children is lonely when away and misses the home folks. He smokes, and at once his loneliness is gone. Tobacco fills the place of home and family. It kills the fine sentiment that made him long for the home fires and the familiar faces.

The smoker's business is not prospering. He is worried. He ought to find out the cause and remove it. He smokes instead. He is no longer worried. All is well. But the business fault is not corrected. More business enterprises have run aground in a fog bank of tobacco smoke than have been wrecked by hard times or business panics. Tobacco is an enemy of business as well as of morals. . . .

The college "smoker" is a devil's den, a snare which has lured many thousands of promising young men to mental and moral ruin. The smoking room is sister to the saloon and must be eliminated along with its iniquitous relative, if civilization is to be saved from the demoralization which threatens it.[4]

Contrast this with the public's attitude today! With eight out of ten men and one out of three women smoking, the *nonsmoker* is almost

---

[3] Frank Neumann, *Earthquake Investigation in the United States*, Special Publication No. 282 (rev. [1953] ed., U.S. Department of Commerce, U.S. Coast and Geodetic Survey), p. 32.

[4] "The Immorality of Smoking," *Good Health*, December, 1922.

an oddity! Public acceptance of smoking is so strong, in fact, that, despite numerous grave warnings by health authorities that lung cancer and other serious diseases are likely to be related to smoking, annual tobacco sales (500 billion cigarettes and 6 billion cigars) are the highest in history!

Our attitudes about dress are equally transient. This mandate on beach apparel was rigorously enforced in 1925 by the Wilmette (Illinois) Park District:

> For women, blouse and bloomer suits may be worn, with or without skirts, with or without stockings, providing the blouse has one-quarter arm sleeve, or close fitting arm-holes and providing the bloomers are full and not shorter than four inches above the knee.
>
> Men's suits must have skirt effect or shirt worn outside of trunks, except when flannel knee pants with belt are worn. The trunks must not be shorter than four inches above the knee, and the shirt must not be shorter than two inches above the bottom of the trunk.

Changes in Business

One of the most dynamic aspects of American life is business. Fluctuation is the rule. Booms and busts, sellers' markets and buyers' markets, inflations and deflations—nothing stands "still" for very long. The television market is a dramatic example. Hardly more than a dozen years ago 7- and 10-inch sets were being snapped up at dear prices. Today, in TV-saturated areas, dealers are driven to incredible lengths to move their merchandise. One is currently offering a 21-inch set for one hundred dollars, no down payment. He is doing a brisk business, but only because of his special enticement: a no-interest five hundred dollar loan goes with each set! His advertisement: "Pay off your doctor and grocer bills; buy shoes for the kids, make payments on your house, car, and appliances—and have TV, too!"

In summary, if there is anything *constant* about the world and the people in it, it is the *constant change* they undergo.

The Influence of Language

It seems strange that such a palpable fallacy as the notion of non-change may persist. Let us examine the role that language may play in nurturing this insidious assumption.

Language and thought are intimately related. As Lister Sinclair expressed it:

> . . . But always we begin by speaking as we think, and end by thinking as we speak. Our language is an expression of our culture, shaped by the way

we are brought up; and on the other hand, the way we are brought up is shaped by our language.[5]

Trace back to the roots of our language and you will discover many clues as to why we talk—and *behave*—as we do. The basic form and structure of the English language were laid down in ancient Greece. Now consider what life must have been like then—comparatively slow, static, and unchanging. Not much written history to read to get a sense of process. To us the average Athenian's life would seem quite placid—one day very much like any other.

Consider, then, that our language was spawned from this relatively constant society. Is it any wonder that they created a language which reflected their static existence? The result is that, although we live in an enormously more dynamic environment, we still use a language which strongly implies non-change, rest, and permanence—thus we are enticed to overlook change.

Note how incredibly easy it is in our language to speak or write (or listen or read) without taking "time" into account. Read each of the paragraphs below and quickly decide the date line (within five years, plus or minus) of each. After you have dated all three, read the answers which follow:

POPE CONDEMNS USE OF NEW "HORROR" WEAPONS

Vatican City—Prompted by widespread fears that new weapons of mass destruction might wipe out Western civilization, the Pope today issued a bull forbidding their use by any Christian state against another, whatever the provocation.
Date_____

* * * *

MORAL ROT ENDANGERS LAND, WARNS GENERAL

Boston—The head of the country's armed forces declared here today that if he had known the depth of America's moral decay he would never have accepted his command. "Such a dearth of public spirit," he asserted, "and want of virtue, and fertility in all the low arts to obtain advantages of one kind or another, I never saw before and hope I may never be witness to again."
Date_____

* * * *

"UNITE OR DIE," U.S. STATESMAN WARNS EUROPEANS

Philadelphia—Only by uniting immediately into one great state can Europe end the wars and trade struggles that are destroying her, the grand

---

5 Lister Sinclair, "A Word in Your Ear," *Ways of Mankind,* ed. Walter Goldschmidt (Boston: Beacon Press, 1954), p. 24.

old man of American politics declared here today. The sole solution, he declared, is for Europe to call at once a constitutional convention which would "combine all her different states and kingdoms into one federal union."

Date_____

Perhaps you will agree that these paragraphs *could* apply to contemporary affairs. According to the author,[6] however, they referred to (1) "Pope Innocent II in 1139; the weapon was neither germ warfare nor the hydrogen bomb"; (2) "George Washington, in 1775"; (3) "Benjamin Franklin, who urged a union of Europe on the American model in 1787."

And therein lies an important inadequacy of our language system —the prevailing failure to specify time:

Hollywood's legion of columnists, correspondents and reporters crowded into the Beverly Hills Hotel last week for movie journalism's traditional big night. It was the annual award-to-actors banquet put on by *Photoplay,* venerable pioneer (founded in 1911) of movie magazines. Master of Ceremonies Ronald Reagan, president of the Screen Actors Guild, rose for his polite remarks about *Photoplay,* then astounded the journalists with a diatribe against the "irresponsible press" of Hollywood. . . .

The *Daily News* made its own unjournalistic retort four days later. For a story headlined EX-ACE JAILED ON A CHARGE OF BANK ROB-BERY, the *News* dug up an old picture of Reagan talking to one Byron Kennerly, an ex-Air Force officer who had been arrested on a charge of robbing an East Los Angeles bank. (Reagan had posed with Kennerly nine years before, when the airman was technical advisor on one of Reagan's pictures.)[7]

This letter-to-the-editor containing a tongue-in-cheek speech might be merely good fun if it did not so closely resemble some *actual* political oratory. Note the author's ridiculous but artful implication that, had the Republicans remained in power, there would have been no technological change:

Voters! Think back! Recall the days of Horrible Herbert! Take, for example, such a commonplace item as your family car of 1932 and compare it to the one which 20 years of Democratic administration has brought you.

Did your dilapidated Republican car have automatic shift or overdrive —I ask you—did it? No! It took the good old Democrats to bring those things to you! Did your Republican car have air conditioning, or push-button window lifts, or crash-pad dash, or torque conversion, or Hollywood wheels? Of course not!

---

[6] Willard R. Espy, "Say When," *This Week,* July 13, 1952. Reprinted from *This Week* magazine. Copyright 1952 by the United Newspapers Magazine Corporation.

[7] *Time,* February 26, 1951, p. 56. Reprinted by permission.

All of those things came to your car during the progressive Democratic administration! And in truth, voters, had the Republicans been in power all these years, you would still have 30 by 3 high-pressure tires on your Model T!

Make this test, if you doubt the progress which Democratic foresight has brought—go to a used-car lot and you'll find you can buy the best car ever put out under a Republican administration for 25 bucks! That in itself is proof of the improvements which the Trumanvelt forces have provided!

So don't let them take it away! Scan your ballot carefully! Maybe somebody will be running on the Whig ticket. If so, and he's elected, history will be rolled back 100 years! Sure, it will! They'd come out and take out your telephone, your lights, your radio, and you'd be forced to wear a beaver hat and grow a spade-shaped beard! Please, Mr. Voter, you don't want to grow a spade-shaped beard, do you?[8]

And speaking of politics, a national magazine once published statements to the effect that all the presidents through Franklin D. Roosevelt in their combined 156 years of administration took from the public only 248 billion dollars. Harry Truman, on the other hand, in his 6 years took 260!

The statements may not have been intentionally deceptive, but they were certainly misleading. The obvious implication was that Mr. Truman's administration had been incredibly extravagant. Specifically (and to spare you the arithmetic), Mr. Truman received 27 times more tax dollars per year than that required by the average pre-Truman president.

All of this, of course, is based on the *frozen evaluations* that "a dollar is a dollar" and "an administration is an administration." If we side-step these misevaluations, we will get a rather different picture. Consider these among the extenuations:

1. The value of the dollar has greatly diminished over the years. The dollar at the time of the magazine's statements (1951), for example, was only half the value of the 1939 dollar.
2. Much of Truman's expenditures were inevitable and due to an evolution in the responsibilities of the federal government.
   a) Our population had grown tremendously—a 30,000 per cent increase since 1790. Governing our nation had become correspondingly more expensive.
   b) The *nature* of the administration had changed. Over the years the federal government had come to play a greater and greater role in the national economy. This role required bureaus and personnel —and money.

---

8 *Chicago Daily News,* August 8, 1952, p. 8.

c) The character of our government in world affairs had changed. Only recently had we become a leader fighting (and spending) for *world* freedom.

3. World War II, the most costly in history, was fought during F.D.R.'s time, but much of it was *paid for* during Truman's.

4. And let us not forget the extraordinary expenses of the Korean War, the national remobilization, and the rehabilitation of half the world.

CORRECTIVES

The previous two chapters described the need for discriminating among people, qualities, traits, etc., *without* regard for time differences. The current chapter calls for *time* differentiation. Let me say this a little differently.

The *frozen evaluation* was defined as a judgment set in concrete—an evaluation which remained constant and inflexible despite changes in its object. The basic problem, therefore, is to keep one's evaluation in pace with past and future changes in the person, situation, etc.—whatever it is that he is evaluating. When the object changes, then the evaluation ought to change correspondingly. How can we accomplish this? How can we keep from freezing our evaluations and how can we "thaw" those already frozen?

Accept the Premise of Change

Substitute the conscious premise of *change* for the unconscious notion of *non-change*. Believe firmly in the process nature of man, of situations, of things, etc., and you will be more likely to keep your evaluations *up to date*.

Apply the When Index

A very simple, yet effective, device for implementing the awareness of change is the *When Index*. Using the *When Index* is simply assigning a *date*. For example, the following Associated Press release appeared in 1950:

WILLIAMS SIGNS WITH RED SOX FOR
RECORD BASEBALL PAY OF $125,000

Boston, Feb. 7 (AP)—Ted Williams, the Red Sox slugger, today signed the highest salaried contract in baseball history—for an estimated $125,000. Babe Ruth's $80,000 salary in 1930 and '31 was tops in the old days.[9]

---

[9] Appeared in the *New York Times*, Feb. 8, 1950. Reprinted by permission of the Associated Press.

At first glance Mr. Williams seems to have fared considerably better financially than Mr. Ruth. But the Foundation for Economic Education, Inc., made a revealing analysis by *When-Indexing* (i.e., dating) the purchasing power of the take-home dollar.

DOLLAR SALARIES	TAKE-HOME PAY	WHAT THE TAKE-HOME WILL BUY
This is a comparison of Ruth's and Williams' dollar salaries.	But after federal income taxes, this is a comparison of their take-home pay.	Inflation has shrunk the buying power of the dollar since 1931, so Williams' real take-home pay is only a little over half of Ruth's—57%.

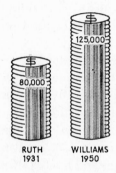

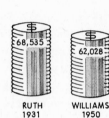

| RUTH 1931 | WILLIAMS 1950 | RUTH 1931 | WILLIAMS 1950 | RUTH 1931 | WILLIAMS 1950 |

If Ted Williams were to have as much buying power in 1950 as Babe Ruth had in 1931, he would have to be paid $327,451.

—THE FOUNDATION FOR ECONOMIC EDUCATION, INC.

The *When Index* (which may be expressed as a mental or even explicit superscript, e.g., the U.S. ^{1933} is not the U.S. ^{1960}) is a reminder of the process nature of life. It reminds us of the constant flux that is characteristic of the world. It is such a versatile little tool that the following three brief cases will only suggest its usefulness:

THE CASE OF RICHARD ROE[10]

Richard Roe embezzled ten thousand dollars in 1950 and was soon apprehended, convicted and sentenced. Roe in 1960 has served his term. Roe ^{1960} is not Roe ^{1950}. There are bound to have been changes. But this does not mean that a prospective employer does not have the right to investigate Roe thoroughly before hiring him. Indeed, it would be imprudent, usually, to fail to do so. But no employer, it seems to me, has the *moral* justification to *refuse* to hire him *without* an investigation. To dismiss Roe summarily as an undated "ex-convict" may not only deprive the employer of an able worker but, more importantly, it may contribute to Roe's destruction as a useful citizen.

---

10 Fictitious.

THE CASE OF EUGENE PLONKA

Eugene Plonka, 40 . . . fell 25 feet to his death from a second-story fire escape door in the Cameron Can Machinery Company. . . .

Police believed Plonka, an assembler, was unaware when he stepped from the door that the fire escape had been removed for repairs. Employees said Plonka frequently spent his "rest break" on the fire escape.[11]

Even a structure as seemingly unchangeable as a fire escape is not always the same. "Fire escape ^{yesterday}" is not "fire escape ^{today}." Had Mr. Plonka ingrained the habit of *When-Indexing*, he would have been prompted to *look* before stepping out onto a fire escape which was not there.

THE CASE OF DAVID

Six-year-old David had had his experiences with inoculations, so his mother was not too surprised that he protested vigorously when she told him he was to receive a polio shot the following afternoon.

"David," she countered, "I know how you feel, and I am willing to make a bargain with you. Now, the shot is not going to hurt you today or tomorrow morning, is it?" "No," he admitted. "And it isn't going to hurt when we leave the house and while we are driving to the doctor's office?" "No." "And it isn't going to hurt when we are sitting in the waiting room, reading the comic books?" "No." "Or when the doctor rubs your arm with alcohol and gets the hypodermic ready?" "No." "Then there would be no sense in crying or yelling at any of these times, would there?" "No, I guess not." "But it *will* hurt when he sticks the hypodermic into your arm, right?" "Yes!" "Well, young man, *at that time* you may yell your head off!"

David agreed, and when the inoculation actually occurred, a relaxed David considered the prick hardly worth yelling about, and his *When-Indexing* had spared him needless anxiety.

Try this sort of *When-Indexing* on yourself the next time you make a dental appointment or anticipate some other unpleasant experience. A wise old professor of mine expressed his feeling about anxiety a little differently: "I'm never late until I get there!"

SUMMARY

A *frozen evaluation* is one which is spread unconsciously (or perhaps deliberately) over the future and/or over the past, without regard for change. The effects of the *frozen evaluation* may take on a great variety of forms, not the least serious of which are those which have to do with our evaluations of ourselves. Evidently, underlying most *frozen evaluations* is the assumption of *non-change*—a fallacious

---

11 *Chicago Daily News*, December 12, 1953, p. 12. Reprinted by permission.

and often unconsciously held notion that there is rest, permanence, constancy. A simple device, the *When Index*, reminds us to take *change* into account in our evaluations—to distinguish among time^1, time^2, time^3, etc.

INCIDENTS

ORDEAL IN LONDON[12]

Subtract 8 days, 23 hours and 31 minutes from 29 days, 15 hours and 7 minutes.

If HMFL spells JOHN in a particular code, how does that code work?

Four men, Smith, Robinson, Jones and Brown, all grow vegetables. All four grow lettuce. All but Smith and Robinson grow potatoes. Smith and Brown grow cabbages. Robinson grows peas. Which two vegetables does Robinson grow? Which two does Smith grow? Which man grows potatoes, lettuce, cabbage, but no peas?

For 2½ hours, one day last week, 32,000 little Londoners, aged 10½ to 11½, sat at their school desks puzzling over such questions as these. Their puzzlement was fierce, as if they thought their very lives depended on their answers. In their estimate of the seriousness of the test, the young Londoners were pretty much right.

The examinations they were taking were the awesome "selection tests"—Britain's new way of finding out just what sort of secondary education each child should have. If he does well, he will win a coveted "place" in one of the "grammar" schools, and there he will get a solid academic education that may eventually lead him to a university. If he does not do so well, he will be sent to a "central" or "secondary technical" school where he will spend more time on vocational training. The bottom 60% of the children will end up in a "secondary modern" school. There, formal academic training is at a minimum.

The selection system started in 1944, when the British government decided that every child should get a free secondary education. Before that, parents paid the bill, and most children merely stayed on in elementary schools until they could legally drop out at 14. Now all children must go on to secondary school at eleven. Since too few grammar schools exist, the government has had to set up a rigid system of selection. But by last week, as the London exams fell due some Britons were asking whether the system is really worthwhile.

Teachers were willing to admit that the tests could winnow out the bright and the quick. But they still did not pick out the hard-working or the talented. They gave no quarter to the late bloomers, made no

---

12 *Time*, February 4, 1952. Reprinted by permission.

allowances for children who happened to be overwrought during the exam. Cried one parent last week: "The test gets the child so worked up. My Patricia went out of the house white as a sheet, and couldn't eat any breakfast." Added another: "It's terrible to think that what a boy does at eleven will govern his whole life."

MONEY TROUBLES[13]

The money market can be treated in the same way as any commodity market. In general, when the supply of money is plentiful, its price (which is the rate of interest) will be lower than when its supply is short. This however, is only part of the story, since it is widely known that federal controls on money supply are in force. This incident arose out of the changing price on money. As a farm loan appraiser for an insurance company's mortgage loan department, I am charged with several duties. Perhaps the most important of these is the recommendations of new loan business.

In April of 1956, money supplies were diminishing and mortgage money developed into a tight situation. Those of us in the field were aware of the tighter money market but no policy change in regard to interest rate was issued from the Home Office. In my own case, I had two farm loan applications on my desk, to be submitted at the then prevailing interest rate of 4%. These would be sent to the office for approval as soon as the appraisal report was completed and as soon as proper credit checks were made. The following day I mailed these cases into the office and made assurances to the applicants that their cases would be approved.

In that same day's mail a memorandum was received stating that "all farm loan applications must be submitted at a 4½% interest rate, effective as of the date of this memorandum."

The two loan applications that were submitted at 4% were committed and mailed to the applicants bearing at 4½% rate. Both applicants were very unhappy with the change in their applications. They felt they had been "doubled-crossed." There is no question that the Company and I lost considerable good will not only with these people but with many of their friends to whom they complained about our treatment of them.

---

[13] Printed by permission of the author, whose name has been withheld by request.

THE "GOOD OLD DAYS"[14]

DEAR MAZIE:

Mike and I walked down the road to Mollie and Bill's last night to see if they'd like to play a game of Scrabble, but Bill wasn't in the mood for Scrabble—he was hopping mad about a $27 bill he had received from a plumber for a small job in the house—"that wouldn't have cost a third as much in the Good Old Days." Mollie merely laughed at him and said, "Serves you right—if you weren't so lazy you would have done the job yourself."

Then Mike aired his latest gripe about the cost of some minor repairs to his car last month and the sloppy way it was done. "All a workman today thinks of is his pay check—he has no pride in his work—once it's out of his hands he doesn't care how soon it falls apart—"

So then we all got into the game and enjoyed a Complain Session about "Labor" in general. We all agreed that such household equipment as refrigerators, stoves, washing machines, vacuum cleaners, etc. are not made as well as they used to be. Neither the materials nor the workmanship are in them. Nothing seems to be made to LAST any more. "Including children's toys," says I—thinking of all the broken plastic toys around the house already since Christmas.

But Mollie, who is a very fair minded person, felt that even though all this may be true—still, we wouldn't want to go back to the so-called "Good Old Days" of our grandparents. So she went to the bookcase and found a little printed card—brittle with age."I want to read this to you," she said. "These are the rules given each new employee—my father was one—way back in the 80's, by what is now one of Chicago's largest department stores. Listen to this and I don't think you'll wonder why Labor rebelled:—

Store must be swept and counters and base shelves and show cases dusted. Lamp trimmed, filled and chimney cleaned; pens made; doors and windows opened; a pail of water and a scuttle of coal must be brought in by each clerk before breakfast.

Store must not be opened on the Sabbath Day unless absolutely necessary and then only for a few minutes.

---

14 *Wilmette Life*, January 17, 1957. "Dear Mazie" is a regular feature of the weekly *Wilmette Life*. Reprinted by permission of Lloyd Hollister, Inc., publishers.

Any employee who is in the habit of smoking Spanish cigars, getting shaved at a Barber Shop, going to dances and other such places of amusement will most certainly give his employer reason to be suspicious of his integrity and all around honesty.

Each employee must pay not less than $5 per year to the Church and must attend Sunday School every Sunday.

Men employees are given one evening a week for courting purposes, and two if they go to prayer meeting regularly.

After 14 hours of work in the store, leisure time must be spent in reading good literature.

Nobody said anything for a minute after Mollie finished reading. I guess we were all trying to digest this form of dictatorship. Then Mike said, "Well, I guess that does it! And I thought we were getting too much regimentation in the past few years. Looks like we're just beginning to know what freedom is."

Yours 'till next week,

Mitzi

THE KNIGHT MANUFACTURING COMPANY[15]

The Knight Manufacturing Company is the manufacturer of clocks and cameras. Last summer the Company was in the midst of the largest selling campaign in its history.

As is the custom with the firm, the comptroller began his weekly breakdown of the finished goods inventory with the perpetual inventory clerk. Everything was checked and accepted. However, the clerk related that the #501 clock was getting out of proportion.

(This clock comes in two styles, #500 and #501. When first produced, the #501 was in greater demand than the other. This factor influenced the management to make a mold that would have one stationary cavity of the #501 and the other cavity could be either the #501 or #500. The result was that it was possible to cast simultaneously either a #501 and a #500 or two #501.

However, there was a complete reversal in sales, the #500 which was not selling became the big seller. The orders were coming in at a rate of 5 to 1 and the inventory of the #501 began to mount because of the construction of the mold; at least one #501 (for which there

---

15 All names have been disguised. Printed by permission of the author, whose name has been withheld by request.

was little demand) had to be cast every time a casting of #500 was made.)

The comptroller then reported this disproportion in the clock inventory to the plant manager. However, he had reported the wrong style number. The comptroller even when told could not get used to a different seller in this line.

The plant manager upon receiving the comptroller's memo called the production manager in for a review. The plant manager wished to know why there was such a great disproportion, when there were orders for every #500 in the warehouse. After considerable confusion the situation was clarified.

SPRING WOOING[16]

For the 50,000 engineers who met in Manhattan last week at the annual convention of the Institute of Radio Engineers, 800 expensive exhibits had been carefully set up. But the convention's most popular exhibition—before which engineers daily stood two or three deep—was a makeshift affair; it was a 15-ft. display of hundreds of white cards tacked on a wall beneath the sign "Job Opportunities."

For many engineers the convention was less a chance to study new developments than an opportunity to get new jobs. For their part, engineering firms, hard-pressed by a steadily increasing shortage of engineers (*Time*, May 30), used the convention as a rich hunting ground for talent. Page after page of display ads in Manhattan newspapers and trade journals invited engineers to investigate a wide variety of engineering jobs offering tempting salaries up to $15,000. Though open recruiting was forbidden at the convention, several companies complained that engineers were being "pirated" right at the convention's exhibit booths. But most of the recruiting went on behind the scenes.

Prize Catch. In Manhattan hotels dozens of engineering firms set up plush suites and "hospitality rooms," where liquor and food were plentiful. Radio Corp. of America alone hired nine rooms at the Waldorf-Astoria, kept ten people busy interviewing some 250 engineers. Said RCA Employment Manager John R. Weld: "Convention time recruiting is our largest single effort." Motorola, which last year

---

16 *Time*, April 1, 1957, p. 82. Reprinted by permission.

hired 32 engineers as a result of convention interviews, talked to 234 applicants. Bendix spent $10,000 for its convention recruitment program, which included a six-room hotel suite.

Some firms, recognizing the danger of exposing their men to such temptations kept them away from the convention altogether. Many sent engineers to the convention for only one day, hoping to keep them from shopping around. This often played right into the hands of the recruiters; the one-day man was obviously a man a company valued—and therefore a good man to steal.

Why Change? Most engineers wanted to change jobs simply to make more money. Though the young engineer just out of college starts at a good salary (currently from $432 to $500 a month), raises are sometimes slow in coming. "Your own company can never understand why you're worth much more two years after being hired," said a 34-year-old electronics engineer on the lookout for a new job, "whereas another company figures that they're getting real experience." Said a Curtiss-Wright engineer: "The general opinion is that if you want more money—change jobs."

The irony of the scramble is that companies must keep hiring not only for expansion but simply to replace engineers who have been wooed elsewhere. While firms were hiring new engineers at the I.R.E. convention, their own men were being hired away by other firms. As a result, hiring and training a new man in an increasingly tight engineers' market generally costs more than a raise for the older man. Many engineers insist that they would be less ready to change jobs if they could be assured of regular raises and increasing responsibilities. Said a young electrical engineer: "What I'd like to see them do is to spend more time interviewing the people who are leaving than worrying about hiring new people."

Chapter **IX**

INTENSIONAL ORIENTATION I
(A GENERAL STATEMENT)

THIS chapter, unlike the others in this book, does not deal with a specific pattern of communication difficulty. The purpose here is to describe and discuss a general orientation toward the relationship between words and what they stand for—between "the map" and "the territory." In the two following chapters we shall examine a number of forms of misevaluation and miscommunication to which this orientation can lead.

One way to define the *intensional* (the *s* is inten*t*ional) *orientation* is to show it in action.

THE GRAHAM UNIVERSITY TAX CASE[1]

Graham is a large private university located in Allyn, a pleasant suburb. For years, town-gown relations had been quite amicable except for one point of friction—taxation.

Graham held two types of exemption from real estate taxation. Exemption$_1$ concerned its educational property, i.e., property used directly for educational purposes, such as classrooms, libraries, administration buildings, dormitories, athletic fields, etc. No one quarreled over this exemption, however, for it was granted to all schools and colleges in Allyn.

Exemption$_2$, on the other hand, covered Graham's investment properties. These were real estate holdings which were *not* directly used for educational purposes, although the income from them was. It was around this exemption that the friction revolved. Interest in the issue waxed and waned, but there was always an underlying current of resentment among many of the townspeople. It was generally believed that the university's exemption had removed a sizable portion of the suburb's real estate from the tax rolls, thus increasing the taxation on the individual's property.

---

1 The names have been disguised; otherwise the details are factual.

The debate became especially heated during election years. One aldermanic candidate, for example, published a statement in the *Allyn Times* to the effect that Graham's exemption$_2$ was depriving Allyn of tax revenue from 6 per cent of its area and 10 per cent of its assessed value. Other published statements, letters to the editor, etc., contended that the exemption covered as much as 50 per cent of Allyn's real estate.

And there were citizens who supported the exemption. "So what if we have to pay more taxes," they argued, "isn't it worth it? Graham has put Allyn on the map, made us a cultural center. Moreover, Graham's thousands of students contribute to the economic health of the community with their purchases in Allyn."

And so the discussing and the contending and the arguing continued until the *Times* decided to do something about it. It hired competent real estate taxation specialists to determine the status of tax exemptions in Allyn. After a comprehensive survey the specialists submitted their report: 16 per cent of the total of Allyn's real estate was tax-exempt. This included not only Graham's property, educational and investment, but that of the other colleges, private and public schools, the churches, the municipal buildings, the libraries, the hospitals, the parks, etc. The subject of debate—Graham's investment property—constituted only one half of 1 per cent of Allyn's real estate!

The friction disappeared almost immediately. Even the most ardent disputants admitted: "If that's all it amounts to—it's hardly enough to fuss about."

INTENSION AND EXTENSION

The Graham case involved a problem which was approached in two vitally different ways. For years people had been verbalizing, theorizing, speculating about Graham's exemption$_2$. They talked, they discussed, they disputed. The more they talked about the problem, the farther they seemed to move away from *it*. They became so absorbed in their own personal *maps of the territory* that it became increasingly difficult for them to examine *the territory itself*. They were *intensionally oriented*—more concerned, that is, with the feelings, thoughts, suppositions, beliefs, theories, etc., *"inside* their skins" than with the life-facts, the "reality" *outside*.

Finally, the *Allyn Times* took a radically different tack. "Look," said the publisher, "all this *talking about* the problem has only succeeded in aggravating the situation. Let's quit *talking* for once and go out and do some *looking*—let's go out and *see* just what this exemption amounts to." The publisher's "stop talking and start looking" approach is characteristic of the *extensional orientation*.

One is *oriented intensionally* when he is predisposed to become absorbed with the map and to neglect the territory. This tendency is epitomized in this charming fable of the recession of 1957–58.

A Man Lived by the Side of the Road . . .
. . . and sold hot dogs.
He . . . had no radio.
He had trouble with his eyes, so he had no newspaper.
But he sold good hot dogs.
He put up a sign on the highway, telling how good they were.
He stood by the side of the road and cried: "Buy a hot dog, mister." And people bought.
He increased his meat and bun orders, and he bought a bigger store to take care of his trade.
He got his son home from college to help him. But then something happened.
His son said: "Father, haven't you been listening to the radio? There's a big depression on. The international situation is terrible, and the domestic situation is even worse."
Whereupon his father thought: "Well, my son has been to college. He listens to the radio and reads the papers, so he ought to know."
So, the father cut down his bun order, took down his advertising sign, and no longer bothered to stand on the highway to sell hot dogs.
His hot-dog sales fell almost overnight.
"You were right, son," the father said to the boy. "We are certainly in the middle of a great depression."[2]

Extensional orientation, on the other hand, is the predisposition to inspect the territory *first*—and *then* to build verbal maps to *correspond with it*. One of the greatest extensionalists in history was Galileo. Time and again he refused to be governed by the revered maps—the theories and postulates—of his time and went instead to observe "the territory" for himself. The Aristotelian Law of Falling Bodies was one of these unquestioned maps. Postulated more than nineteen centuries before, it held that the velocity of falling bodies was directly proportional to their weight—a notion consistent with the prevailing theory of gravitation. But Galileo had to *see* for himself and proceeded to the Tower of Pisa, where he exploded the "Law" and started the world thinking about a new theory of gravity.

---

2 From a Quaker State Metals Co. advertisement, courtesy of *Newsweek* (February 24, 1958, p. 77).

INTENSIONALITY: SOME MANIFESTATIONS

Basically, one behaves *intensionally* when he responds to his "maps" (his feelings, imaginings, visualizations, formulations, attitudes, theories, preconceptions, evaluations, inferences, etc.) *as if* he were responding to the territory (objects, people, happenings, relationships, things, etc.). Trouble tends to come when the map is an inadequate representation of the territory. Take the case of a young southern soldier in World War II. Seriously wounded at the front, the unconscious boy's life hung in the balance. He desperately needed a transfusion, but blood of his unusual type was unavailable, and there was scant hope of acquiring some in time. Fortunately, a Negro in a neighboring battalion heard about the boy's condition and volunteered for a transfusion. His blood type was suitable; the transfusion was made, and the young soldier's life was saved. On the road to recovery several days later, the young Southerner was told of the Negro who had given his blood. The boy became almost uncontrollable with fear and rage. He was overwhelmed by a lifelong delusion that the Negro's blood in his veins would change the color of his skin and even alter the shape and size of his lips and nose, the texture of his hair, etc.

Instead of reacting to the territory, a situation in which he was generously given life-saving blood, the young man responded in terms of his fallacious map.

To a greater extent than most of us are aware we are conditioned to react *intensionally* by the phenomena of our environment. Society's customs, traditions, norms, mores, etc., are maps—sometimes spurious ones—which become so ingrained in us that we often treat them as territories.

I can still recall the hubbub a few years ago when a college professor married a woman who had attended one of his courses a year before. The man, an exceptional scholar and teacher, was forty, and his lovely and intelligent bride was thirty-two. Though entering matrimony relatively late in life, they were obviously well suited to each other, and their marriage has since proved eminently successful.

This was the territory, but some people paid more attention to their specious maps. One newspaper headlined the wedding story with a ridiculous, cradle-snatching implication: "Teacher Marries Pupil." Many readers, largely ignorant of the facts of the situation, raised their eyebrows, clucked their tongues, and some even wrote letters of protest to the college president. They had become so distraught at the imagined violation of a social taboo that they were hardly able or willing to examine the territory behind their fallacious maps.

Sometimes we behave *intensionally* because we want to. It is a relief, occasionally, to escape to our inner self-made worlds. There is value in daydreams, movies, television, novels, etc., when they serve as *temporary* safety valves. There is danger, however, when the world of make-believe becomes accepted as real. Children are perhaps the most susceptible. A mother caught her seven-year-old son pouring ground glass into the family stew. He wanted to see if it would "really work" as it had with the characters in a television play he had seen.[3] Another youngster accidentally hung himself while attempting to free himself from a trick knot from which a comic book hero had escaped.[4] And still another boy caused a $100,000 warehouse fire by using a clever incendiary made of a burning cigarette inserted in a book of matches. He had learned the trick from a movie.

But some adults are almost as prone to delude themselves—to react to faulty or fictional maps as if they were the actual territories. Milton Caniff, originator of the comic strip, "Terry and the Pirates," tells of the time one of the characters, "Hot Shot Charlie," was sent to the United States for a period. Always a precisionist, Caniff depicted him as quartered at an actual apartment in Boston. One day the strip showed "Hot Shot" receiving a cable with the apartment's address clearly visible on the wire. The next panels showed him packing and leaving for overseas.

A day or so later Caniff received an urgent request from the apartment-house owner. "Please print a block in your comic strip," he pleaded, "and explain that there is no vacancy at _____ St.!" The poor man had been deluged with eager inquiries about "Hot Shot's vacant apartment!"

And Bing Crosby gives an amusing illustration of the undeniable effect of another kind of map, the motion picture:

I'd heard of the public identifying actors and actresses with roles, but this was the first time I'd got the full treatment myself. Not long after *Going My Way* was released, I attended a dinner party at the home of my friend Jack Morse. Before dinner, cocktail canapés and hors d'œuvres were served, among them toasted frankfurters on toothpicks. They were served by a gray-haired, motherly-looking maid from the Ould Sod. It happened to be Friday, and when I absent-mindedly took one of the frankfurters, I

---

3 Norman Cousins, "The Time Trap," *Saturday Review of Literature,* December 24, 1949, p. 20.

4 "Tell Hanged Boy's Boast He Could Do Escape Trick," *Chicago Sun-Times,* January 15, 1955, p. 4.

thought she'd have a stroke. "Holy Mother! Father Crosby!" she burst out, "you're not going to eat one of those!" Obviously she was subconsciously thinking of me as the priest I'd played, and the fact that "Father O'Malley" would eat a meat canapé on Friday upset her.

The other guests collapsed with laughter, and she retreated in confusion to the kitchen. I was a little confused myself.[5]

Unfortunately, the impact of the motion picture and other forms of entertainment is not always so delightful. Their chief danger to our children and young people, writes Sidney J. Harris, is not immorality, as many fear, but "the totally false impression of love, marriage and adult relations in general":

A child cannot so easily be corrupted by "dirtiness" as he can be seduced by romanticism. Young people usually laugh at "sexy" movies; but they lap up romantic ones with credulous ecstasy. And this is the basic betrayal of the film-makers.

Most pictures end just where life itself begins—with the romantic clinch and the march up the marriage aisle. "They lived happily ever after" is a more dangerous line than any of the sadism and sensuousness to be found in a "tough" picture.

What creates most of the devastation and despair among young adults is not their tendency toward immorality but their lack of emotional preparation for living. Fed during their formative years on the romantic pap of the film, the serial story, the radio and TV play, they are woefully unequipped to deal with the reality of marriage and social pressures of all sorts.

They always see the lovers laughing and kissing; they never see the quarrels and conflicts that are inevitable between any two personalities. They are "enchanted" by romantic pictures; but the terrible thing about enchantment is that it must inevitably come to an end.[6]

But the most pathetic victims of the celluloid chimera are perhaps some of the stars themselves. Living in the fanciful world created by press agents and celebrity-worshippers, their maps become tragically out of joint with the facts of life. The too frequent results are nervous breakdowns, broken marriages, and suicides.

Generally speaking, *intensionality* is most likely to lead to undesirable consequences (1) when one's map inadequately represents the territory and (2) when he is unaware that he is responding to his map rather than to the territory.

Every medical student knows that the length of the small intestine is 22 feet or thereabouts, for his textbook has taught him so. But Dr.

---

[5] Bing Crosby as told to Pete Martin, *Call Me Lucky* (New York: Simon & Schuster, 1953), pp. 186–87. Reprinted by permission.

[6] Sidney J. Harris, "Calls False Romance Worst Film Offense," *Chicago Daily News*, March 3, 1954, p. 14.

Betty Underhill has revealed this "map" as a dangerous fallacy. In 100 autopsies she found that men's intestines ranged from 16 to 25 feet 9 inches, women's from 11 feet to 23 feet 6 inches. Differences such as these, she asserted, can be life-and-death matters in surgery.[7]

CORRECTIVES

As the problem of *intensional orientation* has been stated only generally, at this point we can offer only general advice for dealing with it. We shall reserve for the next two chapters the task of defining *intensionality* in its more specific forms and of offering techniques for preventing or diminishing their consequences.

The basic advice is to *"get extensional."* Develop the "show me" or "let me see" attitude. Develop a healthy distrust of preconstructed maps—go to the territory, look, observe, explore, probe, examine— *then* make your maps. This is the tenor of the homey advice World Court Justice John Bassett Moore once gave radio-television commentator, Edward R. Murrow: "When you meet men of great reputation, your judgment of them will be greatly improved if you view them as though they were in their underwear."

Extensionality is the *sine qua non* of the scientist. He makes hypotheses (tentative maps), yes, but usually on the basis of previous observation of the territory, and then he checks them against the territory again—and again—and again. If the map matches the territory, well and good; but if it does not, he alters his map or discards it and builds another, and another, until it adequately represents the territory.

This is the scientific attitude, the territory-first-then-map approach; but surely there is great need for it well beyond the confines of the laboratory.

SUMMARY

Intensional orientation is a general term for the tendency to be guided primarily, if not exclusively, by one's maps rather than by the territory. Trouble, confusion, and danger are most likely to occur (1) when the map inadequately represents the territory and (2) when the individual is *unaware* that he is dealing with the map rather than with the territory.

---

[7] From *Time*, December 5, 1955, p. 65.

The basic technique for preventing or minimizing the injurious effects of *intensional orientation,* simply stated, is to develop an *extensional orientation*—a readiness to seek out the territory rather than a willingness to be mesmerized by one's often fallacious maps. *Extensionality,* in short, is the propensity to "look first—then talk."

INCIDENTS

THE "WATER-AMERICAN"[8]

At my first admission into this printing-house I took to working at press, imagining I felt a want of the bodily exercise I had been us'd to in America, where presswork is mix'd with composing. I drank only water; the other workmen, near fifty in number, were great guzzlers of beer. On occasion, I carried up and down stairs a large form of types in each hand, when others carried but one in both hands. They wondered to see, from this and several instances, that the *Water-American,* as they called me, was *stronger* than themselves, who drank *strong* beer! We had an alehouse boy who attended always in the house to supply the workmen. My companion at the press drank every day a pint before breakfast, a pint at breakfast with his bread and cheese, a pint between breakfast and dinner, a pint at dinner, a pint in the afternoon about six o'clock, and another when he had done his day's work. I thought it a detestable custom; but it was necessary, he suppos'd, to drink *strong* beer, that he might be *strong* to labor. I endeavored to convince him that the bodily strength afforded by beer could only be in proportion to the grain or flour of the barley dissolved in the water of which it was made; that there was more flour in a pennyworth of bread, and therefore, if he would eat that with a pint of water, it would give him more strength than a quart of beer. He drank on, however, and had four or five shillings to pay out of his wages every Saturday night for that muddling liquor; an expense I was free from. And thus these poor devils keep themselves always under.

"GET OFF ROUTE 25, YOUNG MAN"[9]
By Charles F. Kettering

My home is in Dayton, Ohio, and I was a friend of the Wright family and learned to fly on the very early Wright airplanes. Their

---

[8] From *The Autobiography of Benjamin Franklin* (New York: D.C. Heath & Co., 1908). Reprinted by permission.

[9] *Colliers,* December 3, 1949, pp. 13–14. Reprinted by permission.

first flight was on the 17th of December, 46 years ago. Everyone was perfectly sure that it was a crazy thing to try. The undertakers moved into Kitty Hawk with a number of caskets because they thought the Wrights would kill themselves.

When they made those first three flights on December 17, 1903, they wired their sister that they had succeeded, that they were very happy, and that they should be home for Christmas.

She thought it was a world-shaking event, so she very excitedly called a Dayton newspaper on the telephone. She rang and rang and rang. The newspaper boys were playing pinochle, but finally one of them answered.

He said, "Yes?"

She said, "This is Katherine Wright speaking," and very excitedly read the telegram.

He said, "Good. Glad to hear the boys are going to get home for Christmas," and hung up the telephone.

The newspaperman said to the others: "Nobody's going to catch me on that, because it has been proved mathematically that a heavier-than-air machine can't fly."

*   *   *   *

I had a friend who was the research and development man for one of the British railroads. He came to this country to deliver a commencement address at a technical university. After the address he came to Detroit to see our laboratories.

"Ket," he said, "when you were over in London last year you told me some things you fellows were doing with Diesel locomotives and you lied to me."

I said, "Not intentionally."

"But," he said, "you told me you were running these locomotives about a hundred miles an hour."

I said, "We are."

"And that you were taking power on the front wheels; that is, the wheels that are ahead."

I said, "We are."

He said, "I have the formulas in my portfolio that say you can't do that."

I said, "For Heaven's sake, don't let the locomotive know about it."

I said to him, "I won't argue with you at all." I took the telephone, called Chicago and get him transportation from Chicago to Denver, and flew him to Chicago to make the connection. He made the trip to Denver, where I had him ride part way on the Diesel engines.

He stopped in to see me on his way back. He was returning to England. I said, "I didn't expect to see you again. Did you ride that locomotive?"

"Yes," he said.

"Did it go a hundred miles an hour?"

"It did."

"Well," I said, "that's the reason I didn't expect to see you back. Maybe you forgot to take the portfolio with the equations in it."

He said, "The thing that amazes me is why we could be so one hundred per cent wrong."

I said, "You weren't wrong. You didn't start in right."

The two of us got out his formulas. He wasn't talking about our locomotive at all. Our locomotive uses an ordinary truck like a streetcar's. He was talking about a locomotive with a rigid frame which would normally have a small-wheel lead truck in front of it.

I said, "What's the use of using mathematics on one kind of thing and then applying it to another which is in no way related? It isn't even a second cousin to it."

*   *   *   *

When we first put self-starters on automobiles I attended a meeting of the American Institute of Electrical Engineers. They asked me if I would make a little talk on the self-starter, and I did.

One fellow got up and said, "No wonder you made your self-starter work; you profaned every law of electrical engineering."

I didn't profane any fundamental laws of electrical engineering. All I did was make the starter work. Those laws had nothing whatever to do with self-starters; they were written for something entirely different.

*   *   *   *

As I said before, my home is in Dayton, and we have had our laboratories for years in Detroit, which is several hundred miles away. I keep my home in Ohio and drive back and forth week ends.

Some of the people who work with me also drive between Dayton and Detroit. One said, "I understand you drive from here to Dayton in four and one-half hours."

I said, "I can do that once in a while, depending on traffic."

He said, "I don't believe it."

I said, "But I do it."

He said, "I'm a much better driver than you are, and I can't do it."

I said, "I'm going down Friday. Why don't you ride along with me?"

So we rode into Dayton in about four and one-half hours, or a little more, and he said, "Hell, no wonder you can do it. You didn't stay on Route 25!"

Now, Route 25 is the red line that is marked on all the maps between Detroit and Dayton. If you are a stranger, that's the road you should take. It never occurred to my colleague that you could take any other road on either side of Route 25. There's a lot of country on either side of it; in fact, half the earth is on each side of it. . . .

REPORT FROM RAINBOW LAND[10]

For millions of British newspaper readers, the U.S. is "Rainbow Land," a world of dazzling fluff and foolishness. The man who paints it that way is Britain's favorite Manhattan columnist, a sleekly combed English reporter named Don Iddon, who writes his weekly "Don Iddon's Diary" for the *London Daily Mail* (circ. 2,293,565) and a string of other papers on the Continent and through the British Commonwealth. Since British newspapers generally do an indifferent job of covering the U.S., many readers rely on Iddon's hodgepodge of gossip, pressagentry and political hip-shooting for much of their U.S. news. Over the weeks, he leaves the impression that most Americans guide their lives by astrology, gorge themselves on thick steaks, give their daughters $10,000 debuts and are all ready to jump into aluminum pajamas and lead-foil brassieres at the first hint of atomic attack.

Such airy servings, neatly calculated to confirm preconceived British notions, have won Iddon the Fleet Street title of "Britain's Walter Winchell." Since 1943, bumptious Reporter Iddon ("Let's face it I'm a terrific egotist") has been doing his diary the way his bosses and readers seem to like it—by skimming the foam from the U.S. scene. Last week, in England on a refresher trip, Reporter Iddon looked about him and blandly remarked: "There seems to be a surprising amount of ignorance about America. People here seem to think Americans eat

---

10 *Time,* May 28, 1951, p. 52. Reprinted by permission.

nothing but steak and ride in enormous cars. Of course, that's nonsense." Then he went to work to plug his new book, Don Iddon's America (Falcon Press, London; 12s, 6d), a collection of his columns which have been carefully edited with the wisdom of hindsight. Some still unedited Iddon items:

"The electric chair is working overtime and Sing Sing's Death Row is jammed as detectives round up gun-happy youths hepped up with dope."

"The sleeping-pill habit is getting widespread [in Hollywood]. Actors and actresses take them to get a few hours' rest and then swallow benzedrine in the morning to do their work."

"The simple truth about the Negro in America . . . is that he is treated as sub-human . . . [Negroes] live worse than the white man's dog."

(Explained Iddon later: "I probably meant an Englishman's dog. After all Britons treat their dogs very well. . . .")

THE TRIALS OF GALILEO

Galileo is perhaps most widely known and remembered for his astronomical studies. Early in life he became a convert to the Copernican ideas, ideas that conflicted with the medieval conception of the universe as established by Ptolemy. Ptolemy declared that the earth was an immovable sphere, fixed in the center of the universe, with the sun and the stars revolving about it. For many centuries the Ptolemaic system was almost undisputedly accepted. Not only did it seem to agree with the perception of the senses but it was also in harmony with the homocentric doctrine of theology, which recognized man as the principal object of divine concern. The entire universe was conceived as having been created to serve man's needs. Hence it was but natural to regard the earth, the abode of man, as the center of the universe. . . .[11]

It was not until he made a number of discoveries by means of the telescope that he boldly championed Copernicanism. Apprised that a contrivance had been invented in the Dutch Netherlands by which distant objects could be made to appear much nearer and larger, he set to work and soon constructed a telescope, becoming the first scien-

___

[11] From *Europe from the Renaissance to Waterloo* by Robert Ergang (New York: D. C. Heath & Co., 1939). Reprinted by permission.

tist to apply it to astronomical observation. With the new instrument Galileo made a number of important discoveries. He found that the moon, instead of being self-luminous, owed its light to reflection; also he proved its surface was deeply furrowed by valleys and mountains. The latter discovery shattered the Aristotelian idea that the moon was a perfect sphere, absolutely smooth. Especially noteworthy was Galileo's discovery of the four satellites of Jupiter, whose revolutions confirmed by analogy the Copernican explanation of the solar system. Galileo also perceived movable spots on the disc of the sun, inferring from them the sun's axial rotation and by analogy the rotation of the earth on its axis.

After making his discoveries with the telescope Galileo could not restrain his enthusiasm for the Copernican system. So persistent were his activities in behalf of it and so unsparing was his ridicule of its opponents that the Church, which still adhered to the Ptolemaic theory, became alarmed. In 1615 he was ordered by the Inquisition to desist from further advocacy of the doctrine "that the earth moves around the sun and that the sun stands in the center of the world without moving from east to west." Galileo submitted, and for the next sixteen years remained silent. Meanwhile, however, he was writing the great work of his life, which he published in 1632 under the title *Dialogue Concerning the Two Chief Systems of the World*. The main reason for his choice of a dialogue between three persons as the medium for his thought was probably a desire to avoid committing himself openly. The work presented overwhelming proof of the Copernican theory. When it was examined by the ecclesiastical authorities, Galileo was immediately summoned to appear before the Inquisition at Rome. Near seventy and broken in spirit, he was forced in the presence of the full Congregation to abjure on his knees the doctrines defined as contrary to the Holy Scriptures. The oath of recantation read in part, "I, Galileo Galilei . . . swear that with honest heart and in good faith I curse and execrate the said heresies and errors as to the movement of the earth around the sun and all other heresies and ideas opposed to the Holy Church; and I swear that I will never assert or say anything either orally or in writing, that could put me under such suspicion." A story has it that after he recited the abjuration Galileo muttered under his breath, "Eppur si muove (But it [the earth] does move)." Though the legend is unsupported by historical evidence, it indicates the value of the renunciation which was obtained under duress and expresses the general belief as to what went on in Galileo's mind.

The last years of his life Galileo devoted to the study of dynamics, publishing in 1636 his famous *Dialogues on Motion*, a consolidation of his earlier work on the subject. This book not only laid the foundation for the study of mechanics but specifically served as the preliminary work for Newton's laws of motion. Soon after publishing it Galileo became blind and also partially deaf. Yet he continued to work until his death on January 8, 1642, at the age of seventy-eight. Many historians of science regard Galileo as the founder of experimental science. His investigations of nature discredited dependence upon accepted authority, particularly upon Aristotle. Galileo's fight for the Copernican system did much to promote its acceptance and win supporters for it.[12]

THE HALL-BARWELL LETTERS (A)[13]

In September, John Turley, Research Engineer with the Hall Mfg. Co., Riverdale, Nebraska, wrote the Barwell Mfg. Co. of Madison, Wisconsin, regarding an abrasive saw Barwell Manufactures. He received an illustrated pamphlet on the machine, a price list, a questionnaire, and the following letter.

September 27, 1955

The Hall Mfg. Co.
Riverdale, Nebraska

Attention: Mr. John Turley, Research Engineer

DEAR MR. TURLEY:

You asked for information on our saw and deburring combination. Here it is.

We find most people want to know about this machine for one of two reasons. Either because they want something for their files or because they feel they need help with a problem.

If you have a cutting problem I want to give you all the help our company can give. Your problems may be similar to those dozens of others have had. In that case I can help you quickly.

At this point, however, I am at a serious disadvantage. I don't know enough. I have to "know more."

---

12 *Ibid.*, 1954 edition. Reprinted by permission.

13 All names and organizational designations have been disguised. Northwestern University cases are reports of concrete events and behavior, prepared for class discussion. They are not intended as examples of "good" or "bad" administrative or technical practices. Copyright 1958 by Northwestern University. Reprinted by permission.

You can tell us your story one of two ways. Write us or phone us. I prefer the latter myself because then we can talk with each other. We can "get together" easier by phone. We can exchange ideas.

Please feel free to call us collect. Our number here is Butler 2-5000. However, we also have a questionnaire enclosed.

The questionnaire is designed to make it easier for you to tell us enough so that we can tell which, if any, of the machines we make would be best for your work.

We will be glad to cut and return to you any cuttable material you would like to have as samples.

You get the information we need to us. We will get the information back to you that will enable you to get the results only abrasives can produce.

> Yours, very truly
> BARWELL MFG. CO.
>
> T. J. WINSTON, *President*

Turley returned the questionnaire with this notation:

We have a special problem. We are interested in obtaining a small cutoff machine for sectioning models and samples of both ferrous and non-ferrous materials and also plastics and glass. Most of these models are of irregular shape and size.

This sequence of letters followed:

> October 25, 1955

Hall Manufacturing Company
Riverdale, Nebraska

Attention: Mr. John Turley, Research Engineer

DEAR MR. TURLEY:

I have the air mail reply letter that went with the letter we mailed you on October 7.

I'm happy to know about your interest in getting a cutoff machine for sectioning models, although I'm going to be perfectly frank with you and tell you I don't know what you mean. Would it be possible to send me some samples of the things you want to cut and/or lacking that, photographs and/or lacking that, some sketches so that I can tell whether we are in a position or could make ourselves in a position to help you. I hate to be so indefinite but to be absolutely honest I don't know enough about what you want to do to be much more intelligent.

Awaiting your comments and/or your samples, which I can assure you will receive as prompt attention as this letter did, I am,

> Sincerely,
> BARWELL MFG. CO.
>
> T. J. WINSTON

November 9, 1955

Barwell Mfg. Co.
Madison, Wisconsin

Attention: Mr. T. J. Winston

GENTLEMEN:

We wish to thank you for the interest you have shown in our problem.

Specifically, we are looking for an economical means of sectioning components and complete assemblies of the various products we manufacture. Under these circumstances, it would be almost impossible to describe exactly what we need. The machine would be used in our research laboratory and you can well imagine the wide variety of products which flow through a department of this kind.

Our manufactured goods range from tiny eyelet shells with a wall thickness of .005″ to large shells with a wall thickness of .125″ on up. Also, we would want to section assemblies such as lipstick cases, and aerosol valves. The valves would be mounted on cans and bottles and we would expect to be able to section these containers.

In the past, we have done this sectioning with an ordinary hack saw, but this method causes quite a bit of deformation of the parts. In many cases, the parts also contained plastic and rubber which melted from the heat of the operation.

If this still leaves any doubt in your mind of what we require, I suggest you mentally consider sectioning the different toilet goods on the market. That is our problem.

Very truly yours,

THE HALL MANUFACTURING COMPANY

JOHN TURLEY
Research Assistant Engineer
Valve Division

*   *   *   *

1. How do you size-up the situation so far?

2. Assume Mr. Winston still does not understand Mr. Turley's problem. What should he do now?

THE HALL-BARWELL LETTERS (B)

November 16, 1955

The Hall Mfg. Co.
Riverdale, Nebraska

Attention: Mr. John Turley, Research Assistant Engineer, Valve Division

DEAR MR. TURLEY:

I've gotten your letter of November 9, and I'm going to come back again and ask you once more what I thought I asked you last time. Could you take some of these things that are bothering you, i.e., valve samples, make up a package and send it to us?

If so, when we get it I can assure you that the best people in our organization will go to work on figuring out ways to cut it. Having tried it, we can tell you what we can do. I have found an abrasive tool a most ineffective instrument when used to cut through verbal description of things that I can't visualize.

On the other hand, abrasives have proved themselves to be efficient cutting devices when applied to specific situations.

Could you get some material together that is perhaps not acceptable as to performance, etc., that we could put one of our saw cutting specialists on? Any information we get we'll be more than happy to send you. In the meantime, I just don't know what to do next except cut.

Sincerely,

BARWELL MFG. CO.

T. J. WINSTON

December 12, 1955

Barwell Mfg. Co.
Madison, Wisconsin

Attention: Mr. T. J. Winston

GENTLEMEN:

I am very sorry not to have answered your request for samples sooner. An emergency leave of two weeks set me behind in my work.

I am sending to you, under separate cover, two samples of aerosol containers with valves attached which we would like to section. These are, in our opinion, the two most difficult in our line of products. What we would like to do is take a quarter section out of the valve and container, thereby exposing the working parts for observation purposes.

The exact shape of the cut is important only insofar as it exposes the inner works without disturbing their relative positions. It is not necessary to section the container all the way to the bottom. One of the containers is ordinary metal such as used in common canned goods. The bottle is glass with a thin plastic coating on the outside.

As a word of caution, the valves contain rubber and plastic components which will melt and distort at high temperatures.

A few valve assemblies are being sent to you with the containers. The internal parts are the same for both types, the only difference is in the metal cup containing the valve.

Very truly yours,

THE HALL MFG. CO.

JOHN TURLEY
Research Assistant Engineer
Valve Division

THE HALL-BARWELL LETTERS (C)

February 3, 1956

The Hall Manufacturing Co.
Riverdale, Nebraska

Attention: Mr. John Turley, Research Engineer, Valve Division

DEAR MR. TURLEY:

Thank you very much for your letter of December 12th and the several samples of aerosol containers and valve assemblies.

We have done quite a bit of experimenting, trying different procedures in cutting your units to expose the working parts for observation. Frankly, we have run into the problems you mentioned in your letter. Although, our cutting temperatures are relatively low, there were definite signs of fusing of the rubber and plastic parts.

Also, it was impossible to obtain a clean cut at the center of the valve where the assembled parts are rather small.

However, our experiments may be of some help to you since a definite possibility occurred to us. There are several companies manufacturing small air or electric high speed hand tools. These tools are used for model and intricate die work. Attachments for these high speed rotating tools include very small abrasive wheels and toothed metal blades. These wheels and blades are approximately 1″ in diameter. Because they run at such high speeds it is quite possible that such a tool could be used in sectioning your containers.

I believe you can obtain information on these hand tools from any hobby shop and I personally have such a unit which was purchased from Sears, Roebuck and Co.

I hope that some of our experiments have been of some help to you even though our standard equipment does not fit the application. Perhaps a hand tool as described above will be an answer.

We wish to thank you for your interest and hope that in the future a Barwell cutoff machine will fit better into your cutting work.

Sincerely,

BARWELL MFG. CO.

FRED KROVINE[14]

NEGRO-WHITE DIFFERENCES[15]

In connection with the qualitative characteristics of the brain, the

---

[14] A Barwell salesman who specialized in saws.

[15] From chap. ii, "Ethnic Differences," *Social Psychology,* by Otto Klineberg (New York: Henry Holt & Co., 1954). Reprinted by permission.

early investigations of Bean[16] have focused attention upon possible Negro-White differences. In a series of studies Bean arrived at the conclusion that the frontal area of the brain was less well-developed in the Negro than in the White, and the posterior area better developed. He believed that this difference paralleled the "known fact" that the Negro is inferior in the higher intellectual functions and superior in those concerned with rhythm and sense perception. Another important difference was in the depth of the convolutions of the cortex, those of the Negro being much shallower and more "childlike" than those of the White. There were also differences in the shape of the corpus callosum, which connects the two hemispheres of the cerebrum, and in the temporal lobe, but these were not regarded as having any direct psychological significance. It happened that these studies were carried out at Johns Hopkins University under the direction of Professor Mall, head of the Department of Anatomy. Mall was for some reason uncertain of Bean's results, and he repeated the whole study[17] on the same collection of brains on which Bean had worked; he took the precaution, however, of comparing the brains without knowing in advance which were Negro and which were White. When he and his associates placed in one group those brains which had rich convolutions, and in another those with convolutions which were shallow, they found exactly the same proportions of Negro and White brains in the two groups. When further they measured the size of the frontal and posterior lobes in the two groups of brains, they found no difference in their relative extent. As a consequence Mall came to the conclusion that Bean's findings had no basis in fact, and that it had not been demonstrated that Negro brains differed in any essential manner from those of Whites.

PROFITS—THE IMPORTANCE OF HOW MUCH[18]

How much does the boss make? To the boss, that has long been an understandably important question. But in the postwar fight over wages, another important question has bobbed up: how much do the

---

[16] R. B. Bean, "Some Racial Peculiarities of the Negro Brain," *American Journal of Anatomy*, Vol. V (1906), pp. 353–432.

[17] F. P. Mall, "On Several Anatomical Characters of the Human Brain," *American Journal of Anatomy*, Vol. IX (1909), pp. 1–32.

[18] *Time*, August 26, 1946. Courtesy *Time*, copyright Time, Inc., 1946.

workers think the boss (i.e., the "proprietors," the managers, and the stockholders) makes?

To find the answer, the Los Angeles Merchants and Manufacturers Association recently hired a professional pollster to ask a cross-section of Los Angeles residents. Of some 1,000 who were interviewed, more than half thought the employers must get around 50¢ out of every incoming dollar. Almost a third thought they got upwards of 75¢. Barely one tenth of them were reasonably close to the nationwide average: 9½¢ out of every dollar (according to the latest figures—September 1945—of the Department of Commerce).

In its current monthly bulletin, the Guaranty Trust Co. of New York deplores these "shocking misconceptions," and management's failure to do anything about them. Said the *Guaranty Survey:* "The effects of industrial unrest are tragic enough in any case, but they are doubly tragic if they arise from such profound misconceptions as these. . . ."

MAKING GLAMOR SELL GLAMOR[19]

At a fashion show in Houston, Texas, not long ago, the commentator matter-of-factly began her pitch: "Gown by Ceil Chapman, body by Slenderella."

Six years ago, nobody would have known what she was talking about. Today, thousands of women know. Last year they haunted Slenderella reducing salons to gross more than $12-million (at $2 a throw) for Slenderella International, founded and headed by Lawrence L. Mack, 38, of Stamford, Connecticut.

Mack is living evidence that in a plush economy, the sizzle counts for more than the steak. If the steak is rather thin, the sizzle gains importance. What Slenderella offers is more a state of mind than a product. . . .

His sales objective has been twofold: To take the curse off the unsavory reputation that some reducing concerns had earned in the past, and to build up a steady flow of repeat customers. To do this, Mack called into play every psychological tactic in his book.

His pitch is to underplay the reducing angle. "We are in the figure proportioning business, not reducing," he says. He isn't much inter-

---

19 *Business Week,* August 11, 1956. Reprinted by permission.

ested in the woman who has become grossly overweight; "She needs a doctor," he says. "We sell dress sizes. If a woman once wore a size 10 or 12, and now needs a 14, that's the lady we like to help."

The typical Slenderella patron, he says, is pretty intelligent; she's in her 30s, with a child or so; she's about 15 lbs. overweight; she once had a good figure and is smart enough to want it back.

Three Ply—The "treatment" consists of three items. Key to it is a muscle-toning table, developed, Mack says, at a Midwestern university. Then there's diet—Slenderella prefers to call it a "menu," which the company is smart enough to require the client's own doctor's O.K. on. The doctor invariably approves it, says Mack, because it's a good basic diet, high in protein, low in carbohydrates.

The third ingredient is a mint wafer to provide minerals and vitamins. On these again Mack calls psychology into play. The patron is asked to eat one mint five times a day. The dose could just as well have been one wafer, five times more potent. But the repetitions serve to keep the woman's mind on her job.

Aura of Respectability—Obviously, there's nothing here that a woman couldn't do on her own if she would. How, then, do you parlay a mechanical table, a menu, and some mint tablets into a business that is expected to gross $20-million this year?

With the cardinal need of establishing an aura of social respectability, Slenderella salons themselves are a show-case. The decor is tasteful, the lighting subtle; Muzak lulls the client. Mack still places stress on the fact that the system involves no personal massaging, that the customer gets her passive exercise fully clothed. . . .

THE STAR SPANGLED BANNER[20]
By Alma Johnson Sarett

On a Saturday evening in December, 1941, shortly after Pearl Harbor, I had a dinner date with another graduate student. We went to a restaurant which had a small dance floor at the end of the room farthest from the entrance and which employed a small orchestra on week-ends. We sat at a table next to the dance floor.

During an intermission three young men in Navy uniforms, who occupied a table near us and who had each downed several drinks from

---

20 Printed by permission.

the bar since our arrival, went out on the dance floor and began an impromptu floor show. Their horseplay included several apparently unintentional sprawls on the floor and the "emcee's" speech came out as "Laszh'n'szhen'lemen," etc. Suddenly one of them seized a trumpet from the deserted orchestra stall and began playing a wavering but recognizable version of "The Star Spangled Banner." With his two companions following, he began a stumbling parade up and down the dance floor. By the time the trumpeter had reached the second or third bar of the anthem, everybody in the restaurant had risen to his feet— except my escort. When I realized that he had remained seated, I sank back down into my own chair. One of the men in uniform stopped, looked at us, and called "Shtan' up! Shtan' up!" but we remained silent and seated. After they had returned to their table, my escort said, "I will not take part in dishonoring a symbol of my country." Shortly afterward, we rose to leave. As we made our way the length of the room to the door, it seemed to me that all talk ceased and that the eyes that followed us were filled with hostility and suspicion.

Chapter X

INTENSIONAL ORIENTATION II
("POINTING" AND "ASSOCIATING")

A DEPARTMENT-STORE manager once received a shipment of high-quality handkerchiefs and, in an experimental mood, placed half of them in a pile at one end of a sales counter with a sign: "Fine Irish Linen— 50¢ Each." He stacked the other half at the opposite end of the counter with a sign: "Nose Rags—3 for 25¢." The "Irish Linens" outsold the "nose rags" five to one!

A delicatessen operator performed somewhat the same sort of "experiment" with some first-rate cheese. He cut two large wedges from the same round and placed them in his showcase. One wedge he labeled "Imported English Cheddar," and the other, "Smelly Cheese." The former, at twice the price, far outsold the latter.

And Haldeman-Julius, publishers of the little five-cent "Blue Books," discovered years ago that changing titles may have a salutary effect on sales:

Title	No. of Copies Sold*
Markheim	100
Markheim's Murder	7,000
The Mystery of the Iron Mask	100
The Mystery of the Man in the Iron Mask	11,000
The Art of Controversy	100
How to Argue Logically	30,000
Fleece of Gold	6,000
Quest for a Blond Mistress	50,000

* During equal periods of time.

It is obvious that the way we react to the *words* by which things are called can affect very considerably the way we react to the *things* themselves. You will recall from Chapter II that the students in Dr. Lee's classes responded quite differently to the foods they were eating *after* they were told that the foods were "dog biscuits" and "grasshopper cookies."

One way of understanding how our response to words can affect our evaluations of things is to recognize the versatility of language use. Among other uses we employ and react to words as *pointers* which call attention to something. We use and react to them also as *evokers* of associations.

Suppose you and I are riding through the country and I see a small pool of water and say, "Look at that swimming hole over there." My words may serve the purpose of a pointing finger and call your attention to the pool that you might otherwise have missed.

But if you happen to associate certain memories, experiences, and feelings, pleasant or otherwise, with the phrase "swimming hole," then it is entirely possible that my words would "stir" you up a bit. Moreover, they might suggest to you a great deal beyond the physical pool to which I was referring.

For convenience, we will use the terms *pointing* and *associating*, respectively, to represent these two functions of language. However, we must guard against the artificial dichotomy that words are used *either* as pointers *or* as associators. They are ordinarily used and reacted to as both. The situation is a case of double contraries.

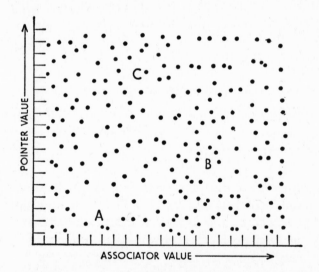

Take the term "sulfuric acid." For A, who has never studied chemistry and is not especially acquainted with the words in any other context, the term may have little pointer or associator value; for B, whose face was once badly burned when somoene threw sulfuric acid at him, the words might usually have great associator value but perhaps comparatively little pointer value; C, a chemist, may ordinarily use and react to the term with largely pointer value and practically no associator value; etc.

Theoretically, depending upon the individual, time, place, verbal context, and other circumstances, one may use or react to a given word or phrase with values anywhere along the infinitely graded double continua.

Even though our terms *pointers* and *associators* imply a fallacious polarization, they provide a useful distinction for describing and coping with serious patterns of miscommunication. I shall henceforth use the words in quotes to remind the reader of the multivalued and interrelated sense in which I am intending them. Let the quotation marks remind us also that *people* (not words) do the "pointing" and "associating" with words.[1]

It is clear, then, that when people "send" and "receive" them, words may have many functions; "pointing" and "associating" are prominent among them. The crux of this chapter, then, is that, *when communicators forget or are unaware that both "pointing" and "associating" are usually involved in communication, confusion, misunderstanding, and other kinds of trouble may not be long in coming.*

The failure to recognize the "pointing-associating duality" of language may lead to several patterns of miscommunication. Three prevalent and troublesome forms are the *"pointing-associating"* confusion, *"name-calling,"* and *"associative" by-passing.*

THE "POINTING-ASSOCIATING" CONFUSION

The most common experience of deluding ourselves with words occurs when we confuse the "associating" and "pointing" functions. We often react to the associations evoked in us by the label *as if* we were reacting to what the label was "pointing" to—the object itself. Most Americans shudder at the prospect of eating rattle-snake meat or snails or bumblebees. Is it because they dislike the taste? Hardly, for most have never eaten these foods, which, incidentally, are regarded as delicacies by some people. It is obvious that they are reacting not to the foods themselves but to their *names* and to the associations they make with the names. Consider whether you would not be somewhat more favorably disposed toward a "sirloin steak" than toward a slice of "dead cow," even though both labels "point" to the same piece of meat.

---

[1] The reader has probably assumed that I am deliberately refraining from using the words *denotations* and *connotations*. These terms have come to suggest so strongly a polarized view of language use that it seemed advisable to avoid them.

Euphemisms and Malphemisms

To *euphemize* is to substitute an inoffensive, mild, or pleasant "associator" for one which may produce an opposite reaction. When one euphemizes, he figuratively "puts a good face" on something. Calling a liquor store a "package store" does not change the store, its contents, or its function, but it may soften the *impression* for many. The *malphemism,* if I may be permitted a coinage, is the counterpart of euphemism. It puts a "bad face" on the thing. Calling the same establishment a "booze store" still doesn't change the store, but it may change the way some people feel about it.

There are many occasions when euphemisms or malphemisms, used judiciously, may serve good purposes—or at least expedient ones. When consoling a friend who has just lost someone near, you would almost certainly use "passed away" rather than "croaked" or "kicked the bucket." And surely it is kinder to refer to a thin woman as "on the slender side" than as "skinny" or "spindly." More appealing titles for people's jobs, as one wit pointed out, may also have their value:

Yesterday	Today	Tomorrow*
Typewriter	Stenographer	Visual transcriptionist
Bookkeeper	Comptroller	Tax avoidance researcher
Garbage man	Sanitary engineer	Excess materials manager
Telephone girl	Switchboard operator	Audio connection supervisor
Head clerk	Office manager	Coffee break coordinator

---

* Harold Coffin, from "Look on the Lighter Side," ed. Gurney Williams, *Look,* August 21, 1956, p. 116. Reprinted by permission of the author and *Look* magazine.

On the other hand, a man running for election might not be reluctant to use malphemisms in describing his determined, liberal, intellectual opponent as "that stubborn, radical, egg-head." Your children and mine may be equally energetic, but if I don't happen to like you, I may prefer to describe yours as "wild" and my own as "active." Your wife may be a "gabby gossip," but mine is an "enthusiastic conversationalist." And, while my home may have that "lived-in look," yours is just "shabby."

One of the most acute dangers of euphemisms-malphemisms and, in general, of reacting to "associators" as if they were "pointers" is that we tend to lose sight of the "things" being represented. We become so mesmerized by the *name* that the "thing" becomes obscured. On some campuses the *name* of one's sorority or fraternity apparently looms very large in extracurricular matters. Fraternity men have told me that the dating of sorority women of other than the "better" houses is frowned upon by their brothers. Ironically, the "Eta Byta Pi" label on a girl sometimes seems a more important criterion for date selection than the unique characteristics and traits of the girl herself. But is this behavior less rational than voting a straight party ballot without any apparent concern for the qualifications of the individual candidates? Speaking of politics, have you heard of the Democratic nomination for treasurer in a Michigan county a few years ago? Democrats discovered that they had nominated a T. Edward Aho, fifty-two, an inmate of a state mental hospital! Aho, an unemployed worker, was not prominent in the county, but his Finnish name had vote appeal among the Finnish voters!

There are many who readily capitalize upon our tendency to react to "associators" as if they were "pointers." You would find some of the most skillful of them writing advertising copy. With deft pens poised, these word-magicians sift through hundreds of words to find the term or phrase most likely to elicit quickly the desired response to their products. They overlook few possibilities for word appeal. In the automobile industry, for example, even the car's colors are verbally glamorized. It is no longer possible to buy a "black" or a "red" or a "green" or a "blue" auto. But you can get one in "Onyx Black," "Carnival Red," "Fern Mist Green," or "Regatta Blue." My personal prize goes to the inventor of the name for a certain yellow color that one manufacturer used a few years ago. To me, at least, the color was a bilious gray-yellow, reminiscent of dusty mustard. Its name—the stroke of a master—was "Sunglo!"

Classified advertisers are generally not as adept as their distant cousins in the agencies, but they too contrive studiously to find the "right word." The favorite terms for describing a house for sale, according to a survey of 8,000 ads in eight major United States daily newspapers, are "cute," "a cutie," "adorable," "exquisite," "elegant," "a dandy," "magnificent," "glamorous," "spic and span," "clean as a pin," "a rare find," and a "real bargain." A farm was seldom a "farm" but a "rural hideaway," a "rustic retreat," or a "secluded estate." There were few "jobs" in the Help Wanted columns, but "openings" and "positions" were plentiful. A lost dog was frequently the "pet of an invalid grandmother" or belonged to a "heartbroken little girl." Dogs for sale were advertised variously as "love that money can't buy," "darlings," "cuddlies," and "swell pets." Possibly the most refined touch of all was the term for a bitch with a litter of pups—she was listed as a "matron."

Even the farmer who was busily building an unusual structure on his "east forty" had a flair for "associators." "What's it going to be?" asked a neighbor. "It all depends," was the reply. "If I rent it, it's a pastoral lodge—if I don't, it's a cowshed." And if you happen to write restaurant menus, you had better watch your "associators," for they determine to some extent how much you can charge for the food.

IT ALL DEPENDS ON WHERE YOU EAT*

Hamburger $0.50
Salisbury Steak 1.00
Chopped Tenderloin Steak 1.50
Charcoal-Broiled Chopped Tenderloin Steak 2.50
Prime Tenderloin Steak, Charcoal Grilled (Chopped) 3.50
Du Bœuf Haché Grillé au Charbon de Bois 4.50

---

* Carl H. Nilson, from "Look on the Light Side," ed. Gurney Williams, *Look*, July 10, 1956, p. 83. Reprinted by permission of the author and *Look* magazine.

"NAME-CALLING"

There is a species of the "pointing-associating" confusion which merits special attention. It concerns the "associating" labels which people apply to one another and to themselves. The "names" we call others or by which we are called can profoundly influence our evaluations and behavior.

The Double Burden

The child's retaliation, "Sticks and stones may break my bones, but names can never hurt me," is unfortunately only half correct. Names *can* hurt us, even more grievously, on occasion, than "sticks and stones."

Consider the youngster who survives polio with a withered leg. The physical pain of walking and the psychic pain of watching other children run may be as nothing compared with the burden of a thoughtlessly imposed nickname such as "Limpy" or "Gimpy." Or consider the youngster scarred by acne. His disfigured face is a sufficient trial, but a label such as "Scarface" may well double his burden.

Adults are not, of course, exempt from carrying a double burden. A psychologist who serves as an employee counselor with a manufacturing firm recently described the case of a young, intelligent, and attractive stenographer who came to him for help. Until recently she had been considered by her supervisor to be a superior worker, but during the last few months she had grown nervous and irritable. Her work began to deteriorate, and her supervisor finally recommended that she speak with the counselor. He learned that the young woman had been divorced three years previously but seemed to have made a satisfactory adjustment. In recent months, however, her social life was more than she could bear. Breaking down, she sobbed: "I've dated four men in the last year, and in each case things were going fine until my boyfriend found out I had been married. Two of them dropped me like a hot potato, and the other two began taking such liberties that I had to drop them. Why don't men give divorcees a chance to start over? Look, I'm decent and I intend to stay that way but they make it pretty rough."

Living Up to the Labels

This young woman is resisting her "name," but this is not always the case. People, often unconsciously, tend to *live up to their labels*. I shall never forget an experience in a group dynamic course in college. There were about twenty in the class, and we met twice weekly in two-hour discussion sessions. Our basic purpose was to study group dynamics by observing the dynamics of our own group. Along about the sixth week, one member of the group made a statement to this effect: "It has occurred to me that certain people in this group tend to play certain roles. I have noticed that whenever someone is being picked on, Kathy will step in to defend him—she's sort of a protector of the underdog. And when we begin to argue and the tension begins to build, have you noticed that it's often Bill who tries to relax us with a comical remark? And Don usually backs anyone who wants a change—he's 'Mr. Progressive!' " He continued to categorize three or four other members. The group responded with some chaffing of the "underdog protector," "the jokester," etc., and the subject was forgotten—apparently. But, as the weeks went on, it became obvious that some of those labeled were increasingly portraying their "roles"! Kathy was defending underdogs more vehemently than ever; Bill was joking more than ever—even when there were no tensions to be broken, etc.

Unhappily, living up to one's labels can have far graver consequences:

I got a reputation as the town's bad girl. Sure, I did some of the things they said I did. But not until I had been blamed for a lot of things not my fault. After that I didn't care.[2]

The double burden has become so oppressive for adolescents in trouble that authorities have been moved to speak out against such incriminating labels as "juvenile delinquent." Joseph Lohman, sociologist and, for four years, sheriff of Cook County, Illinois, has said: "The name juvenile delinquent . . . sets the young person apart and

---

[2] Penny Gaielyrd (psuedonym) as told to Norma Lee Browning, "Story of a Bad Girl," *Chicago Tribune Magazine*, September 19, 1954, pp. 18 ff.

may motivate further misbehavior." Mrs. Newton P. Leonard, president of the National Congress of Parents and Teachers (PTA), a few years ago, exhorted her nearly nine million members to discard the label. "Juvenile delinquents, so-called, are children in trouble, children in conflict—with the law, with society, with themselves," she said. "The last thing they need is to be branded with a dehumanizing label and a matching set of attitudes from members of the community."

Living Down the Labels

Living *up* to one's labels may result in quite irrational and tragic behavior, but the consequences of living them *down* can be equally foolish and dangerous. For instance, a Claremont, California, youth became so embarrassed when he failed his driver's license test that, to prove himself to his ridiculing friends, he stole a car and drove it—to Philadelphia! But, for a more poignant example, consider the case of a seventeen-year-old who stabbed a fourteen-year-old boy to death. A typical attack-by-bully incident? If one were to look behind the glaring headlines, he would find a very different kind of explanation. He would discover the story of a life in torment—the story of a boy pathetically small for his age, frail since infancy, a boy prevented by malnutrition from entering school until he was eight, a boy now seventeen who weighed only ninety pounds and stood four feet eleven in his shoes. One could see the image of a lad taunted by his playmates with the stinging labels of "Half-pint," "Short-stuff," and "Flyweight."

Pink-cheeked Adrian Konecki, 17, twirled in the witness chair today as he told a jury in Judge Pope's court how he stabbed a friend to death after being called a "runt."

Adrian weighs 90 pounds and his victim, Michael Bucsko, 8600 Houston Av., though three years younger weighed 140. . . .

On the fateful day, the boy said, he went to church, then sought out friends in a bowling alley, then started home and encountered "Mickey" Bucsko and Thomas Karczewski, 14, (5 feet 11, 135 pounds). . . .

"They said they'd been drinking and using toothpaste to cover it up. Mickey sneered, 'You can't drink, you runt! I said, 'Say that again.' He did, and asked, 'You wanta make something out of it?'

"I said 'Yes' and slapped him. Mickey started for me and Tommy went to the side. I backed up and pulled my knife."

The weapon was a three-inch switchblade knife which Adrian said he found in a vacant lot and used to open boxes in the grocery store where he works.

He went on: "They were bigger than me and I thought they were gonna jump me and beat me up. I hadda use something to protect myself. He kept coming and I stabbed him."

His feet swinging clear of the floor, Adrian kept staring at the jurors with interest but without emotion. His face clouded as he suddenly recalled his tormentors also had called him an imp, a weasel, and "wimpy."[3]

Positive Labels

These sobering illustrations of the possible consequences of living up to or of living down one's labels are not intended as evidence that such behavior is *necessarily* negative and destructive in its effect. On the contrary, labels may sometimes have definite positive influence. I am firmly convinced that a fair share of the "good" in people is derived from the "good" that was *expected* of them as children. Many a child, I am confident, has become an honest, responsible, generous adult partly, if not largely, because others, notably his parents, teachers, and playmates, *expected* such qualities of him and *communicated* their anticipations to him. By making clear to a child that you know he is truthful and that you genuinely trust him, you are implicitly, if not explicitly, labeling him as a "truth-teller," and chances are that he will live up to the label.

But even positive labels may be dangerous. Unrealistic positive labels may entice one to overreach his capabilities and thus lead to disillusionment and tragedy. Consider the case of the young man described in the *polarization* chapter, who, on the eve of his high-school graduation, was found hanged in his attic. An outstanding personality, the boy had been president of his class, active in school affairs. He had just been accepted for enrollment by one of the nation's leading universities and had been given a new convertible by his proud parents. What could conceivably have driven him to suicide? Authorities uncovered a probable reason: He had missed being elected to the National Honor Society by a fraction of a point. His self-image (his self-labels, if you will) and this overwhelming "failure" were evidently irreconcilably polarized in his tortured mind.

"ASSOCIATIVE" BY-PASSING

The "pointing-associating duality" of language offers still another possibility for communication difficulty. An earlier chapter described *by-passing* as the miscommunication pattern whereby people miss one another with their meanings. We were concerned with words which were being used and reacted to as primarily "pointers." It is now perti-

---

[3] Elgar Brown, "Boy Tells Jurors He 'Had to Kill,'" *Chicago American*, September 19, 1957, p. 5. Reprinted by permission.

nent to discuss the tendency of people to miss one another's *"associative"* meanings.

"Associative" By-Passing Becomes Possible

1. When the sender (speaker, writer, etc.) assumes that, because he intends his words as merely "pointers," they will necessarily have little or no "associative" value for his receiver (listener, reader, etc.):

In the earlier years of commercial aviation a stewardess would warn her passengers: "We're flying through a *storm*. You had better fasten your *safety* belts; it will be less *dangerous*." She might have intended nothing more than merely "pointing" with her words, but you may be sure the novice passengers "associated" a great deal more. Today, stewardesses are trained to elicit pleasant and secure associations with: "We're flying through some *turbulence* now, and if you fasten your *seat* belts you will be more *comfortable*."

2. When the receiver interprets words as largely or solely "pointers," whereas the sender intended them to be "associative":

If you have ever complained: "Oh! You take things so literally," you have probably been involved in this sort of *"associative" by-passing*. It is the pathetic miscommunication which occurs when the young lady vainly tries to encourage her shy date with "Johnny, I'm cold." Whereupon her gallant escort whips off his jacket and slips it around her shoulders. She had wanted the jacket, all right, but with Johnny's arms still in the sleeves!

This is the pattern, too, of sarcasm which fails. A sales manager was busily preparing for a trip which was to take him away from the office for the day. He called his filing clerk, pointed to a small pile of correspondence, and instructed: "Please file these letters." And, hoping to jar her from her usual lethargy, he added wryly: "Be sure to take all day with the job!" She did.

3. When the communicator (sender or receiver or both) assumes that words have the *same* "associative" value for the other fellow as they have for him:

Illustrative is the case of the hospital patient who was awaiting major surgery. He was toying with breakfast as he worried about the operation. Suddenly a nurse appeared at his door, noticed the barely touched food, and said: "Better eat—*while you can!*" The poor man immediately assumed the worst. But the nurse had only meant to imply that the food service attendant would soon pick up the breakfast tray!

A POSSIBLE MISUNDERSTANDING

If in discussing these particular pitfalls of language I have given the impression that "associators" are "bad" or that they are to be avoided or abolished, I have not intended to. In the first place, "associating" is not a "thing" which can be destroyed. It is a function of words, and it has no existence apart from *people* using and reacting to words. As long as people have "imaginations," as long as they have the agility to leap beyond the immediate objects of their senses, there will be "associating." And let us be everlastingly grateful for it. The world would be unbearably prosaic without humor (an enormous portion of which is based upon association) and without poetry, drama—literature, in general—which is designed to elicit rich associations from us. "I love you" (among the most highly "associative" phrases in our culture) would be just so many flat, commonplace words if the sender and receiver were not able to transport themselves beyond mere "pointers."

No, this chapter has not been calculated to annihilate "associators" (even if it were possible). And certainly there has been no intention of debasing or minimizing their value and usefulness. On the other hand, it is clear that there are occasions when it is important, even imperative, to be *aware* of when "associators" are being used and to know how to cope with them. It is for these purposes that the following corrective measures are offered.

CORRECTIVES

It is the major thesis of this chapter that words can be used and reacted to both as "pointers" and as "associators." When communicators forget, ignore, deny, or, for any reason, are unaware of this "duality," patterns of miscommunication become possible which may lead to confusion and trouble. Among these patterns are the *"pointing-associating"* confusion, *"name-calling,"* and *"associative"* by-passing. The suggestions which follow should be helpful in recognizing and dealing with these patterns.

The "Pointing-Associating" Confusion

Make a Habit of Distinguishing between Labels and "Things." Living and communicating with labels as we do, we are frequently enticed to accept them as the "things" they represent. Communicators must be wary of reacting to labels as if they were more than representations (and often misleading representations, at that). In this vein, give Mrs. Haney credit for a sensible adjustment to what had been a distinctly distasteful task for her. As a child it was occasionally her lot to fish the potato peelings, carrot scrapings, and assorted remains from the dinner dishes out of the sink. This was referred to in the family as "cleaning out the garbage," a chore (and phrase) which distressed her to the point of nausea. At Girl Scout camp a year or so later, she gained an insight. There the girls were instructed to scrape the "left-over food" off their plates. On returning home, she discovered she could remove the "garbage" from the sink with scarcely a qualm so long as she reminded herself that it was "left-over food" she was touching.

Remember, the map is *not* the territory; words are *not* that which they are being used to represent. Ask yourself: "Am I responding to the *object* or to the *association* I have for its *name?*"

Don't Permit the Label to Obscure the "Product." Develop the extensional habit of looking "behind" labels to see the "product" more clearly. Manufacturers who assume that consumers usually look beyond the labels have been known to "have their fingers burned." Several years ago a new chocolate dessert topping came on the market. The product was tasty and inexpensive, but many customers adamantly refused to try it, apparently because they were unable or unwilling to look beyond its rather descriptive name—"Goop!"

Some companies, however, learn the lesson less painfully. "Mrs. Japp's Potato Chips" had been distributed throughout greater Chicago for sometime before World War II. But shortly after Pearl Harbor sales began to sag. It didn't take Mrs. Japp (a Danish name) long to find the answer and change the name to "Jay's Potato Chips." The product has prospered ever since.

It came as no great surprise to the sports world that the National League Cincinnati Baseball Club in the era of congressional investigations of Communists changed its name from "Reds" to "Redlegs." This, incidentally, was the same word-wise organization which felt "bleachers" was a somewhat unattractive name for its uncovered stands. Since 1954 the stands have been known as the "Sun-Deck," and its patrons are permitted to wear beach costumes!

Another convincing illustration of the role that a label plays in the acceptance of its product occurred several years ago when Hopalong Cassidy was riding into fame and fortune on millions of television screens. It happened at the time that a certain Boston restaurant, catering to families, was featuring a children's-size meat potpie. But the kids were recalcitrantly uninterested until a bright young assistant manager clapped a new label on the potpies. With the menu featuring the "Hopalong Casserole," the kitchen was unable to keep up with the demand!

"Name-Calling"

The basic advice is to recognize "names" for what they are—merely tags, often inaccurate, and always incomplete representations of the flesh-and-blood persons to whom they are appended. Remember that the labels in themselves are utterly powerless and meaningless. It is our *reactions* to the labels of others (and to our own) that can have profound effects on our evaluations and behavior. It is incredibly easy for those who do the labeling and for those who are labeled to assume that the labels are valid and complete.

More specifically, if the labels assigned to you are negative and unfavorable, refuse to live up to them, to resign yourself to them. Resist them, contradict them with your behavior (actions are usually more convincing than words). But, on the other hand, avoid overreacting to them and assuming a manner or characteristic which is equally or more objectionable than the trait originally labeled. If your labels are positive, recognize that they may serve as a beneficial stimulant, but be wary of overreaching your capacities.

If you are doing the labeling, if label you must, be careful in your selection of "tags." Negative labels are seldom useful and often dangerous, while positive labels are often, but not invariably, beneficial. If you want someone to be honest, let *him* know you trust him.

"Associative" By-Passing

"Associative" by-passing occurs when communicators miss one another with their "associative" meanings. As such, "associative" by-passing is similar to by-passing (the missing of "pointer" meanings), and the reader is encouraged to review the correctives section in the by-passing chapter.

But, in addition, remember:

1. Words to which you "associate" little or nothing may be highly "associative" for the other person:

Labor contract negotiators have learned to be alert to some of the "red-flag" words which upset the other party. In meeting with company representatives, union negotiators, for example, refrain from mentioning the union "demand" and substitute union "proposal" when softer associations seem in order. They find, too, that discussions with management in terms of what "your employees want" rather than what "the union (or 'we') wants" are often carried on with more equanimity and objectivity.

2. Words "associating" a great deal to you may "associate" little or nothing to the other person—they may merely *"point"* for him:

Before making his final decision on a proposal to move to new offices, the head of a large company, called his top executives for a last discussion of the idea. All were enthusiastic except the company treasurer who insisted that he had not had time to calculate all the costs with accuracy sufficient to satisfy himself that the move was advantageous. Annoyed by his persistence, the chief finally burst out:

"All right, Jim, all right! Figure it out to the last cent. A penny saved is a penny earned, right?"

The intention was ironic. He meant not what the words denoted but the opposite—forget this and stop being petty. For him this was what his words connoted.

For the treasurer "penny saved, penny earned" meant exactly what it said. He put several members on his staff to work on the problem and, to test the firmness of the price, had one of them interview the agent renting the proposed new quarters without explaining whom he represented. This indication of additional interest in the premises led the agent to raise the rent. Not until the lease was signed, did the agency chief discover that one of his own employes had, in effect, bid up its price.[4]

3. Your receiver (or sender) may not be "associating" with his words as you are:

Employed by a tool and die works, a young engineer was assigned to study the plant's production procedures in general and to devise improvements. Tool and die men are the aristocracy of factory workers, and their foremen are of correspondingly high standing. The engineer was aware of this and took great care to show respect.

When he found one department where he thought he could make considerable improvement, he first set about making friends with the workmen and their foreman. Once he had gained their acceptance he got the foreman to call the men together so that he could outline his plans to the whole group. Because he thought that several of the men might resist change, he sought to allay their fears by saying:

"Of course, at this stage what I'm proposing is only an experiment." ...

The men not only dragged their heels but actively sabotaged his attempted innovations. Finally, the foreman went to the production manager. The gist of his complaint was that the engineer was trying to use him and his men as "guinea pigs."

You may be tempted to dismiss this as an unthinking reaction on the part of the men. But it was the engineer who sought to communicate something to them, not they to him. He wanted to make them feel that he was proposing only tentative changes which would not become permanent unless they proved successful.[5]

---

[4] From Robert Froman, "Make Words Fit the Job," *Nation's Business*, July, 1959, p. 78. Reprinted by permission.

[5] *Ibid.*, pp. 76–77.

INCIDENTS

GALVANIZED SHEETS[6]

From 1940 to 1953 the manufacturers of galvanized sheeting were experimenting with new methods of galvanization. The object was to develop a process which would be quick, inexpensive and yet would coat sheeting in such a manner that it could be bent sharply without the galvanizing peeling off. One company finally developed a process which met these qualifications.

Their method was to manufacture sheeting in a continuous roll in order that it could be galvanized as it rolled through the galvanizing pit. The sheeting was then cut to specifications.

The company felt it had a superior product but decided upon a marketing test as a precautionary measure. A few salesmen in certain pilot territories were instructed to begin selling the new products to their customers, i.e., sheet metal shops, ventilating firms, etc. Since no trade name had as yet been selected, the salesmen were told to refer to the new product as "continuous roll galvanized sheets."

Customer reaction ranged from apathy to resistance. The salesmen returned to the plant and complained that the average customer had a firm conviction that the "rolling process"[7] would flatten out the galvanizing to the point that it would be too thin to withstand severe bends without peeling.

The salesmen tried in vain to explain that the "continuous roll" of their new galvanizing process didn't really involve "rolling" in the *thinning* sense at all. The reports were disturbing, but the company, convinced of the superiority of its product, decided to gamble. The continuous roll process was adopted throughout the plant. The product was trade-marked "Flex-tite" in the hope that it would offset prejudices. Production began in full swing while management crossed its fingers and waited.

Within two years it was obvious that the gamble had paid off. The company, now producing "Flex-tite" exclusively, had doubled its total sales of galvanized sheeting.

---

[6] All names have been disguised.

[7] "Rolling" in the metals industries generally referred to the process of thinning strips of metal as they passed between sets of rollers. The rollers exerted great pressure on the strips and literally squeezed them down into thinner gauges.

199

CASE OF THE GROWING BOY[8]

Even in maturity, long-leggey (6 ft. 6 in.) Clarence E. McVey, 49, a carpenter of Graham, N.C. (pop. 5,000) could not forget the misery of his schooldays. He had grown so fast that he towered above all his classmates, was so gangling and awkward that he became the butt of their jokes. He swore that his five-year-old son David, already over four feet tall, would never have to suffer from the family curse of being "too big for his age."

Just to make sure, he decided last fall to start David in school a year early, even though North Carolina law forbids pupils to enter before they are six. At first, no one was the wiser, and David became one of the best pupils in the first grade. Then one day someone told David's dreadful secret.

The teacher asked Clarence McVey to take five-year-old David out of school. McVey flatly refused. A few weeks later, the county school board made the same request, but McVey still refused. Last week, when he ignored a formal order from North Carolina's Tenth District Superior Court to keep David at home, he was hauled off to jail. Said McVey: "I'll stay here and rot before I take little David out of school." This week, there he stayed—and David stayed in school.

SEEK TO CHANGE NAME OF CICERO[9]

Cicero town officials have decided that they just can't bury Al Capone.

"He's been gone 30 years, he was here only six months and yet our town still is burdened by his reputation," said town attorney Nicholas Berkos.

To help lay the Capone legend to rest, the members of the town board will meet Monday night to hear arguments pro and con on changing the name of their town. They feel that a new name may erase the old black marks.

After the meeting, citizens of Cicero will circulate petitions to urge the name change. If more than half of the voters in the last election ap-

8 *Time*, April 9, 1951. Reprinted by permission.
9 *Chicago Sun-Times*, September 14, 1952, p. 3. Reprinted by permission.

prove it, the name will be changed after a search to discover if there are any similarly named places in the state.

Most prominently mentioned as new names for the old town are Electra—to mark the place as a center of the electrical industry—and Normandy—reminiscent of a beachhead and a brave, new start.

"We have one of the lowest crime rates in the country," Berkos said. "Juvenile deliquency here is non-existent."

"And yet a kid from Cicero can't get into a fraternity or a sorority at a college because of the town's reputation. Real estate value is held down because of the unearned bad repute."

"No politician can get elected to any job outside if he's from Cicero. People everywhere think we're just a bunch of hoods. Maybe a name change will help."

Opponents of the plan to change the town's name contend it would be a cowardly act and feel sure that they can live down the dark associ- ations with the word Cicero in time.

"We're not trying to force the thing," Berkos said. "If more than half of the people don't want to change the name, then Cicero still will be Cicero."

STICKS AND STONES . . .[10]

Despite the child's defiant jingle, names hurt more than sticks or stones: a man can more easily bear an attack on his body than an offense to his feelings, and will remember an insult long after he has forgotten an injury.

—SIDNEY HARRIS

LIVE WIRE. In Christchurch, New Zealand, haled into court on a charge of using foul language to a telephone operator, an angry sub- scriber countercharged that the girl "just laughed and laughed" after he obliged her by spelling his name: Montmorency de Villiers.

ANY OTHER NAME. In Calgary, Alta., George and Rosie Big Belly asked the Provincial Secretary what could de done for them under the provisions of "The Change of Name Act."

TYPO. In Philadelphia, when INQUIRER Columnist Frank Brookhouser reported that Hubert B. Wolfeschlegelsteinhasenberger- dorff had registered to vote in the November elections, Hubert wrote

---

10 All items except the Harris quotation are from *Time* and are reprinted with per- mission.

in indignantly to say that a "u" had been left out: his name was Wolfe-schlegelsteinhausenbergerdorff.

In Washington, Mrs. Alben Barkley told reporters that she did not like to be addressed as "The Veepess": "Somehow or other it sounds like a snake. I guess I connect it with the word viper. I'd really much rather be called Mrs. Veep."

In New Haven, Conn., Yale Graduate Student Edmund D. Looney petitioned the superior court for permission to change his name, claimed that it might interfere with the practice of his future profession—psychiatry.

TIRED OF LIVING IN SNAKE DEN. Johnston, R.I. Residents of Snake Den Rd. complained to the City Council of the "frightful" name of their street. The council ordered the name changed to "Belfield Dr."

SOUTHERN HOSPITALITY. In Birmingham, when the judge asked him what the initials stood for, Juryman W. J. Weaver recalled; "My mother and daddy had eleven daughters in a row. They decided to call me Welcome John."

THE MANATEE[11]

The flesh of the manatee is light-colored and tastes much like fresh pork. It is such excellent eating that the animal was in danger of being exterminated by the settlers and tourists. Kirk Monroe related how he had introduced a bill in the legislature in which he left out its common names and put in only the scientific one, Trichechus latirostris, a bill which made the penalty for killing one $500.00. The measure hung fire until the last day of the session. Then one senator got up and declared:

"If there is a beast with any such name as that in the State of Florida it ought to be protected." Everyone agreed with him, and the manatee became a protected animal.

THE FOUR GOALS OF LABOR[12]

Recently FORTUNE staged an informal experiment—and of a

---

11 From *The World Grows round My Door* by David Fairchild (New York: Charles Scribner's Sons, 1947), p. 64. Reprinted by permission.

12 From "Is Anybody Listening? *Fortune*, September, 1950, p. 82. Reprinted by permission.

type the reader can easily try out on his associates. A cartoon chart of "The Four Goals of Labor" was clipped from a C.I.O. newspaper and photostated. A new legend, however, was attached at the bottom: "From June 3 N.A.M. Newsletter." Twenty C.I.O. members were then shown the ad and asked if they thought it was a fair presentation of labor's goals. Four grudgingly said it was and two couldn't make up their minds. The remaining fourteen damned it as "patronizing," "loaded," "paternalistic," "makes me want to spit." . . .

NAME IT A NAME[13]

A bowling enthusiast was telling us the other day how the game happens to be played with tenpins. Seems that during the early 19th century, the popular pastime of ninepins was made illegal, probably to conserve manpower or raise the price of talcum powder or something.

Man, the ingenious, promptly added another pin, and presumably the outwitted lawmakers quit, figuring that bowling enthusiasts could add pins to the game faster than they could add amendments to the law.

Speculating upon this human capacity for solving difficulties by a new name—such as "26" instead of dice—we wondered why it has not been applied to more of the day's bitter controversies.

For instance, let the proponents of the Bricker amendment outlaw "executive agreements" entirely. Then the executive branch could make "memoranda of understanding" with foreign governments, and everybody could be happy.

For further instance, repeal the disputed Taft-Hartley law, and pass it again under the sponsorship of Sen. Green and Rep. Hope. This new Green-Hope act could recognize that maybe sometime, somewhere, a union would have to be restrained. But since such restraints are the most hated feature of the law, it could replace the rude "injunction" with "civil sanctions," and perhaps the Atomic Age would give way to that greater marvel, the Era of Labor Peace.

PRESTIGE FOODS[14]

"Prestige foods," attractively packaged fruits, fowl, meats, etc., have

---

13 *Chicago Daily News*, February 18, 1954, p. 14. Reprinted by permission.
14 All names have either been disguised or omitted.

found widespread favor as business gifts. The foods are generally of high quality and and even more highly priced. The gift is invariably accompanied by a piece of sales literature. The following were sent with a smoked pheasant and a box of apples, respectively:

SMOKE DREAMS COME TRUE

Rembrandt stewed over his canvas—a regular fuss-budget about deep, rich browns. Stradivari swooned over a violin, working for a tone of pure gold. But they weren't in it with the way *we* toil, turning out our smoked bird masterpieces.

Wild life is pampered on our rolling wooded acres. Birds are urged to gorge on the fat of the land. To the plumpest we award the great adventure of the smokehouse and the great wide world, where they make mouths water and gladden hearts.

This succulent creature is ready to eat. It's been slowly smoked over fragrant hickory embers. Lazy little plumes of smoke sealed in the sweet juices, turned the outside crackly brown. We firmly believe you can't get such happy flavor anywhere else.

This bird will keep approximately two or three weeks in the refrigerator. (Hsst! Or a year in a freezer with the wrapper left on. But who's that Spartan?)

Hints for Serving

How to Slice. With any smoked bird it's gourmet-wise (not stingy) to slice it wafer thin. That lets your lucky palate savor every delicious smoky morsel. A good sharp knife will do the trick.

Getting Het up, Whole. If—instead of eating your bird cold, just as it comes—you have a yen to try it hot, here's how. Put it in a roaster with some good strong chicken broth or consomme. Use a moderate oven and baste conscientiously.

Wonderful Canapes. Here's where a smoked bird really preens itself. Try slivers of the tender smoked meat on little squares of fresh buttered toast—goldly brown and fragrant. Top with a dab of horse radish, or better yet, our very own Dippin' Gravy.

Or mince some of the smoked meat and add to softened, well seasoned cream cheese. Spread on crisp crackers.

Or serve thin slices of smoked meat with snowy rings of Bermuda onion on rounds of buttered rye.

Or carry out your own inspirations. This bird can't *help* being delicious!

Fancied Up

Smoked Bird à la King. And we really mean regal. Use your favorite Chicken à la King recipe, substituting whatever smoked bird you're blessed with. Just before serving add a good stiff dose of Sherry or Madeira.

Smoked Bird Rarebit. Nestle slices of smoked bird between pieces of hot buttered toast. Cover with strips of brisk sharp cheese and slide under the broiler till the cheese starts to burble and run. Serve at once.

Smoked Bird and Scrambled Eggs. Mince the meat and add to slightly beaten eggs. Cook in double boiler, stirring thoughtfully.

Smoked Bird Salad. Toss some savory bird shreds in with your favorite mixed salad—crisp greens, dewy tomatoes, shivery cucumbers. Let it glisten with good French dressing and rejoice in a mite of Roquefort.

Glorious Leftovers

Never, NEVER throw out that precious carcass till it's worked magic! Would you toss out platinum? Would you discard diamonds?

'Tis wonderful—that carcass—in soup, beautiful soup. And that goes for the glittering white bones of the most greedily denuded. Try simmering that exposed frame in a kettle of Split Pea Soup. Serve in man-size soup plates, spiked with Sherry. O tempora! O mores! And the same for Black Bean or Lentil.

GREETINGS FROM
SPARKLING BROOK[15]
CALIFORNIA

DEAR EPICURE:—

These "Golden Globe" Apples were sent to you at the request of the person whose name appears on the address label.

They are grown solely by me, in a little hidden valley in the Sierra Nevada Mountains of California. Your donor is able to send them to you through having acquired a Preferred Share in the fruits of my orchard.

When I first found this valley, over twenty years ago, it was an abandoned homestead—so forlorn that folks poked fun at me, and said: "What are you going to raise, Joe—sagebrush or rabbit weed?"

But here I had found one old apple tree, with a heavy crop on it. And a native of these parts told me that every fall, for twenty-five years, he had helped himself to apples from it. "Hmm," I thought, "a natural apple spot if there ever was one."

So here I planted a dozen different kinds of apples—including a new one, recently discovered growing wild on a mountain side. And this new one turned out to be just the apple this little valley was waiting for.

Here our golden California sun gives its flesh and skin a golden tinge. Here our cold mountain nights develop its fruit sugars, and make it so crisp that every bite crackles. Here the volcanic ash in the soil gives it a tang no other apple has. And here the pure mountain springs from which its growth is watered fill it with a cider-like juice which is nature's true champagne.

---

[15] All names have been disguised.

Because this "Golden Globe" Apple is a luxury fruit which can be gotten nowhere else, apple lovers all over America now send to me for it. If, after eating these, you would like information on my various packs, and Preferred Rights to them, I will be glad to send it.

Sincerely yours,
JOE WILSON

FLIGHT FROM SCORN[16]

—A Tale of 2 Boys

Oklahoma City—(AP)—A 13-year-old Enid (Okla.) boy didn't like being called "fatty" by his schoolmates.

Five months ago, Dean Roberts weighed 105 pounds—not too hefty for his 5-foot-5 frame, but in his own mind, just a bit too chunky. He decided to reduce and practically stopped eating.

At first, his parents thought nothing of it. But when his weight dropped to 62 pounds, they took him to a hospital.

Finding no glandular trouble, doctors ordered him fed through tubes. He gained 10 pounds in five days.

Then the story came out. He had been worried about being teased.

Now he's up to 74 pounds and doctors have let him go back home for another crack at Mom's good home cooking.

Schoolmates at Maryville Academy, Des Plaines, teased Orville Culp about his eyes.

Orville, 11, has one brown eye and one blue eye.

The boys at Maryville got to calling him "old brown and blue eyes," Orville told police.

On Monday, Orville couldn't take it any longer. He ran away.

But two nights of sleeping under porches on the Near West Side were even worse than the teasing.

So Orville gave himself up Wednesday night to Warren Ave. police. He was turned over to juvenile authorities pending his return to Maryville, a home and school for dependent children.

---

16 *Chicago Daily News,* August 8, 1954, p. 10. Courtesy of Associated Press.

McCALL COLLEGE[17]

McCall College is a small eastern liberal arts college. For many years its Theatre Department had enjoyed an excellent and well-deserved reputation among the student body and faculty and among the community in which the college was located. The Theatre Department presented eight or nine plays yearly, the season beginning in October and ending in May. Each play was presented for six performances—one each night from Wednesday through Sunday and a matinee on Saturday. The average attendance over the years had been gratifyingly high, 85 per cent of capacity, ranging from 60 to 65 per cent to frequent standing-room-only audiences.

In 1958 the Theatre's director, Doug Lawson, decided that for one of the mid-season productions he would present a collection of excerpts from several plays rather than one single play. The theme was to portray the changes in theatrical production from classic Greece up to the twentieth century. He titled the production, accurately enough, *Theatre Styles Review*, and chose excerpts from Euripides' *Hippolytus*, representing the classic Greek theatre; *Everyman* (medieval morality play); Shakespeare's *Midsummer Night's Dream* (sixteenth century); Molière's *The Would-Be Gentleman* (seventeenth century); Sheridan's *School for Scandal* (eighteenth century); Stowe's *Uncle Tom's Cabin* (nineteenth-century melodrama); Ibsen's *Ghosts* (nineteenth-century realism); and Wilde's *The Importance of Being Earnest* (nineteenth-century comedy of manners).

Lawson designed the sets and carefully rehearsed the cast. After several weeks of hard work everyone from Lawson to the student curtain-puller eagerly anticipated the audience reaction.

Finally, on opening night Lawson peeked through the act curtain to "count the house." The auditorium was virtually empty! It seemed incredible. The weather was typically unpleasant for February, but audiences had turned out on much more inclement nights. No one could think of a competing attraction in town that night and yet there they were—(or weren't!)—an audience of only 20 per cent capacity!

But the show must go on—and so it did, admirably. The sparse audience thoroughly enjoyed the presentation, and Lawson, despite his disappointment with the size of the audience, was justifiably proud

---

[17] All names have been disguised.

of his company. He had rarely seen an opening night at McCall so brilliantly and flawlessly executed.

After the performance the director, cast, and crew sat down together to ponder. The only possible answer, everyone agreed, must lie in freakish chance. It just happened, someone offered, that everyone decided, for one reason or another, that he would attend on some night other than the first. But just wait, some promised bravely, we'll have over-flow crowds the rest of the week!

But there were no over-flow crowds. To be specific, the audiences ranged between 20 and 35 per cent of capacity. Lawson was stunned. Didn't people like the excerpt format? He had had good audience reactions to it on several previous occasions. Were the performances poor? Certainly his own judgment and the demonstrably appreciative, though scant, audiences precluded this as a reason. What then? Lawson called his company together and began:

As you all know we have just had the greatest attendance flop in the fifteen years I have been here. Now why? Don't tell me the audiences, what there were of them, didn't love it. And you people did marvelously. Now the purpose of this meeting is to decide what went wrong, correct it, and run the show again in May. I gambled with it once and lost but I'm just stubborn enough, and confident enough of my product, to gamble again. Now, what went wrong?

Several suggestions for minor changes in dialogue, business, and sets were made. Someone suggested that the title might be changed. Lawson invited the group to think of a better name. Some suggestions: *Lagniappe, Grease Paint Review, Sex through the Ages, Euripides Goes Wilde, 2600 Years of Grease Paint.* Finally, *Athens to Broadway* was selected, and the production was repeated during a week in May.

The attendance soared to the old standard. The audiences ranged from 70 to 85 per cent of capacity during the six performances.

Chapter XI

INTENSIONAL ORIENTATION III (BLINDERING)

A GOOD way to get the essence of this chapter under your skin is to make an earnest effort to solve this problem:

Objective: To draw through all nine of the dots.

Restrictions:

1. Start with your pencil on any one of the dots.
2. Draw four straight lines without removing your pencil from the page.
3. You may cross over lines but you may not repeat them, i.e., trace back on them.

Most people have difficulty with the problem because they unconsciously add a fourth restriction—one which renders the problem insoluble.

Did you perceive the nine dots as a *square* (left figure)?

Most people in our culture would see it as such.[1] But did you then proceed to restrict your drawing of lines to the boundaries of *your* square? Did you assume that you could not draw *beyond*?

If you did (and most of us would), you were, of course, severely hampering your progress toward a solution. Once you remove the self-imposed restriction, the solution comes easily (see right figure).

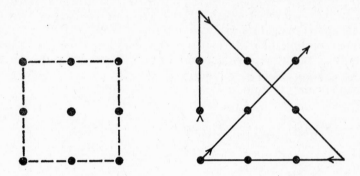

The nine-dot puzzle illustrates one of the key difficulties in problem solving—one's tendency to restrict his view of the problem.

Very clearly, one of the most important reasons why the problem solver restricts his perception of a problem grows out of his definition of the problem. (Most people define or think of the problem we just considered as that of the "nine-dot *square*.") David A. Levine, while a mathematician for the National Advisory Committee for Aeronautics at Langley Memorial Laboratories, Virginia, found that an inaccurate term for a phenomenon apparently misguided even scientists who were studying it:

I began to notice semantic flaws in certain theory. The one particular problem I was interested in at the time dealt with what is called "boundary layer theory." According to the vernacular of the science when an airfoil, like the wing of an airplane passes through the air, the air does not slip over the surface of the wing. The air right next to the wing surface sticks to the surface thus forming a layer or blanket of sluggish, slow-moving air as opposed to the swiftly flowing stream farther out from the wing. The picture this brings to mind is something like this:

---

1 There is evidence to indicate that people in some cultures fail to see such connecting lines and would see, in this case, simply an aggregate of isolated dots. See Dorothy Lee's discussion of the Trobriand Islanders' nonlineal apprehension of reality, "Lineal and Nonlineal Codifications of Reality," *ETC: A Review of General Semantics,* Vol. VIII, No. 1 (Autumn, 1950), (pub. December, 1950).

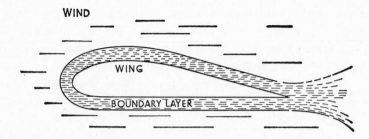

The boundary layer apparently forms a *discrete* blanket or layer over the wing surface according to this picture.

Upon examining the *mathematics* of the boundary layer I got a similar but vitally different picture. According to the mathematics the air stuck to the wing surface, but did not form a sluggish *layer*, but a sluggish *region*. This mathematical picture looks something like this:

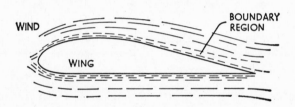

There is a vital difference in the two pictures. A boundary *layer* implies a *discrete blanket* with a definite defining thickness. A boundary *region* implies a *continuous*, nondiscrete sluggish *region* which has no definite thickness.

Of course this is well-known, old-hat stuff to aeronautics men, but the point is I found one scientist had *unconsciously assumed* a discrete layer because of the incorrect symbolism, boundary *"layer."*[2]

In short, the *words* we use to define a problem or situation may act as *blinders* (à la Dobbin) in our approach to the problem or situation.

SOME CONSEQUENCES

Roughly speaking, *blindering* may lead to two broad kinds of consequences. Blindering may (1) delay or impede solutions and (2) lead to solutions which are undesirable.

Delayed Solutions

If you are still in the mood for puzzles, try this one.[3] Two cyclists

---

2 David A. Levine, "A Student's Progress Report on Some Applications of Korzybskian Methodology," *General Semantics Bulletin*, Nos. 10 and 11 (Autumn–Winter, 1952–53), p. 65. Reprinted by permission of the Institute of General Semantics.

3 From Stuart Chase, *Guides to Straight Thinking* (New York: Harper & Bros., 1956).

are separated by thirty miles of straight, flat road. They begin pedaling toward each other simultaneously. At the same time, a fly takes off from the handlebars of one of the cyclists, flies to the second, turns instantaneously, flies back to the first, etc. The fly continues to make these alternating flights as the cyclists continuously decrease the distance between themselves. Finally, the fly is smashed between the handlebars as the cyclists collide. Both cyclists were traveling at fifteen miles per hour and the fly at forty—all at constant rates of speed. The problem: How far did the fly fly? (Don't read further until you have tried to work out the problem for yourself.)

If you arrived at an incorrect answer or at no answer at all, or at the correct answer in more than fifteen seconds, something must have impeded your progress. Examine the assumptions you made about the problem. Did your reactions fall into one or more of the categories below?

1. "The problem is difficult. It requires computation—paper and pencil work."
2. "The problem is incomplete. I don't have all of the necessary data."
3. "The problem is silly. I won't waste my time and energy."
4. The technicality finder: "A fly couldn't fly that fast." "How could the fly turn instantaneously—he would lose some speed." "He couldn't be smashed between the handle bars—the cyclists' front wheels would bump first!"

Probably underlying each of these expressions (although only the first admits it) is the assumption that the problem is *complex*. Once one *defines* a problem as complex, he is more likely to search (if he searches at all) for an answer by using complex techniques, for example, by computing the sum of the decreasing distances of the fly's individual flights.

The problem, however, is quite simple—*if one defines it as such*. The cyclists are thirty miles apart and pedaling at fifteen miles per hour. They will thus collide in one hour. The fly which travels at forty miles per hour will, of course, have flown forty miles.

In all fairness let me admit that I *helped* you to blinder yourself by asking "How *far* did the fly fly?" thus focusing attention on distance and away from time. Had the question been "How long did the fly fly and, therefore, how far?" the correct answer would probably have come much more rapidly and easily.

The phenomenon of *blindering* as a factor in impeding progress is suggested by M. W. Ball's book, *This Fascinating Oil Business:*

Oil men, through some queer quirk of herd psychology, have been great respecters of political boundaries. When oil is found in a state they are likely to search that state with enthusiasm and thoroughness, ignoring areas of equal promise just over the state line. Perhaps this explains why no oil was produced in New York until five years after its discovery in Northern Pennsylvania. . . .[4]

Down in Texas, close to the southeast corner of New Mexico, the year that saw Maljamar discovered saw the discovery of the Hendricks field, one of the great fields of the West Texas Permian basin. The field was scarcely more than a stone's throw south of the New Mexico border, on a structural feature that obviously extended into New Mexico, yet for nearly three years the state line stopped the oil men cold.[5]

Blinder Names.   One cannot help wondering how long progress has been retarded by the assignation of inappropriate names. How much time was lost and how many lives were squandered by the term *malaria?* Contracted from the Italian words *mala aria* ("bad air"), it perpetuated the erroneous notion that the disease was caused by the bad air of the swamps. And how long were the properties of *oxygen* concealed because of its misleading name? Oxygen stems from the Greek terms for acid-producer—but, unfortunately, oxygen does not produce acid! And how many bright and willing scientists were inhibited from even dreaming of the possibility that the atom (from the Greek for *indivisible*) *could* be split largely because its *name* said it could *not* be divided?

Undesirable Solutions

Blindering may not only retard or prevent the finding of appropriate, constructive solutions, but it may steer us toward improper, unintelligent, even dangerous, solutions. As an analyst for an insurance company, Benjamin Lee Whorf was solely concerned at first with the physical factors in fires and explosions, e.g., defective wiring, presence or lack of air spaces between metal flues and woodwork, etc. But he soon began to notice certain *human* factors as well. He found that the way people defined or labeled a situation greatly influenced their behavior toward it. For example, he found that people tended to be extremely cautious around what they called "gasoline drums." Great care was taken to prevent smoking or striking matches in their vicinity. But when the drums were emptied and were thus now labeled *"empty gasoline drums,"* caution was thrown to the winds. Cigarettes were smoked with abandon because the situation was now *defined* as safe.

---

4 From *This Fascinating Oil Business,* by Max W. Ball, copyright 1940, used by special permission of the publishers, The Bobbs-Merrill Company, Inc., p. 342.

5 *Ibid.,* pp. 358–59.

Ironically, the "empty" drums were *full* of gasoline vapors, and one spark could be sufficient to explode them—an enormously more dangerous circumstance than when they contained the liquid gasoline.[6]

Among other similar incidents, Whorf cited the case of the tannery drying room:

A drying room for hides was arranged with a blower at one end to make a current of air along the room and thence outdoors through a vent at the other end. Fire started at a hot bearing on the blower, which blew the flames directly into the hides and fanned them along the room, destroying the entire stock. This hazardous setup followed naturally from the term "blower" with its linguistic equivalence to "that which blows," implying that its function necessarily is to "blow." Also its function is verbalized as "blowing air for drying," overlooking that it can blow other things, e.g., flames and sparks. In reality a blower simply makes a current of air and can exhaust as well as blow. It should have been installed at the vent end to draw the air over the hides, then through the hazard (its own casing and bearings) and thence outdoors.[7]

CORRECTIVES

It is obvious that blindering may be a serious hindrance in business, education, government, science, even in our personal lives. How, then, can we cope with it? How can we eliminate it or at least minimize its destructive influence? The following suggestions are offered:

Remember, Defining = Neglecting

Blindering may be described as the process of narrowing one's perception, of channeling one's vision of a situation, problem, phenomenon. These restrictions are frequently introduced by the verbal (and nonverbal) *definitions* that he assigns to the situation, etc. *To define* is "to mark the limits or boundaries of." Thus, when I define the chair I am sitting on as a "piece of office furniture," I am setting up certain restrictions. I am calling attention to those attributes my chair has in common with other "office furniture," such as that it is usually found indoors, in offices (rather than in homes or on lawns), that it is largely utilitarian (as opposed to decorative), etc. At the same time, however, my definition is neglecting a host of other aspects which my chair does *not* share with "office furniture" in general. My definition *distracts*

---

[6] From "The Name of the Situation as Affecting Behavior," by B. L. Whorf. Published in "The Relation of Habitual Thought and Behavior to Language," in *Language, Culture, and Personality: Essays in Memory of Edward Sapir,* ed. Leslie Spier *et al.* (Menasha, Wis.: Sapir Memorial Fund, 1941). This article is reproduced in its entirety in the "Incidents" section following this chapter.

[7] *Ibid.*

attention from a host of details unique to my chair—among them, its specific colors, weight, textures of the plastic and steel surfaces, tensile strengths of the various materials, style, molecular structures, cost, resale value, origins of materials, etc. In short, the process of defining inevitably involves the neglecting of some (actually, most) details.

The crux is that, while it is unavoidable that definitions neglect aspects, it is nevertheless essential that we *do* define, delimit, categorize, classify, organize our data and experience. The practical implication, therefore, is that it is dangerous to *forget* that defining, by its function, is a process of restricting and neglecting. Remember, in other words, that you are abstracting.

Does My Definition Blinder Me?

Hunt[8] reports an interesting experiment conducted with college students. One group was confronted with the problem of removing a ping-pong ball from the bottom of an upright rusty pipe. They were not to change the position of the pipe in any way. In the room were a hammer, pliers, rulers, soda straws, pins, and a bucket of dirty water. After several futile attempts with the various "tools" to fish the ball out, they struck upon the idea of pouring the dirty water into the pipe and floating the ball up.

A second group of students was given the same problem, but with one change. Instead of the bucket of dirty water, a large pitcher of clear ice water, surrounded by crystal goblets and set on a clean table cloth, was placed in the room. They never solved the problem. In this case they defined the water as *drinking water*—and their definition blindered them from other possible uses.

The same phenomenon is illustrated by the popular scissors and strings experiment. The experimenter hangs two strings from the ceiling as in Figure *1*. The objective is to tie the two ends together as

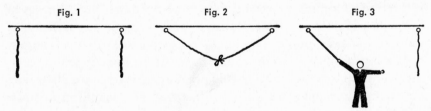

Fig. 1	Fig. 2	Fig. 3

in Figure *2*. The strings are far enough apart, however, that the performer cannot quite reach string *B* while holding *A*, or reach *A* while holding *B* (Fig. *3*). He is now given one instrument with which to

---

[8] Morton M. Hunt, "How to Overcome Mental Blocks," *Mayfair,* December, 1956.

solve the problem—a pair of scissors. Some individuals promptly snip off a length from one string and tie it to the other. The addition permits them to move closer to where the end *was*, but, alas! they find that the shorter string is now too high for them (Fig. *4*).

Fig. 4

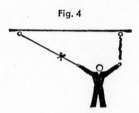

Their definition of scissors as a "cutter" inhibits their thinking of it as anything else. A pair of scissors, after all, is also a *length*, and tying it to the end of one of the strings might have given the additional length necessary to reach the second string. It is also a *weight*, and tying it to a string which could then be set in motion as a pendulum would be an effective solution for the problem (Fig. *5*).

Fig. 5

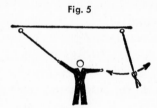

It may be exceedingly helpful on occasion to ask one's self: "Am I blindering myself, restricting my approach to the problem by my definition, my 'sizing-up' of the problem?"

How to Recognize Our Blinders

This is the crux, of course. How can one cope with his blinders if he does not recognize that he is being blindered? We laugh at the old wives' tales of yesteryear, but is it not possible that unwittingly we still accept a good many chimeras as valid? Consider the alumnus who returned to visit his old physics professor. After looking over some of the examination papers the old gentleman was grading, he was prompted to remark: "Why, professor, these are the same questions I had when I was a student twenty years ago!" Whereupon the old man smiled indulgently and said: "Yes, the *questions* are the same, but the *answers* are different now!"

Is it not true that the answers of today often become the problems of tomorrow? Reflect on the tremendous resistance against William Harvey's discovery of the circulation of blood. His findings contradicted "the prevailing beliefs that the blood ebbed and flowed in the vessels, that there were two sorts of blood and that the blood was able to pass from one side of the heart to the other."[9]

Harvey was fearful that the news of his discovery would not find receptive ears, and his fears were well founded. He suffered ridicule and abuse, and his practice suffered considerably. It required twenty years of ceaseless struggle before his discovery became accepted.

Are there any practical, day-to-day techniques which will help us to uncover and eliminate our blinders? Here are a few that are often useful:[10]

1. *Talk with an Outsider.* There are times when all of us have difficulty "seeing the forest for the trees." We become so immersed with a problem that we become quite unable to see it from other vantage points. One of the chief values of an outside consultant to a business institution is the freshness of outlook he brings with him. As a dispassionate observer, unencumbered with the minutiae of problems, he is often able to suggest views and insights that have eluded men closer to the situation. The Bell System Laboratories deliberately assign a new man to a research team from time to time in order to get the benefit of his naïveté, his ignorance, if you will. He is often able to stir up the thinking of the scientists who have been at the problems longer and thus prompt them to arrive at new and better approaches.

But the outsider need not always be a professional or even well versed with a particular problem area. Often a wife, a friend, a parent, even a child, can help one see a problem in a new light. And not infrequently, as in nondirective counseling, the very process of explaining the problem to another, of making the effort to get someone else to see his problem, helps one to break through his self-created encasements.

2. *Kill "Killer Phrases."* This apt coinage is by Charles H. Clark of the Ethyl Corporation, who has compiled a list of phrases which squelch a new idea before it has a chance to be examined. "Let's be practical," "we've never done anything like that," and "the customers won't stand for it" are examples. Granted, some suggestions prove to be worthless or worse. But some, ridiculous or impractical at first

---

9 W. I. B. Beveridge, *op. cit.*, p. 103.
10 Suggested by Morton M. Hunt, *op. cit.*

hearing, may have a nugget of gold in them—something which, if combined with other ideas, might prove exceedingly useful. The point is that the killer phrase will decapitate the infant idea before anyone has had the opportunity to dig for its gold, to give it a fair appraisal.

3. *Brainstorm with a Group.*   Brainstorming, an idea-generating technique which swept the nation a few years ago, acquiring many advocates and not a few antagonists, has definite blinder-finding potential. The rules of the game are quite simple. A group of people meet to make suggestions relevant to a given problem area. The goal is quantity—not quality—the more ideas, the better. No one evaluates or censures their worth. Only afterward are the ideas sifted through for possible pearls. The key antiblindering feature of brainstorming is the interpersonal excitement and stimulation generated among the group. Mr. A may say something that sets off Miss B and Mr. C, who in turn mention something that triggers ideas from D, E, and F, etc. The upshot is that ideas may appear that might never have occurred to the same people working as solitary thinkers.

However, brainstorming is not without its own blindering dangers. Without skilled leadership, the flow of ideas may get started down one relatively narrow channel—one idea merely pressing another deeper into this specialized rut. Good leadership can guide the ideas through a more comprehensive and useful area.

4. *Start Anywhere—But Start.*   How many times have you tackled a creative project and had difficulty in beginning? Perhaps it was a term paper, an essay, or a report, and the main heading or the lead sentence simply did not come, regardless of your efforts to grind it out. I have wasted hours, I am embarrassed to say, because I could not begin a chapter or an article or even a paragraph in a way that satisfied me. I have discovered at this late date what others have known for years—that it is rarely *necessary* to begin at the *beginning*. The important thing is to start—start anywhere, middle, end, but start. Often when I start *where I can make a start*, I come back to the beginning, and the chapter title or the lead line, or whatever it was that had me blocked, falls into place.

5. *Break the Tension Cycle.*   Sometimes you find yourself working on a problem, making reasonable headway, when suddenly there's a brick wall. You are blocked, stymied. Most people back off a few feet and run headlong at the wall to butt it down. It doesn't give, so they try it again—and again—and again. Ironically, the more frustrated one becomes in attacking problems, the tenser he becomes. The more tense, the less insight—the less likelihood of noticing that there may

be other ways of dealing with a brick wall, perhaps of going over, under, or around it. And thus the tension cycle, one of the most effective
deterrents to problem solving to which man is subject, takes over.

There are several ways to break the tension cycle—leaving the area
of frustration, learning to relax physically the individual members of
the body, participating in an unrelated activity, etc. The last is my
favorite. If I find myself stymied in my work and beginning to grow
tense, I shift to another area of the same work. If this is not effective,
I pull out of my desk a list of previously planned short-term and
reasonably agreeable tasks. Then I spend twenty minutes taking a
book to the library—or out of the library, or answering a letter, or
reorganizing my bookshelves, or just taking a walk around the block.
When I return to my original work, I am invariably more relaxed,
and quite often I can now see a solution to the problem that I had not
noticed before. Regardless of what you call it—intuition, subcon-
scious, what-have-you—there *does* appear to be something working
inside of us even if we are not fully aware of it, and often it works
more efficiently when we are not consciously holding the reins.

Dead Lines. One of the greatest sources of personal tension in our
modern world is the well-known dead line. But the relationship between dead-line tension and blindering is not always clear. How is it
that some people seem to work well under "dead-line pressure" while
others go to pieces? Part of the confusion may lie in the ambiguity of
"dead line." There are at least three types of dead lines.

1. *Those That Are Externally-Imposed and Unavoidable.* Some
people, such as newsmen, work with these dead lines hanging over
them constantly. Evidently they accommodate themselves to the pressures of time and work with great efficiency and surprising ease. For
most of us, however, unavoidable dead lines are rare occurrences. Most
of our dead lines are of the latter two kinds.

2. *Those That Are Self-Imposed.* Among individuals who tend
toward perfectionism there is the inclination to set up arbitrary dead
lines for themselves. Before long, the dead lines seem to become quite
demanding, and the tension cycle is likely to set in. Self-imposed dead
lines may be helpful stimulators and guides, so long as we recognize
them as such; but if we let them take on the guise of externally imposed unavoidable dead lines, we are inviting tension and blindering.

3. *Those That Are Created through Procrastination.* There must
be students who do not procrastinate, but they seem to have successfully avoided my classes. These dead lines actually exist, of course, but
better planning could have made them less formidable. But advice of

this sort is usually futile, for procrastinators usually rationalize that they work better under pressure anyway—and perhaps they do. Like the newsmen, they have had a great deal of experience under these conditions!

*   *   *   *

The motto of the Air University is "Proficimus more irrenti," usually translated as "Progress unhindered by tradition." Major General M. K. Deichelmann phrased it more pragmatically as "Stay loose, boy —stay loose."

INCIDENTS

THE RAWLEY COMPANY[11]

The Rawley Company, manufacturers of custom-made metal forming machinery, have been in business for over half a century. It is located in a large midwest city and employs approximately one hundred
persons. Executives of Rawley have become aware that their company sales have fallen considerably short of its full production capacity. Stimulated by the company's president, James Howe, a dynamic man with an inquiring mind, the firm has decided to approach
the problem through the cooperative efforts of a group of persons
henceforth known as the Sales Council.

The Sales Council is to be composed of representatives of various
departments of the firm, some of which are not conventionally concerned with sales. The representatives and their departments are as
follows:

James Howe, *president* (designer, engineer, sales)
Donald Brewster, *vice-president* (asst. general manager, manager of
    sales)
Raymond Prescott, *treasurer*
Clifford Carlin, asst. vice-president (production manager)
Ralph Goodwin, asst. vice-president (warehouse manager)
Arthur Howard, asst. sales manager
Chester Green, eastern sales
Fred Lemec, charge of machinery orders
Russell Thurston, engineer and salesman

The Sales Council is to operate on the basic assumption that ultimately every employee is directly or indirectly related to the sale
of the company's products. Consequently, the combined thinking of
representatives of these various sections might produce helpful suggestions for their common objective, increased sales.

In order to expedite the meetings of the Sales Council a professor
of interpersonal communication from a local university has been called
in to act as moderator. It was felt that he should act as disinterested

---

11 All names have been disguised. Printed by permission of the author, whose name
has been withheld by request.

chairman whose primary responsibility was simply to help the members of the group to understand one another as clearly and as accurately as possible. Specifically, he was to repeat and/or paraphrase the statement of each speaker immediately after the speaker had finished making it. This was to give the speaker the feeling that at least one person understood what he had tried to communicate. Furthermore, all other members were to have the opportunity to agree or to disagree with the accuracy of the moderator's restatement of the speaker's statement until, theoretically, everyone was satisfied that he had understood the speaker.

Shortly before the first Sales Council meetings were to be held, some of Rawley's executives and the professor met for a preliminary meeting. The meeting was to explain to the professor what the Sales Council was, what its objectives were, and what the professor's role as moderator was to be.

After each executive present had expressed his view of these points the professor, David Wilson, asked to have the floor.

WILSON: Gentlemen, I'd like to try to sum up what I think you have been saying about the Sales Council so that you can tell me if you think I understand you. As I get the picture you are proposing an experiment in group problem-solving. Casting this approach in my own frame of reference this is going to be essentially a group—something like the conventional classroom situation in which the lines of communication are directly between teacher and students and only indirectly from student to student. . . .

HOWE, acting as chairman, breaks in: I see heads shaking in disagreement, Dave. Ralph?

GOODWIN: Dave, I don't like your analogy. This is not going to be a classroom situation at all. The moderator isn't supposed to act as an autocrat. He's trying to achieve the cooperation and communication of the group at a high level. . . .

WILSON: I think you're right about the analogy being a poor one, but I only used it to describe the direction of the communication lines as I see them in the Sales Council. . . .

CARLIN: No offense meant, Dave, but you can't presume to act the role of a teacher, the subject-matter expert. You don't have the company background for it.

Ten minutes later.

WILSON: Now, getting specifically to the role of the moderator. . . . The way I get it he is to listen to Speaker A, filter through his personality and background what he thinks A has said and express it to the group. . . .

GOODWIN: You don't filter anything. Your job is to repeat what A has said.

CARLIN: Well, he's to *paraphrase* what A has said so that A will know that at least one person has understood him.

WILSON: I get that, but how can I possibly relay a man's statement, other than through the sheer repetition of his exact words, unless I interpret, size-up what he has said. In other words isn't it inevitable that I filter what comes to me through my own nervous system, my personality, my background?

GOODWIN: Filtering is changing the substance you are conveying— that isn't your job.

CARLIN: You don't *filter*—you *reflect* what has been said.

WILSON: Perhaps "filter" has been a bad figure of speech but even in reflecting the other fellow's statement, must I not determine his meaning for myself—and how can I size up his meaning unless I relate his words to my own unique frame of experience?

At this point dinner was announced, and the subject was dropped.

THE NAME OF THE SITUATION AS AFFECTING BEHAVIOR[12]
By B. L. Whorf

There will probably be general assent to the proposition that an accepted pattern of using words is often prior to certain lines of thinking and forms of behavior, but he who assents often sees in such a statement nothing more than a platitudinous recognition of the hypnotic power of philosophical and learned terminology on the one hand or of catchwords, slogans, and rallying-cries on the other. To see only thus far is to miss the point of one of the important interconnections which Sapir saw between language, culture, and psychology. . . . It is not so much in these special uses of language as in its constant ways of arranging data and its most ordinary every-day analysis of phenom-

12 From "The Relation of Habitual Thought and Behavior to Language," in *Language, Culture, and Personality: Essays in Memory of Edward Sapir*, edited by Leslie Spier, A. Irving Hallowell, Stanley S. Newman, pp. 75–77. Menasha, Wisconsin, Sapir Memorial Fund 1941. Reprinted by permission.

ena that we need to recognize the influence it has on other activities, cultural and personal.

I came in touch with an aspect of this problem before I had studied under Dr. Sapir, and in a field usually considered remote from linguistics. It was in the course of my professional work for a fire insurance company, in which I undertook the task of analyzing many hundreds of reports of circumstances surrounding the start of fires, and in some cases, of explosions. My analysis was directed toward purely physical conditions, such as defective wiring, presence or lack of air spaces between metal flues and woodwork, etc., and the results were presented in these terms. Indeed it was undertaken with no thought that any other significances would or could be revealed. But in due course it became evident that not only a physical situation *qua* physics, but the meaning of that situation to people, was sometimes a factor, through the behavior of the people, in the start of the fire. And this factor of meaning was clearest when it was a *linguistic meaning*, residing in the name or the linguistic description commonly applied to the situation. Thus around a storage of what are called "gasoline drums" behavior will tend to a certain type, that is, great care will be exercised; while around a storage of what are called "empty gasoline drums" it will tend to be different—careless, with little repression of smoking or of tossing cigarette stubs about. Yet the "empty" drums are perhaps the more dangerous, since they contain explosive vapor. Physically the situation is hazardous, but the linguistic analysis according to regular analogy must employ the word "empty," which inevitably suggests lack of hazard. The word "empty" is used in two linguistic patterns: (1) as a virtual synonym for "null and void, negative, inert," (2) applied in analysis of physical situations without regard to, e.g., vapor, liquid vestiges, or stray rubbish, in the container. The situation is named in one pattern (2) and the name is then "acted out" or "lived up to" in another (1); this being a general formula for the linguistic conditioning of behavior into hazardous forms.

In a wood distillation plant the metal stills were insulated with a composition prepared from limestone and called at the plant "spun limestone." No attempt was made to protect this covering from excessive heat or the contact of flame. After a period of use the fire below one of the stills spread to the "limestone," which to everyone's great surprise burned vigorously. Exposure to acetic acid fumes from the stills had converted part of the limestone (calcium carbonate) to calcium acetate. This when heated in a fire decomposes, forming inflammable acetone. Behavior that tolerated fire close to the covering was induced by use of the name "limestone," which because it ends in "stone" implies noncombustibility.

A huge iron kettle of boiling varnish was observed to be overheated, nearing the temperature at which it would ignite. The operator moved it off the fire and ran it on its wheels to a distance, but did not cover it. In a minute or so the varnish ignited. Here the linguistic influence is more complex; it is due to the metaphorical objectifying (of which more later) of "cause" as contact or the spatial juxtaposition of "things"—to analyzing the situation as "on" versus "off" the fire. In reality the stage when the external fire was the main factor had passed; the overheating was now an internal process of convection in the varnish from the intensely heated kettle, and still continued when "off" the fire.

An electric glow heater on the wall was little used, and for one workman had the meaning of a convenient coat-hanger. At night a watchman entered and snapped a switch, which action he verbalized as "turning on the light." No light appeared, and this result he verbalized as "light is burned out." He could not see the glow of the heater because of the old coat hung on it. Soon the heater ignited the coat, which set fire to the building.

A tannery discharged waste water containing animal matter into an outdoor settling basin partly roofed with wood and partly open. This situation is one that ordinarily would be verbalized as "pool of water." A workman had occasion to light a blow-torch nearby, and threw his match into the water. But the decomposing waste matter was evolving gas under the wood cover, so that the setup was the reverse of "watery." An instant flare of flame ignited the woodwork, and the fire quickly spread into the adjoining building.

A drying room for hides was arranged with a blower at one end to make a current of air along the room and thence outdoors through a vent at the other end. Fire started at a hot bearing on the blower, which blew the flames directly into the hides and fanned them along the room, destroying the entire stock. This hazardous setup followed naturally from the term "blower" with its linguistic equivalence to "that which blows," implying that its function necessarily is to "blow." Also its function is verbalized as "blowing air for drying," overlooking that it can blow other things, e.g., flames and sparks. In reality a blower simply makes a current of air and can exhaust as well as blow. It should have been installed at the vent end to *draw* the air over the hides, then through the hazard (its own casing and bearings) and thence outdoors.

Beside a coal-fired melting pot for lead reclaiming was dumped a pile of "scrap lead"—a misleading verbalization, for it consisted of the lead sheets of old radio condensers, which still had paraffin paper between them. Soon the paraffin blazed up and fired the roof, half of which was burned off.

Such examples, which could be greatly multiplied, will suffice to show how the cue to a certain line of behavior is often given by the analogies of the linguistic formula in which the situation is spoken of, and by which to some degree it is analyzed, classified, and allotted its place in that world which is "to a large extent unconsciously built up on the language habits of the group." And we always assume that the linguistic analysis made by our group reflects reality better than it does.

ARNO ANNELLO, MACHINIST[13]

The standards department of the Schoonway Machine Company recommended that Arno Annello, who operated a battery of automatic gear-cutting machines, be discharged for failure to attain required minimum production as set by the standards department. The foreman in whose department Annello was employed objected to the recommendation. The matter was placed before the production manager for final decision.

Arno Annello came to this country from Finland. He had received the equivalent of a grade-school education in his native land but had practically no knowledge of the English language. He secured a job as a floor cleaner in the Schoonway plant. He showed himself to be industrious and thorough, and the foreman of the milling and gear-cutting department became interested in him. One day he suggested to one of Annello's friends that the floor sweeper should apply for a better job. When Annello heard this, he signified his desire to become an operative of the automatic sharpening machines. These machines were used to sharpen the teeth of cutters after the cutters were otherwise finished. They were automatic in operation, and with proper setup there was very little danger of spoiling the work. The foreman or an experienced assistant personally supervised each setup. The opera-

---

13 Reprinted by permission from *Introduction to Industrial Management*, by Franklin E. Folts, Copyright 1949, McGraw-Hill Book Company, Inc.

tive inserted and removed the work, started and stopped the machines, and dressed the emery wheels when necessary. He operated from four to eight machines, depending on the character of the work.

When a vacancy occurred in the department, the foreman decided to give Annello a chance, and obtained his transfer (on trial) from the cleaning department. Over a period of several months, Annello, with the assistance of the foreman, became proficient in operating the machines, and he was given a permanent job. For the next two years Annello showed steady improvement. He became known in the department as a first-class operative of automatic cutter-sharpening machines and finally developed into a skilled machine setter. While he improved as a machinist, Annello showed no aptitude in mastering the English language, and any extended or involved conversation had to be handled through an interpreter. The foreman, however, believed that Annello had the makings of a first-class machinist and was willing to put up with this inconvenience.

The company decided to install a new battery of gear-cutting machines for milling the teeth in cutters, and the foreman was confronted with the task of getting additional operatives to run these machines. The work of operating the automatic gear-cutting machines required considerably more skill than was necessary to run automatic cutter-sharpening machines. The machine attendant had to set up the indexing mechanism for the cutter blank, set the tooth-milling cutter at the correct distance off the center line of the blank, see that the cutter was properly sharpened, and set the machine for the correct stroke. The machine fed and indexed automatically, but considerable care was necessary on the part of the operative to keep the indexing at exactly the proper adjustment. The foreman approached Annello with the suggestion that he prepare himself to work on the new machines. Annello was highly pleased and put in all his spare time trying to familiarize himself with the work. He succeeded so well that by the time the machines were finally installed the foreman felt that Annello was sufficiently qualified and gave him a place on the new battery. Here Annello worked along with the other workmen, all of whom had been trained at one time or another by the foreman. He appeared to do average work and was well liked by the other men.

The standards department of the Schoonway Machine Company decided to institute a series of studies relative to the operations of gear-cutting machines for milling teeth in cutters. After the routine research had been made, the standards engineer announced the minimum amount of output which a worker must attain in order to be considered efficient. No bonus could be earned until this standard was exceeded.

During the period in which the studies were made, Annello was nervous. He appeared unable to keep his machine in proper adjustment. The pieces which he turned out were inferior in quality, and the total number gradually fell below the point at which the minimum standard was finally set. Engineers from the standards department, knowing that Annello was a protege of the foreman, sought to ascertain the cause of his trouble, but he was unable to make an intelligible explanation. They warned him of the seriousness of the situation. For several days there was no change. Then, at the suggestion of the foreman, time-study men retimed Annello, in an endeavor to find the cause of his failure. His showing was worse than ever. The engineers began to question whether or not he had the native ability to do the work. The head of the standards department expressed that doubt to the foreman. The foreman insisted that Annello was a first-class workman. The standards department believed that the foreman was prejudiced because he did not object when they suggested that Joseph Smith be discharged. Smith had been employed on the new battery for about the same length of time as Annello and his output was not so low.

With their watches concealed in their pockets so as not to arouse Annello's suspicion, the time-study men clocked him for a third time. Still he showed no improvement. After that, the standards department became insistent that Annello be discharged. The foreman was obdurate, and the standards department appealed to the production manager for a final decision. The latter listened to the recommendations of the standards department and to the objections which the foreman raised, and then made a ruling that at the end of one week the standards department was to make another clocking of Annello's work. If it still was unsatisfactory, the foreman was to be given an additional week in which he could take any measures he chose in attempting to bring the machinist's work up to standard. If he failed to do this within the allotted period, Annello was to be fired for inability to attain the minimum standard.

At the end of the first week the new timings were made. Annello showed no improvement. When the foreman received this information, he went to Annello accompanied by a friend of the latter's, who acted as interpreter. The foreman told the machinist that his work was coming along well and that he had no need to fear the time-study men, that they would bother him no more. He said he would see to it personally that nothing happened to Annello and that as long as he tried his best he always could have a job with the Schoonway Machine Company. Annello thanked the foreman profusely and said that he always tried to do his best. The next morning he appeared at work smiling and happy. His output for the day was just at the minimum standard, but the quality was excellent. The next day his output increased. At the end of the week he was earning a good bonus. Six months later the standards department, as well as the foreman, rated him as the best worker on the automatic gear-cutting machines.

YOU GET WHAT YOU WANT[14]
By Robert Froman

A little more than a year ago the maker of a popular kitchen gadget for mixing waffle batter, milk shakes, and such decided to improve on his product. He put engineers to work designing a new model more powerful than the old and almost completely noiseless. When the redesigning was completed, at a cost of thousands of dollars, he invested more thousands in retooling part of his plant.

Several months later the first of the new models reached the retail stores. And there most of them remained. You, the members of the great buying public, simply weren't interested.

Much disturbed, the manufacturer sent out investigators to learn why. They returned with a flabbergasting answer.

"Darn' thing doesn't seem to have any power," one potential purchaser who had changed his mind summed it up for all. "Doesn't make any noise."

And that was that. The manufacturer had to withdraw the new models and rebuild them so that they made a little more noise. That was the way you wanted them, so that was the way they had to be. Attempting to argue with you in such matters, once you have made up your mind, leads only to bankruptcy court. . . .

There are occasions when you react most unexpectedly, but you still have your way. Early automobile fog lights had amber-colored lenses on them. Some years later the Westinghouse Electric Corporation brought out a more powerful fog light and used a clear lens.

14 From the article of the same name, in *Colliers,* April 17, 1951. Reprinted by permission of the author.

You weren't interested. By then fog lights meant amber lights to you. Westinghouse tried an advertising campaign, pointing out that its clear lens produced the same road-hugging light pattern as the amber and had other advantages. The campaign failed almost completely. Today, the company sells four fog lamps with amber lenses for every one with a clear lens, though it has to charge more for the amber.

The United States Rubber Company has had a somewhat similar experience with inner tubes. Before World War II the tubes were made of natural rubber and were red in color. During the war natural rubber inner tubes disappeared and were replaced by gray, synthetic butyl tubes. Many of you automatically assumed that the synthetic tubes were inferior and, as soon as natural red rubber became available again after the war, began clamoring for tubes made of it.

Actually, says U.S. Rubber, butyl tubes hold air 10 times longer and are more resistent to tearing than those made of natural rubber. What's more, the red tubes' price is considerably higher, because natural rubber costs more than butyl. . . .

In many similar matters you adamantly resist any change whatsoever. Over the years, for instance, would-be innovators in the manufacture of playing cards have attempted such novelties as replacing the usual effigies of king, queen and jack with photographs of such personalities as Babe Ruth, Lana Turner and Jimmy Durante. Any who went so far as to invest money in such an endeavor probably lost every penny of it. You like the faces of playing cards the way they are, and that's that. . . .

Some problems which result from your demands are quite irrelevant to the basic nature and purpose of the products concerned. When synthetic detergents first went on the market for household use in the thirties, they proved excellent for many washing purposes. Huge advertising and publicity campaigns broadcast this news far and wide. You were sufficiently impressed to give the detergents a trial, but you weren't very enthusiastic.

The puzzled manufacturers turned to the market researchers. You just didn't know, the latter found, whether detergents were as good as they were supposed to be.

Why not? the researchers wanted to know. Didn't they do a good cleaning job?

Well, that might be, you temporized. But the stuff didn't make suds. You had got used to the idea that the more suds a soap produced, the better job it did.

So back went the detergents to the laboratories. If you wanted suds, the chemists had to find a way of making detergents produce them. And they finally turned up a sudsing agent which could be blended into the detergents without interfering with their action. It convinced you, and sales soared.

You are seldom content for long, however, with a big new development like detergents, and in a field as highly competitive as the soap business the manufacturers have to keep finding something new. The Lever Brothers Company, for one, maintains a continuous study of family washday habits in thousands of homes in order to find out what changes in its products will please you.

"If Mrs. Consumer were to start demanding a soap which would do everything from the breakfast dishes to putting the cat out at night," says Lever's director of marketing research, "we'd have to try to find it."

Occasionally, you grow downright capricious in your demands. When the makers of foam rubber first adapted the material for pillows, they made them as soft as possible on the theory that the whole purpose of a pillow is softness. But many of you objected. You liked "hard" pillows. So the manufacturers made some firmer, some more yielding.

The result was confusion compounded. When those of you who like your pillows soft found foam-rubber ones which were firm, you took the notion that *all* pillows of this material were too hard for you. You finally drove The Dayton Rubber Company, which makes Koolfoam pillows, to desperate measures. The company has adapted the Goldilocks story and now puts out a Baby Bear pillow labeled very soft, a Mama Bear pillow which is medium soft and a Papa Bear pillow which is quite firm.

At the opposite extreme from items on which you make such outrageous demands are those about which you don't know very clearly what you want. Automobile manufacturers spend millions every year to coax from you a few hints on what you expect of a car. But they have found that you can be oddly equivocal about what you want. When you consider a car in the abstract, you say one thing. But when you set out to buy one, you often do the opposite.

One company's questionnaire, for instance, lists 10 general automobile features such as dependability, economy, comfort and appearance, and asks which you consider the most important. You nearly always put dependability or economy near the top of the list and appearance near the bottom. But when you buy a car, say the dealers, appearance almost always seems to be your chief and sometimes your only concern. And you can be contradictory about appearance. When asked about chrome trimming, most of you say the less the better. But when the chrome on a new model is cut down, its sales drop precipitately.

One of the most elaborate systems for trying to sound you out on a new product is the General Electric Company's Consumer Advisory Council. This is composed of 2,000 families scattered all over the country and representing every income group and cities of all sizes. Usually, GE first asks these people what they think of a new idea, then, if they like it, sends them samples to try out.

What makes this arrangement so useful is that odd, unpredictable quirks constantly turn up in your reactions to new products. When GE decided to try a foot pedal for opening the door of its refrigerator, one member of the council had a singular complaint: "I don't like foot pedals," she announced. "My cat thinks he's people. He'll sit on it and open the door to cool off."

So, before General Electric put refrigerators so equipped on the market, it designed the pedal to take more pressure than cats or other house pets could apply.

Perhaps the oddest of all your quirks is your occasional insistence on being hoodwinked. Champagne labeling is a case in point. Both United States producers and importers have entered a sort of half-open conspiracy with you not to call things by their right names.

What lies behind this is that most people who drink champagne like it to taste fairly sweet. But there's a general belief that a true champagne connoisseur wants it to taste dry. Naturally, most people who drink it want to think of themselves as connoisseurs. So the champagne men label their product "Brut"—which means absolutely dry —when very little sweetening has been added, "Dry" when it's a bit sweeter and sometimes "Extra Dry" when it's sweetest.

Along the same line is your frequent refusal to believe in a new product until it is dramatized for you. Such dramatizing is one of the chief functions of industrial designers like Raymond Loewy.

Not too long ago a new client turned up at Loewy's office. He was the maker of a device for automatically cooking and vending hot dogs and hamburgers. When a customer inserted a coin, the wrapped sandwich dropped into view, was cooked from the inside out electronically in a little over a minute and was then ready to eat.

The machine worked perfectly, did everything it was supposed to do. But most people flatly refused to believe in it. On being questioned they admitted that the sandwiches were delivered hot and seemed to be cooked. But, said the customers, they couldn't *see* anything happening. So they suspected some trickery. Loewy's solution was simple. He installed orange-red lights which glowed while the sandwich cooked. They had nothing to do with the cooking process, but they convinced you that something was happening.

THE ROBERTS MACHINE COMPANY[15]

It was customary for the Sales Department of the Roberts Machine Company to meet for dinner about every other month. A hotel private dining room was engaged and after dinner a business meeting was conducted by Gordon Swift, Sales Manager. Present at the October meeting in 1957 were Swift, Al Rockland, Assistant Sales Manager, and ten salesmen of the department, six of whom had more than fifteen years of service with Roberts. Also present was James Jacobs, Sales Manager of Electro-Products, Inc., manufacturers of electrical components for home appliances. Jacobs, a personal friend of Swift's and known to most of the men, had been invited to observe the meeting. Swift had previously accepted a similar invitation from Jacobs.

The agendum for the meeting was the consideration of a new method for communicating product information to Roberts' dealers. The new technique was a phonograph record to accompany the firm's catalog. The catalog-record idea was for the dealer, in his own shop or home, to play the record as he leafed through the Roberts catalog. Swift felt the pictures and written words of the catalog alone could not communicate as adequately as the record and catalog combined. The record, in his words, "added another dimension to product communication."

Swift opened the meeting by explaining the purpose of the catalog-record technique and asked the salesmen to play the role of the dealer as they listened to the record. The salesmen leafed through the catalog as the record called their attention to certain aspects about the products.

---

15 All names and organizational designations have been disguised. Northwestern University cases are reports of concrete events and behavior, prepared for class discussion. They are not intended as examples of "good" or "bad" administrative or technical practices. Copyright 1958 by Northwestern University. Reprinted by permission.

When the record ended, Swift asked for comments about the technique. Most of the men contributed to the informal discussion which followed. Mr. Jacobs did not participate.

Various pros and cons of the technique were discussed but the majority of the men seemed to agree that the catalog-record idea was basically a good one. Most of them approved of the method as a way of communicating to the dealer in two media, visually and aurally, simultaneously. A few, however, wondered if it might be too difficult for a man to listen, look at pictures, and read at the same time.

There was some disagreement as to whose voice should appear on the record. Several felt a professional announcer should do the job while the majority preferred that Mr. Swift be the narrator. They suggested that his voice would add a note of warmth and make the process seem more personal than the usual media such as catalogs, pamphlets, newsletters, etc.

Some thought the record offered a special advantage in increasing the accuracy of the communication. They said the emphasis and inflection of the narrator's voice on certain words would help to convey information more precisely than would the written word alone. One man wondered if the average dealer would have the facilities for playing the record but others felt almost every home had a 78 rpm record-player these days.

About thirty minutes after the discussion began, one of the younger salesmen, Ed Knoll, commented: "As long as we're talking about dealer communication, I think we could capitalize on the visual communication angle, too. I wonder if we couldn't take some film clips of several of our machines in action."

There was an audible groan from several of the men. The next person to speak referred to another topic and the subject of film clips never arose again.

Jacobs was somewhat puzzled about the apparent apathy and even negative reaction to the film clip idea. While it was not strictly relevant to the catalog-record technique, it did appear to Jacobs that the idea had potential value for Roberts' overall sales program. The Roberts machines were intricate; a motion picture of them in action could convey what words and still pictures could not possibly communicate. Moreover, Jacobs had always considered Knoll as a bright, hard-working young man who had expressed sincere interest in Roberts during his three years with the firm. But Jacobs remained silent and the meeting continued for another hour.

Eventually, Swift said: "Well, gentlemen, I think we've kicked this around long enough and I certainly appreciate your comments. Al and I will get our heads together next week and we'll let you know whether or not we decide to go ahead with the catalog-record idea.

"But right now, I'd like to hear what our friend, Jim Jacobs, has to say about the performance we put on for him. He's been sitting here soaking it all in. Any reactions, Jim?"

"You're right, Gordon, I have been soaking it all in, which is a bit unusual for me. I'm ordinarily running the show rather than watching it—and I certainly appreciate your invitation. I'd like to do this more often.

"Now, if you don't mind, Gordon, I wonder if I could impose upon you and your men for about three minutes."

"Go right ahead, Jim. Got something cooked up?"

"Well, in a way. You men all know how enthusiastic Gordon is on the subject of communication. And most of you know that I'm pretty much the same way myself. As a matter of fact Gordon and I have spent hours at a time talking about the problems of communication in a business and heaven only knows we've got them in our plant— and in my own department, too. Now, there was one point in this meeting that particularly interested me. Do you all recall that remark of Ed Knoll's about film clips? Well, I wonder if you'd oblige me by writing a short sentence or two about your reaction to Ed's comment. Don't bother to sign your name."

Each man wrote a brief note and passed it to Jacobs who said: "Thank you very much, gentlemen. You might be interested in what I'm up to. Frankly, it's just a little 'experiment' I thought of while I was sitting with my ears open for a change instead of my mouth. I really don't know what to expect from it.

"But Gordon is giving me a lift home so I imagine you'll be getting the results through him."

"Fine, Jim," Swift replied, "This might be interesting at that. And now, unless anyone has anything else to add, let's adjourn the meeting."

Swift began speaking with two or three of the salesmen at the door while the others were collecting their papers and getting into their coats. Jacobs called Knoll over and said: "Ed, I wonder if you would tell me just what you had in mind with that film clip idea?"

"Well, Mr. Jacobs, I thought we could shoot a short film on our own —probably wouldn't run more than ten or fifteen dollars. I have a 16mm camera and if the company would buy the film and help me rig up a few lights—"

"Were you suggesting that the film would be coordinated with the record?"

"Oh, no—it would be entirely apart from the catalog and record. It would be just another way of communicating with our dealers and their customers, too. Our machines are too big, too expensive, and there are too many models for our dealers to stock them. The film would be a way of communicating the actual operation of our machines.'

Jacobs thanked Knoll and went over to Swift who was waiting to drive him home. As they rode Jacobs read the statements aloud. There were eleven of them:

"COST!!!"[16]
"Oh, no! Not the movie boys again!"
"That isn't the kind of thing we can afford to do now."
"Coupled with the record and preview of the catalog the film would be a sharp idea."
"Necessity of having a projector and screen besides a phonograph—too much apparatus."
"Completely irrelevant in terms of a critique of the record idea."
"The idea is for catalogs and records to be sent out and heard. If they are going to show movies you don't need catalogs."
"Vision with the record sounded like a good idea."
"A sound film would be better than a film with a separate record."
"Book, voice, and pictures—too much to observe."
"That's all we need—another unusable film!"

FLIES, TYPHOID, AND PUBLICITY[17]

It was while I was working at the Memorial Institute that an opportunity came for me to bring my scientific training to bear on a problem at Hull House. (My efforts in the baby clinic could not be called scientific.) This was in the fall of 1902, when I came back from Mackinac to find Chicago in the grip of one of her worst epidemics of typhoid fever. At that time the water, drawn from the Lake, was not chlorinated; the only precaution taken against dangerous pollution was to make daily cultures of samples from the different pumping stations

---

16 Jacobs discovered from Swift that the Roberts Company had had a very unpleasant and costly experience with a product film prepared by a film production firm. The film had cost $7,500 and for various reasons had never been used.

17 From *Exploring the Dangerous Trades* by Alice Hamilton, M.D. (Boston: Little, Brown & Co., 1943). Reprinted by permission.

and the next day, when the cultures had had time to develop, publish the results and tell the public whether or not to boil water. It was assumed that housewives would look up these instructions every day, and act accordingly, but the actual result was that typhoid was endemic in Chicago and periodically it reached epidemic proportions. On this particular occasion Hull House was the center of the hardest-struck region of the city—why, nobody knew. Miss Addams said she thought a bacteriologist ought to be able to discover the reason.

It was certainly not a simple problem. The pumping station which sent water to the Nineteenth Ward sent it to a wide section of the West Side, the milk supply was the same as that for neighboring wards. There must be some local condition to account for the excessive number of cases. As I prowled about the streets and the ramshackle wooden tenement houses I saw the outdoor privies (forbidden by law but flourishing nevertheless), some of them in backyards below the level of the street and overflowing in heavy rains; the wretched water closets indoors, one for four or more families, filthy and with the plumbing out of order because nobody was responsible for cleaning or repairs; and swarms of flies everywhere. Here, I thought, was the solution of the problem. The flies were feeding on typhoid-infected excreta and then lighting on food and milk. During the Spanish-American War, when we lost more men from typhoid fever than from Spanish bullets, Vaughan, Shakespeare, and Reed had made a study of conditions in camps—open latrines, unscreened food—which led them to attribute an important role in the spread of typhoid fever to the house fly. That was what started the "Swat the fly" campaign.

Naturally, my theory had to be put to the test, so, with two of the residents to help me, Maude Gernon and Gertrude Howe, I went forth to collect flies—from privies and kitchens and filthy water closets. We would drop the flies into tubes of broth and I would take them to the laboratory, incubate the tubes, and plate them out at varying intervals. It was a triumph to find the typhoid bacillus and I hastened to write up the discovery and its background for presentation before the Chicago Medical Society. This was just the sort of thing to catch public attention: it was simple and easily understood; it fitted in with the revelations made during the Spanish War of the deadly activities of house flies, and it explained why the slums had so much more typhoid than the well-screened and decently drained homes of the well-to-do.

I am sure I gained more kudos from my paper on flies and typhoid than from any other piece of work I ever did. Even today I sometimes hear an echo of it. In Chicago the effect was most gratifying; a public inquiry resulted in a complete reorganization of the Health Department under a chief loaned by the Public Health Service, and an expert was put in charge of tenement-house inspection. But unfortunately my gratification over my part in all this did not last long. After the tumult had died down I discovered a fact which never gained much publicity but was well-authenticated. My flies had had little or nothing to do with the cases of typhoid in the Nineteenth Ward. The cause was simpler but so much more discreditable that the Board of Health had not dared reveal it. It seems that in our local pumping station, on West Harrison Street, near Halsted, a break had occurred which resulted in an escape of sewage into the water pipes and for three days our neighborhood drank that water before the leak was discovered and stopped. This was after the epidemic had started. The truth was more shocking than my ingenious theory, and it never came to light, so far as the public was concerned. For years, although I did my best to lay the ghosts of those flies, they haunted me and mortified me, compelling me again and again to explain to deeply impressed audiences that the dramatic story their chairman had just rehearsed had little foundations in fact.

Chapter XII

TRIGGER TO DISPUTE

The problem of human disagreement is as old as man. Much has been discovered about the nature of disputes, their benefits and evils, their causes and consequences, how they may be instigated, utilized, conciliated, avoided. Rather than present a comprehensive exposition on dispute, this chapter is restricted to one major contributing factor and to the suggestion of techniques by which undesirable dispute may be avoided or ameliorated. It will be useful to classify disputes into two arbitrary categories.

INTENTIONAL DISPUTE

Some disagreements occur largely, if not solely, because the disputants desire them. They find it in their own interests or in the interests of groups they represent to enter into conflict. When company and union representatives meet for contract negotiations, it is generally accepted that each side will take more extreme positions than they intend untimately to assume. This is the nature of bargaining, whether it occurs at a summit conference of the major world powers or at the corner pawnshop.

But not all intentional dispute is based upon self-interest. A favored technique among many teachers is to play the role of the "Devil's Advocate." The teacher may assume a position, with which he may actually disagree, simply to stimulate students to defend or clarify their own positions.

NONINTENTIONAL DISPUTE

Much human disagreement is largely nondeliberate.[1] The disputants differ without intending to do so. The so-called "honest disagree-

---

[1] The categories of "intentional" and "nonintentional" are by no means mutually exclusive. It is unlikely that any given dispute would not involve at least some aspect of "intent" and "nonintent." The dichotomy is merely a convenient one for this chapter's purpose, which is to focus on disputes of a primarily nonintentional nature.

239

ments" fall into this classification; people quarreling with one another because they sincerely believe themselves "right" and the other fellow "wrong."

This chapter takes the position that a major contributor to non-intentional disagreement is *differing perceptions*.

Differing Perceptions

There is an abstract painting hanging in my office. I don't particularly care for it myself, but I keep it there because I enjoy observing my visitors' reactions to it. A photograph of the picture is shown on pages 242–43. And here are verbatim samples of unsolicited comments:

"Where did you find that monstrosity?"
"There's a lot of emotional impact there."
"Looks like someone did that with the brush between his toes."
"That's very well done, isn't it?"
"My five-year-old brought home something like that from kindergarten yesterday!"
"What are you doing—covering up a hole in the wall?"
"You can tell that the artist has had training."

My visitors' reactions differed markedly despite the probability that the impacts of stimuli upon their respective nervous systems were very similar. *Differing perceptions*—different ways of appraising, interpreting, evaluating the experience they were having—is a plausible explanation of the phenomenon. A case for differing perceptions as a trigger to nonintentional dispute can be made quite logically.

1. Perceptions influence external behavior, overt reactions. (If you perceive the painting as ridiculous, for example, would you not be inclined to react accordingly with a grimace, or grunt, or an uncomplimentary remark?)

2. Different people may perceive an object, situation, person, happening, etc., differently. (What did *you* think of my picture?)

3. Therefore, differing perceptions of the object, etc., tend to lead to differing overt reactions to it.

4. And when people's overt reactions to an object, etc., differ, the setting is ripe for confusion and dispute. (Imagine my uninhibited "art critics" expressing themselves at the same time and place!)

Why Perceptions Differ

The next question, then, is What causes perceptions to differ? How can people view a picture or hear a piece of music or political oration and respond in such diverse ways? Two factors seem paramount:

Which part of the event happening one sees, hears, etc., and *how* he interprets that portion.

Which Details Are Abstracted. No one sees *all* of a happening, situation, person, object, etc. Some aspects are inaccessible to him, and, of the others, he inevitably selects some and discards or neglects the remainder. Often the fragment one sees is determined by chance and by timing and location. In the movie, *Production 5118*,[2] the company president has decided to ship some machines from one plant to another division of the firm. His purpose is to bring in new and better machines which will increase production, upgrade employees, etc. But the employees in the first plant have been told only that the machines are to be shipped. In the absence of any explanation, they conclude that their plant is to be shut down and make arrangements to take jobs elsewhere. Their perceptions differed from those of the president because they had been excluded from a significant part of the situation.

The differing perceptions of union and management develop partly because the two groups are often not looking at similar aspects in their relationship. For example, what the union hears from employees is frequently not what management hears from them. And in many cases union-company differences may evolve partially because the union is not in a position to observe the innumerable intricacies, pressures, and forces with which management must deal in its administration of the firm.

Of course, we, in our habits of *attending*, exclude parts of a situation from ourselves. It is said that a doctor at home asleep or engrossed in reading may hear a telephone ring, but not his baby's crying. His wife, under similar circumstances, might hear the baby but not the telephone.

Physiological Differences. Chance, timing, location, and habits of attending are not the sole determinants of which details are abstracted by the perceiver. Differing physiological limitations and deficiencies may play a role as well. To illustrate this point in the classroom, I usually distribute small squares of white paper to my students with the request that they chew them and try to determine the taste. If the class is representative, a good share of them describe the paper as tasteless, another large group taste it as distinctly bitter, and the remainder taste it variously as sweet, sour, or salty. I then explain that the paper had been impregnated with the chemical, phenyl-thio-carbamide

---

2 Produced by the Champion Paper and Fibre Company as a public service.

(P.T.C., for short). The paper, which is harmless, is prepared by the American Genetic Association[3] to trace hereditary traits. If a student failed to receive a definite taste sensation, it does not mean that he is going to enjoy a steak any less than anyone else, but it does indicate that he has apparently failed to inherit the sensory apparatus necessary to distinguish P.T.C. from other "tasteless" paper (no great loss). The demonstration does illustrate, however, that our senses do differ (color blindness and faulty vision and hearing are more obvious and serious examples), and thus our perceptions are accordingly affected. I have had a few mild disputes, for example, with my wife who "alleged" the presence of a shrill whistle in the television set. Since I did not hear it I, logically enough, denied that it existed. This, however, was before I submitted to an audiometric examination and discovered that, like so many others who worked near artillery during the war, I had lost the capacity to hear tones of extremely high pitch.

How Details Are Interpreted.   One's perception, then, is obviously influenced by which aspects he abstracts from a given situation. There is, however, another factor which contributes to the phenomenon of differing perceptions. *How one interprets* what he abstracts is equally important.

How we size up, evaluate, and appraise the data and experiences we have may be affected by numerous influences—among them, learning, set, and language habits.

Learning. "Learning" is intended here in its broadest usage—including not only one's formal education but all his experience, his background, his culture—any facet of his environment which has helped to shape him. Especially with respect to social phenomena, no two of us learned quite the same things in quite the same way and never develop, therefore, precisely the same attitudes and feelings about certain things. Take the subject of alcoholic beverages, for example. Some people look upon drinking as inexcusably sinful, others as a pleasant relaxation, others as an extravagance, others as an opportunity for companionship or conviviality, and still others as an escape from it all.

For more dramatic examples of how learning affects perception, compare different cultures. Suppose a child is misbehaving and its mother is about to tell it to behave properly. If the family is an English-speaking one, the mother would most likely say: "John, be *good!*" or words to that effect. That is, the English-speaking mother has *learned*

---

3 The P.T.C. papers may be obtained at a nominal price from the Association at 1507 M St. N.W., Washington 5, D.C.

to perceive misbehaving children as *bad, wicked, naughty.* This is also true for Greeks and Italians. The French-speaking mother, however, would say: "Jean, sois sage!"—"be wise." The French child who misbehaves is not considered bad or naughty; it is *foolish, imprudent, injudicious.* In Scandinavian countries it is still different. A Swedish mother would typically say: "Jan, var snell!" and a Norwegian: "Jan, ble snil!" Both mean about the same: "Be *friendly,* be *kind."* The Scandinavian child who misbehaves is seen as *unfriendly, unkind,* and *unco-operative.* But how different in Germany: "Hans, sei artig!"— "be in line!" The misbehaving child is *out of line, out of step, not conforming.* And the Hopi Indian mother has a similar feeling but expresses it more gently when she says: "No, no, no, that is not the Hopi way." The Hopi way is the *right,* the *proper* way.[4]

Clearly, these mothers could watch the same child and yet *perceive* his conduct quite differently. They have *learned* through one of the greatest (and most subtle) of teachers—their respective cultures—to perceive differently.

Set. A *set* is defined as a predisposition to respond in a certain manner. We tend to perceive a situation as we want to see it or as we are prepared to see it. Munn described a personal experience in which his *set* obviously influenced his perception:

> I once had a colony of white rats in the attic of the psychology building. One afternoon I found several rats outside of their cages. Some were dead and partly eaten. It occurred to me that, however the rats had escaped, they must have been eaten by wild rats. I went downstairs to get some water and was climbing the stairs again when I saw before me, and directly in front of the cages, a large wild gray rat. It was standing tense and trembling, apparently having heard me ascend the stairs. Very slowly I raised a glass jar that was in my right hand, and aimed it at the rat. Much to my surprise, the animal failed to move. Upon approaching the object, I discovered it to be a piece of crumpled-up grayish paper. Without the set induced by my suspicion that gray rats were in the attic, I should undoubtedly have seen the paper for what it was, assuming that I noticed it at all.[5]

A common psychological defense mechanism—*projection*—is the tendency of a person to perceive his own thoughts and desires in others. The college student who cheats in examination has the *set* to "see" other students cheating. And the husband who "strays" may, without foundation, accuse his wife of unfaithfulness.

---

4 See "A Word in Your Ear," *Ways of Mankind* by Lister Sinclair *et al.* (Boston: Beacon Press, 1954), pp. 28–29.

5 Norman L. Munn, *Psychology: The Fundamentals of Human Adjustment* (Boston: Houghton Mifflin Co., 1946), p. 327. Reprinted by permission.

People with different *sets*, then, will tend to perceive differently. Workers and foremen apparently perceive job conditions in quite different ways. The table below shows how they ranked the importance of various job conditions.

Job Conditions	Worker Rating	Foreman Rating*
Appreciation for good work	1st	8th
Feeling "in" on things	2nd	10th
Help with personal problems	3rd	9th
Job security	4th	2nd
Good wages	5th	1st
"Work that keeps you interested"	6th	5th
Possibilities for promotion	7th	3rd
Personal loyalty to the workers	8th	6th
Good working conditions	9th	4th
Tactful discipline	10th	7th

* Prepared by the Labor Relations Institute of New York and published in *Human Understanding in Industry* by William C. Menninger and Harry Levinson (Chicago: Science Research Associates, Inc., 1956), p. 12. Reprinted by permission.

Note that the three job conditions rated *first* by the employees were rated *last* by the foreman.

Language Habits.   When people are engaged in dispute, certain patterns of language (aside from profanity) tend to occur quite frequently. Here are examples of disagreement on two widely separated planes.

One of the most widespread disputes of the century occurred in the spring of 1951 when President Truman ordered General MacArthur from his Pacific command. Few events within memory have led to such controversy and divided opinion. *Time,* in an article titled "Jubilation & Foreboding," quoted dozens of newspapers, radio broadcasts, people in the street, as they gave their reaction to the MacArthur dismissal. The following is a sampling from the article:

. . . In the Communist world, jubilee was mostly high and unrestrained. "Victory for the Chinese and Korean people in the fight to resist American aggression," crowed Radio Peking. Rome's Red organ *l'Unita* echoed: "The criminal MacArthur fired because of the protest of the whole civilized world." The satellite Budapest press chanted a litany of satisfaction over the dismissal of a "bloody-handed hangman, murderous, carnivorous fascist." Only Moscow struck the suspicious as well as triumphant note. "Having removed the general who failed," warned the *Literary Gazette* for the ears of the Communist faithful, "Wall Street does not intend to renounce his risky policy."

In the free world, there was also jubilation—and foreboding. A vast sigh of relief rose from Europe and Britain, where MacArthur had long been the symbol of an American urge to get entangled in Asia, plunge into World War III.

"With all his merits," said a complacent Dutch housewife, "he was a nuisance."

"He was *muy macho*" (a brave fellow), shrugged a Spaniard. "He won a war of guns and lost a war of words."

The Athens *Kathimerini* editorialized: "The sacking of an American military leader as a sacrifice for the British lion does not bring about unity."

In Japan, it was as though a fatherly friend and mentor had departed. The *Nippon Times* said: "The Japanese people owe General MacArthur an eternal debt of gratitude." The national Diet sent a letter: "Deepest gratitude. . . . We shall remember you as our greatest benefactor."

Filipinos, who felt very close to MacArthur, were saddest of all. Sighed a Manila hack driver: "It is like being told that Uncle Sam is no more." A small-town storekeeper asked: "This man Truman doesn't make sense. Why is it that he is tough and cruel to a brother American like MacArthur, yet is bashful to an enemy like Stalin?"[6]

And now a disagreement on quite another level:

Fifteen-year old Jerry Sikon of Macomb County, Michigan, watched a TV horror mystery as he cleaned his shotgun. Four of his brothers and sisters were also looking on. His father, Deputy Sheriff John Sikon, a former preacher, objected to the program. His mother said it wasn't harmful. Words between the parents led to blows. After the deputy sheriff struck the wife with a paint roller, Jerry slipped a shell into his shotgun and fired at his father. "Don't blame the boy. I was wrong," said the father just before he died.[7]

- The "Is" of Predication.   Note in each dispute the explicit and implicit recurrence of the grammatical form in which a noun and an adjective are connected by a form of the verb *to be*. Statements and implications such as these were plentiful:

MacArthur was brave.
MacArthur was bloody-handed.
The program is harmful.
The program is harmless.

This particular use of *is* (or the verb *to be* in any tense or number) is called the *"is of predication"* because it predicates a quality (which is represented by the adjective) to the subject (which is represented by the noun). Thus the *is* in the statement, "the tomato is red," predicates "redness" to the tomato, suggesting that the "redness" *belongs to* or *exists in* the tomato. This is a troublesome notion for two reasons: (1) It expresses a fallacious relationship. (2) People are usually un-

---

6 "Jubilation & Foreboding," *Time*, April 23, 1951, p. 34. Reprinted by permission.
7 *Time*, February 4, 1952, p. 13. Reprinted by permission.

aware, especially in the heat of dispute, that they are basing their thinking and actions on such a fallacy. Thus they may be led into unreasonable, immature, unintelligent, and destructive behavior.

A Fallacious Notion. Does "redness" exist *in* the tomato? If "redness" is contained in the tomato as, say, water is contained in a pitcher; then it ought to remain there regardless of any external factors we might vary, such as changing the color of the light we shine upon it. That is, we would hardly expect the water to cease to exist in the pitcher just because we throw blue or green light upon it. But let us try it with the tomato, which supposedly "contains" the "redness." Beam a blue or green light on a ripe "red" tomato in an otherwise darkened room, and it will appear black! Where has the "redness" gone? Obviously, it wasn't in the tomato in the first place. But where, then, is the "redness"?

To return to our high-school physics, the reason we *call* a tomato "red" or a banana "yellow," a plum "purple," etc., is because these objects have the property of reflecting certain wave lengths of light but not others. These reflected light waves impinge upon one's retina and are eventually translated into inside-the-head experiences. It is these personal experiences that are labeled "redness," "yellowness," "purpleness," etc.[8] Colors and qualities in general, then, exist neither in the object nor exclusively in the observer but rather *in the observer in his relation to the observed*—as a *joint phenomenon* of the two.

Perceptions, therefore, have to do not only with the *observed* but with the *observer*, as well. The *is* of predication form of language would lead us to believe otherwise, that perception is concerned only with the observed—that "redness" is *in* the tomato apart from the observer; that "beauty" is in the painting regardless of the viewer; and that "excellence" in the stage play, irrespective of the critic.

A Lack of Awareness. The *is* of predication, then, promulgates a fallacy. A fallacy is usually harmless if it is recognized as such. Unfortunately, such is not often the case with the *is* of predication. As with the other erroneous assumptions we develop and hold through the influences of our language habits, we rarely challenge them. We seldom question the notion that the "gaudiness" is *in* the tie, that the

---

8 This explains why a "red" tomato appears "black" when a "green" or "blue" light is thrown upon it. "Red" pigments have the property of reflecting "red" light but of absorbing "green" and "blue" light. In the darkened room all *available* light was absorbed by the "red" pigment, none was reflected, thus giving the appearance of "black." A ripe tomato usually *appears* "red" because we usually see it bathed in "white" light (which contains all light colors, including "red," and thus the "red" light waves are reflected while the "blue" and "green" light waves are absorbed).

"silliness" is *in* the poem, and that the "impracticality" is *in* the company policy.

How easy it was for the unfortunate Sikon parents to see "harmfulness" and "harmlessness" *in* the television program rather than in *themselves as they viewed it.*

If one assumes that qualities (e.g., honesty, loyalty, selfishness, courage, laziness, stupidity, friendliness, treachery, trustworthiness, talent, etc.) are solely in the persons he is observing, then it is quite logical for him to assume that what he sees in them is what everyone else will or should see. According to this reasoning, anyone who disagrees with him (i.e., sees the person differently) must be misinformed, stupid, or perverse or just plain ornery. And if the other fellow is burdened by the same fallacy, you can imagine the prospects for conflict. Let us put this more concretely.

Suppose Mr. Andrews and Mr. Baker, employees of a firm, know that Mr. Carson, another employee, has the habit of taking company property for his own use. They know he would never touch the personal possessions of his fellow workers, nor would he take a company item of considerable value. But he does carry home small quantities of rubber bands, pencils, stamps, carbon paper, etc.

Now Mr. Andrews, a product of a strict religious upbringing, may perceive this behavior as sinful, dishonest, inexcusable. Mr. Baker, in such matters, is strongly influenced by his military service during World War II, in which a widespread code was that "you can rob from the Service—but don't take a nickel from another Serviceman." Baker might very conceivably see Carson's actions as quite acceptable, a bit risky perhaps, but perfectly justified—just taking advantage of certain "informal perquisites" which go with working for the firm.

If neither Andrews nor Baker is aware of the nature of perception— that the qualities of "dishonesty" and "honesty" they may respectively see *in* Carson are really *in themselves as they view him*—then conflict is virtually assured. And the "Carson-is-dishonest"—"Carson-is-honest" pattern of thought and talk which triggers their dispute will only intensify their differences.

Two Useful "Is'es." Before concluding this discussion of the *is* of predication, let me make it clear that I do not suggest that we abolish the word, *is*! It is an exceedingly useful word in two senses:

1. As an auxiliary in the formation of tenses as in "He *is* eating"; "They *were* window-shopping"; "She *was* working in the garden"; etc.
2. As a synonym for existence or location as in "I live, I exist, I *am*"; "Chicago *is* in Illinois"; "There *are* four persons in this room"; etc.

Neither of these usages of the verb *to be* is harmful or misleading, and both, in fact, are quite necessary.[9]

SUMMARY

We have been concerned with the nonintentional aspects of dispute. Differing perceptions appear to be a prime factor. One's perceptions are determined to a great extent by *which* details he abstracts and *how* he interprets them. Our perceptions may be affected by, among other influences, learning, set, and language habits. One of the more destructive of our language habits is the *is* of predication, which gives a false picture of the perception process.

CORRECTIVES

If one would avoid nonintentional, unconstructive dispute, if he would obviate the loss of time and temper in fruitless argument, the following suggestions should prove of value.

Regard Perception as a Joint Phenomenon

Remember that perception involves the *observer* as well as the *observed*. How one perceives "reality" often depends greatly on the perceiver. Qualities exist not exclusively in the *observed* but in the *observer in his relationship with what he is observing*—qualities exist, if you will, in the *observer's observations*.

Carl Rogers suggests a provocative technique:

The next time you get into an argument with your wife, or your friend, or with a small group of friends, just stop the discussion for a moment and, for an experiment, institute this rule. "Each person can speak up for himself only *after* he has first restated the ideas and feelings of the previous speaker accurately, and to that speaker's satisfaction." You see what this would mean. It would simply mean that before presenting your own point of view, it would be necessary for you to really achieve the other speaker's frame of reference—to understand his thoughts and feelings so well that you could summarize them for him. Sounds simple, doesn't it? But if you

---

9 We use *is* in still another sense which, like the *is* of predication, contributes to faulty and deceptive communication. Lee describes the "is of identification" thus:

". . . The 'is' leads to the *identification* of different levels of abstraction, implying in the utterance that one 'thing' can exist as another. The use has this form: 'Man *is* an animal'; 'Joe *is* a radical'; 'Having done that, she *is* a sinner.' The 'is' of identity serves to link nouns, obscuring the differences between silent and verbal levels. This 'is' serves as a synonym for 'may be called or classified as.' "—Irving J. Lee, *Language Habits in Human Affairs*, p. 229.

try it you will discover it one of the most difficult things you have ever tried to do. However, once you have been able to see the other's point of view, your own comments will have to be drastically revised. You will also find the emotion going out of the discussion, the differences being reduced, and those differences which remain being of a rational and understandable sort.[10]

Beware the Is of Predication

The *is* of predication, of course, is not the only contributor to dispute and conflict, but it does offer a specific means for attacking the problem.

Develop the "To-Me-ness" Attitude. An effective way to cope with nonintentional dispute is to develop an awareness of the uniqueness of perceptions.

If I can remain conscious of the fact that my perceptions are the way "reality" *appears to me*—and not *necessarily* to the other fellow—I will find it possible to be a good deal more reasonable and tolerant of other points of view. One way to gain this awareness and to communicate it to others is to substitute in your talking, writing, and *thinking*, "appears to me" for the *is* of predication. Instead of "Carson *is* dishonest," make it "Carson *appears to me* dishonest." By doing so, not only do you heighten your own awareness of the "to-me-ness" nature of perception, but your remarks becomes less irreconcilable for the fellow whose perception differs from your own.

It is a useful technique for the receiver, as well. Suppose someone tells you: "A liberal arts education *is* the best preparation for business." And suppose your point of view is diametrically opposed to this assertion. You will find yourself less likely to lose control of yourself if you can translate his statement as "A liberal arts education *appears to him* to be the best . . . etc."

The Concealed Is. A digression is in order here. The *is* of predication does not appear exclusively in the simple noun-is-adjective form. Often it is only implied. Grammatical inversions and elaborations sometimes conceal the *is*, making its influence only more insidious. To cope with the disguised *is*, translate the phrase or statement into the noun-is-adjective form, thus revealing its fallacious implication. Some examples:

---

10 Carl R. Rogers, "Communication: Its Blocking and Its Facilitation," a paper originally prepared for delivery at the Northwestern University Centennial Conference on Communications, held in Evanston, Illinois, October 11–13, 1951. Reproduced here from the Northwestern University *Information*, Vol. XX, No. 25, pp. 9–15.

Type	Statement	Translation	Implication
Adjective in subject rather than predicate	"That arrogant union business agent infuriates me."	"That business agent is arrogant."	The "arrogance" is in the business agent (rather than in the observer as he observes him).
Verb substitution	"The British have an excellent form of government."	"The British form of government *is* excellent."	The "excellence" is in the British form of government.
A quality expressed by an "associative" noun rather than by an adjective.	"My boss takes the prize as the top grouch in this company."	"My *boss is* grouchy."	The "grouchiness" is in the boss.
A quality expressed by an adverb.	"Tom plays tennis brilliantly."	"Tom's *tennis-playing is briliant.*"	The "brilliance" is in the tennis-playing.

A Final Word. "To-me-ness" (and "to-him-ness") as deeply ingrained conditioned responses can, in the view of this author, be exceeding useful in avoiding and reducing unintentional dispute. But, manifested as mere verbal mannerisms, they may be worse than useless. We sometimes hear a person preface his remarks with "It seems to me," "In my opinion," or "It appears to me," and proceed to make quite dogmatic, unqualified, and unreasonable statements. Whether ignorant of his arrogance or deliberately trying to conceal it, he is hardly likely to minimize the possibilities of conflict with such superficial expressions.

If "to-me-ness" is to be truly effective, one must "internalize" it—make it a habitual orientation toward life. This takes time, self-discipline, and constant vigilance, but the results will be well worth the effort. And, of course, as the habit becomes established, it will require less and less conscious effort.

INCIDENTS

IS THIS MAN MAD?[11]

Imagine that the individual described in the following brief case history came to you for treatment. How would you diagnose his ailment and what therapy would you recommend? . . .

All through childhood, K. was extremely meditative, usually preferred to be alone. He often had mysterious dreams and fits, during which he sometimes fainted. In late puberty, K. experienced elaborate auditory and visual hallucinations, uttered incoherent words, and had recurrent spells of sudden coma. He was frequently found running wildly through the countryside or eating the bark of trees and was known to throw himself with abandon into fire and water. On many occasions he wounded himself with knives or other weapons. K. believed he could "talk to spirits" and "chase ghosts." He was certain of his power over all sorts of supernatural forces.

THE ACTUAL DIAGNOSIS

Believe it or not, K. was not found insane, nor was he committed to the nearest institution for the mentally ill. Instead, in due course, he became one of the leading and most respected members of his community.

How this strange turn of events could come about may become more plausible to you if we supply an important bit of information that was purposely left out of the case history on the preceding page.

K., we should have told you, was a member of a primitive tribe of fishermen and reindeer herders that inhabits the arctic wilderness of Eastern Siberia. In this far-off culture the same kind of behavior that we regard as symptomatic of mental illness is considered evidence of an individual's fitness for an important social position—that of medicine man or shaman.

The hallucinations, fits, manic episodes and periods of almost complete withdrawal that marked his early years were considered signs that he had been chosen by some higher power for an exalted role. His

11 *State of Mind,* published by Ciba Pharmaceutical Products, Inc., Summit, N.J., Vol. **I,** No. 1 (January, 1957). Reprinted by permission.

behavioral eccentricities were, in fact, prerequisite to his becoming a shaman, just as balance, solidity, self-confidence and aggressiveness are prerequisite for the young man who hopes to be successful in American business.

Sociologists and anthropologists explain that shamanism serves two socially useful purposes in Siberian society. In the first place, it pro· vides an approved outlet for the person of unstable temperament. It allows him to let off steam through an emotionally satisfying dramatic performance in which he summons spirits and manipulates the supernatural. In the second place, shamanism provides entertainment for other tribesmen and welcome relief from the monotony of their bleak environment.

THE COCKTAIL PARTY[12]

The following conversation occurred at a cocktail party between Fred Lyons and William Baird. Both men were in their early thirties. Lyons had been practicing dentistry for six years, and Baird had just been graduated from law school. Both were veterans of World War II and had received G.I. Bill benefits toward their college educations. Each, however, had worked part-time to supplement his income during his years in college. They had known each other on a casual basis for about a year.

LYONS: Well, Bill, I hear you're about to take your bar examination. What are your plans if you get by them?

BAIRD: There's no *if* about it, Fred. But to answer your question, I'm lining up a practice right now.

LYONS: Do you mean to tell me you have no doubts about passing the bar?

BAIRD: None, really. This is the way I look at it: I attended one of the better law schools in the country and I was one of the better men in my class. So I really don't have any qualms at all.

LYONS: (Slightly sarcastically) And I suppose you have no qualms about succeeding in law, in general.

BAIRD: No, I'm really quite confident that I'll make a go of it.

LYONS: Well, buddy, you've got a lot to learn. (He then began to recount at length some of his own difficulties and disappointments in starting in his profession.) And when you come right down to it, it's

---

12 Adapted from a case prepared by Eleanor Lynch Roeser. Printed by permission.

a plenty tough uphill climb to establish a reputation and a following. Frankly, Bill, you're going to have trouble attracting a clientele with this super-confidence of yours.

BAIRD: There's where you're dead wrong. A man has to have assurance and confidence in himself or no one else will have confidence in him. Do you think a person would want his legal problems handled by a fellow who didn't give the appearance that he was dead certain he knew what he was doing?

LYONS: To be honest, I think the average man would be repelled rather than attracted by this attitude. Your client, the man on the street, wants to feel that his lawyer is his type of man. You've got to speak his language in order to convince him you understand his problem. Here, I'll give you a test. Suppose I come to you with a problem. (He then posed a legal question concerning income tax.) How would you handle it?

BAIRD: I can't give you an opinion on that. I'd have to have a good many more facts and I'd have to study them.

LYONS: Now, do you see? Be honest with yourself, Bill. You don't have the experience and if you parade around with that cocksure attitude of yours, you're not going to get to first base.

BAIRD: (Both men were somewhat angered by now.) Now, listen, Fred. Law is a science of the mind. Dentistry is more of a mechanical science where you might expect to solve some problems immediately. And even in dentistry you can't pass judgment on an oral problem without an examination and maybe even an X-ray.

LYONS: Well, all I can say, Bill—if you don't learn a more humble approach; if you don't bring your speaking and attitude down to the level of the average man, you're asking for trouble.

BAIRD: Well, if you ask me, the "average man" isn't going to have much confidence in anyone who is *too* average.

The afternoon was "saved" by a third person who broke into the conversation and managed to switch the subject to baseball.

THE ACCIDENT[13]
By E. C. St. John

The scene is the personnel office of an industrial firm. Sam, the

---

13 All names are disguised. Printed by permission.

personnel manager, is questioning the second shift printing foreman about an accident which had occurred the previous night. Dave, the printing foreman, is a middle-aged man who has come up from the ranks. He is conscientious, energetic, and proud of his production record.

"Sam, I don't know what makes these guys pull these crazy stunts," Dave said as he lit his cigarette. The cuticles of the hand holding the match were stained from years of wash-ups and make-readys on the presses. "You front office guys are always harping on this 'Why do accidents happen?' business too much anyway," he continued. Leaning forward in his chair eager to make his point, he waved a stubby finger under the personnel manager's nose. "Accidents are bound to happen," he stated. "I've been trying to tell you ever since you came to this plant. You take this one you're asking about now. Ross just did a dumb thing that's all. He knew better than to adjust the gate on the hopper while the press was running but he just didn't think. Stupid, I guess."

"Stupid?" the personnel manager questioned. "Oh, I don't mean stupid really," Dave continued. "He's got more education than I have and when it comes to figuring he's tops but last night he just didn't care."

"It must have played the devil with your production to have a man almost lose his finger. Beside the time taken getting him to first aid, you had to run the press a man short," Sam sympathized.

"Well, no," Dave said as he tapped his cigarette out. "You see when they came in I cornered the whole bunch and told them we had this big beer ad run to get out and I wanted these presses running red hot. I remember telling Ross he wouldn't have time to worry about that baby that's coming soon, cause we were gonna hang up a record for the first shift to shoot at. I had to climb him a little later for taking so long with his make-ready. Then at lunch break he said he was having trouble with his register. I told him not to kid me, I'd run presses when he was reaching for a bottle and I knew he could finish that order if he wasn't too lazy. He didn't get hurt until about an hour and a half after lunch. By then we had two-thirds of the order run, so by holding the guys for half an hour, we finished it."

"You say he hurt his hand because—" Sam questioned. "—Cause he's just plain careless," Dave interrupted.

"O.K., Dave," the personnel manager said, "I think I understand."

"THEY DON'T DO IT OUR WAY" [14]
By Dr. Ina Telberg

"What the Distinguished Lady Representative has just suggested proves that women can be more than decorative—they can also be useful."

With this jovial remark, a United States Delegate looked at his Soviet Colleague in the Population Commission of the United Nations and awaited a smile of response. None came. The Russian sat stiff and unsmiling. In Russia there are no jokes about women drivers or women delegates, so beloved by the Americans. The Russian conception of courtesy, therefore, forbade the Soviet Delegate to do anything but freeze into a silent disapproval. The well-meaning American attempt to find common ground by means of a joke thus increased, rather than decreased, the psychological distance between the two delegations. . . .

ONE MAN'S MEAL . . .

One of the most deeply rooted, and largely unconscious, features of any culture is what the psychologists call the *time perspective*. Within the United Nations, at least three different time perspectives operate.

"Gentlemen, it is time for lunch, we must adjourn," announces the Anglo-Saxon chairman, in the unabashed belief that having three meals a day at regular hours is the proper way for mankind to exist.

"But why? We haven't finished what we were doing," replies—in a puzzled manner that grows rapidly more impatient—an Eastern European Delegate, in whose country people eat when the inclination moves them and every family follows its own individual timetable.

"Why, indeed?" placidly inquires the Far Eastern representative, hailing from a country where life and time are conceived as a continuous stream, with no man being indispensable, with no life-process needing to be interrupted for any human being, and where members of electoral bodies walk in and out of the room quietly, getting a bite to eat when necessary, talking to a friend when pleasant; but where meetings, theatre performances, and other arranged affairs last without interruption for hours on end, while individuals come and go,

14 Reprinted by permission from *UNESCO Courier*, May, 1950.

are replaced by others, meditate or participate as the occasion requires, without undue strain, stress, or nervous tension.

As one or the other group persists in its own conception of the time perspective, as the Anglo-Saxons demand that the duration of meetings and conferences be fixed in advance and that meals be taken regularly at fixed hours, and as the Russians sit irritated and the Latins puzzled and the Secretariat frantic—as this condition continues, mutual friction grows, murmurs of "unreasonableness" are heard around the room; and, when the issue under discussion is an important one, overt accusations are hurled across the room of "insincerity," "lack of a serious approach to the problem," and even "sabotage."

IRONY OR POETRY

Another frequent source of irritation, rooted deeply in the cultural differences among nations, is the *length and the style of oration*.

The Latins are usually accused of unnecessary length and of equally unnecessary flights of poetic fancy. The Russians are disliked both for the length of their speeches and for the irony and sarcasm of the speeches' content. The utilization of irony in political speeches is a long-standing tradition of *public oratory in Russia*. It has nothing to do with the Soviet Government. Mr. Vishinsky, for example, most noted for this type of oration, was born, trained, and had had considerable success as trial lawyer and political orator, long before the establishment of the Soviet Government.

It was in November, 1946, that I was flown to Lake Success from the Nurnberg Trials. I was tired, sleepy, and a stranger to the United Nations. On November 15th Vishinsky was delivering his now-famous veto speech in the Political Committee at Lake Success. A regular interpreter failed, and I was rushed to the microphone in the middle of the speech. I remember how my voice trembled when I first began to speak. I knew that I was on the air, and that many of my friends in America and England were listening. In a few minutes, however, I lost every trace of self-consciousness as Mr. Vishinsky's Russian carried me away by its sheer beauty, force, and richness of expression. Latin quotations, Russian proverbs, even Shakespearian poetry, were utilized for the purposes of his attack on the British and the American positions.

Next day I was startled by the press reactions. I myself even received some fan mail: a couple of letters that denounced me as a Communist for having interpreted the speech with such fervor, and another one that praised me for same. I realized then how unnecessarily vitriolic, aggressive, and offensive the address was when translated: in fact, how ill-adapted was the Russian oratorical style to delivery in a foreign tongue. It was not the language itself, however, that was the obstacle. It was the tradition behind the language; what I have since learned to call *speech etiquette.*

SETTLING A "GRAVE" ISSUE

The Latins, on the other hand, far from employing sarcasm, prefer to sprinkle their speeches with a liberal amount of poetic imagery, metaphysical expressions, and literary allusions.

During the General Assembly meetings in Paris, a Latin-American delegate pleaded for the inclusion of the phrase, "from the cradle to the grave," in the Article of the Declaration of Human Rights dealing with social security. He wanted to insure that a worker, or rather, a citizen, should be covered by measures of social protection in just that manner: from the cradle to the grave. He meant precisely, literally, what he said.

"Such phrases have no place in a serious document," pronounced a Western European delegate.

"But the Declaration should be beautifully worded," argued another Latin delegate.

"It's a legal document—not a poem," muttered a Benelux member.

A member of the United States Delegation whispered darkly into a neighbor's ear:

"Why not 'from womb to tomb'? At least it rhymes!"

Before the final text of the Article was settled upon, several other poetical versions were suggested. Some others, quite unprintable, shortly made the rounds of the corridors outside the conference rooms. ....

THE ORIGIN OF MAN

Life itself is prized differently in different cultures. To die of peaceful old age is the ideal life pattern in some parts of the world. Death for a country or an ideal is the desirable social behavior in others. Nowhere have these differences been made so manifest as in the drafting of the Declaration of Human Rights.

"Man is of divine origin, endowed by nature with reason and conscience," argued several Latin-American delegates.

"All life is of divine origin, not only human life," a representative of a Buddhist state murmured gently. *"Is it not vanity to attribute divine origin to human life alone?"*

"Man is not divine. He is rooted in the very land he tills, in the soil that bred him," once stated an Eastern European Delegate from a preponderantly agricultural area. The Soviets suggested tactfully that science had reservations on the whole subject. The Anglo-Saxon bloc, evidently not quite definite on the subject of human divinity, kept still.

CONFUSION OVER CHINA

Humour relief is not infrequently provided by the very cultural differences that are usually so productive of misunderstandings.

On one occasion, a misunderstanding was particularly startling:

"Gentlemen, gentlemen, let us not act in this matter like an elephant in a china shop!"

As this remark was being rendered from the Russian into English, a language in which the Chinese Delegate was following proceedings, he promptly raised his hand.

"Mr. Chairman, I should like the Soviet Delegate to explain just what China has to do with his objections."

"Mr. Chairman, I said nothing whatever about China. The Chinese Delegate must have misunderstood."

"Mr. Chairman, I distinctly heard my country mentioned. I request an explanation." . . .

ON A CERTAIN BLINDNESS IN HUMAN BEINGS[15]
By William James

Some years ago, while journeying in the mountains of North Carolina, I passed by a large number of "coves," as they call them there, or heads of small valleys between the hills, which had been newly cleared and planted. The impression on my mind was one of unmitigated squalor. The settler had in every case cut down the more man-

---

[15] From *Essays in Faith and Morals*, by William James (New York: Longmans, Green & Co., Inc., 1943). Reprinted by permission.

ageable trees, and left their charred stumps standing. The larger trees he had girdled and killed, in order that their foliage should not cast a shadow. He had then built a log cabin, plastering its chinks with clay, and had set up a tall zigzag rail fence around the scene of his havoc, to keep the pigs and cattle out. Finally, he had irregularly planted the intervals between the stumps and trees with Indian corn, which grew among the chips; and there he dwelt with his wife and babes—an axe, a gun, a few utensils, and some pigs and chickens feeding in the woods, being the sum total of his possessions.

The forest had been destroyed; and what had "improved" it out of existence was hideous, a sort of ulcer, without a single element of artificial grace to make up for the loss of Nature's beauty. Ugly, indeed, seemed the life of the squatter, scudding, as the sailors say, under bare poles, beginning again away back where our first ancestors started, and by hardly a single item the better off for all the achievements of the intervening generations.

Talk about going back to nature! I said to myself, oppressed by the dreariness, as I drove by. Talk of a country life for one's old age and for one's children! Never thus, with nothing but the bare ground and one's bare hands to fight the battle! Never, without the best spoils of culture woven in! The beauties and commodities gained by the centuries are sacred. They are our heritage and birthright. No modern person ought to be willing to live a day in such a state of rudimentariness and denudation.

Then I said to the mountaineer who was driving me, "What sort of people are they who have to make these new clearings?" "All of us," he replied. "Why, we ain't happy here, unless we are getting one of these coves under cultivation." I instantly felt that I had been losing the whole inward significance of the situation. Because to me the clearings spoke of naught but denudation, I thought that to those whose sturdy arms and obedient axes had made them they could tell no other story. But, when *they* looked on the hideous stumps, what they thought of was personal victory. The chips, the girdled trees, and the vile split rails spoke of honest sweat, persistent toil and final reward. The cabin was a warrant of safety for self and wife and babes. In short, the clearing, which to me was a mere ugly picture on the retina, was to them a symbol redolent with moral memories and sang a very paean of duty, struggle, and success.

I had been as blind to the peculiar ideality of their conditions as they certainly would also have been to the ideality of mine, had they had a peep at my strange indoor academic ways of life at Cambridge.

SPEECH EXPERTS VARY IN RATING MacARTHUR[16]

By M. W. Newman

Speaking professionally, Chicago speech experts differed Tuesday in sizing up Gen. MacArthur's keynote address to the Republican convention.

Some thought it was a fine job. Others thought he put his foot in his mouth.

The *Daily News* asked them to comment on the speech only from the professional point of view, leaving politics out.

Dean James H. McBurney of the Northwestern University School of Speech said it was "a very strong speech, well-constructed and well-presented." "He gives the impression of utter clarity and warmth. He was in command all the way."

Dean McBurney said MacArthur probably didn't have to rehearse much, either, for his TV and radio oratory.

"He's convinced and that came through, whether you agree with him or not," said the dean. "It's not an act."

Another viewpoint was taken by three members of the University of Chicago English department, Mrs. W. R. Ebbitt, Gwin J. Kolb and Stuart Tave.

"The attack against the administration was all-inclusive and well organized," they said. "But the speech was much too long, it was repetitive, and the end—when it finally came—was anti-climactic."

Bess Sondel, a University of Chicago communications expert, took a mixed view of the speech.

"Gen. MacArthur is an 'orator,' " she commented. "His magnificent choice of valuative and even incitive language make his listeners forget entirely the absence of strictly informative terms.

"This is oratory as conceived by the generation of MacArthur. We live in a new day."

Prof. A. G. Pierrot of the Roosevelt College speech department said the speech was "very high-grade and beautifully phrased."

"It was well organized," said Prof. Pierrot.

"You knew where he was going and when. He was dignified and his voice was well rounded."

---

16 *Chicago Daily News*, July 8, 1952, p. 4. Reprinted by permission.

Prof. John Bettenbender, chairman of the Loyola University speech department, found MacArthur's talk "quite disappointing."

"He was much more dynamic and impassioned when he spoke before Congress last year," said Prof. Bettenbender.

"His speech to the convention seemed long, formal and a bit dull. He didn't let go."

Chapter XIII

UNDELAYED REACTIONS

OUR culture tends to place a premium on the "man of action," the "quick thinker." And, to be sure, there are circumstances when the "snap" decision is to be desired over the delayed response or no action at all. On the other hand, the consequences of some undelayed, unreasoned reactions have ranged from mild embarrassment to some of the greatest catastrophes in history. Consider the tragic phenomenon of panic. Take the famous Iroquois Theatre fire (Chicago, 1903), for example. It is generally conceded that a considerable portion of the terrible death toll (almost 600) could be attributed to the crush of fear-crazed persons who jammed the exits.

Doors, windows, hallways, fire escapes—all were jammed in a moment with struggling humanity, fighting for life. Some of the doors were jammed almost instantly so that no human power could make egress possible. Behind those in front pushed the frenzied mass of humanity, Chicago's elect, the wives and children of its most prosperous business men and the flower of local society, fighting like demons incarnate. Purses, wraps, costly furs were cast aside in that mad rush. Mothers were torn from their children, husbands from their wives. No hold, however strong, could last against that awful indescribable crush. Strong men who sought to the last to sustain their feminine companions were swept away like straws, thrown to the floor and trampled into unconsciousness in the twinkling of an eye. Women to whom safety of their children was more than their own lives had their little ones torn from them and buried under the mighty sweep of humanity, moving onward by intuition rather than through exercise of thought to the various exits. They in turn were swept on before their wails died on their lips—some to safety, others to an unspeakably horrible death.[1]

Veteran writer Ben H. Atwell, an eyewitness, gave testimony of the senseless loss of lives:

Piled in windows in the angle of the stairway where the second balcony refugees were brought face to face and in a death struggle with the occupants of the first balcony, the dead covered a space fifteen or twenty feet square and nearly seven feet in depth. *All were absolutely safe from the*

---

[1] *Chicago's Awful Theatre Horror* by the Survivors and Rescuers (Chicago: Memorial Publishing Co., 1904), p. 36.

fire itself when they met death, having emerged from the theatre proper into the separate building containing the foyer. In this great court there was absolutely nothing to burn and the doors were only a few feet away. There the ghastly pile lay, *a mute monument to the powers of terror. . . .*

To that pile of dead is attributed the great loss of life within. The bodies choked up the entrance, barring the egress of those behind. Neither age nor youth, sex, quality or condition were sacred in the awful battle in the doorway. The gray and aged, rich, poor, young and those obviously invalids in life lay in a tangled mass all on an awful footing of equality in silent annihilation.[2]

If that calamity seems remote, consider the more recent Cocoanut Grove night-club fire:

To a week already overcrowded with gruesome news pictures from the war, Boston added a terrible climax of civilian tragedy on Saturday night (Nov. 28) when more than 400 people[3] lost their lives in a fire at a midtown night club. It was the worst U.S. disaster of its kind since the 1903 Iroquois Theatre fire in Chicago.

A thousand merrymakers were packed in the Cocoanut Grove celebrating football victories and "getting away from the war" at 10:15 P.M. when the floor show was scheduled to start. A bus boy struck a match to see how to screw a light bulb back into its socket. A tinsel palm tree nearby caught fire and havoc took the stage. The guests' mad headlong rush for the two inadequate exits ended by completely clogging all escape. *More than the flames and stifling smoke, it was the hysteria and panic of the screaming, clawing crowds which piled up the dead like a dam.* One chorus boy kept his head in the pandemonium, directing entertainers to the safety of an adjacent roof through a second story window.[4]

Panic, of course, is not exclusively a group phenomenon. The individual may experience "solo panic" which can lead to destructive consequences. I am looking at a newspaper clipping which tells of a businessman who was dozing as his commuter train carried him home. The train stopped at the station just below his own and started up again, awakening the man. Startled and thinking he was missing his station, the man dashed out the forward door of the coach. He stumbled and fell under the train, and its wheels cut off his feet at the ankles. He was taken to a hospital, where authorities said his condition was critical.[5]

Riots, lynchings, and many other forms of mob or individual vio-

---

2 *Ibid.,* pp. 41–42. Italics are mine.

3 A subsequent article ("After Cocoanut Grove," *Atlantic Monthly,* Vol. CLXXI, No. 3 [March, 1943], pp. 55–57) totaled the fatalities at just under 500, the hospitalized at 250.

4 "Boston Holocaust," *Life,* December 7, 1942, © Time Inc., p. 44. Reprinted by permission. Italics are mine.

5 "Leaps Off Train, Loses Feet," *Chicago Sun-Times,* September 23, 1954, p. 66.

lence or inaction[6]—unsanity, in any case—are almost invariably earmarked by irrational, impulsive behavior.

THREE CLASSES OF BEHAVIOR

The question is: How is it possible that normally civilized, law-abiding, peaceful, sane, and adult persons sometimes act like fear-crazed or enraged animals? How can humans, collectively or individually, "lose their heads" or "fly off the handle" and, as a consequence, effectively contribute to the harm and destruction of themselves and of others? A way of approaching the problem is to compare three broad classifications of human behavior.

I. Reflex Responses

Shine a light into someone's eyes and watch his pupils contract. Draw a pointed instrument across the sole of his foot and note the reaction of his toes. Tap his knee just below the patella and watch his lower leg jerk. These simple reactions are called *reflex responses.* Involving no "thinking," they are uncontrolled (and largely uncontrollable), direct and immediate responses of the organism to stimuli.

II. Voluntary Responses

Now ask the same person to spell his full name backward, to multiply forty-three by nine, and to estimate your weight. Assuming that he had had no special preparation for these tasks, his responses will have the opposite characteristics of reflexes. They will involve some "thinking"; they will be delayed, controllable (and controlled), responses.

III. Reflex-like Responses

Compare these two forms of behavior with a third:

We enlisted men were at bat in a hotly contested baseball game with our officers, when a private hit what looked like a single to short right field. Instead of stopping at first, however, he foolishly started a wild dash for second. Realizing, then, that he couldn't make it, he scrambled back toward first. Now he was being chased in a rundown between the lieutenant playing first and the colonel playing second.

It looked like a sure out, but just as the lieutenant flipped the ball back to the colonel, the private snapped to attention, saluting the colonel. Automatically, the colonel snapped a salute back—and muffed the catch.[7]

---

6 See Meerloo's discussion of "Frozen Panic" in Joost A. M. Meerloo, M.D., *Patterns of Panic* (New York: International Universities Press, Inc., 1950), pp. 28–30.

7 Cpl. Bill O'Brian in *True,* quoted in *Reader's Digest,* May, 1958, p. 166. Reprinted by permission of Fawcett Publications, Inc.

The colonel's reaction appears to be a cross between a reflex response and a voluntary response. Like a reflex, his reaction was undelayed, uncontrolled, and apparently involved little or no thought. On the other hand, it resembled a voluntary response, in that his action was *controllable* (albeit largely uncontrolled in this instance). In short, his response *could* have been delayed, controlled, and premeditated— in other words, it *could* have been a voluntary response, but years of conditioning and habit militated against it. A reflex-like response, then, may be considered a *potential* voluntary reaction which, through habit, panic, conditioning, surprise, etc., tends to resemble reflexes.

Useful Reflex-like Responses. Reflex-like responses often begin as conscious, voluntary actions. One learns to drive a car, play a musical instrument, type, throw a baseball, etc., quite consciously and perhaps laboriously at first. But with repetitions these actions so habituated that they may be carried on with virtually no conscious control. Our capacity for learning these responses is invaluable to us. Consider driving an automobile. If the driver had to maintain conscious control of his steering, braking, accelerating, etc., he might have considerable difficulty in coping with, say, the added complexity of the car in front stopping quickly. One simply does not have the time, under these conditions, to decide with due premeditation that he must slow up or stop his car, and to do this he must take his foot off the accelerator, that he must put it on the brake, that he must press the brake pedal hard enough to stop in time but not hard enough to skid his car into oncoming traffic, that he must be looking for possibilities of steering around the stopped car, that he must take into account the actions of the drivers behind and beside him, etc. If he is an experienced driver, he has so thoroughly habituated many of these actions that he will perform them without pre-thought and therefore will have time and concentration for coping with the less familiar aspects of the situation. A good typist, for example, is unaware of the specific movements of her fingers. In fact, if she began to *will* that certain fingers strike certain keys, her rate would fall off markedly, and her errors would probably increase. In short, there is a great deal to be said for properly trained reflex-like responses. If a punch-press operator had to make conscious decisions before stamping each piece, you can imagine the decrease in his productivity.

Dangerous Reflex-like Responses. There are occasions, however, when reflex-like responses can lead to trouble. There was, for example, the incident of the rookie police officer who was assigned to night duty in a downtown shopping district. He was making his rounds, checking the rear doors of the shops, when he found the door of a furniture store unlocked. He swung the door open and noticed with a start that the figure of a man loomed in the darkness inside. The officer quickly went for his gun and was astonished to see the "other man" go for his. The policeman *immediately* pulled his revolver and fired—and the "man" disappeared amid the sound of shattering glass. Upon investigating, the young officer discovered that he had destroyed a ninety-five dollar mirror!

Most of us might argue that we would have done the same thing as the embarrassed rookie—and so we might, for we would have been "rookies," too. But veteran policemen tell us that the situation could have been handled more skillfully. They say that they have learned from experience to suspect immediately the possibility of a mirrored image. They say that there are ways of weaving, ducking, and dodging —while reaching for one's gun—which (1) make one a difficult target if the "man" should turn out to be actually there and (2) permit a check on the suspected mirror. Of course, if the other "man" *doesn't* weave, duck, and dodge as you do, you may have a problem on your hands! But, the veterans insist, you are certainly in a better position to cope with it.

The undelayed, unthinking response can sometimes have far graver consequences than minor property damage and embarrassment. These tragedies might be appropriately labeled "The Quick and The Dead."

ALBANY, TEX.—(UP)—A schoolgirl raced for her life trying to get off a railroad trestle as the freight train bore down on her Friday. But she stumbled and was killed, sheriff Jack Moberley reported Saturday.

Margie Dell Macon, 12, became frightened when she felt the trestle vibrate as the train rumbled onto it with its brakes on. She started to run. Her sister, Barbara, 14, remained where she was—crouched on the edge of the trestle. The train didn't touch her. . . .[8]

Fear of a snake crawling along the roadside cost the life of a 6-year-old boy.

Romeo Ramos was killed Wednesday when he darted into the path of an oncoming car at Wilke and Kirchoff Rds. in Arlington Heights.

His brother Roel, 11, told the police he and Romeo were walking along the shoulder of the road when they spotted the snake. He said Romeo, afraid, ran onto the road.

Police said the snake apparently was one of the harmless "grass snake" type.

---

[8] "Girl Races Train on Trestle, Dies," *Chicago Daily News*, December 18, 1954, p. 1. Courtesy of United Press.

Isadore J. Valente, 35, of Elmwood Park, driver of the car, was not held by police.[9]

THE PROBLEM OF UNDELAYED REACTIONS

The problem of undelayed reactions does not, of course, involve true reflexes, which, for the most part, consist of harmless and often self-protective[10] behavior. Nor are we concerned with properly trained and habituated reflex-like actions which increase one's efficiency in repetitive tasks and, in fact, facilitate his handling of unusual situations, as in driving an automobile, as previously discussed.

The undelayed reactions which are of concern here are those which *can* and *ought* to be delayed, controlled, and premeditated. If the girl on the trestle, for example, had delayed for a moment, as her sister apparently did, and considered possibilities other than a headlong, panic-stricken rush from the train, she might be alive today.

The correctives which follow, then, apply to the reflex-like responses which, in the interest of saving tempers, time, energy, money, and lives, could and ought to be delayed, conscious, voluntary responses.

CORRECTIVES

Instantaneous Action—Rarely Necessary

First of all, let us recognize that very few emergencies require an immediate action. This chapter has cited numerous examples of critical circumstances ranging from a policeman's reflection in a mirror to the unforgettable Iroquois Theatre fire. In no case was immediate, unthinking response necessary. In fact, in every case, had those involved delayed their reactions for even a moment to "size up" the situation, the consequences might have been a good deal happier.

The Habit of Delay

Bishop Samuel Fallows, on the aftermath of the Iroquois Theatre catastrophe, wrote:

Let every safeguard that human ingenuity can devise be furnished and yet there always remains the personal element to be taken into account.

---

9 "Auto Kills Boy Fleeing from Snake," *Chicago Daily News*, July 8, 1954, p. 43. Reprinted by permission.

10 As in the case of the gagging reflex, pupillary contractions and dilations, eye winks, etc.

Habitual practice of self-control in daily life will help give coolness and calmness in times of peril. Keeping one's head in the ordinary things prevents its losing when the extraordinary occurs.[11]

The *"habitual practice of self-control in daily life"* is precisely what is advocated here. Frequently practice the technique of delaying your response, if only for an instant. It is especially helpful to discipline one's self under "semi-emergency" circumstances. If, for example, someone makes a remark which seems offensive, resist the impulse to respond—instead, let your *initial* reaction be *delay*. Give yourself time to size up the situation—Did he really mean that? Will it be wise to retaliate in kind? What are his reasons for saying it? Could he be only joking? Hadn't I better give him a chance to clarify this? Chances are with you that your delayed reactions will be appreciably more intelligent, mature, and, in the long run, effective than your impulsive response would have been. The point is not simply to "count to ten" but to *size up the situation—to analyze, get more data, look for other alternatives, date, index, distinguish inferences from observations— while doing so.*

Since many of our harmful, overquick responses are vocal, a good habit to practice is to clench a pen or pencil crosswise in your teeth when the urge to "pop off" comes upon you. While the wear and tear on the writing instrument may be considerable, this little technique not only reminds one of the wisdom of delaying but rather effectively inhibits the verbal outburst!

Advance Preparation for Emergencies

The best general provision for emergencies is the deeply ingrained habit of delay-while-sizing-up, but more specific preparation is often possible. Generally speaking, an emergency *is* an emergency because it involves circumstances which are unexpected, unfamiliar, and with which we feel unprepared or unable to cope. To the extent that the circumstances are anticipated and made familiar and to the extent that we are equipped to cope with them, they are no longer overwhelming crises. Training for combat is an excellent example of this. The recruit spends weeks going through many of the activities of warfare, firing his rifle, throwing grenades, forced hikes with full field pack, bayonet drill, crawling through the infiltration course,[12] etc.

---

11 *Chicago's Awful Theatre Horror*, p. xv.

12 The infiltration course is a simulated battlefield. The trainee crawls fifty yards or so under barbed wire, with a brace of machine guns firing real bullets a few inches above his head. As an added fillip, charges explode sporadically throughout the field, showering him with grit or mud, as the case may be.

The object is to acquaint him with as many of the aspects of combat as possible, in order that the actual experience will not seem overpoweringly complex and terrifying.

Speech training is another good example of advance preparation for "emergencies." The beginning speaker is advised to familiarize himself in advance, insofar as he can, with the components of the speaking situation. He is urged, for example, to master the speech (in many cases this will require committing the ideas and their connectives, [not the exact wording] to memory); to learn in advance what he can about the audience (size, age, sex, interests, prejudices, etc.); to know the purpose of the occasion, the topics of any previous and subsequent speakers, and the role his own talk will play; to acquaint himself with the physical aspects (acoustics, arrangement of audience, position of speaker's stand, lighting, etc.). In short, one becomes able to cope with difficult and critical situations to the extent that he has predicted, prepared for, and controlled factors in advance.

Anticipate the Undelayed Responses of Others

So far, we have been concerned with measures one can take to encourage his own delayed reactions. Let us now consider how to deal with the harmful undelayed responses of others. First of all, it should be recognized that the tendency to react overquickly varies from individual to individual, and *within* the individual, from time to time. In other words, *index* and *date* the other fellow's propensity to fly off the handle. While Sam seemed to stand up under pressure last week, there is no guarantee that he will be as serene now.

Second, if you anticipate a potential flareup, use the most "snap reaction-proof" medium of communication possible. For example, it is extremely easy for a man who loses his temper on the telephone to cut you off in an instant and proceed to act foolishly and destructively. A memo or letter, under some circumstances, with no chance of immediate feedback from the other person or possibility of control on your part, may be even worse. But a face-to-face communication gives you a chance to see the storm clouds forming and to forestall them. And even if the other fellow does "blow his top," you are *there* to help him regain his composure.

Third and most important, don't match the other fellow's undelayed response with one of your own. As sorely tempting as it may be at times, double overquick reactions may make reconciliation considerably more difficult. And, after all, if you are "right," you can afford to keep your temper; if you are "wrong," you can't afford to lose it.

A Group Technique

In the chapter on *by-passing* I described a special conference technique.[13] While the clarification of communication among the participants was the prime objective, an important by-product emerged. The executive meetings of this particular firm characteristically had been marred by frequent angry exchanges among the conferees. But not long after the installation of the "moderator system" it became evident that something had happened—the outbursts had disappeared. In fact, the meetings moved along with amazing tranquillity. The reason was soon apparent. The system required the moderator to paraphrase a speaker's remark *before* anyone else was permitted to respond. It was clear that this necessary delay, plus the likelihood of clarifying the communication, forced the quick responder to delay, to reconsider his response! And when he was finally allowed to speak, he was invariably more cool-headed and objective than he would have been, had he been permitted to respond immediately.

And perhaps there is a moral in this experience for the individual a swell as for the group. If you feel you disagree or disapprove of what someone has just said, *take the time* to make sure you understand him correctly. This can have at least three salutary effects. You may find that you *have* misunderstood and are not actually in disagreement; your attempt to understand will tend to communicate respect for the other person, and he may be likely to return the consideration; and, finally, the delay may have given you both time to be more intelligent and reasonable in your differing.

---

13 See pp. 58–59.

INCIDENTS

THE LOGAN COMPANY[14]

The Logan Company,[15] a manufacturer of television and radio receiver sets, employs some 2,000 persons. The firm, which had been privately owned for over thirty years, was sold to a large electronics holding corporation approximately four years ago. The firm was permitted to retain substantially the same management after the sale had been made. However, after three rather unsatisfactory years the president of Logan retired and the holding corporation installed a new general manager from outside the firm but within the corporation. Eric Stone, the new general manager, was given the rank of vice president although he actually carried out the functions of the president, an office now vacant. Stone soon initiated extensive personnel changes in the upper management levels including the product-line managers. The current situation, then, may be said to be one of flux and readjustment.

*   *   *   *

Among the responsibilities of the Industrial Engineering Department is the supervision of the installation of production lines as new products or changes in products are called for. One of these new lines was a conveyor assembly line for the television tuner. In passing, it might be explained that formerly the tuner had been assembled by the conventional bench assembly method, the workers being compensated on an individual incentive schedule. The new method required a strictly uniform rate of assembly by the fourteen female assemblers on the line who were paid on a group incentive basis. These employees have expressed considerable dissatisfaction with the new methods, their major complaint that their take-home pay had been markedly reduced.

Ray Edwards, the industrial engineer in charge of installing the conveyor line, found on Tuesday that an adjustment in the rate of the

---

14 All names have been disguised. Printed by permission of the author, whose name has been withheld by request.

15 The ages and lengths of service with Logan of the characters in this case are as follows:

Eric Stone, 43 (6 months)	Ray Edwards, 35 (6 years)
Roy Sheldon, 48 (19 years)	Fred Peterson, 36 (2 months)
Tom Flynn, 38 (13 years)	

conveyor was necessary in order to train the assemblers properly. Realizing that Fred Peterson, product line manager in whose division the tuners were assembled, was under considerable pressure to get out production, Edwards phoned to discuss the intended adjustment. He phoned at 11 A.M. and was unable to reach him. While waiting for Peterson to return the call, Edwards mentally constructed four alternatives for choosing a time for making the change:

1. Have the firm's maintenance men make the adjustment after work hours today. To Edwards this did not appear to be a very satisfactory choice for it involved overtime pay at time and a half for the maintenance men. This pay would be charged against the Industrial Engineering Department whose budget for such expenses had already been severely strained for the fiscal period.
2. Have the salesman of the adjustment equipment make the change during work hours. Since the salesman would be paid by his own firm, the maintenance expense would not be charged to the Industrial Engineering Department budget. The obvious disadvantage, however, was that production would be shut down on the tuner during that period, and the incentive-paid workers would not be paid during the shut-down period, thus provoking more complaints from them.
3. Have the salesman make the change during the lunch period of the assembly group. Edwards favored such a plan because it not only removed the burden of over-time pay fom his department's budget, but it also provided for a minimum of shut-down time and loss of worker's pay. However, Edwards wanted to inform Peterson that there was a possibility that the change would require a somewhat longer time than the lunch period—thus preventing the assemblers from returning to work immediately.
4. The final alternative, Edwards felt, would be to wait until Saturday (a non-working day) and have the maintenance men make the installation. Their over-time pay would then be charged to the Miscellaneous Budget. While the plan necessitated no loss of production time, or worker's pay, and relieved the Industrial Engineering Department of the over-time charge, the delay in installing the change presented a very serious problem in regard to operator training. There would then be a period of three and a half days during which the operators would be hampered in their training because of the improperly regulated line. Edwards felt that the third alternative was the best at the moment.

Peterson had spent the morning in conference in the office of the vice-president in charge of Manufacturing, Roy Sheldon. Also present was Tom Flynn, manager of the Industrial Engineering Department (and Edwards' superior). At 12:45 P.M., Peterson left Sheldon's office and was stopped by Miss Larson, Sheldon's secretary, who gave him Edwards' message. This had been relayed to Miss Larson by Peterson's secretary.

Peterson immediately picked up the phone on Miss Larson's desk and called Edwards.

PETERSON: Ray, I understand you called—just got the note.
EDWARDS: (By now it was evident that the third alternative was no longer possible because the operator's lunch period had ended.) Yes, Fred—say, we're going to have to regulate the tuner line. As you know, it has been going too fast for the girls.
PETERSON: Yeah? (Suspiciously)
EDWARDS: Well, we've purchased some new gearing that should do the trick. Now, as far as when to make the change, I have a few ideas to sound out with you.
PETERSON: Shoot.
EDWARDS: First, we could have the maintenance men do the job to-night. Frankly, I'm opposed to this and so is Flynn. Their time would be charged to us, and we're up to the hilt right now in over-time charges. I don't think Tom would stand for it. So I thought—.

CLICK! Peterson had hung up. He charged angrily back into Mr. Sheldon's office and, in the presence of Sheldon, Peterson's and Flynn's superior, proceeded to unbraid Tom Flynn for trying to shut down his production line in order to avoid overtime costs.

THE MID-WESTERN TELEPHONE COMPANY[16]

The General Staff of the Mid-Western Telephone Co. decided upon a revision in the company's billing procedure. Formerly, billing machine symbols had appeared on four portions of the bill. The change consisted in using symbols on only one section of the bill. Thus, it was necessary to have three sets of symbols removed from each of the firm's billing machines.

Late Friday afternoon the General Staff notified the United Office Machine Co., who serviced the machines, to send out a repairman at the beginning of the week to remove the unneeded symbols. The General Staff also contacted the Division Staff who were told to notify the District Heads and Supervising Accountants of each of the districts of the change. Each of the Supervising Accountants was to have relayed the information to the Supervisor under him.

These lines of communication are charted below:

---

16 All names have been disguised. Printed by permission of the author, whose name has been withheld by request.

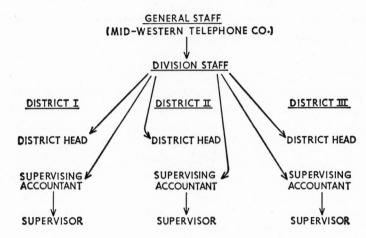

Ted Jennings, a Division Staff man, tried to contact George Lowrey, the District Head in District I, and was unable to reach him. Jennings then called Al Hanson, Supervising Accountant in District I, and gave the message to him and requested him to notify Bart Long, the Supervisor whose unit was involved.

At the time he was called, Hanson was wrestling with a production problem and was several hours behind schedule. He did not contact Long and did not take any notes.

Monday morning the repairman walked into Long's unit and told him that he was there to remove something but he was hazy on whether he was to remove all of the symbols or only some of them from the machines. Long, who had not been contacted about the matter, tried to call Hanson, but he was not at his desk. Long then called Mr. Lowrey to ask him what to do. Hanson happened to be in Lowrey's office when Long's call came in. Lowrey, knowing nothing of the situation, told Hanson that Long was asking what to do about symbols on the billing machines. He asked if Hanson could handle the situation.

Hanson flushed with embarrassment as he suddenly recalled his failure to pass the staff man's message to Long. He vaguely remembered something about the removal of symbols but because he felt Lowrey was already holding him responsible for his current production problem he dreaded admitting his error in the presence of his superior. He clutched the phone and told Long that all of the symbols were to be removed. He silently resolved to stop the repairman and check with Jennings as soon as he left Lowrey's office. Unfortunately, the District Head began a prolonged discussion of Hanson's production difficulty. Hanson became so preoccupied with Lowrey's remarks that the symbols incident slipped his mind. Meanwhile Long relayed Hanson's instruction to the repairman who proceeded to remove all of the symbols.

Some time later in the morning, Jennings, following up to see if the work had been done, discovered what had happened. Upon checking with the United Office Machine Co., he was told that the correct symbols could be replaced at $35 per machine and that the machines would have to be brought into the shop for the replacement.

The end result was that the ten machines of the unit were taken out of production for several days and that a cost of $350 was necessary for the replacement of the symbols.

AIR JUDGE'S CHARGE OF ABUSE BY POLICE[17]

An investigation was under way Tuesday into Criminal Court Judge John T. Dempsey's charges against two Park District policemen.

He was "roughed up" by one of the officers, the judge said, while the other was present and did nothing to prevent it.

Judge Dempsey gave this account of the incident:

He said that he was walking his 8-month-old fox terrier, Bibelot, in the park, which is about a half mile from his home at 2530 Richmond.

"It was about 4:30 P.M., just about dusk," said the judge. "I was throwing a tennis ball for my dog to catch when Policeman Kuhter came over." He said Kuhter yelled, "Say, I want to talk to you." "Almost before I could answer him," said Judge Dempsey, "he grabbed me and said, 'You come along with me.' "

Judge Dempsey said Kuhter refused to tell him why he was arresting him. He said that just as the other policeman, Cummings, came along, Kuhter started to push and shove him.

"When I told him to stop, he told me to shut up and pulled out his club," said Dempsey.

"When I again asked the policeman what it was all about, Kuhter pushed me into the bushes. When I got up he pushed me into the bushes a second time.

"Brandishing his club over my head, he said, 'I told you to keep quiet. Don't say another word. If you do I'll let you have it.' "

17 *Chicago Daily News*, November 17, 1953, p. 3. Reprinted by permission.

When he identified himself as a judge, he said he was told by Kuhter that "it made no difference."

Judge Dempsey said that when he asked to be taken to a superior officer, he was told by Kuhter:

"You are going to talk to me before anyone else. You have to talk to a patrolman in charge first."

Dempsey said as the three walked through the park, Kuhter said, "I'll book him for not having his dog on a leash and I'll think of something else before we get there."

The judge said just before they started to cross Humboldt Blvd., Kuhter reached over and "grabbed me by the jacket."

"When we reached the other side of the street, I again asked what it was all about. Kuhter pulled out his club again and said:

" 'I've taken enough of this cheap _____. I think I'll give it to you right now.' Dempsey said he was led into what had formerly been a police station in the park.

He said either Kuhter or Cummings used a key to open the place.

He said Kuhter shoved him on a bench and refused to let him use a telephone.

"Every time Officer Cummings said I could use the phone, Kuhter said, 'What are you trying to do, be nice to him?' "

Judge Dempsey said that after an hour, they permitted him to use the phone. He said he was able to reach Lt. Ralph Riley at the Garfield Park Station.

"When I told Lt. Riley who I was," said Dempsey, "he said, 'My God, tell them to let you go.'

"I told the lieutenant that I wanted to talk to him. When he got there he offered to drive me home, but I told him my car was parked in the park."

Judge Dempsey said that when he talked to Capt. Duffy about the incident, the captain asked if Dempsey would accept an apology.

"I told him no," said the judge. "This man, Kuhter, is dangerous and shouldn't be on the force.

"If he would do this to me, what would he do to an ordinary citizen?"

Judge Dempsey said that Cummings at no time took part in the pushing and shoving.

"His part was minor," said Dempsey. "My impression was that Kuhter was the boss and the other officer was afraid to do anything.

"Cummings tried two or three times to be nice to me."

Judge Dempsey said, in making his statement Monday night, he expressed willingness to appear at any hearings into the matter.

"I want to protect other citizens from similar outrages," he said.

Capt. Duffy said statements also were taken from Kuhter and Cummings. They, too, will be sent to Chief Otlewis.

He said the contents will not be revealed until then.

*   *   *   *

Subsequent newspaper accounts reported the following developments in the case. Both Kuhter and Cummings were rookie policemen. Kuhter was 26 years old and Cummings was 27.

As a consequence of the incident, the two officers were suspended without pay; Kuhter for 30 days and Cummings for 10.

Dempsey called this punishment a travesty and pressed criminal charges. Kuhter was charged with assault and battery, false imprisonment and extortion. Cummings was charged with accessory before the fact of assault and battery and false imprisonment.

Cummings later accused Kuhter of committing assault without provocation.

A statement taken from the two officers indicated that they had seized the judge because they thought he resembled a sex offender they had been looking for. (State's Attorney Gutnecht said Cummings quoted Kuhter's description of the man and that it did not fit Dempsey in several respects.) George T. Donoghue, Park District general superintendent, announced that policeman Kuhter had been investigating a complaint that a man with a dog annoyed a girl in the park. He also stressed that there was nothing to indicate that Judge Dempsey was that man.

YOUR EYES CAN DECEIVE YOU[18]
By Arthur Bartlett

George Smith got home from a date with his girl about midnight. His mother was not at home. Probably she was out playing cards with friends, George thought. That had been her favorite recreation ever

---

18 Reprinted by permission from the American Weekly, © 1951 by Hearst Publishing Company, Inc.

since her divorce, when George was six. Working all day in the candy factory, she liked to relax in the evenings. Now that George was 20, and working, and had a girl to occupy his attention, she often stayed out fairly late. So George went up to his own front room, undressed, got into bed and lay there reading the newspaper.

A bus stopped across the street, and George pulled aside the window shade and looked out. Under the street light, he could see his mother descending from the bus. A tall, heavy-set man got out behind her. The bus moved on. George was about to drop back on his pillow when his startled eyes stopped him. The man was reaching for his mother, trying to put his arms around her. George saw her push at him and try to step back off the curb; saw him grab her again and start pulling her towards him.

George leaped out of bed, pulled on his trousers and rushed down the stairs to the front door. Across the street, the man was still attempting to embrace his mother and she was struggling against him. George dashed to the rescue. Clenching his fist as he ran, he leaped at the man and punched with all his strength, hitting him squarely on the jaw. The man toppled backward and uttered a groan as his head hit the sidewalk. Then he lay there, still.

What happened next filled George with utter confusion. Dropping to her knees beside the unconscious man, his mother looked up at him with anguish in her eyes. "George," she cried, "what have you done? This is Howard Brower. . . . Howard, the candymaker at the factory . . . the man who asked me to marry him." . . .

The boy stared at his mother across the crumpled figure on the pavement. "He wasn't attacking you?" he demanded, dully.

"Of course not," she told him. "We'd been out together all evening. He brought me home. He wanted a good-night kiss, that's all. I was just teasing him."

An ambulance took Howard Browser to the hospital, but he never regained consciousness. He died the next day. George Smith spent that night in a jail cell.

The authorities finally decided not to prosecute. George, the investigation proved, didn't know Browser; had never seen him before. He had honestly thought that what he saw was a man attacking his mother.

But he had been misled by what he saw. His imagination exaggerated the evidence presented by his own eyes and converted it into something that wasn't true at all. As a result he had killed his mother's suitor. . . .

Take the case of Matthew J. Flaherty, a Boston policeman, some years ago. Shortly after being appointed to the force, Matt Flaherty took a bride and they moved into their own home on Newcastle Road. Eleanor Flaherty loved the house, but she was nervous about being alone in it at night, waiting for Matt to come home from his late tour of duty. Every little noise made her think that there was someone in the house or trying to get in. When Matt got home she was usually so upset that he would search the whole house, from cellar to attic, though smiling at her fears.

"No burglars," he would assure her, "except in your pretty little head."

Still, he couldn't help feeling anxious. If anyone really were prowling around his house while he was away nights. . . .

One night—they had been living in the house about two months then—he made the usual fruitless search and went to bed. But he had hardly dropped off to sleep, it seemed, when he woke with a start. What had awakened him? Naturally, his first thought was of a prowler. Listening tensely, he heard a sound—the creaking of a floor board—on the other side of the closed bedroom door. Quietly, he reached for his gun and eased himself up in bed.

Sure enough, the door began to push open. Somebody was coming right into the room.

"Who's there?" Matt Flaherty yelled, taking careful aim. There was no answer but a startled gasp and he started shooting. It was too dark to see the figure beyond the half-opened door, but whoever it was fell with a thump to the floor.

Then Matt turned on the light. That was when he realized, for the first time, that Eleanor was not there in the bed beside him.

She was lying just outside the door, dead.

[Is it your *eyes* which deceive you?—W. V. H.]

TORMENT IN A NEIGHBORHOOD[19]
By *Walter B. Smith*

What made James Lee, the Chinese laundryman, go berserk?
Why did he shoot three men, two of them police, then try to fight off

---

19 *Chicago Daily News*, February 13, 1954, p. 3. Reprinted by permission.

150 more cops before falling with a bullet wound through the skull?

Lying Saturday in County Hospital, his head throbbing and his left ankle shackled to the bed frame, Jimmy Lee gave his explanation of why he did it.

"I was scared," he said.

He was scared, he said, because he thought the three men had come to beat him up and perhaps take his money because he had slapped a boy.

And he slapped the boy, Lee said, because he finally had become fed up with the way neighborhood kids in general tormented him with squirt guns, name-calling, door-banging and other mischief.

The furious gun battle took place just a week ago in Lee's laundry at 2705 Diversey.

The city was shocked—the more so because such violence is so rare among Chicago's law-abiding Chinese.

Today two of Lee's victims are dead—detectives Jeremiah Lucey and Roman C. Steinke.

The third victim, truck driver Steven Malenk, 40, father of the slapped boy, has recently been discharged from a hospital.

The 42-year-old Lee has a sewed-up hole in his head where a bullet went right through. Doctors expect him to recover, but he may be paralyzed on one side for life.

Lee started the shooting when the two policemen went to the laundry with Malenk to arrest Lee on a warrant charging assault.

The warrant stemmed from an incident three nights earlier when Lee had slapped Malenk's son Steve Jr., 11.

For months, Lee said, neighborhood kids had badgered him. Sometimes they spit on the floor, sometimes they threw things, sometimes they called him obscene names.

On the evening of Feb. 3, Lee said, the Malenk boy and a companion were heckling him. (The boys say they were just looking in the window.)

Lee chased them and caught Steve, slapping him.

Soon afterward Steve came back to the laundry with his father. Lee said the truck driver threatened him and they struggled. The laundry-man admits he batted Malenk with a flatiron, breaking his wrist.

Malenk went to the Shakespeare police court next day and got the warrant charging Lee with assault.

Lee said he did not know about that when the officers came to get him last Saturday. Why didn't he go along peacefully to the Police station?

"I was scared," Lee said. "All I knew was that these three men were coming to get me and wanted me to pay them $125. I thought they were going to beat me up."

He said he did not know that the men with Malenk were police. They wore civilian clothes.

"All I could think of was to shoot first."

The mention of $125 apparently was a misunderstanding of the policemen's statement that Lee would have to post $125 bail at the police station.

Lee said he kept the pistol and shotgun with which he fought the police as protection against burglars.

He lived alone at the laundry. He has no relatives in Chicago.

Lee told his story twice. First it was in halting English to a *Daily News* reporter. Then it was in Chinese to the Rev. Philip Lee, no relation, who is pastor of the Chinese Christian Union Church at 23rd St. and Wentworth.

The wounded man's chief worry was about his laundry. The Rev. Mr. Lee assured him that arrangements would be made with a Chinese friend to see that the customers get back their shirts.

The clergyman said Chinese welfare organizations were making plans to give Lee the help he needs.

Lee said he was brought to America in 1914, at the age of 2. After three years in New Jersey he was brought to Chicago, where he has lived ever since.

He said he had had his laundry at the Diversey address for six years, but that the trouble with the youngsters did not start until last September.

An inquest into the death of Detective Lucey has been continued to March 9.

*   *   *   *

James Lee died two-and-a-half months later from his wounds. A newspaper account included the following:

Lee said he went berserk because he was afraid the officers were going to beat him up. However, a fingerprint check showed Lee was sought as an Army deserter, and police said that might have been the reason he feared arrest.

DYER PUBLIC RELATIONS, INC. (C)[20]

In March, 1958, Robert Dyer was speaking to a Northwestern University case writer, Ralph Stewart. "You're certainly welcome here," he said. "If you can uncover anything constructive about our communications and human relations, we'd be very grateful. Believe me, we certainly need it—especially me. I would suggest that you might want to talk to our people about what we now call the 'Office Boy Incident.' Our people know you're here, and I've requested them to be completely frank in their interviews with you."

As Ralph Stewart began to question members of Mr. Dyer's firm, he recalled some general previously acquired information about the company.

Dyer Public Relations, Inc., was founded fourteen years ago in a large west coast city by Mr. Dyer (then 31)—a driving, ambitious, dynamic young man with seemingly inexhaustible energy. Due primarily to his exceptional salesmanship the company had become a nationally recognized firm grossing $1.5 million annually. Dyer Inc., employed approximately forty persons.

In addition to Mr. Dyer, the following persons are involved in the case:

Mark Taylor—47, treasurer, joined Dyer thirteen years ago. Mr. Taylor also maintains a private accounting practice. He has a working agreement with Mr. Dyer that he will spend approximately half of his time on the Dyer accounts and the other half on his own practice. These percentages are never adhered to rigidly. Sometimes, over a month's time, Mr. Taylor spends more than 50 per cent of his time on Dyer affairs, sometimes less. This has been an established arrangement between the two men for some time and both seem satisfied with its operation.

William Frey—27, holds a Ph.D. in industrial psychology. Is in charge of Personnel Services, including testing and placement for clients and Dyer staff. Dr. Frey joined the Dyer firm two years ago. His predecessor, Kenneth Elson, had served both as director of personnel services and as office manager. Dr. Frey assumed the responsibilities of the former, but those of the latter were given to Mrs. Lane.

Miriam Lane—26, office manager for the firm and personal secretary to Mr. Clawson. She came to Dyer six years ago and has been office manager for the past two and one-half years. The firm's general clerical work flows through her desk. She assigns it to secretaries who are not already busy with duties for their immediate supervisors. She has direct responsibility for Russell Harmon, office boy.

Russell Harmon—25, office boy, a university student majoring in business management has been working approximately 30 hours per week with Dyer for the past year.

Dyer Public Relations, Inc.
Partial Organization Chart*

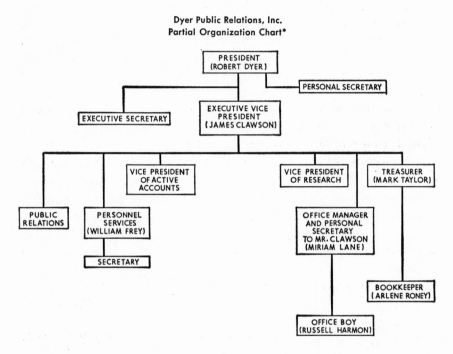

* The chart does not completely express the working relationships within the firm. In addition to the lines of organization, Mr. Dyer frequently communicates directly with Mr. Taylor, the two vice presidents, and Mrs. Lane. Each of these persons also communicates directly with Mr. Dyer. Mr. Dyer also communicates directly with Dr. Frey and the public relations director. These two men, however, rarely initiate direct communication with Mr. Dyer.

THE OFFICE BOY INCIDENT

Over the past several months, because of financial complications, Mr. Taylor had been devoting considerably more than the normal 50 per cent of his time to the Dyer firm. One day while preparing to take a trip for Dyer, he was attempting to clear up a few personal affairs. He handed a typed letter regarding his professional fraternity to his bookkeeper, Arlene Roney, with the instruction that she have twenty-five copies made. Miss Roney had been with the firm only two weeks and knew nothing of the firm's duplicating procedures except that the actual reproduction work was done by the office boy, Russell Harmon.

She knew the firm owned a photo-copying machine but was unaware that the company also had an offset duplicator.[21] She assumed the letter was to be photo-copied, called to Harmon as he was passing her desk, and handed the letter to him. She said, "Mr. Taylor would like twenty-five copies of this."

Harmon had just been instructed by Frey to make some deliveries to an office building several blocks away. He glanced at the letter, realizing that in its present form (without mat) he could only photo-copy it, a job requiring forty to forty-five minutes, and said, "I can't do that now. I've got to run an errand. If I get back in time, I could do it before closing time, but I doubt if I can make it that soon. Guess it'll have to wait until tomorrow."

Miss Roney felt she could do no more about the situation and placed the letter on her desk. A few minutes later Mr. Taylor approached her. "Did Russell run off those copies of the letter yet?"

Miss Roney answered, "No, he said he didn't have time and said he probably couldn't do it until tomorrow."

Mr. Taylor, visibly angered, walked directly to Mr. Dyer's office. "Say, Bob, now I know this is my own personal work, but I would think I could get a little cooperation from the personnel around here—especially when you consider the amount of time I've been putting in for you."

DYER: What do you mean? What kind of co-operation?

TAYLOR: Why, Harmon just refused to run off twenty-five copies of a personal letter for me.

DYER: (Considerably disturbed) Where is he? We'll just see what the hell's going on here!

Dyer walked to Mrs. Lane's desk in the main office and demanded loudly, "Where is Harmon?"

MRS. LANE: Why—I don't know. I imagine he's out on an errand for Dr. Frey (pointing toward Frey's office.) He's been sending Russell to the Weber building on the other side of the city.

Mr. Dyer turned and strode into Frey's office. "Why can't Harmon do this work for Mark?"

Frey was nonplussed. This was the second time that day that Mr. Dyer had appeared to hold him personally responsible for the conduct

---

21 The two machines served different purposes. The photo-copies, requiring no stencil or mat, reproduced directly from the material to be reproduced. Its chief advantage for the Dyer firm was that it could reproduce quickly one or a few copies of the material without the necessity of typing the material on a stencil or mat. However, the offset duplicator was faster and less expensive for situations requiring a quantity of copies.

of persons over whom, in his opinion, he had been given no authority. Earlier in the day, Mr. Dyer had come to him with complaints about errors in the work of the secretaries. Moreover, Frey had noticed through the glass partition of his office that Mrs. Lane had apparently directed Mr. Dyer to him. He was suddenly angered with Mr. Dyer's accusations and Mrs. Lane's evident "buck-passing" and snapped, "I don't know! Harmon doesn't work for me! He works for Lane!"

Mr. Dyer stamped out of Frey's office and headed for his own. As he passed Mrs. Lane's desk he shouted, "When Harmon comes back, tell him I want to see him!"

Mrs. Lane was suddenly incensed with Frey, for she assumed he had sent Mr. Dyer back to her. She got up and followed Mr. Dyer into his office. "Do you have to make a scene about this?" she asked. Mr. Dyer slammed his office door behind Mrs. Lane and himself and said, "Who in the hell does Russell Harmon think he is! If Harmon refuses to work for Mark Taylor, he can just get his rear-end out of this office!"

MRS. LANE: What's this all about?

MR. DYER: Mark brought something to Harmon to reproduce and Harmon refused to do it. Now, I want to see this kid, now!

MRS. LANE: I'll find out from Russell about this.

DYER: *I'll* ask him!

Mrs. Lane returned to her desk. Shortly afterwards, Mr. Dyer, who had an outside appointment, left the office for the day before seeing Harmon, who returned just before quitting time. When told of the incident, Harmon was bewildered. He felt betrayed by Dr. Frey who had not, in his words, "stuck up" for him by telling Mr. Dyer that he was on an errand. About Miss Roney he remarked to a friend, "I was never even introduced to the girl, and it looks like she's trying to cut me down. Why, I don't even know her!"

Mrs. Lane questioned Harmon about the affair and said she would explain everything to Mr. Dyer in the morning.

By coincidence, Dr. Frey, Mrs. Lane, and Russell Harmon were scheduled to work overtime that evening. Harmon was still very disturbed and was talking to Mrs. Lane at the water cooler. Dr. Frey saw them through his glass partition and went out to join them.

HARMON: What I can't understand is why Mr. Taylor didn't come to me. I could have explained everything and the whole thing could have been prevented. But, boy! I guess I'm in the soup now. I want to see Mr. Dyer. It doesn't seem fair that he should only hear one side of the story.

FREY: Speaking about "sides of the story," maybe you would be interested in mine. (Frey proceeded to recount how Mr. Dyer had charged into his office and upbraided him for Harmon's conduct.)

MRS. LANE: If you ask me, I'm the gal with the responsibility. I've got to see Mr. Dyer first thing tomorrow morning.

The three continued to compare their versions of the "Office Boy Incident." Dr. Frey and Mrs. Lane were able to reconcile their suspicions of one another although neither offered a formal apology to the other. Harmon, however, still felt upset. He repeatedly stated that nothing could clear up the situation until he has a chance to explain the matter directly to Mr. Dyer. This he wanted to do the first thing the following day.

Early the next morning, Mrs. Lane explained the confusion to Mr. Dyer. At first he became angry with Mr. Taylor for not giving him the complete account of the affair and said, "That's poor communication. If Mark is having trouble with his girl, I'll give him a pamphlet on how to communicate!"

Later he grew aggravated with himself and finally became contrite: "I'm sorry—that's one of my failings. I should be able to control myself."

The case writer was told that Mr. Dyer frequently made this sort of statement after a flareup.

When Russell Harmon reported to work the next morning, he walked to Mrs. Lane's desk.

HARMON: Is Mr. Dyer in yet?

MRS. LANE: Well, yes, but the situation is all cleared up.

HARMON: Would it be all right if I saw him—I'd like to explain the thing to him.

MRS. LANE: Russell, I don't think you should do that. He knows that you weren't to blame, and I really think you should let the thing blow over.

After assurances from Mrs. Lane that he was "in the clear," Harmon decided to let the matter drop.

Chapter XIV

OVERVIEW

WE HAVE been examining human communications (the encoding and decoding phases, in particular) as they are influenced by assumptions held by the communicators involved. Some of these assumptions are destructive and troublesome because (1) they are false and imply an inadequate, distorted view of the world and (2) the communicator is usually unaware that his evaluations and communications are being influenced by them. Under these conditions, patterns of misevaluation and miscommunication are prone to occur and recur. It may be helpful to summarize the patterns we have considered.

INFERENCE-OBSERVATION CONFUSION

The *inference-observation confusion* occurs when one somehow acts upon his inference *as if* it were his observation. In essence he takes a risk without being aware that he is taking one and is off-guard, therefore, against the possibility that his inference is erroneous. The situation is not unlike that of walking downstairs in the dark—of striding off the last step, "certain" that you had reached the floor level!

Probably one of the key reasons we often find it easy to accept inference for observation is that our *statements* of inference can be readily confused with *statements* of observation. That is, there is nothing in the nature of our language (grammar, spelling, pronunciation, syntax, etc.) which inescapably distinguishes between them. Thus the habit of differentiating *statements* of inference from *statements* of observation should go far in training one's acuity for distinguishing between inferences and observations, on nonverbal levels.

BY-PASSING

By-passing occurs when communicators miss one another with their meanings—either by using the same words while meaning different things or by using different words while meaning the same thing. By-

289

passing appears to happen most frequently when communicators are unconsciously influenced by two fallacious assumptions: (1) that words are used in only one way (the respective communicator's way, of course) and (2) that words have meanings. To guard against by-passing, the communicator can supplant these assumptions with two others which represent much more adequately the relation between words and meanings: (1) most words, with the exception of some technical terms, are used in *more* than one way; (2) meanings exist not in words but only in the *people* who speak, hear, write, and read them. Querying, paraphrasing, and being alert to contexts, verbal and situational, are ways of implementing these premises.

ALLNESS

Allness is a sort of evaluational "disease." It occurs when one unconsciously assumes that it is possible to know and to say everything about something; that what he is saying (or writing or thinking) covers *all* there is (or all that is important) about the subject. The assumption is manifestly fallacious, and yet it is an extremely difficult one to dislodge if one does not recognize that he is inevitably and continuously abstracting.

To abstract is to select some details of a situation while neglecting all others. We abstract when we observe (see, hear, smell, etc.), talk, listen, write, read, "think," etc.

When one fails to realize that he is abstracting, i.e., leaving out details, he is in distinct danger of believing that he has left out nothing—nothing of consequence, at any rate. Arrogance, intolerance of other viewpoints, and closed-mindedness are very frequent consequences of such false assurances.

If one were to intensify his awareness of abstracting, he would find "remembering the ETC." a simple, yet effective, device.

DIFFERENTIATION FAILURES

I. Indiscrimination

Indiscrimination occurs when one fails to recognize *differences* among the *similarities*. The frequent result is that one reacts to Negroes, policemen, politicians, businessmen, Jews, etc., as if they were all identical—or at least enough alike to preclude any important differences. But people, situations, happenings, things, theories, etc., are unique. No two of anything are totally identical. And often there are differences which make a difference. The basic device for warding off dogmatic, unreasonable in discriminations is the *Which Index*— Negro$_1$ is not the *same* as Negro$_2$, etc.

II. Polarization

Polarization is the result of the confusion of *contraries* (situations involving graded variations, middle ground, alternatives) for *contradictories* (strict either-or, no-middle-ground affairs). It is the tendency to evaluate and communicate in black-and-white terms when shades of gray would be more appropriate. The *How-Much Index*—the habit of ascertaining "how much" or "to what degree" in seeming either-or situations can be an effective counter against polarization.

III. The Frozen Evaluation

The frozen evaluation generally occurs when one assumes nonchange. It tends to happen when one unconsciously believes that the way it (a person, a process, a situation, an object, etc.) is now is the way it has always been—or always will be. This can be a troublesome and dangerous premise because literally nothing (especially human beings) remains the same. Perhaps the only constant aspect about the world in which we live is its inconstancy.

We can keep ourselves alert to the process nature of life by habitually *When-Indexing* (dating) our thoughts and statements. Man$_1$, [1950] after all, is not the same as Man$_1$. [1960]

INTENSIONAL ORIENTATION

I. A General Statement

The chapter on intensional orientation did not deal with a specific pattern of miscommunication but rather with a general approach to "reality." One is *intensionally oriented* when he goes primarily, if not solely, by his "maps" (verbal and otherwise) of the "territory" rather than by the "territory" itself. An intensional parent, for example, would be guided by hazy memories of his own childhood, by the theories in Sunday supplement articles, and, by various child-rearing notions and nostrums of his generation to the virtual exclusion of his firsthand observations of the behavior of his child.

Intensional orientation invites trouble, confusion, and conflict because (1) often one's "maps" (his child-care theories and notions, for example) inadequately and fallaciously represent the "territory" (the flesh-and-blood child; his feelings, evaluations, actions, etc.) and (2) one may be *unaware* that he is dealing primarily with these "maps" and not with the respective "territories" they represent. He may thus be led to react to the "territory" inappropriately, unintelligently, and even dangerously.

The basic remedy for diminishing the destructive effects of intensional orientation is to "get extensional." That is, develop a readiness to go out and examine the "territory" rather than be content to be deluded by one's often spurious "maps." The byword of extensionality is to "look first—then talk."

II. "Pointing" and "Associating"

Among the ways we use words are these: (1) simply to point to, or call attention to, what we are representing by the words and (2) to evoke associations (memories, feelings) for what we are referring to. "Jail," for example, may be used to point, figuratively, to the physical structure where prisoners are housed. But it may also be used to elicit an emotional response, as when one is threatened with "jail."

When one is unaware that words may be used for these dual purposes, there is the possibility of a number of miscommunication patterns, including the "pointing-association" confusion (the tendency for one to respond to the associations evoked in him by words *as if* he were responding to what was being represented by the words); "name-calling" (the tendency for one's evaluation of a person to be influenced by the "associative" labels which have been applied to that person); and "associative" by-passing (the tendency for communicators to miss each other's "associative" meanings).

III. Blindering

One's definition (i.e., his interpretation, sizing-up, perception, appraising, etc.) of a problem greatly influences his attempts at solving the problem. But a definition is inevitably an abstraction, a leaving-out of details. If, then, in defining a problem, one is unaware that he is leaving out details (especially if they are important or vital details), he is in danger of becoming blindered—of unconsciously permitting his narrowed perception to restrict his attack on the problem. The basic correctives are (1) to remember that definitions inevitably involve the neglect of details (perhaps crucial ones) and (2) to recognize and remove one's blinders. How to do the latter was discussed more specifically in the chapter.

TRIGGER TO DISPUTE

Futile, exasperating quarrels and arguments probably constitute an expenditure of time and nervous energy far beyond our most liberal estimates. When one considers the toll in frayed nerves, injured feelings, and residual resentment, it seems clear that measures for avoiding and ameliorating dispute are essential.

This chapter takes the viewpoint that a key contributor to needless, destructive dispute is differing perceptions. If your perception and mine differ, we are likely to *respond* differently to the "same" situation. Differing overt responses provide a highly fertile ground for dispute if we fail to recognize that we may be quarreling over our perceptions (our subjective evaluations) rather than about objective, external "realities."

The chapter discusses the role of such influences as learning, set, and language habits as they contribute to perceptions. The remedy is not to discourage differing perceptions but to understand how and why they occur and to take them into account when dealing with the viewpoints of others.

UNDELAYED REACTIONS

Some undelayed reactions, such as reflex responses, are largely unavoidable, harmless, and even self-protective. Others, such as many reflex-like responses, may be highly useful when they have been properly conditioned and employed—the numerous actions of driving an automobile, for example. But some reflex-like responses—for instance, those manifested in fear and rage—are often destructive in their consequences. It is the latter which should be controlled if we are to avoid contributing to the harm of ourselves and others.

In some respects this was the key chapter of the book. Whereas the other chapters recommended various techniques, habits, and devices for avoiding and correcting the patterns of misevaluation and miscommunication, this chapter urged the basic setting for using them—the habit of delay-while-evaluating before action.

*   *   *   *

Our basic corrective methods, then, have been to suggest techniques for becoming (and remaining) *aware* of the insidious assumptions that

influence our evaluation and communication and, second, to recommend the substitution of new, more adequate premises.

To implement these premises, we have suggested a number of evaluational habits as substitutes for, or modifications of, some existing
habits. Let the reader be cautioned, however. The firm, enduring ac-
quisition of these deceptively "simple" habits will not come easily.
They will require practice and persistence. The experience will not
be unlike that of the person who for years has typed with two fingers
who is now learning the touch system of ten-finger typing. He may
become discouraged, for his efficiency will decrease *at first*. But eventually he will develop a typing facility of which he had never thought
himself capable.

With cultivation, then, these evaluational habits (Which, When,
and How-Much Indexing; remembering the ETC.; querying and paraphrasing; distinguishing inferences from observations; etc.) can become "second-nature" conditioned responses that will pay handsome
rewards in terms of more intelligent, safe, productive, and mature
communicative behavior.

A BIBLIOGRAPHY ON COMMUNICATION
AND RELATED AREAS

COMMUNICATION AND HUMAN RELATIONS

ALLEN, ROBERT. "Communicative Skills and Applied Imagination," *Journal of Communication,* Vol. VIII, No. 3 (Autumn, 1958).

ANDREWS, KENNETH R. (ed.). *The Case Method of Teaching Human Relations and Administration.* Cambridge, Mass.: Harvard University, 1953.

ARENSBERG, CONRAD M., *et al. Research in Industrial Human Relations: A Critical Appraisal.* New York: Harper & Bros., 1957.

ARGYRIS, CHRIS. "The Individual and Organization: Some Problems of Mutual Adjustment," *Administrative Science Quarterly,* June, 1957.

————. *Personality and Organization.* New York: Harper & Bros., 1957.

AYER, A. J.; HALDANE, J. B. S.; *et al. Studies in Communication.* London: Martin Secker & Warburg, 1955.

BABCOCK, C. MERTON. "A Dynamic Theory of Communications," *Journal of Communication,* Vol. II, No. 1 (1952).

————. *The Harper Handbook of Communication Skills.* New York: Harper & Bros., 1957.

BAKER, HELEN; BALLANTINE, JOHN W.; and TRUE, JOHN M. *Transmitting Information through Management and Union Channels.* Princeton, N.J.: Princeton University, Industrial Relations Section, 1949.

BARLOW, WALTER G. "Measuring the Effectiveness of Communication," *Key Problems in Human Relations.* American Management Association General Management Series, No. 181. 1956.

BENJAMIN, ROBERT E. "Communication Barriers between Employee and Employer," *Journal of Communication,* Vol. III (1953).

BENNETT, W. E. "Communication in Industry," *Journal of Communication,* Vol. II, No. 2 (1952).

BERELSON, BERNARD. *Content Analysis in Communication Research.* Glencoe, Ill., 1952.

BERRIEN, F. K., and BASH, WENDEL H. *Human Relations: Comments and Cases.* New York: Harper & Bros., 1957.

BRETH, ROBERT D. "Human Relations and Communications Are Twins," *Personnel Journal,* December, 1952.

BROADBENT, D. E. *Perception and Communication.* New York: Pergamon Press, 1958.

BRYSON, LYMAN. *The Communication of Ideas.* New York: Harper & Bros., 1948. See especially HAROLD D. LASSWELL's "The Structure and Function of Communication in Society."

Building a Balanced Communications Program. General Management Series, No. 170. New York: American Management Association, 1954.

BURLING, TEMPLE. "Aids and Bars to Internal Communication," *Hospitals,* Vol. XXVIII (November, 1954).

CABOT, HUGH, and KOHL, JOSEPH A. *Human Relations,* Vol. I. Cambridge, Mass.: Harvard University Press, 1953.

CADY, EDWIN LAIRD. *Creative Communication.* New York: Reinhold, 1956.

CALHOUN, RICHARD P.; NOLAND, E. WILLIAM; and WHITEHILL, ARTHUR M., JR. *Cases on Human Relations in Management.* New York: McGraw-Hill Book Co., Inc., 1958.

CARTIER, FRANCIS A., and HARWOOD, K. A. "On Definition of Communication," *Journal of Communication*, Vol. III (1953).

Cases in Business Administration: Intercollegiate Bibliography, published and distributed on behalf of the Intercollegiate Contributors and the American Association of Collegiate Schools of Business. Boston: Harvard University Graduate School of Business Administration, Vol. I (1957) through IV (1960). See especially cases listed under "Human Aspects of Administration."

CASSELS, LOUIS. "You Can Get Your Ideas Across," *Nation's Business*, December, 1957.

Channels of Employee Communication: Part I. New York: General Electric Co.

CHAPIN, RICHARD E. *Mass Communications.* East Lansing: Michigan State University Press, 1957.

CHERRY, COLIN. *On Human Communication.* New York: Technology Press of Massachusetts Institute of Technology and John Wiley & Sons, Inc., 1957.

CHASE, W. HOWARD. "Human Relations—Key to a New Era," *Journal of Communication*, Vol. I, No. 1 (1951).

CHASE, STUART. *Power of Words.* New York: Harcourt, Brace & Co., 1954.

———. *Roads to Agreement.* New York: Harper & Bros., 1951.

COATES, R. H. "Human Communications," *British Management Review*, Vol. XIII (October, 1955).

Communicating with Employees. Studies in Personnel Policy, No. 129. New York: National Industrial Conference Board, 1952.

"Communication and the Communication Arts," *Teachers College Record*, Vol. LVII (November, 1955). A "Selected Bibliography" appears on pp. 140–49.

Communication in Business and Industry. New Brunswick, N.J.: Johnson & Johnson, 1949.

Communication within the Management Group. Studies in Personnel Policy, No. 80. New York: National Industrial Conference Board, 1947.

COOK, P. H. "An Examination of the Notion of Communication in Industry," *Occupational Psychology*, Vol. XXX (January, 1951).

CORSON, JOHN J. "The Role of Communication in the Process of Administration," *Public Administration Review*, Vol. IV (Winter, 1944).

CROCKER, LIONEL. "The Employer as a Communicator," *Journal of Communication*, Vol. VI (1956).

DAHLE, THOMAS L. "An Evaluation of Communication Skills Training," *Journal of Communication*, Vol. IX, No. 3 (September, 1959).

———. "Transmitting Information to Employees: A Study of Five Methods," *Personnel*, Vol. XXXI (November, 1954).

DANDENEAU, RICHARD J. "How to Set Up an Employee Communications Program," *Management Methods*, Vol. IX, No. 3 (December, 1955).

DAVIS, KEITH. "Communication *within* Management," *Personnel*, November, 1954.

———. *Human Relations in Business.* New York: McGraw-Hill Book Co., Inc., 1957.

———. "Management Communication and the Grapevine," *Harvard Business Review*, September–October, 1953.

———, and SCOTT, WILLIAM G. *Readings in Human Relations.* New York: McGraw-Hill Book Co., Inc., 1959.

DAVITZ, JOEL R., and DAVITZ, LOIS JEAN. "Correlates of Accuracy in the Communication of Feelings," *Journal of Communication*, Vol. IX, No. 3 (September, 1959).

DEFLEUR, MELVIN L., and LARSEN, OTTO N. *The Flow of Information: An Experiment in Mass Communication.* New York: Harper & Bros., 1958.

DEUTSCH, KARL W. "On Communication Models in the Social Sciences," *Public Opinion Quarterly*, Vol. XVI, No. 3 (Fall, 1952).

DEUTSCHMANN, PAUL J. "The Sign Situation Classification of Human Communication," *Journal of Communication*, Vol. VII, No. 2 (Summer, 1957).

The Dollars and Sense of Human Relations in Industry, by the Editors of *Industrial Relations News*. New York: Industrial Relations Newsletter, Inc., 1956.

DOOHER, M. JOSEPH, and MARQUIS, VIVIENNE. *Effective Communication on the Job*. New York: American Management Association, 1956.

DOVER, C. J. "An Analysis of Interpretative Communication Management," *Journal of Communication*, Vol. VIII, No. 3 (Autumn, 1958).

————. *Effective Communication in Company Publications*. Chicago: Bureau of National Affairs, 1959.

DOUGLASS, PAUL. *Communication through Reports*. Englewood Cliffs, N.J.: Prentice-Hall, Inc., 1957.

DUBIN, ROBERT. *Human Relations in Administration*. New York: Prentice-Hall, Inc., 1951.

Education, Vol. LXXII (March, 1952). Entire issue deals with communication.

Effective Communication on the Job: A Guide to Employee Communication for Supervisors and Executives. New York: American Management Association, 1956.

Employee Communication: Executive Summary. New York: General Electric Co.

Employee Communications for Better Understanding. Rev. ed. (Pamphlet published by the National Association of Manufacturers, 14 W. 49th St., New York 20, N.Y.)

ESTES, CHARLES. "Communication in Industry," *Journal of Communication*, Vol. I, No. 2 (1951).

EXTON, WILLIAM, JR. "Human Communication: Non-verbal and Supra-verbal," *General Semantics Bulletin*, Nos. 6 and 7 (Spring–Summer, 1951).

————. "Taking the Double-Talk Out of Communicating," *Factory Management and Maintenance*, April, 1957.

FESSENDEN, SETH. "How Can We Teach Listening?" *Journal of Communication*, Vol. I, No. 2 (1951).

FESTINGER, LEON, *et al.* "Study of Rumor: Its Origin and Spread," *Human Relations*, Vol. I (August, 1958).

The Flow of Information among Scientists: Problems, Opportunities, and Research Questions. New York: Bureau of Applied Social Research, 1958.

FREDRIKSEN, C. W., and MARTINSON, HELMER. "Helping Supervisors Train Themselves in Human Relations," *Personnel*, January, 1955.

FREEDMAN, WILLIAM A. "A Study in Communication," *Journal of Communication*, Vol. IX, No. 1 (March, 1959).

FROMAN, ROBERT. "How to Say What You Mean," *Nation's Business*, May, 1957.

————. "Make Words Fit the Job," *ibid.*, July, 1959.

"Fundamentals of Communications," *NICB Management Record*, September, 1954.

FUNK, H. B., and BECKER, R. C. "Measuring the Effectiveness of Industrial Communication," *Personnel*, November, 1952.

GARDNER, BURLEIGH B., and MOORE, DAVID G. *Human Relations in Industry*. 3d ed. Homewood, Ill.: Richard D. Irwin, Inc., 1955.

GERBER, GEORGE. "Toward a General Model of Communication," *Audio-Visual Communication Review*, Vol. IV (Summer, 1956).

GLENN, EDMUND S. "Interpretation and Intercultural Communication," *ETC: A Review of General Semantics*, Vol. XV, No. 2 (Winter, 1957–58).

GLOVER, JOHN DESMOND, and HOWER, RALPH M. *The Administrator: Cases on*

Human Relations in Business. 3d ed. Homewood, Ill.: Richard D. Irwin, Inc., 1957.

GRACE, HARRY A. "Confidence, Redundancy, and the Purpose of Communication," *Journal of Communication,* Vol. VI (1956).

GRACEY, HARRY F. "Effective Communications—One Road to Productivity," *Journal of Communication,* Vol. II, No. 1 (1952).

GRAY, ROBERT D., and SORENSON, L. ROBERT. "Practicing Supervision," *Personnel,* May, 1954.

HABBE, STEPHEN. *Communicating with Employees.* Studies in Personnel Policy, No. 129. New York: National Industrial Conference Board, 1952.

HACKETT, HERBERT, *et al. Understanding and Being Understood.* New York: Longmans, Green & Co., 1957.

HERON, ALEXANDER R. *Sharing Information with Employees.* Stanford, Calif.: Stanford University Press, 1942.

HINDS, GEORGE L. "The Communicative Behavior of the Executive," *Journal of Communication,* Vol. VII, No. 1 (Spring, 1957).

HOSLETT, SCHUYLER DEAN. *Human Factors in Management.* Rev. ed. New York: Harper & Bros., 1951.

How to Improve Business Communications. Detroit: Wayne University Press, 1950.

Human Relations. Quarterly. London and Ann Arbor, Mich.: Vol. I, 1947/48
———.

"Human Relations: Where Do We Stand Today"—("Human Relations: How Far Have We Come?" by THOMAS G. SPATES); ("Human Relations: How Far Do We Have to Go?" by PETER F. DRUCKER); ("Human Relations: A Look into the Future," by CHRIS ARGYRIS), *Management Record,* March, 1959.

Improving Management Communication. General Management Series, No. 145. New York: American Management Association, 1950.

JACKSON, JAY M. "The Organization and Its Communication Problem," *Advanced Management,* February, 1959.

JANIS, JACK HAROLD (ed.). *Business Communication Reader.* New York: Harper & Bros., 1959.

JENNINGS, ELIZABETH, and JENNINGS, FRANCIS. "Making Human Relations Work," *Harvard Business Review,* January, 1951.

JOHNSON, KENNETH G. "Understanding the Communication Process," *Extension Insights* (Newsletter of the University of Wisconsin Extension Division, Madison, Wisconsin).

JOHNSON, ROY IVAN; SCHALEKAMP, MARIE; and GARRISON, LLOYD A. *Communication: Handling Ideas Effectively.* New York: McGraw-Hill Book Co., Inc., 1956.

JOHNSON, WENDELL. "The Fateful Process of Mr. A Talking to Mr. B," *Harvard Business Review,* Vol. XXXI, No. 1 (January–February, 1953).

KAHN, ROBERT L., and CONNELL, CHARLES F. " 'Nobody Tells me Anything!': Getting the Facts You Need for Decision," *Dun's Review and Modern Industry,* November, 1957.

KATZ, D. "Psychological Barriers to Communication," *Annals of the American Academy of Political and Social Sciences,* 1947.

———. "Human Relations Skills Can Be Sharpened," *Harvard Business Review,* Vol. XXXIV (July–August, 1956).

KEGEL, CHAS. H. and STEVENS, MARTIN. *Communication: Principles and Practice.* San Francisco: Wadsworth, 1959.

KIRK, JOHN. "Communication Theory and Methods of Fixing Belief," *ETC.: A Review of General Semantics,* Vol. X, No. 4 (Summer, 1953).

KNOWER, FRANKLIN H. (ed.). *Proceedings of the First Ohio State University Conference on Communications Research and Training in Business and Industry.*

Columbus: Ohio State University.

KOLB, HARRY D. "Creating the Organizational 'Atmosphere' for Improved Communications," *Personnel*, May, 1954.

LAIRD, DONALD A., and LAIRD, ELEANOR C. *The Technique of Handling People.* New York: McGraw-Hill Book Co., Inc., 1943.

LARSEN, S. A. (ed.) *How to Improve Business Communications.* Detroit: Wayne University Press, 1951.

LAWRENCE, PAUL R. "How to Deal with Resistance to Change," *Harvard Business Review*, May–June, 1954.

LEE, IRVING J. *Customs and Crises in Communication.* New York: Harper & Bros., 1954.

———. *How to Talk with People.* New York: Harper & Bros., 1952.

———. "Procedure for 'Coercing' Agreement," *Harvard Business Review*, Vol. XXXII, No. 1 (January–February, 1954).

———, and LEE, LAURA L. *Handling Barriers in Communication.* New York: Harper & Bros., 1957.

LILLYWHITE, HEROLD. "Toward a Philosophy of Communication," *Journal of Communication*, Vol. II, No. 1 (1952).

LINDGREN, HENRY C. *Effective Leadership in Human Relations.* New York: Hermitage House, 1954.

LONGLEY, ARNOLD. "Communications from the Viewpoint of the Industrial Engineer," *Journal of Communication*, Vol. II, No. 1 (1952).

MACRORIE, KEN. *The Perceptive Writer, Reader, and Speaker.* New York: Harcourt, Brace & Co., 1959.

MAIER, NORMAN R. F., *et al. Communication in Organizations.* Ann Arbor: Foundation for Research on Human Behavior, 1959.

MAIER, NORMAN R. F. *Principles of Human Relations.* New York: John Wiley & Sons, 1952.

MAIZE, RAY C. "A Military Program in Communications," *Journal of Communication*, Vol. II, No. 1 (1952).

MARROW, ALFRED J. *Making Management Human.* New York: McGraw-Hill Book Co., Inc., 1957.

MARSTON, E. C., *et al. Business Communication.* New York: Macmillan Co., 1949.

MAYO, ELTON. *The Human Problems of an Industrial Civilization.* Boston: Harvard University, Graduate School of Business Administration, 1945.

———. *The Social Problems of an Industrial Civilization.* Boston: Harvard University, Graduate School of Business Administration, 1945.

MCGREGOR, DOUGLAS. "The Human Side of Enterprise," *Adventure in Thought and Action* (Proceedings of the 5th Anniversary Convocation of the School of Industrial Management, Massachusetts Institute of Technology, April 9, 1957).

———. *Line Management's Responsibility for Human Relations.* New York: American Management Association, 1953.

———. "The Staff Function in Human Relations," *Journal of Social Issues*, Summer, 1948.

MCLEAN, ALAN. "An Industrial Psychologist Looks at Employee Communications," *Personnel Journal*, Vol. XXXIII, No. 9 (February, 1955).

MCNAIR, MALCOM P. "Too Much 'Human Relations'?" *Look*, October 28, 1958.

MEHLING, REUBEN. "A Study of Nonlogical Factors of Reasoning in the Communication Process," *Journal of Communication*, Vol. IX, No. 3 (September, 1959).

MELLINGER, GLEN D. "Interpersonal Trust as a Factor in Communication," *Journal of Abnormal and Social Psychology*, Vol. LII (May, 1956).

MENNINGER, WILLIAM C., and LEVINSON, HARRY. *Human Understanding in Industry: A Guide for Supervisors.* Chicago: Science Research Associates, 1956.

MILLER, GEORGE A. *Language and Communication.* New York: McGraw-Hill Book Co., Inc., 1951.

MOSER, GEORGE V. "How Not to Influence People," *Management Record*, March, 1958.

MURRAY, ELWOOD. "What Are the Problems of Communication in Human Relations?" *Journal of Communication*, Vol. I, No. 1 (1951).

————. "Human Intercommunication as a Unified Area for Research," *ibid.*, Vol. II, No. 1 (1952).

————. "How an Educator Looks at Industrial Activities in the Field of Communication," *ibid.*, Vol. VI (1956).

————; SORENSON, F.; and PAUL, W. B. "A Functional Core for the Basic Communications Course," *Quarterly Journal of Speech*, Vol. XXXII, No. 2 (April, 1946).

NEWMAN, JOHN B. "Communication: A Dyadic Postulation," *Journal of Communication*, Vol. IX, No. 2 (June, 1959).

NILSEN, THOMAS R. "Research Problems in Communication in Industry," *Journal of Communication*, Vol. IV (1954).

————. "Some Assumptions That Impede Communication," *General Semantics Bulletin*, Nos. 14 and 15 (Winter–Spring, 1954).

NAFZIGER, RALPH O., and WHITE, DAVID M. *Introduction to Mass Communications Research.* Baton Rouge: Louisiana State University Press, 1958.

PARKER, WILLARD E., and KLEEMEIER, ROBERT M. *Human Relations in Supervision.* New York: McGraw-Hill Book Co., Inc., 1951.

PERRY, DALLIS, and MAHONEY, THOMAS A. "In-Plant Communications and Employee Morale," *Personnel Psychology*, Autumn, 1955.

PERRY, JOHN. *Human Relations in Small Industry.* New York: McGraw-Hill Book Co., Inc., 1954.

PETERS, RAYMOND W. *Communication within Industry.* New York: Harper & Bros., 1950.

————. "Management Looks at Communication Again," *Journal of Communication*, Vol. II, No. 2 (1952).

PIGORS, PAUL. "Communication in Industry: A Cure of Conflict?" *Industrial and Labor Relations Review*, July, 1953.

————. *Effective Communication in Industry.* New York: National Association of Manufacturers, 1949.

PLATT, JAMES H. "What Do We Mean, 'Communication'?" *Journal of Communication*, Vol. V (1955).

RAINES, I. I. *Better Communications in Small Business.* Washington, D.C.: Small Business Administration, 1953.

REDDING, CHARLES. "The Most Important Problems of College Courses in Communication," *Journal of Communication*, Vol. I, No. 1 (1951).

REDFIELD, CHARLES E. *Communication in Management.* Rev. ed. Chicago: University of Chicago Press, 1958.

————. "Communication: The Lifestream of Every Organization," *Office Management*, Vol. XVIII (March 15, 1957).

ROETHLISBERGER, FRITZ J. "The Administrator's Skill: Communication," *Harvard Business Review*, November–December, 1953.

————. "Barriers to Communication between Men," *Northwestern University Information*, Vol. XX, No. 25 (April 21, 1952).

————. "Human Relations in Industry: A Problem of Communication," *General Semantics Bulletin*, Nos. 14 and 15 (Winter–Spring, 1954).

————. *Management and Morale.* Cambridge, Mass.: Harvard University Press, 1952.

————, and DICKSON, WILLIAM J. *Management and the Worker*. Cambridge, Mass.: Harvard University Press, 1950.

————; LOMBARD, GEORGE F. F.; and RONKEN, HARRIETT O. *Training for Human Relations*. Boston: Harvard Graduate School of Business Administration, 1954.

ROGERS, CARL R. "Communication: Its Blocking and Facilitation," *Northwestern University Information*, Vol. XX, No. 25 (April 21, 1952).

————, and ROETHLISBERGER, F. J. "Barriers and Gateways to Communication," *Harvard Business Review*, July–August, 1952.

RONKEN, HARRIET O. "Communication within the Work Group," *Harvard Business Review*, July, 1951.

————, and LAWRENCE, PAUL R. *Administering Changes: A Case Study*. Boston, Mass.: Harvard University Graduate School of Business, 1952.

RUESCH, JURGEN. *Communication*. New York: W. W. Norton & Co., 1951.

RUESCH, J., and BATESON, G. *Communication: The Social Matrix of Society*. New York: W. W. Norton & Co., 1951.

————, and KEES, WELDON. *Nonverbal Communication*. Los Angeles: University of California Press, 1956.

SALTONSTALL, ROBERT. *Human Relations in Administration*. New York: McGraw-Hill Book Co., Inc., 1959.

SAYLES, LEONARD R. "Human Relations and the Organization of Work," *Michigan Business Review*, November, 1954.

SCHACHTER, STANLEY, and BURDICK, HARVEY. "A Field Experiment on Rumor Transmission and Distortion," *Journal of Abnormal and Social Psychology*, Vol. L, No. 3 (May, 1955).

SCHRAMM, WILBUR. *The Process and Effects of Mass Communication*. Urbana, Ill.: Free Press, 1953.

————. *Responsibility in Mass Communication*. New York: Harper & Bros., 1957.

SCHUTZ, WILLIAM C. "The Interpersonal Underworld," *Harvard Business Review*, July–August, 1958.

SELEKMAN, BENJAMIN M. *Labor Relations and Human Relations*. New York: McGraw-Hill Book Co., Inc., 1947.

SHANNON, CLAUDE E., and WEAVER, WARREN. *The Mathematical Theory of Communication*. Urbana: University of Illinois Press, 1949.

SHAW, MARVIN E., and GILCHRIST, J. C. "Intra-Group Communication and Leader Choice," *Journal of Social Psychology*, Vol. XLIII (February, 1956).

————, and ROTHSCHILD, GERALD H. "Some Effects of Prolonged Experience in Communication Nets," *Journal of Applied Psychology*, Vol. XL (October, 1956).

SHULL, FREMONT A. *Selected Readings in Management*. Homewood, Ill.: Richard D. Irwin, Inc., 1958. See especially section on "Communication and Control."

SINGER, T. E. R. (ed.). *Information and Communication Practice in Industry*. New York: Reinhold, 1958.

SMITH, BRUCE L., and SMITH, CHITRA M. *International Communication and Political Opinion: A Guide to the Literature*. Princeton, N.J.: Princeton University Press, 1956.

SPITZ, RENÉ A. *No and Yes: On the Genesis of Human Communication*. New York: International Universities Press, 1957.

STEIGLITZ, HAROLD. "Barriers to Communications," *NICB Management Record*, January, 1958.

STEINBERG, C. S. *The Mass Communicators*. New York: Harper & Bros., 1959.

STRYKER, PERRIN. "A Slight Case of Overcommunication," *Fortune*, Vol. XLIX (March, 1954).

TARR, J. C. "Improving Communication in the Air Force," *Journal of Communication*, Vol. IX, No. 2 (June, 1959).

TEAD, ORDWAY. *The Art of Administration*. New York: McGraw-Hill Book Co., Inc., 1951.

TEPLOW, LEO. "Communication as a Way of Industrial Life," *Management Review*, August, 1956.

THISTLETHWAITE, DONALD L.; HAAN, HENRY DE; and KAMENETZKY, JOSEPH. "The Effects of 'Directive' and 'Nondirective' Communication Procedures on Attitudes," *Journal of Abnormal and Social Psychology*, Vol. LI, No. 1 (July, 1955).

THOMPSON, WAYNE N. *Fundamentals of Communication: An Integrated Approach*. New York: McGraw-Hill Book Co., Inc., 1957.

Toward Understanding Men. Topeka, Kan.: Menninger Foundation, Division of Industrial Mental Health, 1956.

VICKERS, SIR GEOFFREY. "Human Communication," *British Management Review*, Vol. XII (January, 1954).

WEAVER, CARL H. "Measuring Point of View as a Barrier to Communication," *Journal of Communication*, Vol. VII, No. 1 (Spring, 1957).

WEAVER, ROBERT G., and ZELKO, HAROLD P. "Talking Things Over on the Job," *Supervision Magazine*, May, June, and July, 1958.

WEBB, WILSE B. "Elements in Individual-to-Individual Communication," *Journal of Communication*, Vol. VII, No. 3 (Autumn, 1957).

WESTLY, BRUCE H., and MACLEAN, MALCOMB S., JR. "A Conceptual Model for Communications Research," *Audio-Visual Communication Review*, Vol. III, No. 1 (Winter, 1955).

WHITAKER, JOHN C. "Talking with People: Getting the Most from Employee Communication," *Building an Effective Workforce*. American Management Association Personnel Series, No. 165. 1955.

WHITEHEAD, T. N. "Human Relations within Industrial Groups," *Harvard Business Review*, Autumn, 1935.

WHYTE, WILLIAM F. *Pattern for Industrial Peace*. New York: Harper & Bros., 1951.

WHYTE, WILLIAM H., and the EDITORS of *Fortune*. *Is Anybody Listening?* New York: Simon & Schuster, 1952.

WHYTE, WILLIAM H., JR. "The Web of Word of Mouth," *Fortune*, Vol. L, No. 5 (November, 1954).

WIENER, NORBERT. *The Human Use of Human Beings*. Boston: Houghton Mifflin Co., 1950.

WILSON, E. B., and WRIGHT, S. B. *Getting Along with People in Business*. New York: Funk & Wagnalls, 1950.

WINN, A. "Training in Administration and Human Relations," *Personnel*, September, 1953.

WOOD, K. P. "Communication in a Communication Service," *Journal of Communication*, Vol. I, No. 2 (1951).

ZELKO, HAROLD P. *Management-Employee Communication in Action*. Cleveland: Howard Allen, Inc., 1957.

COMMUNICATION PROCESSES

SPEAKING

AUSTON, JOHN T. "Improving Everyday Speaking and Listening Efficiency," *Journal of Communication*, Vol. IV (1954).

BAIRD, A. CRAIG, and KNOWER, FRANKLIN H. *General Speech*. New York: McGraw-Hill Book Co., Inc., 1949.

BARBARA, DOMINICK A. *Your Speech Reveals Your Personality*. Springfield, Ill.: Charles C. Thomas, 1958.

BEIGHLEY, K. C. "A Summary of Experimental Studies Dealing with the Effect of Organization and of Skill of Speaker on Comprehension," *Journal of Communication*, Vol. II, No. 2 (1952).

BLACK, JOHN W., and MOORE, WILBUR E. *Speech-Code, Meaning, and Communication*. New York: McGraw-Hill Book Co., Inc., 1955.

BRIGANCE, W. N. *Speech—Its Disciplines in a Free Society*. New York: Appleton-Century-Crofts, Inc., 1952.

BRYANT, DONALD, and WALLACE, KARL. *Oral Communication*. 2d ed. New York: Appleton-Century-Crofts, Inc., 1954.

CASEY, ROBERT S. *Oral Communication of Technical Information*. New York: Reinhold, 1958.

CROCKER, LIONEL. *Business and Professional Speech*. New York: Ronald Press, 1951.

DAHLE, THOMAS L., and DOWLING, FRED R. "Improving Oral Communication," *Journal of Communication*, Vol. VI (1956).

DIETRICH, JOHN E., and BROOKS, KEITH. *Practical Speaking for the Technical Man*. New York: Prentice-Hall, Inc., 1958.

GILKINSON, HOWARD. "Research in Relation to the Teaching of Oral Communications," *Journal of Communication*, Vol. II, No. 1 (1952).

HICKS, MASON A. "Speech Training in Industry," *Journal of Communication*, Vol. V (1955).

HINDS, GEORGE L. "Continuous Speech Education in Industry," *Journal of Communication*, Vol. IV (1954).

HOVLAND, C. L. (ed.). *Order of Presentation in Persuasion*. New Haven: Yale University Press, 1958.

HUSTON, ALFRED D.; SANDBERG, ROBERT A.; and MILLS, JACK. *Effective Speaking in Business*. Rev. ed. Englewood Cliffs, N.J.: Prentice-Hall, Inc., 1955.

MARTIN, JOHN M. *Business and Professional Speaking*. New York: Harper & Bros., 1956.

MAWHINNEY, CLARA KREFTING, and SMITH, HARLEY A. *Business and Professional Speech*. New York: American Book Co., 1950.

McBURNEY, JAMES H., and WRAGE, ERNEST J. *The Art of Good Speech*. New York: Prentice-Hall, Inc., 1953.

McCRERY, LESTER LYLE. "An Experimental Study of the Relationships between Writing and Speaking Performance as Measured by College Grades and Student Rating Scales," *Journal of Communication*, Vol. I, No. 1 (1951).

MICKEN, RALPH A. *Speaking for Results*. Boston: Houghton Mifflin Co., 1958.

MINNICK, WAYNE C. *The Art of Persuasion*. Cambridge, Mass.: Riverside Press, 1957.

MONROE, ALAN. *Principles and Types of Speech*. Chicago: Scott, Foresman & Co., 1955.

———. *Principles of Speech*. 4th ed. Chicago: Scott, Foresman & Co., 1958.

MURRAY, ELWOOD. *Integrative Speech: Speech-Communications in Human Management*. Denver: University of Denver Press, 1949.

NICHOLS, RALPH G., and LEWIS, THOMAS R. *Listening and Speaking*. Dubuque: Wm. C. Brown, 1954.

NIRENBERG, JESSE S. "How to Reach Minds—and Hearts—When You Talk to People," *Sales Management*, December 19, 1958.

OLIVER, ROBERT T. *Effective Speech for Democratic Living*. New York: Prentice-Hall, Inc., 1959.

PHILLIPS, DAVID C. *Oral Communication in Business*. New York: McGraw-Hill Book Co., Inc., 1955.

PROCHNOW, HERBERT V. *The Successful Speaker's Handbook.* New York: Prentice-Hall, Inc., 1951.

SANFORD, W. P., and YEAGER, W. H. *Practical Business Speaking.* 3d ed. New York: McGraw-Hill Book Co., Inc., 1952.

SARETT, LEW; FOSTER, WILLIAM TRUFANT; and SARETT, ALMA JOHNSON. *Basic Principles of Speech.* 3d rev. ed. Boston: Houghton Mifflin Co., 1958.

SCHUBERT, LELAND. *A Guide for Oral Communication.* New York: Prentice-Hall, Inc., 1948.

SMITH, RAYMOND G. *Principles of Public Speaking.* New York: Ronald Press, 1959.

THOMPSON, WAYNE N., and FESSENDEN, SETH A. *Basic Experiences in Speech.* New York: Prentice-Hall, Inc., 1951.

WOLFF, TOM. "Leaders Must Speak Up," *Personnel,* May, 1954.

ZELKO, HAROLD P. *How to Become a Successful Speaker.* New London, Conn.: National Foreman's Institute, 1950.

———. "Practical Training in Effective Speaking," *Journal of the American Society of Training Directors,* January, 1958.

———. "Speech and Conference Leadership Training in American Industry," *Personnel,* September, 1950.

———. "Speech Problems in Customer Relations," *Today's Speech,* November, 1958.

WRITING

CADY, EDWIN LAIRD. *Creative Communication.* New York: Reinhold, 1956.

DEPARTMENT OF THE AIR FORCE. *Preparation of Written Communications.* Air Force Manual No. 10–1. April 10, 1959.

DOUGLASS, PAUL. *Communication through Reports.* New York: Prentice-Hall, Inc., 1957.

DRACH, HARVEY E. *American Business Writing.* New York: American Book Co., 1959.

DRAKE, FRANCIS E. "Teaching Written Communication," *Journal of Communication,* Vol. III (1953).

DUNN, THOMAS. "Preparing an Objective Test of Reading and Writing," *Journal of Communication,* Vol. II, No. 1 (1952).

FORD, NICK AARON, and TURPIN WATERS. *Basic Skills for Better Writing.* New York: G. P. Putnam, 1959.

GAUM, CARL G.; GROVES, HAROLD F.; and HOFFMAN, LYNE S. *Report Writing.* 3d ed. New York: Prentice-Hall, Inc., 1953.

GIBSON, WALTER. *Seeing and Writing: Fifteen Exercises in Composing Experience.* New York: Longmans, Green & Co., 1959.

GODFREY, J. W., and PARR, G. *The Technical Writer.* New York: John Wiley & Sons, 1959.

GREBANIER, BERNARD D. N., and RECTOR, SEYMOUR. *College Writing and Reading.* New York: Henry Holt & Co., 1959.

GUNNING, ROBERT. *Techniques of Clear Writing.* New York: McGraw-Hill Book Co., Inc., 1952.

GUYER, BYRON, and BIRD, DONALD A. *Patterns of Thinking and Writing.* San Francisco: Wadsworth, 1959.

HOVLAND, C. I. (ed.). *Order of Presentation in Persuasion.* New Haven: Yale University Press, 1958.

LINTON, CALVIN D. *How to Write Reports.* New York: Harper & Bros., 1954.

McCRERY, LESTER LYLE. "An Experimental Study of the Relationships between

Writing and Speaking Performance as Measured by College Grades and Student Rating Scales," *Journal of Communication*, Vol. I, No. 1 (1951).

McLEAN, JOHN G. "Better Reports for Better Controls," *Harvard Business Review*, Vol. XXXV (May–June, 1957).

MOORE, ROBERT HAMILTON. *Effective Writing*. 2d ed. New York: Rinehart, 1959.

MUHLENBRUCH, CARL W. "Why Do Engineers Just Write?" *American Business Writing Association Bulletin*, February, 1959.

PERRIN, PORTER G. *Writer's Guide and Index to English*. 3d ed. Chicago: Scott, Foresman & Co., 1959.

SHURTER, ROBERT L. *Effective Letters in Business*. 2d ed. New York: McGraw-Hill Book Co., Inc., 1954.

———. *Written Communication in Business*. New York: McGraw-Hill Book Co., Inc., 1957.

SMART, W. K.; McKELVEY, L. W.; and GERFEN, R. C. *Business Letters*. 4th ed. New York: Harper & Bros., 1957.

ULMAN, JOSEPH N., JR., and GOULD, JAY R. *Technical Reporting*. New York: Henry Holt & Co., 1959.

WALDO, WILLIS H. *Better Report Writing*. New York: Reinhold, 1957.

WEIL, B. H. (ed.). *Technical Editing*. New York: Reinhold, 1958.

WOODFORD, BRUCE P. "A Creative Approach to Remedial Writing," *Journal of Communication*, Vol. II, No. 1 (1952).

WOLSELEY, ROLAND E. *Critical Writing for the Journalist*. Philadelphia: Chilton, 1959.

Writing Guide for Naval Officers. Washington, D.C.: Government Printing Office 1959.

LISTENING

AINSWORTH, STANLEY, and HIGH, CHARLES. "Auditory Functions and Abilities in Good and Poor Listeners," *Journal of Communication*, Vol. IV (1954).

AUSTON, JOHN T. "Improving Everyday Speaking and Listening Efficiency," *Journal of Communication*, Vol. IV (1954).

BAKEN, PAUL, "Some Reflections on Listening Behavior," *Journal of Communication*, Vol. VI (1956).

BARBARA, DOMINICK A. *The Art of Listening*. Springfield, Ill.: Charles C Thomas, 1958.

BIRD, DONALD E. "Bibliography of Selected Materials about Listening," *Education*, January, 1955.

———. "Have You Tried Listening?" *Journal of the American Dietetic Association*, Vol. XXX (March, 1954).

———. "Teaching Listening Comprehension," *Journal of Communication*, Vol. III (1953).

———. "This Is Your Listening Life!" *Journal of the American Dietetic Association*, Vol. XXXII, No. 6 (June, 1956).

BLEWETT, THOMAS T. "An Experiment in the Measurement of Listening at the College Level," *Journal of Communication*, Vol. I, No. 1 (1951).

CARTIER, FRANCIS A. "The Social Context of Listenability Research," *Journal of Communication*, Vol. II, No. 1 (1952).

Education, Vol. LXXV (January, 1955). Entire issue deals with listening.

ERICKSON, ALLEN G. "Can Listening Efficiency Be Improved?" *Journal of Communication*, Vol. IV, No. 4 (Winter, 1954).

FESSENDEN, SETH. "How Can We Teach Listening?" *Journal of Communication*, Vol. II, No. 2 (1952).

HAYAKAWA, S. I. "The Task of the Listener," *ETC.: A Review of General Semantics*, Vol. VII, No. 1 (Autumn, 1949).

IRVIN, CHARLES E. "Motivation in Listening Training," *Journal of Communication*, Vol. IV (1954).

———. "Suggested Activities Designed to Improve Listening Skill," *ibid.*, Vol. IV (1954).

JOHNSON, KENNETH O. "The Effect of Classroom Training upon Listening Comprehension," *Journal of Communication*, Vol. I, No. 1 (1951).

JOHNSON, WENDELL. "Do You Know How to Listen?" *ETC.: A Review of General Semantics*, Vol. VII, No. 1 (Autumn, 1949).

KRAMAR, EDWARD J. J., and LEWIS, THOMAS R. "Comparison of Visual and Non-Visual Listening," *Journal of Communication*, Vol. I, No. 2 (1951).

LARKE, ALFRED G. "How to Learn by Listening," *Dun's Review and Modern Industry*, April, 1955.

LEWIS, MAURICE S. "The Effect of Training in Listening upon Reading," *Journal of Communication*, Vol. III (1953).

NICHOLS, RALPH G. "Listening Is a 10-Part Skill," *Nation's Business*, July, 1957.

———. "Needed Research in Listening Comprehension," *Journal of Communication*, Vol. I, No. 1 (1951).

———. "You Don't Know How to Listen," *Collier's*, July 25, 1953.

———, and LEWIS, THOMAS R. *Listening and Speaking*. Dubuque: Wm. C. Brown, 1954.

———, and STEVENS, LEONARD A. *Are You Listening?* New York: McGraw-Hill Book Co., Inc., 1957.

———, and ———. "If Only Someone Would Listen," *Journal of Communication*, Vol. VIII, No. 1 (Spring, 1957).

PHIFER, GREGG. "Propaganda and Critical Listening," *Journal of Communication*, Vol. III (1953).

ROGERS, CARL R., and FARSON, RICHARD E. *Active Listening*. Chicago: Industrial Relations Center, University of Chicago, 1955.

STRONG, LYDIA. "Do You Know How to Listen?" *Management Review*, August, 1955.

ZELKO, HAROLD P. "An Outline of the Role of Listening in the Communication Process," *Journal of Communication*, Vol. IV (1954).

———. *How to Be a Good Listener* (Booklet). New York: Employee Relations, Inc., 1958.

———. "You Can Be a Good Listener," *Parade*, September 22, 1957.

READING

COSPER, RUSSELL. "Improving Reading Skill," *Journal of Communication*, Vol. III (1953).

———, and GRIFFIN, E. GLENN (eds.). *Toward Better Reading Skills*. 2d ed. New York: Appleton-Century-Crofts, Inc., 1959.

DEE, JAMES P. "Written Communications in the Trade Union Local," *Journal of Communication*, Vol. IX, No. 3 (September, 1959).

DUNN, THOMAS. "Preparing an Objective Test of Reading and Writing," *Journal of Communication*, Vol. II, No. 1 (1952).

GREBANIER, BERNARD D. N., and RECTOR, SEYMOUR. *College Writing and Reading*. New York: Henry Holt & Co., 1959.

GUILER, WALTER S., and RAETH, CLAIRE J. *Developmental Reading*. Philadelphia: J. B. Lippincott Co., 1958.

HEILMAN, ARTHUR. "Reading Emphasis in the Communications Course," *Journal of Communication*, Vol. II, No. 1 (1952).

HILDRETH, GERTRUDE. *Teaching Reading: A Guide to Basic Principles and Modern Practices*. New York: Henry Holt & Co., 1958.

MILLER, LYLE L. *Maintaining Reading Efficiency*. New York: Henry Holt & Co., 1959.

SHELDON, WILLIAM D., and BRAAM, LEONARD S. *Reading Improvement for Men and Women in Industry*. Syracuse, N.Y.: Syracuse University Press, 1959.

SMITH, NILA BANTON. *Read Faster and Get More from Your Reading*. New York: Prentice-Hall, Inc., 1958.

SPACHE, GEO. D., and BERG, PAUL C. *Faster Reading for Business*. New York: Thomas Y. Crowell, 1958.

TUTTLE, ROBERT E., and BROWN, C. A. *Writing Useful Reports*. New York: Appleton-Century-Crofts, Inc., 1956.

WITTY, P. A. *How to Become a Better Reader*. Chicago: Science Research Associates, 1953.

GROUP PROCESSES: DISCUSSION, CONFERENCE, GROUP DYNAMICS

ALLEN, LOUIS A. "The Problem-Solving Conference," *Developing Executive Skills*. New York: American Management Association, 1958.

AUER, J. JEFFERY, and EWBANK, HENRY LEE. *Handbook for Discussion Leaders*. Rev. ed. New York: Harper & Bros., 1954.

BALES, ROBERT F. "In Conference," *Harvard Business Review*, March–April, 1954.

———. *Interaction Process Analysis*. Cambridge, Mass.: Addison-Wesley Press, 1950.

BONNER, HUBERT. *Group Dynamics: Principles and Applications*. New York: Ronald Press, 1959.

BRADEN, WALDO W., and BRANDENBURG, EARNEST. *Oral Decision Making*. New York: Harper & Bros., 1955.

BRADFORD, LELAND, and LIPPITT, GORDON. "The Individual Counts in Effective Group Relations," *National Education Association Journal*, November, 1954.

BROWN, C. S., and COHN, T. S. (eds.). *The Study of Leadership*. Danville, Ill.: Interstate, 1958.

BUSCH, HENRY M. *Conference Methods in Industry*. New York: Harper & Bros., 1949.

CARTWRIGHT, DORWIN, and ZANDER, ALVIN. *Group Dynamics, Research, and Theory*. Evanston, Ill.: Row, Peterson & Co., 1953.

"Committees, Their Role in Management Today," *Management Review*, October, 1957.

COOPER, ALFRED M. *How to Conduct Conferences*. New York: McGraw-Hill Book Co., Inc., 1946.

CORTRIGHT, RUPERT, and HINDS, GEORGE. *Creative Discussion*. New York: Macmillan Co., 1959.

DAVIES, DANIEL R., and HARROLD, KENNETH F. *Make Your Staff Meetings Count*. New London, Conn.: A. C. Croft, 1954.

DICKENS, MILTON. "Basic Principles of Measurement in Human Relations as They Apply to Group Discussion," *Journal of Communication*, Vol. III (1953).

FIEDLER, FRED E. *Leader Attitudes and Group Effectiveness*. Urbana: University of Illinois Press, 1958.

FISHER, WALDO. *Management Conferences—How to Run Them*. Report No. 10, Wharton School of Finance, University of Pennsylvania. Philadelphia, 1947.

GORDON, THOMAS. *Group Centered Leadership, a Way of Releasing the Creative Power of Groups.* Boston: Houghton Mifflin Co., 1951.

GUETZKOW, HAROLD (ed.). *Groups, Leadership, and Men.* Pittsburgh: Carnegie Press, 1951.

——, and GYR, JOHN. "An Analysis of Conflict in Decision-Making Groups," *Human Relations,* Vol. III, No. 3 (1954).

——, and KRIESBERG, MARTIN. "Executive Use of the Administration Conference," *Personnel,* March, 1950.

GYLLENHAAL, HUGH A. "Your Meetings Can Get Results," *Nation's Business,* June, 1957.

HAIMAN, FRANKLYN S. *Group Leadership and Democratic Action.* Boston: Houghton Mifflin Co., 1951.

HOMANS, GEORGE. *The Human Group.* New York: Harcourt, Brace & Co., 1950.

"How to Get the Most Out of Your Conferences," *Advanced Management,* October, 1951.

How to Lead Discussions. Leadership Pamphlet No. 1, Adult Education Association of the U.S.A. (743 N. Wabash, Chicago, Illinois).

JENKINS, RUSSELL L. "Discussional Procedures in Communication," *Journal of Communication,* Vol. II, No. 2 (1952).

JONES, O. GARFIELD. *Senior Manual for Group Leadership.* Rev. ed. New York: Appleton-Century-Crofts, Inc., 1949.

KELTNER, JOHN. *Group Discussion Processes.* New York: Longmans, Green & Co., 1957.

KLEIN, ALAN F. *Role Playing in Leadership Training and Group Problem Solving.* New York: Association Press, 1956.

LEE, IRVING J. *How to Talk with People.* New York: Harper & Bros., 1952.

LIPPITT, GORDON. "What Do We Know about Leadership?" *National Education Association Journal,* December, 1955.

LIPPITT, RONALD. "Methods for Producing and Measuring Change in Group Functioning: Theoretical Problems," *General Semantics Bulletin,* Nos. 14 and 15 (Winter–Spring, 1954).

LONEY, GLENN M. *Briefing and Conference Techniques.* New York: McGraw-Hill Book Co., Inc., 1959.

MCBURNEY, JAMES H., and HANCE, KENNETH G. *Discussion in Human Affairs.* New York: Harper & Bros., 1950.

MOSER, GEORGE. "Avoiding Pitfalls in Conference Leading," *Management Record,* National Conference Board, November, 1958.

MURRAY, JANET P., and MURRAY, CLYDE E. *Guide Lines for Group Leaders.* New York: Whiteside, Inc., 1954.

POSZ, A. CONRAD, and WIKSELL, MILTON J. "Learning to Solve Group Communication Problems," *Adult Leadership,* Vol. VI, No. 6 (December, 1957).

REISMAN, DAVID; GLAZER, NATHAN; and DENNEY, REUEL. *The Lonely Crowd.* Garden City, N.Y.: Doubleday & Co., 1956.

SATTLER, WILLIAM, and MILLER, N. EDD. *Discussion and Conference.* New York: Prentice-Hall, Inc., 1954.

SCHAFFNER, BERTRAM (ed.). *Group Processes: Transactions of the Fourth Conference, 13–16 October 1957.* New York: Josiah Macy, Jr., Foundation, 1959.

SHAW, MARVIN E., and GILCHRIST, J. C. "Intra-Group Communication and Leader Choice," *Journal of Social Psychology,* Vol. XLIII (February, 1956).

STAGEBURG, NORMAN. "Obstacle-Words in Group Conference," *Journal of Communication,* Vol. II, No. 1 (1952).

STRONG, LYDIA. "Meetings and the Manager," *Management Review,* July, 1956.

THELEN, HERBERT A. *Dynamics of Groups at Work.* Chicago: University of Chicago Press, 1954.

Training Group Leaders. Leadership Pamphlet No. 8, Adult Education Association of the U.S.A. (743 N. Wabash, Chicago, Illinois).

Understanding How Groups Work. Leadership Pamphlet No. 4, Adult Education Association of the U.S.A. (743 N. Wabash, Chicago, Illinois).

UTTERBACK, WILLIAM E. *Group Thinking and Conference Leadership.* New York: Rinehart, 1950.

WAGNER, JOSEPH A. *Successful Leadership in Groups and Organizations.* San Francisco: Howard Chandler, 1959.

WALSER, FRANK. *The Art of Conference.* Rev. ed. New York: Harper & Bros., 1948.

ZELKO, HAROLD P. "Speech and Conference Leadership Training in American Industry," *Personnel,* September, 1950.

————. *Successful Conference and Discussion Techniques.* New York: McGraw-Hill Book Co., Inc., 1957.

RELATED STUDIES

GENERAL SEMANTICS

BOIS, J. S. A. "Executive Training and General Semantics," *General Semantics Bulletin,* Nos. 14 and 15 (Winter–Spring, 1954).

BOIS, J. SAMUEL. *Explorations in Awareness.* New York: Harper & Bros., 1957.

BONTRAGER, O. R. "Origins of Verbaiism," *Elementary English,* Vol. XXVIII, No. 2 (February, 1951).

CHISHOLM, FRANCIS P. *Introductory Lectures on General Semantics.* Lakeville, Conn.: Institute of General Semantics, 1944.

ETC.: A Review of General Semantics. This is the quarterly publication (since 1943) of the International Society for General Semantics, 400 West North Avenue, Chicago 10, Illinois.

EXTON, WILLIAM, JR. "Semantics of Industrial Relations," *Personnel,* Vol. XXVI, No. 6 (May, 1950).

FROMAN, ROBERT. "How to Say What You Mean," *Nation's Business,* May, 1957.

————. "Make Words Fit the Job," *ibid.,* July, 1959.

General Semantics Bulletin. This is a periodic publication of the Institute of General Semantics, Lakeville, Connecticut. Numbers 1 and 2 are dated Autumn–Winter, 1949–50.

GLENN, EDMUND S. "Semantic Difficulties in International Communication," *ETC.: A Review of General Semantics,* Vol. XI, No. 3 (Spring, 1954).

HAYAKAWA, S. I. "How Words Change Our Lives," *Saturday Evening Post,* Vol. CCXXXI (December 27, 1958).

————. *Language in Thought and Action.* New York: Harcourt, Brace & Co., 1949.

————. *Language, Meaning, and Maturity.* New York: Harper & Bros., 1954.

————. "The Meaning of Semantics," *New Republic,* Vol. LXXXXIX, No. 1287 (August 2, 1939).

————. "New Techniques of Agreement," *Colgate Lectures in Human Relations.* Colgate University, 1950.

———— (ed.). *Our Language and Our World.* New York: Harper & Bros., 1959.

JOHNSON, WENDELL. *People in Quandaries.* New York: Harper & Bros., 1946.

————. *Your Most Enchanted Listener.* New York: Harper & Bros., 1956.

JOHNSON, WENDELL, *et al.* "Studies in Language Behavior," *Psychological Monographs,* Vol. LVI (1944).

KENDIG, M. (ed.). *Papers from the Second American Congress on General Seman-*

tics. Lakeville, Conn.: Institute of General Semantics, 1943. Some 80 papers on theoretical aspects and practical application; wide-ranging considerations from aesthetics to finance, reading-readiness to journalism.

KEYES, KENNETH S. *How to Develop Your Thinking Ability.* New York: McGraw-Hill Book Co., Inc., 1950.

KORZYBSKI, ALFRED. "General Semantics," *The American People's Encyclopedia,* Vol. IX. Chicago: Spencer Press, 1948.

————. *Science and Sanity: An Introduction to Non-Aristotelian System and General Semantics* (1933). Lakeville, Conn.: Institute of General Semantics, 1948.

————. *Time-Binding: The General Theory.* (Two Papers, 1924–26.) Lakeville, Conn.: Institute of General Semantics, 1949.

————. *Manhood of Humanity* (1921). Lakeville, Conn.: Institute of General Semantics, 1950.

————. "The Role of Language in the Perceptual Process," *Perception: An Approach to Personality* (ed. R. R. BLAKE and G. V. RAMSEY). New York: Ronald Press, 1951.

————, and KENDIG, M. Foreword, *A Theory of Meaning Analyzed.* General Semantics Monographs, No. 3. Lakeville, Conn.: Institute of General Semantics, 1942.

LEE, IRVING J. *How Do You Talk about People?* (Freedom Pamphlet published by Anti-Defamation League of B'nai B'rith, 212 Fifth Avenue, New York 10).

————. *Language Habits in Human Affairs.* New York: Harper & Bros., 1941.

LEE, IRVING J., and LEE, LAURA L. *Handling Barriers in Communication.* New York: Harper & Bros., 1957.

NILSEN, THOMAS R. "Some Assumptions That Impede Communication," *General Semantics Bulletin,* Nos. 14 and 15 (Winter–Spring, 1954).

SONDEL, BESS. *The Humanity of Words: A Primer of Semantics.* Cleveland: World Publishing Co., 1958.

WHYTE, WILLIAM FOOTE. "Semantics and Industrial Relations," *Human Organization,* Vol. VIII, No. 2 (1949).

OTHER RELATED STUDIES

ADAMS, J. STACEY. *Interviewing Procedures: A Manual for Survey Interviewers.* Chapel Hill: University of North Carolina Press, 1956.

ALLPORT, GORDON W., and POSTMAN, LEO. *The Psychology of Rumor.* New York: Henry Holt & Co., 1947.

ANSHEN, RUTH NANDA (ed.). *Language: An Enquiry into Its Meaning and Function.* New York: Harper & Bros., 1957.

BARNLUND, DEAN. "Leadership Evaluation: Some Premises and Procedures," *Journal of Communication,* Vol. III (1953).

BARTLETT, SIR FREDERICK. *Thinking: An Experimental and Social Study.* London: George Allen & Unwin, 1958.

BARTLEY, S. HOWARD. *Principles of Perception.* New York: Harper & Bros., 1958.

BAVELAS, ALEX, and BARRETT, DERMOT. "An Experimental Approach to Organization," *Personnel,* Vol. XXVII (March, 1951).

BEARDSLEE, DAVID C., and WERTHEIMER, MICHAEL. *Readings in Perception.* Princeton, N.J.: D. Van Nostrand Co., 1958.

BEARDSLEY, MONROE C. *Thinking Straight.* New York: Prentice-Hall, Inc., 1950.

BINGHAM, W. VAN D., and MOORE, B. V. *How to Interview.* 4th ed. New York: Harper & Bros., 1959.

BROWER, REUBEN (ed.). *On Translation.* Cambridge, Mass.: Harvard University Press, 1959.

BROWN, DONA W.; BROWN, W. C.; and BAILEY, DUDLEY. *Form in Modern English.* New York: Oxford University Press, 1958.

BROWN, JAMES I., and SALISBURY, RACHEL. *Building a Better Vocabulary.* New York: Ronald Press, 1959.

BROWN, ROGER. *Words and Things.* Glencoe, Ill.: Free Press, 1958.

BRUNER, J. S.; GOODNOW, J. J.; and AUSTIN, G. A. *A Study of Thinking.* New York: John Wiley & Sons, 1956.

CARROLL, J. B. *Language, Thought, and Reality: Selected Writings of Benjamin Lee Whorf.* New York: John Wiley & Sons, 1956.

CHASE, STUART. *Guides to Straight Thinking.* New York: Harper & Bros., 1956.

———. *The Proper Study of Mankind.* New York: Harper & Bros., 1948.

COON, ARTHUR M. "Brainstorming—a Creative Problem Solving Technique," *Journal of Communication,* Vol. VII, No. 3 (Autumn, 1957).

CRAWFORD, ROBERT P. *Techniques of Creative Thinking.* New York: Hawthorn Books, Inc., 1954.

DEAN, LEONARD F., and WILSON, KENNETH G. (eds.). *Essays on Language and Usage.* New York: Oxford University Press, 1959.

DEIGHTON, LEE C. *Vocabulary Development in the Classroom.* New York: Bureau of Publications, Teachers College, Columbia University, 1959.

DEWEY, JOHN. *How We Think.* Boston: D. C. Heath & Co., 1933.

EMERY, F. E., and OESAR, O. A. *Information, Decision, and Action: A Study of the Psychological Determinants of Changes in Framing Techniques.* London: Cambridge University Press, 1958.

ENTWHISTLE, WILLIAM J. *Aspects of Language.* London: Faber & Faber, 1953.

ESTRICH, ROBERT M., and SPERBER, HANS. *Three Keys to Language.* New York: Rinehart, 1952.

FINLAY, WILLIAM W.; SARTAIN, A. Q.; and TATE, WILLIS M. *Human Behavior in Industry.* New York: McGraw-Hill Book Co., Inc., 1954.

FRANCIS, W. NELSON. *The Structure of American English.* New York: Ronald Press, 1958.

GEORGE, A. L. *Propaganda Analysis: A Study of Inferences Made from Nazi Propaganda in World War II.* Evanston, Ill.: Row, Peterson & Co., 1959.

GILMARTIN, JOHN G. *Words in Action.* New York: Prentice-Hall, Inc., 1954.

GRAY, ROBERT D., and SORENSON, L. ROBERT. "Practicing Supervision," *Personnel,* May, 1954.

GUILFORD, J. P. *Personality.* New York: McGraw-Hill Book Co., Inc., 1959.

———. "Some Recent Findings on Thinking Abilities and Their Implications," *Journal of Communication,* Vol. III (1953).

HALL, EDWARD TWITCHELL. *The Silent Language.* Garden City, N.Y.: Doubleday, 1959.

HAPPE, BERNARD F., and KAMINSKY, JACK. *Logic and Language.* New York: Alfred A. Knopf, 1956.

HARRIS, ROBERT T., and JARRETT, JAMES L. *Language and Informal Logic.* New York: Longmans, Green & Co., 1956.

Harvard Business Review. Quarterly. Boston, Vol. XX, 1941———.

HENLE, P. (ed.). *Language, Thought, and Culture.* Ann Arbor: University of Michigan Press, 1958.

HENRY, HARRY. *Motivation Research: Its Practice and Uses for Advertising, Marketing, and Other Business Purposes.* New York: Frederick Ungar, 1958.

HIRST, R. J. *The Problems of Perception.* New York: Macmillan Co., 1959.

HOCKETT, CHAS. F. *A Course in Modern Linguistics.* New York: Macmillan Co., 1958.

HUFF, DARRELL. *How to Lie with Statistics.* New York: W. W. Norton & Co., 1954.

312   COMMUNICATION: PATTERNS AND INCIDENTS

ITTELSON, WILLIAM. *The Ames Demonstrations in Perception*. Princeton, N.J.: Princeton University Press, 1952.

JACOBS, N. J. *Naming Day in Eden: The Creation and Recreation of Language.* New York: Macmillan Co., 1959.

JENNINGS, CHAS. B.; KING, NANCY; and STEVENSON, MARJORIE. *Consider Your Words.* New York: Harper & Bros., 1959.

JOHNSON, ALEXANDER BRYAN. *The Meaning of Words.* New York: Harper & Bros., 1854. Now available in an edition published by John Winston Chamberlin, Milwaukee, Wisconsin.

————. *A Treatise on Language* (ed. DAVID RYNIN). East Lansing, Mich.: University of California Press, 1947.

JONES, M. R. (ed.). *Nebraska Symposium in Motivation, 1955.* Lincoln: University of Nebraska Press, 1955.

KELLEY, EARL. *Education for What Is Real.* New York: Harper & Bros., 1947.

KLUCKHOHN, CLYDE. *Mirror for Man.* New York: McGraw-Hill Book Co., Inc., 1949.

LARRABEE, HAROLD. *Reliable Knowledge.* Boston: Houghton Mifflin Co., 1945.

LAWSON, CHESTER A. *Language, Thought, and the Human Mind.* East Lansing: Michigan State University Press, 1958.

LEAVITT, HAROLD J. *Managerial Psychology: An Introduction to Individuals, Pairs, and Groups in Organizations.* Chicago: University of Chicago Press, 1958.

LEE, IRVING J. *The Language of Wisdom and Folly.* New York: Harper & Bros., 1949.

MAIER, NORMAN R. F. *The Appraisal Interview: Objectives, Methods, and Skills.* New York: John Wiley & Sons, 1958.

MANDER, A. E. *Logic for the Millions.* New York: Philosophical Library, 1947.

MANDLER, GEORGE, and KESSEN, WILLIAM. *The Language of Psychology.* New York: John Wiley & Sons, 1959.

MARTIN, JOHN L. *International Propaganda: Its Legal and Diplomatic Control.* Minneapolis: University of Minnesota Press, 1958.

MARTIN, R. M. *Truth and Denotation: A Study in Semantical Theory.* Chicago: University of Chicago Press, 1958.

MASLOW, A. H. *Motivation and Personality.* New York: Harper & Bros., 1954.

————. "A Theory of Human Motivation," *Psychological Review,* Vol. L (1943).

McBURNEY, JAMES H.; O'NEILL, JAMES M.; and MILLS, GLEN E. *Argumentation and Debate.* New York: Macmillan Co., 1951.

MENNINGER, KARL A. *The Human Mind.* New York: Alfred A. Knopf, 1945.

MILLER, G. A. *Language and Communication.* New York: McGraw-Hill Book Co., Inc., 1951.

MORRIS, CHARLES. *Signs, Language, and Behavior.* New York: Prentice-Hall, Inc., 1946.

OGDEN, C. K., and RICHARDS, I. A. *The Meaning of Meaning.* New York: Harcourt, Brace & Co., 1952.

OSBORNE, ALEX F. *Applied Imagination.* New York: Charles Scribner's Sons, 1953.

PACKARD, VANCE. *The Status Seekers.* New York: David McKay, 1959.

PHILBRICK, F. A. *Understanding English.* New York: Macmillan Co., 1942.

PRESTON, GEORGE H. *Psychiatry for the Curious.* New York: Rinehart, 1940.

REIS, SAMUEL. *Language and Psychology.* New York: Philosophical Library, 1959.

RUSSELL, BERTRAND. *Human Knowledge.* New York: Simon & Schuster, 1948.

SAPIR, EDWARD. "Language," *Encyclopedia of the Social Sciences,* Vol. XIV.

SKINNER, B. F. *Verbal Behavior.* New York: Appleton-Century-Crofts, Inc., 1957.

SKINNER, ROBERT A. *Leave Your Language Alone!* Ithaca, N.Y.: Linguistica, 1950.

SNYGG, DONALD, and COMBS, ARTHUR W. *Individual Behavior.* New York: Harper & Bros., 1949.

STAGNER, ROSS. *The Psychology of Industrial Conflict.* New York: John Wiley & Sons, 1956.

STOGDILL, RALPH M. *Individual Behavior and Group Achievement.* New York: Oxford University Press, 1959.

TABORI, PAUL. *The Natural Science of Stupidity.* Philadelphia: Chilton, 1959.

TOULMIN, STEPHEN E. *The Uses of Argument.* New York: Cambridge University Press, 1958.

VANCE, STANLEY. *Industrial Administration.* New York: McGraw-Hill Book Co., Inc., 1959.

WERKMEISTER, W. H. *An Introduction to Critical Thinking.* Lincoln, Neb.: Johnson Publishing Co., 1948.

WIENER, NORBERT. *The Human Use of Human Beings.* Boston: Houghton Mifflin Co., 1950.

ZALEZNIK, A; CHRISTENSEN, C. R.; and ROETHLISBERGER, F. J. *The Motivation, Productivity, and Satisfaction of Workers.* Cambridge, Mass.: Harvard University Division of Research, Graduate School of Business Administration, 1958.

INDEX

A

Abstracting, 77–79
Affectors, role of, 6–9
Agassiz, 76, 77
Allness
  "All Wall," the, 81–83
  allness and learnability, 81–83
  correctives, 83–84
  underlying assumptions, 75
Ambassador's Report, 83
American Genetic Association, 244
Ames Demonstrations in Perception, The, 21
Appley, Lawrence, 83
Aristotelian Law of Falling Bodies, 164
Aristotle, 122, 130
Armour, Richard, 132
Art of Scientific Investigation, The, 127, 217
Art of Straight Thinking, The, 60
Art of Teaching, The, 77
Associating, 186 ff.
  values of, 195
"Associative" by-passing, 193–94
  conditions for occurrence of, 194
  correctives, 197–98
  distinguished from *by-passing,* 193
Assumptions
  as affectors of behavior, 8
  underlying communication, 3–4
Atlantic Monthly, 265
Atwell, Ben H., 264

B

Ball, M. W., 212
Beecher, Henry K., 7
Bell System Laboratories, 217
Beveridge, W. I. B., 127, 217
Blinder names, 213
Blindering
  consequences, 211–14
  correctives, 214–20
  defined, 214
Bois, J. Samuel, 9, 75
Bowles, Chester, 83
Brainstorming, 218
Brown, Douglas, 2
Brown, Elgar, 193
By-passing
  correctives, 56–62
  defined, 42
  different words—same things, 43

By-passing—*Cont.*
  immediate consequences
    apparent agreement, 45
    apparent disagreement, 45–46
    motives of by-passers, 54–56
    multi-usage of words, 49–53
    same words—different things, 43
    underlying fallacies, 46–54

C

Caine Mutiny, The, 125
Calculated risk, 24
Call Me Lucky, 167
Caniff, Milton, 166
Carroll, Lewis, 54
Chase, Stuart, 83, 211
Chicago's Awful Theatre Horror, 264–65, 269–70
Clark, Charles H., 217
Clarke, Edwin Leavitt, 60
Cocoanut Grove fire, 265
Communication
  in business, 1
  process of, 2–4
Connotations, 187
Consultation Room, 53
"Container myth" of meaning, 47–48
Contexts
  situational, 61–62
  verbal, 59–61
Contradictories, 122
Contraries, 122–23
  double contraries, 132–33
Coughlin, William J., 44
Cousins, Norman, 166
Crosby, Bing, 166–67
Crouse-Hinds Company, 83
Crusade in Europe, 83

D

Davis, Keith, 80
Deadlines, as tension inducers, 219
Deichelmann, Maj. Gen. M. K., 220
Denotations, 187
Discourse on Language, A, 109
Dispute
  correctives, 250–52
  intentional, 239
  nonintentional, 239 ff.
    differing perceptions as key contributor to, 240

Double burden, 190
Double contraries, 132, 133
Duckworth, Pauline, 1

E

Earthquake Investigation in the United States, 147
Eisenhower, Dwight D., 83
Encyclopaedia Britannica, 49, 60
Epictetus, 81
Espy, Willard R., 150
ETC.: A Review of General Semantics, 9, 210
Etymological shifts, 49–51
Euphemisms
    danger of, 188–89
    defined, 188
    uses of, 188–90
Evaluations, 5–9
Explorations in Awareness, 9, 75
Extensional orientation, defined, 164

F

Fallows, Bishop Samuel, 269
Fansler, Thomas, 20
Foreman's Letter, The, 41
Foundation for Economic Education, Inc., The, 153
Froman, Robert, 125, 198
Frost, Robert, 102
Frozen evaluations
    correctives, 152–54
        the *When Index*, 152–54
    defined, 145
    language influence, 148

G

Galileo, 164
General Semantics Bulletin, 9, 19, 21, 211
Goals and Desires of Man, 128
Goethe, 24
Good Health, 147
Guides to Straight Thinking, 83, 211–12

H

Haldeman-Julius, 185
Haney, William B., 19, 21
"Hardening of the categories," 101–4
Harper's Magazine, 44
Harris, Sidney J., 79, 167
Harrison, George Russell, 61
Harvey, William, 217
Hawkins, Dwight Everett, 51
Hayakawa, S. I., 9, 125

Highet, Gilbert, 77
How Much Index, 131–32
How to Talk with People, 9
Human behavior, diagram, 5
Human Relations in Business, 80
Human Understanding in Industry, 246
Humpty-Dumpty attitude, 54
Hunt, Morton M., 215, 217

I

Indiscrimination
    correctives, 107–10
    defined, 101
    language influence, 104–7
    value of seeing similarities, 110–11
    Which Index, 109–10
Inference, 17
Inference-observation confusion, correctives, 20–23
Inferential statements, 17
    distinguished from observational statements, 21
Institute of General Semantics, 9
Intensional orientation
    correctives, 168
    defined, 163–64
International Society for General Semantics, 9
Iroquois Theatre fire, 264–65
"Is" of identification, 250
"Is" of predication, 247–50
    concealed, 251–52
Ittelson, William H., 21

J

Johnson, A. B., 109
Johnson, Wendell, 9
Journal of the American Medical Association, 7
Journal of Criminal Law and Criminology, 14
Juvenile delinquents, 191–92

K

Kilby, Clyde S., 52
Kirsten, Dorothy, 102
Klimov, Maj. Gregory, 45–46
Kluckhohn, Clyde, 106
Korzybski, Alfred, 9, 10

L

Labels
    living down, 192–93
    living up to, 191–92
    positive labels, 193

Language, as influencer of behavior, 9–10
Language, Culture, and Personality: Essays in Memory of Edward Sapir, 214
Language habits, as influencing perception, 246–50
Language Habits in Human Affairs, 9, 250
Language in Thought and Action, 9, 125
Law of Falling Bodies, Aristotelian, 164
Laws of Thought, Aristotle's, 122, 130
Learning, as influencing perception, 244–45
Lee, Dorothy, 210
Lee, Irving J., 8, 9, 47, 108, 185, 250
Leighton, Dorothea, 106
Leonard, Mrs. Newton P., 192
Lerner, Leo, 84
Levine, David, 210–11
Levinson, Harry, 246
Life, 265
Lohman, Joseph, 191
Look, 188, 190
Loomis, Frederic, 53

M

MacArthur, Gen. Douglas, 246–47
Malphemisms
  danger of, 188–89
  defined, 188
  uses of, 188–89
Mandell, Milton M., 1
Map-territory analogy, 9–10, 163 ff.
Mayfair, 215, 217
Mayo, Elton, 124
McCarthy, Senator Joseph, 133
Meerloo, Joost A. M., 266
Menninger, William C., 246
Miscommunication, patterns of, 2–4
  defined, 3
Moore, John Bassett, 168
Munn, Norman L., 245
Murrow, Edward R., 168

N

"Name-calling," 190–93; *see also* Labels
  correctives, 197
National Bureau of Standards, 62
Nation's Business, 83, 125, 198
Navaho, The, 106
Neumann, Frank, 147
Non-change, the assumption of, 146 ff.

O

Observation, 17
Observational statements, 17
  distinguished from inferential statements, 21
Otto, M. C., 14–16

P

Panic, 264–66
  group, 264–66
  "solo," 265
Parade Magazine, 49
Patterns of Panic, 266
Pendulum effect, 126–27
People in Quandaries, 9
Perceptions, differing
  joint phenomenon, 248, 250–51
  as a key contributor to dispute, 240
  reasons for differences, 240–50
    how details interpreted, 244–50
    which details abstracted, 241–44
Personal labels; *see* Labels
Personnel, 1
Personnel Policies and Practices Report, 84
Phenyl-thio-carbamide, 241
Pointing, 186 ff.
"Pointing-associating" confusion, 187–90
  correctives, 195–96
Polarization
  consequences, 123–27
  contributing factors, 127–30
  correctives, 130–33
    How Much Index, 131–32
  defined, 123
Production 5118, film, 241
Promoting Growth toward Maturity in Interpreting What Is Read, 47
Psychology: The Fundamentals of Human Adjustment, 245
Psychology and Life, 146

R

Reader's Digest, 60, 132
Reeves, George, 103
Regional variations, word usage, 51–52
Responses
  reflex, 266
  reflex-like, 266–69
    dangerous, 267
    useful, 267–69
  voluntary, 266
Rogers, Carl, 250–51
Roosevelt, Franklin D., 151
Ruch, Floyd L., 146
Russell, Bertrand, 83

S

Sandburg, Carl, 102
Sarett, Lew, 102
Saturday Review of Literature, 166
Saxe, John G., 78
Schilder, Paul, 128
Science and Sanity, 9

Set, as influencing perception, 245–46
Sinclair, Lister, 105, 149, 245
Some Notes on the Psychology of Pierre Janet, 124
Stereotypes, 102

T

Technical/common usage, 52–53
Tension cycle, 218–19
Terror Machine: The Inside Story of the Soviet Administration, The, 46
This Fascinating Oil Business, 213
This Week, 149
Through the Looking Glass, 54
Tide, 60
Time, 101, 102, 127, 150, 168, 246–47
"To-me-ness" attitude, 251
Traffic Digest and Review, 19
Traffic Review, 20
True, 266
Truman, Harry, 151–52, 246–47

U

Uncalculated risk, 19–20
Uncritical Inference Test, 12–13
    answers, 18

Undelayed reactions
    correctives, 269–72
    problem of, 269
Underhill, Betty, 167–68

W

Walsh, Raoul, 103
Wayne, John, 103
Ways of Mankind, 105, 149, 245
When Index, 152–54
Which Index, 109–10
Whorf, Benjamin Lee, 213–14
Word Study, 51, 52
Word usage
    etymological shifts, 49–51
    regional variations, 51–52
    technical/common usage, 52–53
Words
    as evokers of associations, 186
    as pointers, 186
Wouk, Herman, 125

Y

Your Most Enchanted Listener, 9

INDEX TO INCIDENTS

Accident, The 255
Air Judge's Charge of Abuse by Police 277
Aldermanic Election 91
Ammons v. Wilson & Co. 65
Arno Annello, Machinist 226

Big Business—Pro and Con 85

Case of the Growing Boy 200
Case of the Ledgers, The 29
Case of the Storage Shelves, The 139
Cocktail Party, The 254
Construction of a Sailplane 67

Deadly Force 134
Dixon Company, The 112
Dyer Public Relations, Inc. (C) 284

Evans and Borne 135

False Armistice 37
56 Minutes before Pearl Harbor 25
Flies, Typhoid, and Publicity 236
Flight from Scorn 206
Four Goals of Labor, The 202
Full Circle 113

Galvanized Sheets 199
General Patton and the Sicilian Slapping Incidents 32
"Get Off Route 25, Young Man" 170
"Good Old Days," The 158

Hall-Barwell Letters (A), The 176
Hall-Barwell Letters (B), The 178
Hall-Barwell Letters (C), The 180
Hayden Company, The 98

Intelligence Is for Commanders 97
Interview with Miss Winkler 93
Is This Man Mad? 253

Jack McGuire 70

Kiss and the Slap, The 85
Knight Manufacturing Company, The 159

Logan Company, The 273

Making Glamor Sell Glamor 182
Man and the Desk, The 40
Manatee, The 202
Mayhall House 136
McCall College 207
Mid-Western Telephone Company, The 275
Money Troubles 157

Name It a Name 203
Name of the Situation as Affecting Behavior, The 223
Negro-White Differences 180
New Neighbor, The 120

On a Bus 119
On a Certain Blindness in Human Beings 260
Ordeal in London 156

Prestige Foods 203
Product-Information Program, The 63
Profits—The Importance of How Much 181

Rawley Company, The 221
Report from Rainbow Land 173
Roberts Machine Company, The 233
Room 406 71

Seek to Change Name of Cicero 200
Speech Experts Vary in Rating MacArthur 262
Spring Wooing 160
Star Spangled Banner, The 183
Sticks and Stones 201
Student Answers, The 136
Sturdy Corporate Homesteader, The 72

They Don't Do It Our Way 257
Torment in a Neighborhood 281
Trials of Galileo, The 174
Two Factions 140

Was There a Noise? 63
"Water-American," The 170
Wayland Company, The 117

What's Wrong with the Men? 114
Wright Cleaners and Dyers, Ltd. 115

You Get What You Want 229
Your Eyes Can Deceive You 279

*This book has been set on the Linotype in
11 point Baskerville, leaded 2 points and 10
point Baskerville, leaded 1 point. Chapter
numbers are in 24 point Lydian Cursive and
Lydian Bold and chapter titles in 18 point
Lydian Bold caps. The size of the type page
is 27 by 45½ picas.*